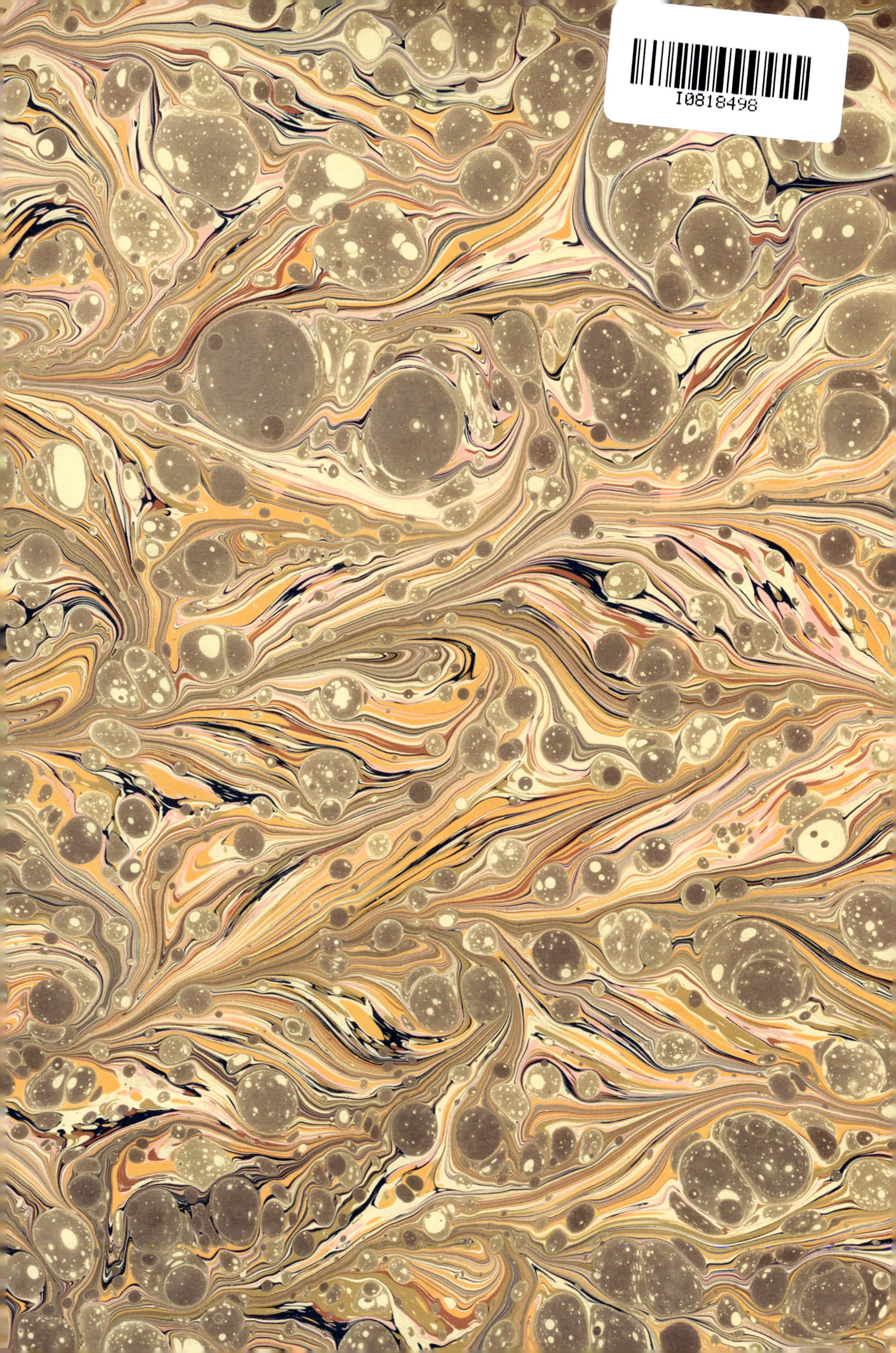
I0818498

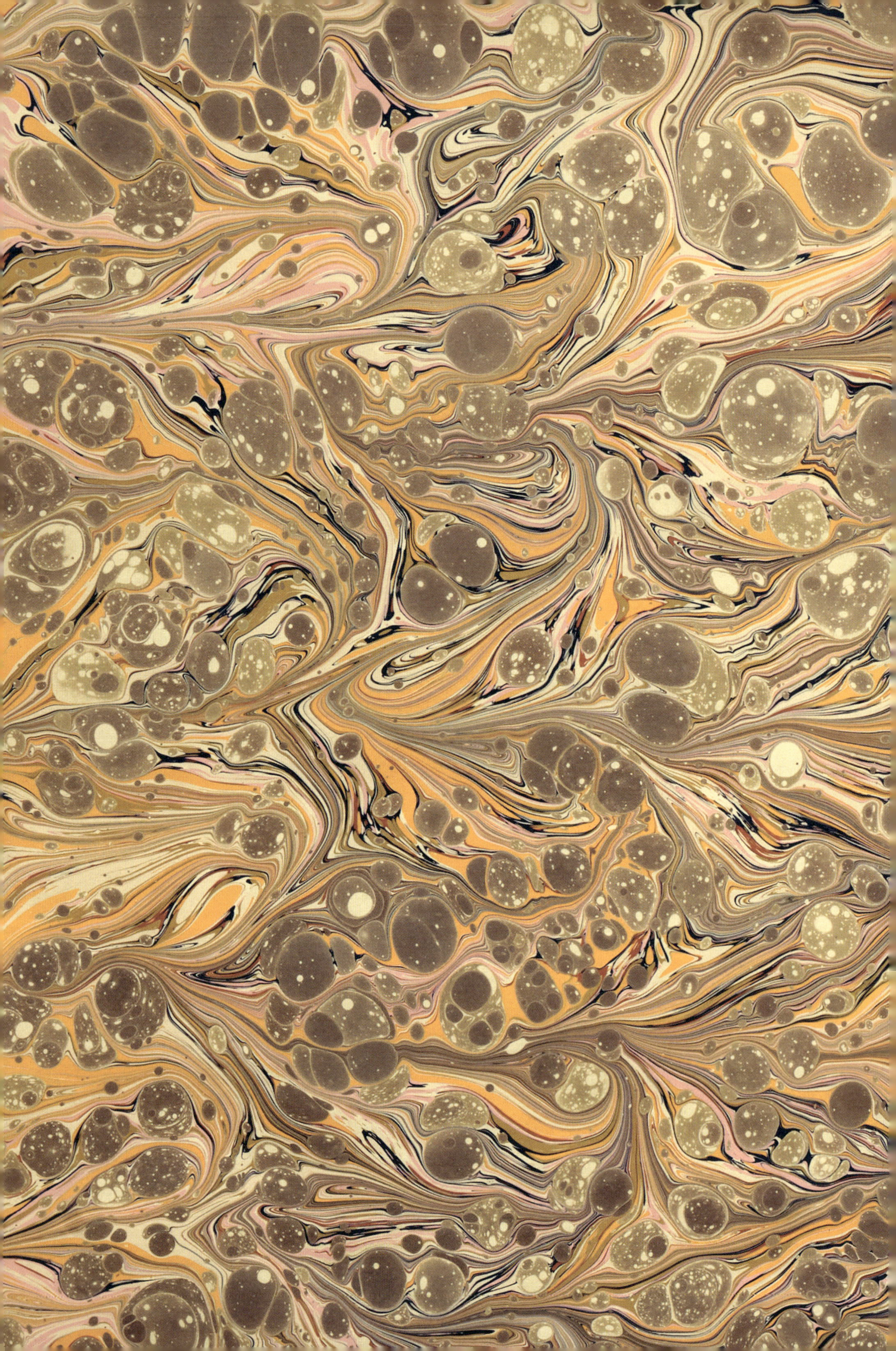

The Gourmand's Mushroom
A Collection of Stories and Recipes

The Gourmand's

Mushroom

A Collection of Stories and Recipes

TASCHEN

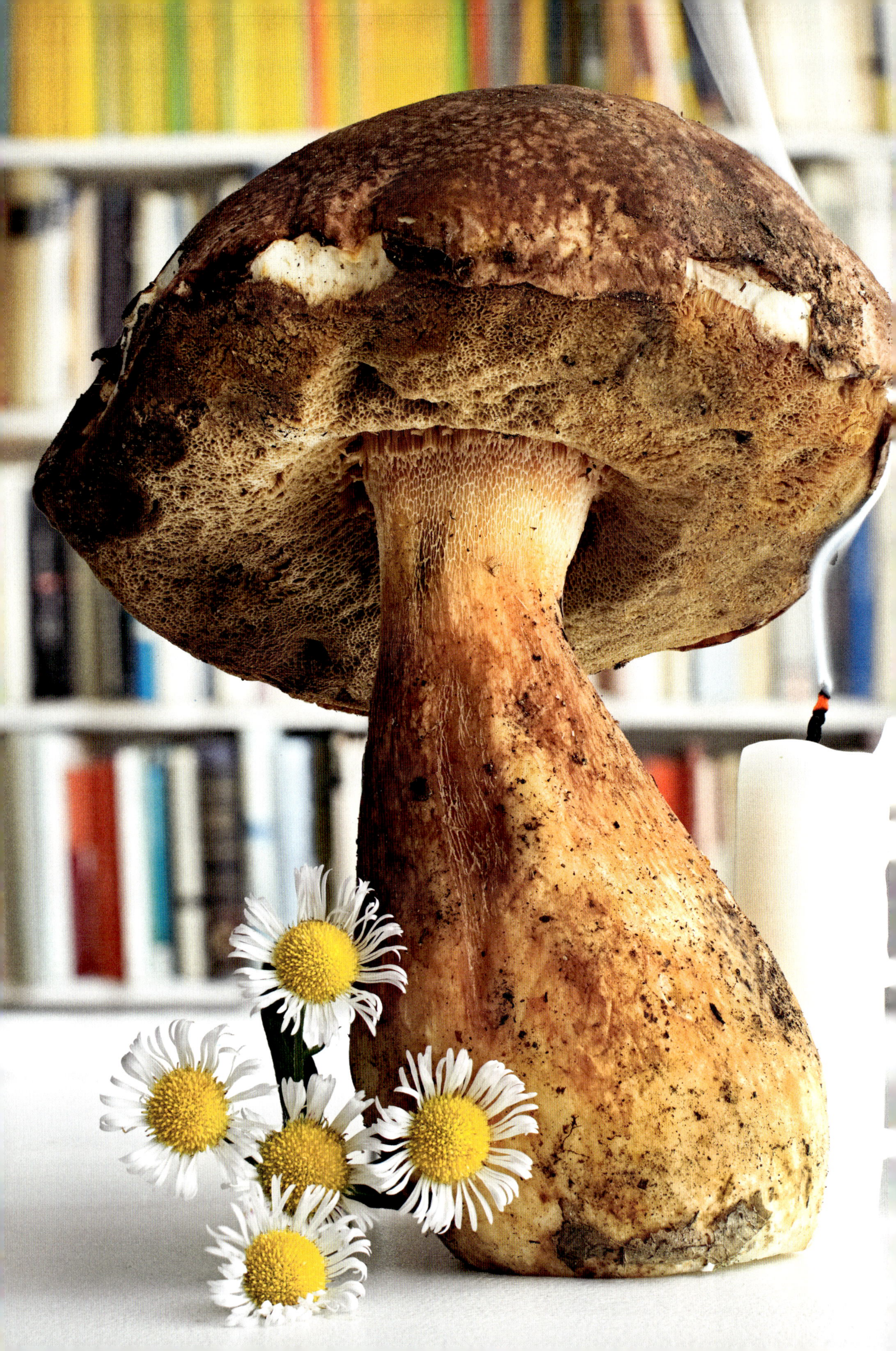

This book is dedicated to everyone who contributed to The Gourmand journal (2012 – 2020)

OPPOSITE **Bobby Doherty**, *Mushroom & Flowers*, 2022
FOLLOWING **Alice Schillaci**, *Untitled*, 2018

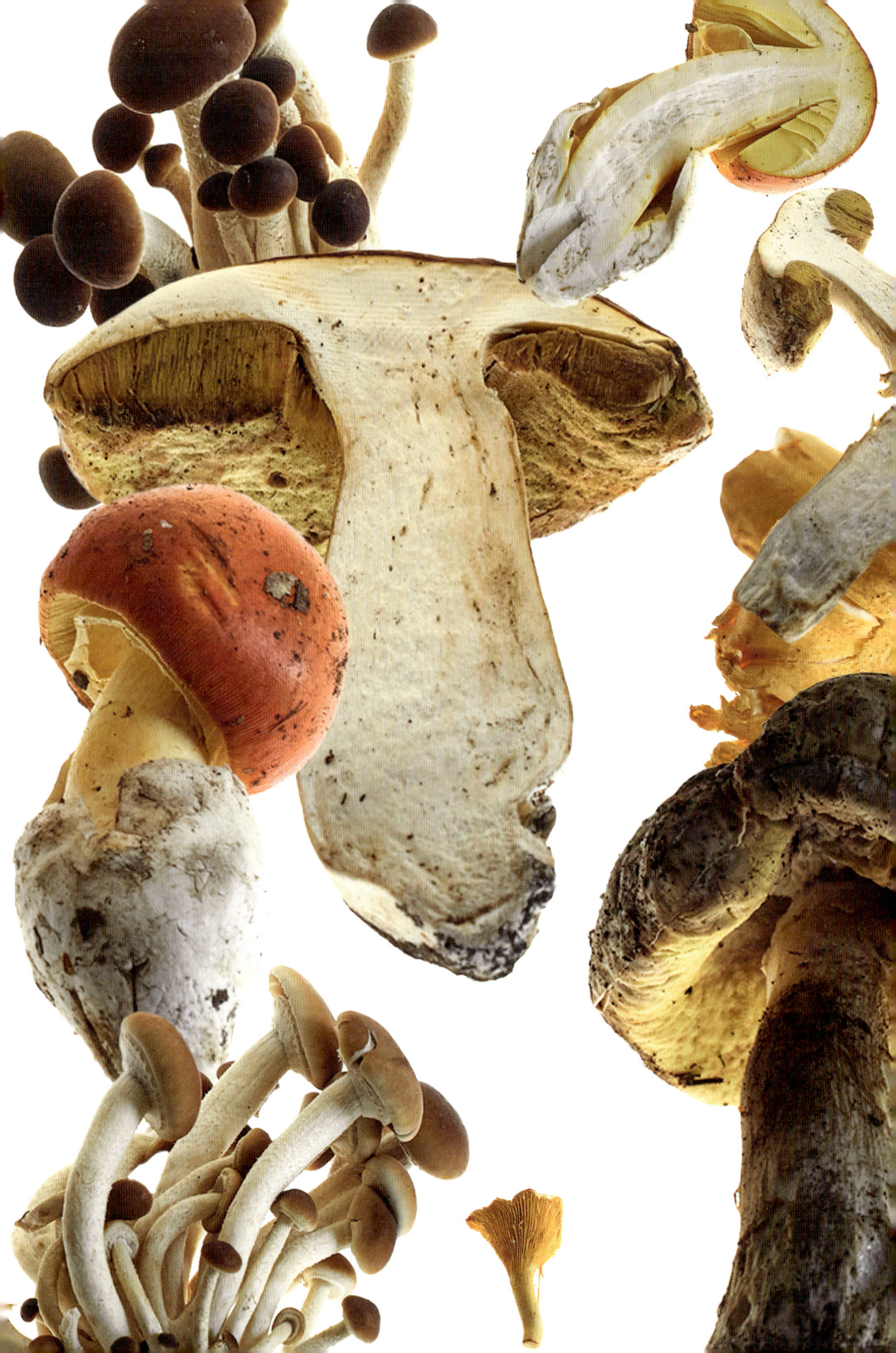

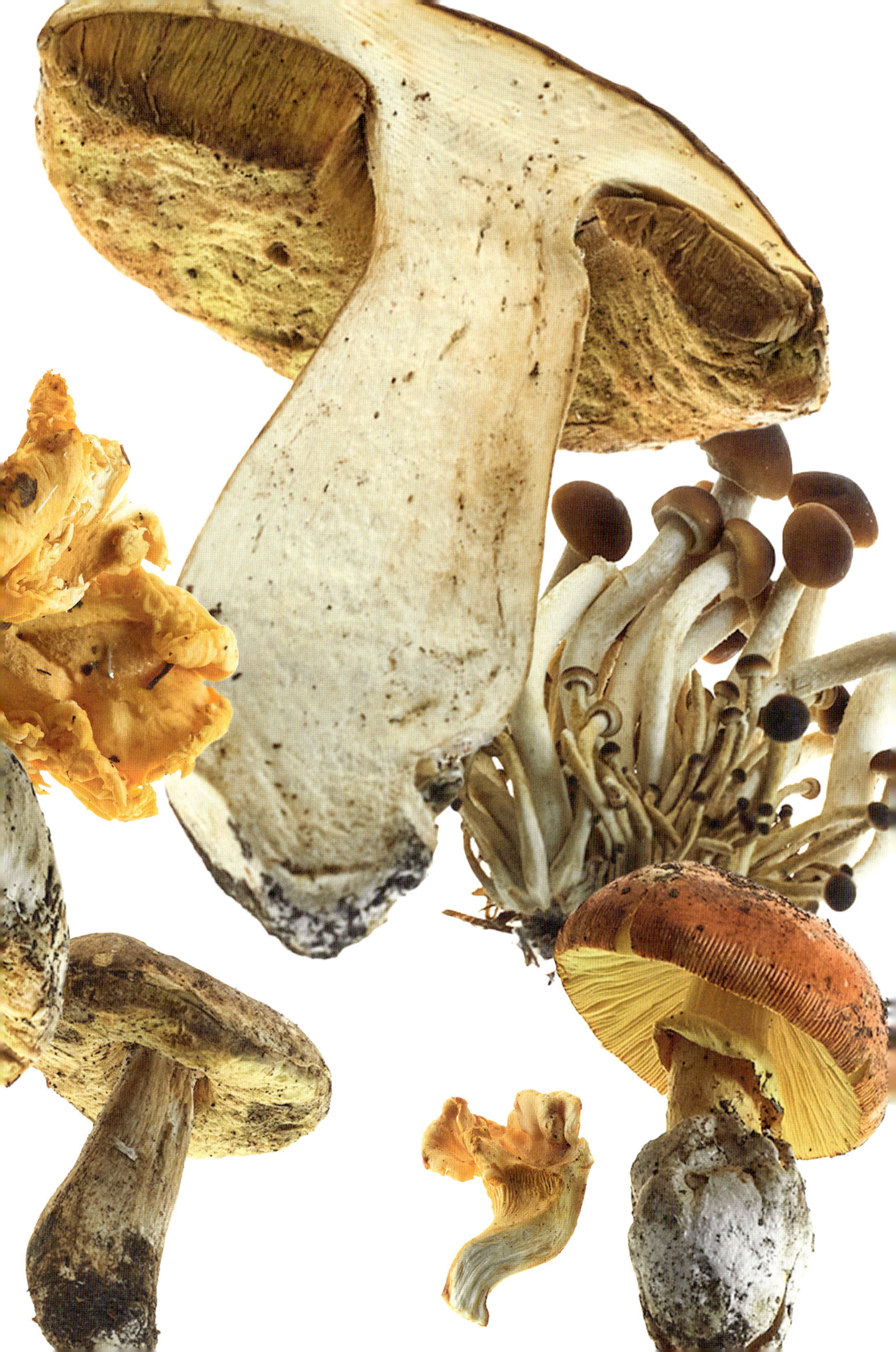

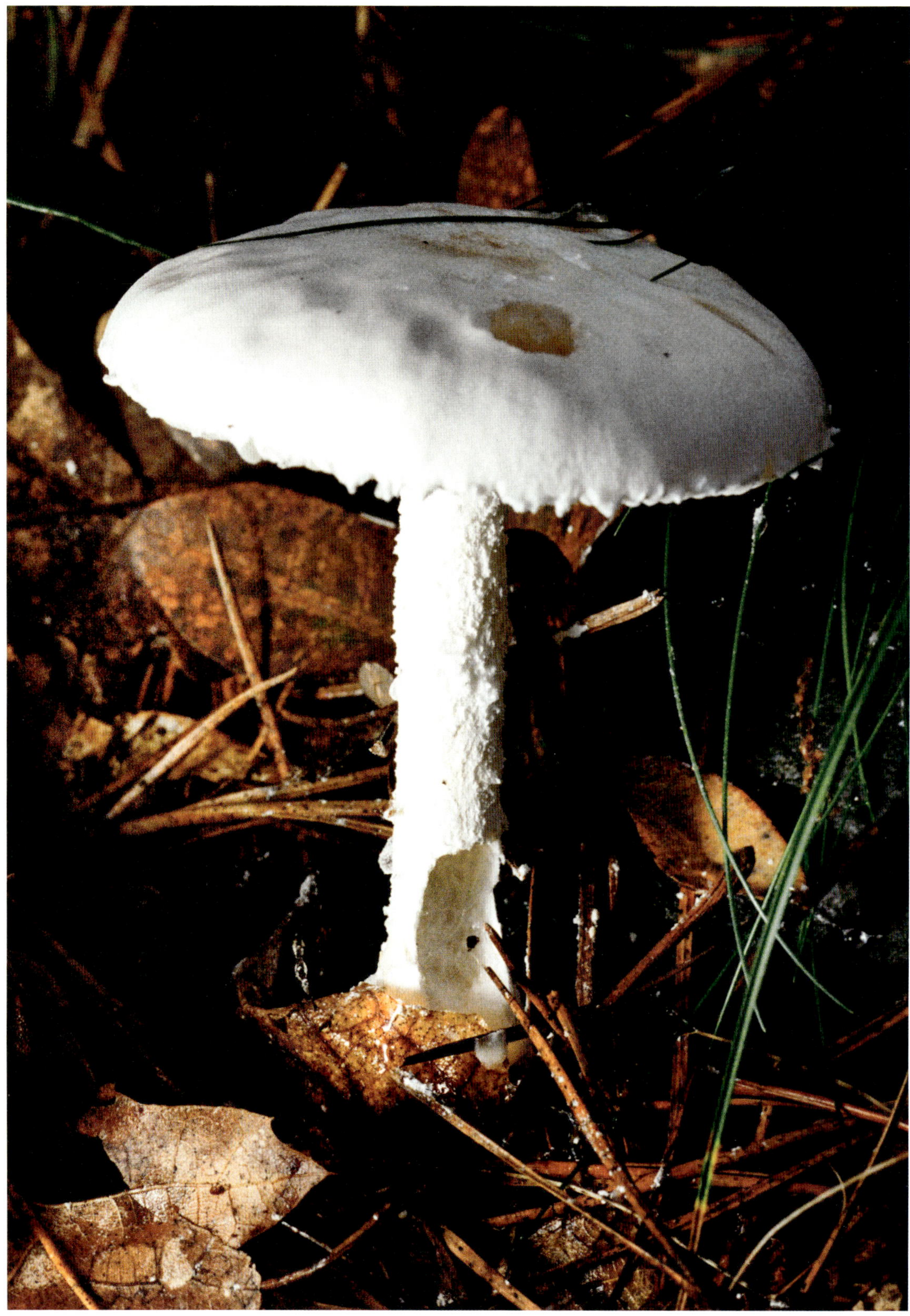

Bobby Doherty, *Untitled*, 2023

Contents

FOLLOWING **Ben Toms**, *Untitled*, 2021
PAGE XII **Bobby Doherty**, *Mushroom on Green Plaid Blanket*, 2024

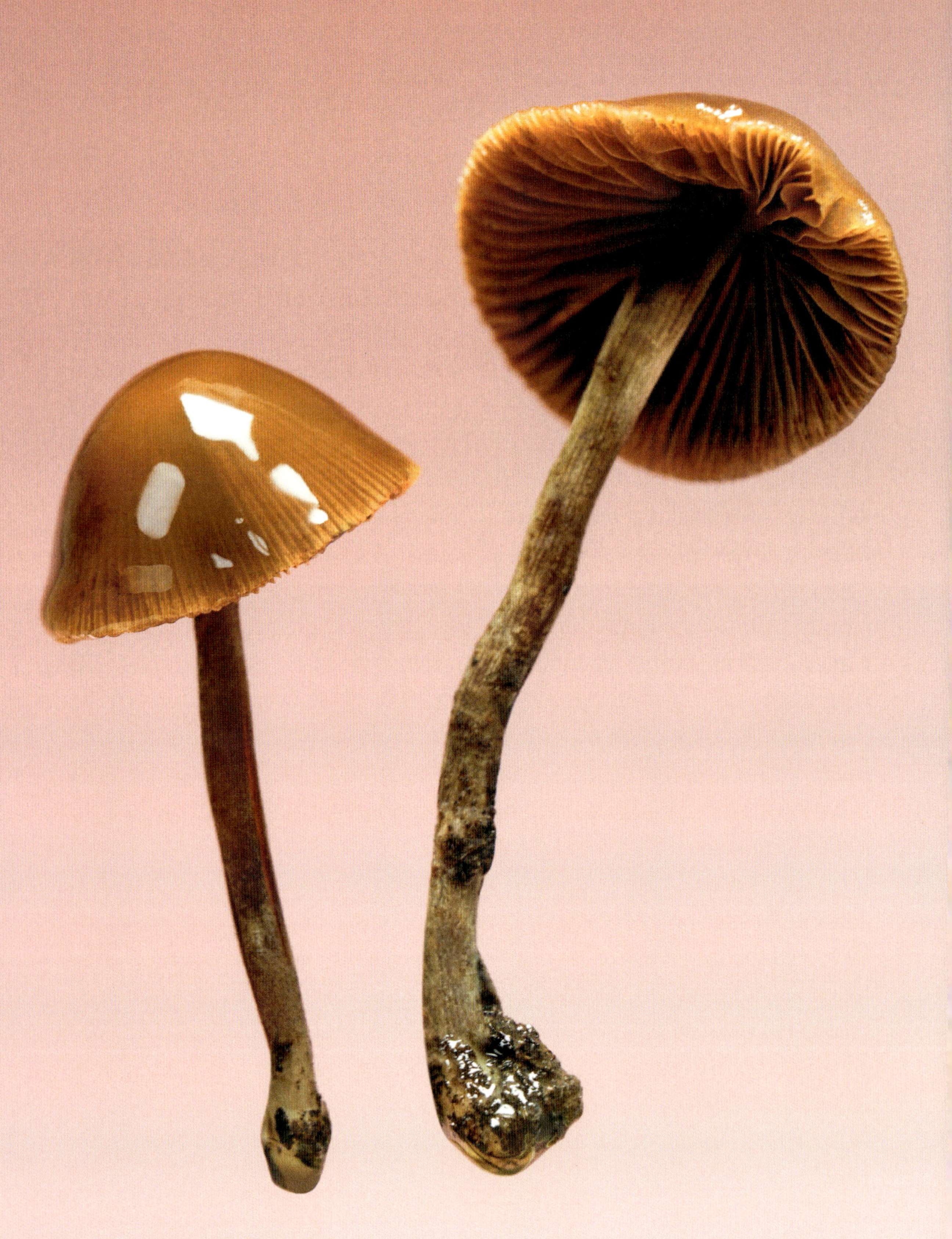

Recipes

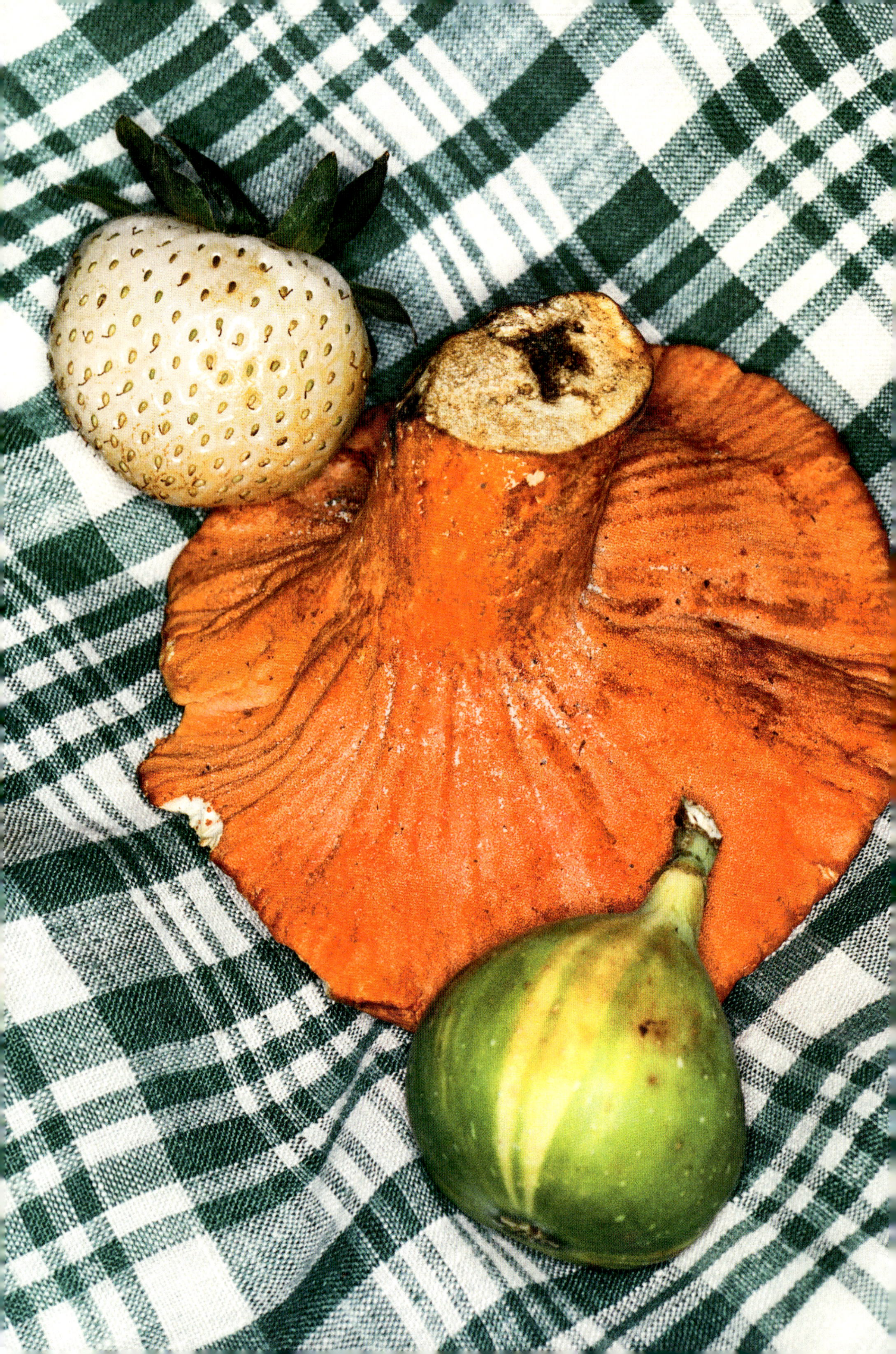

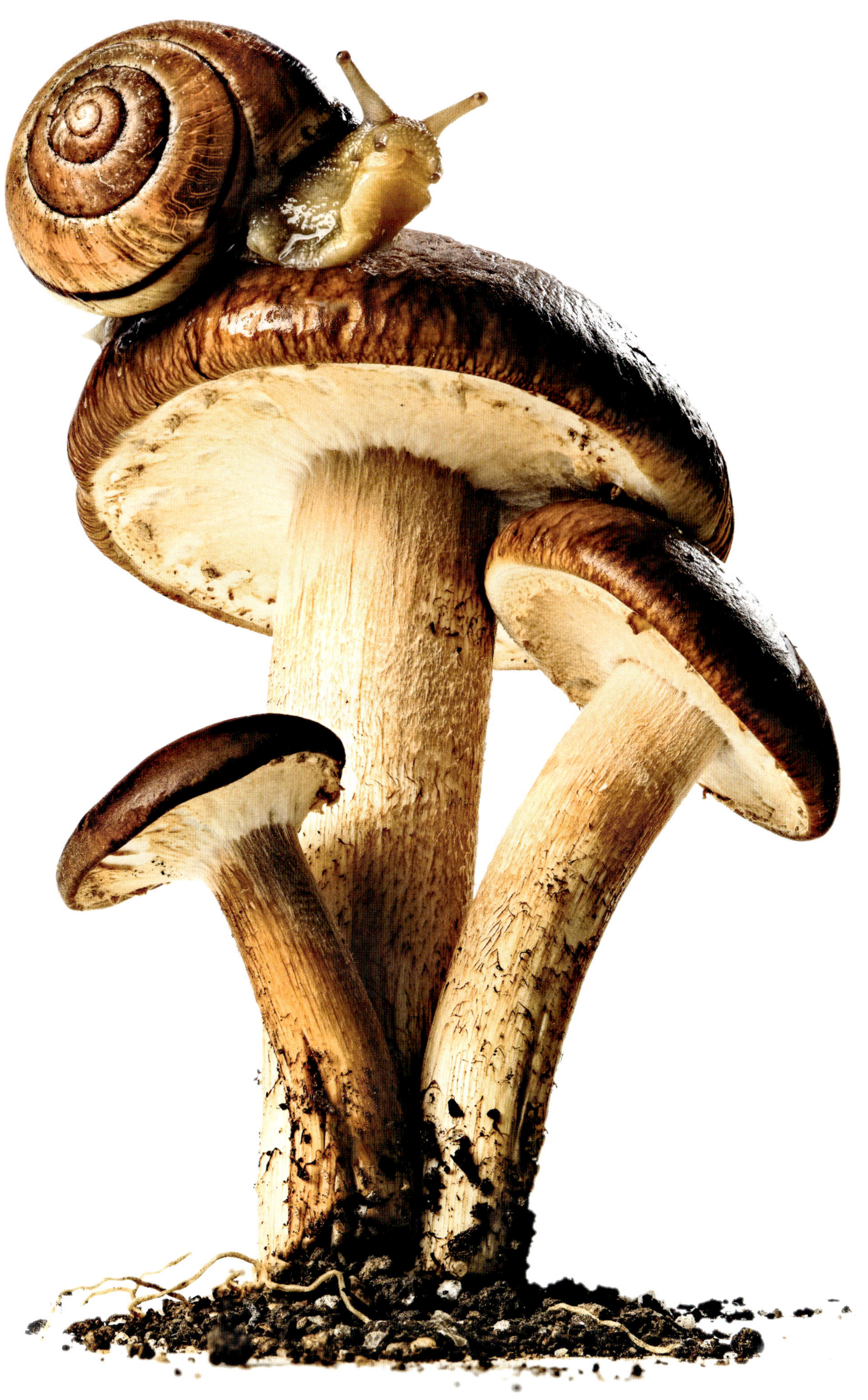

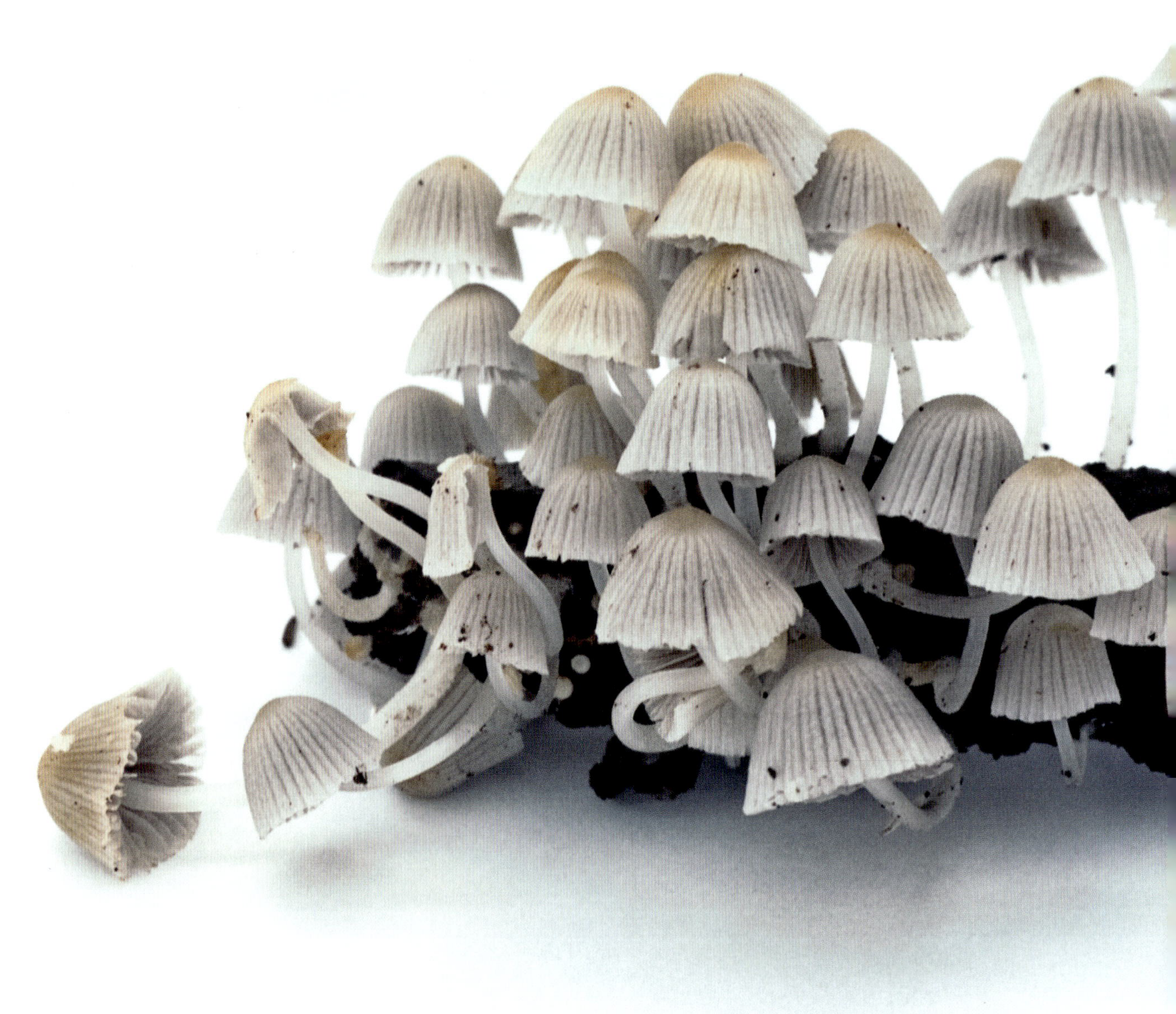

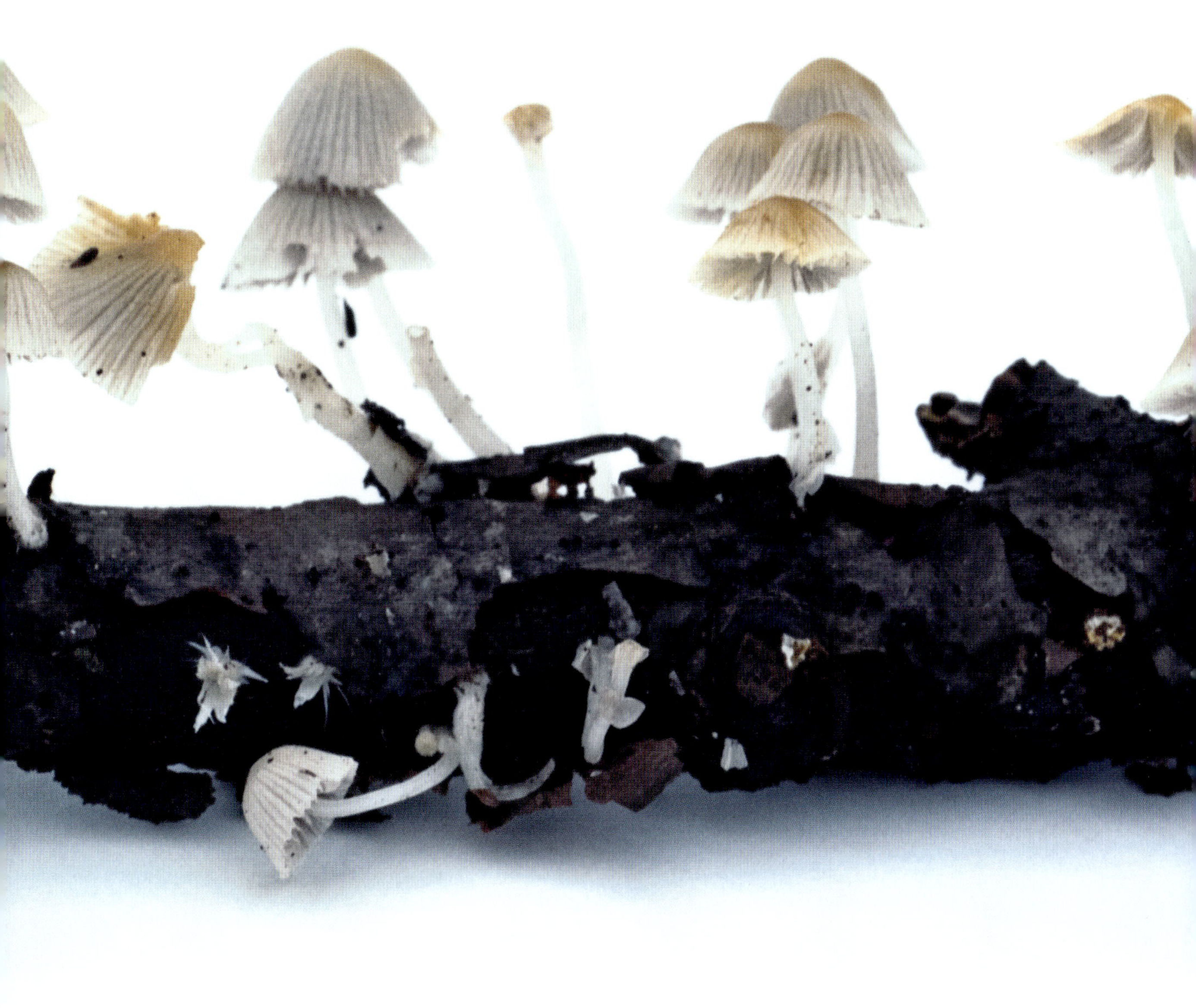

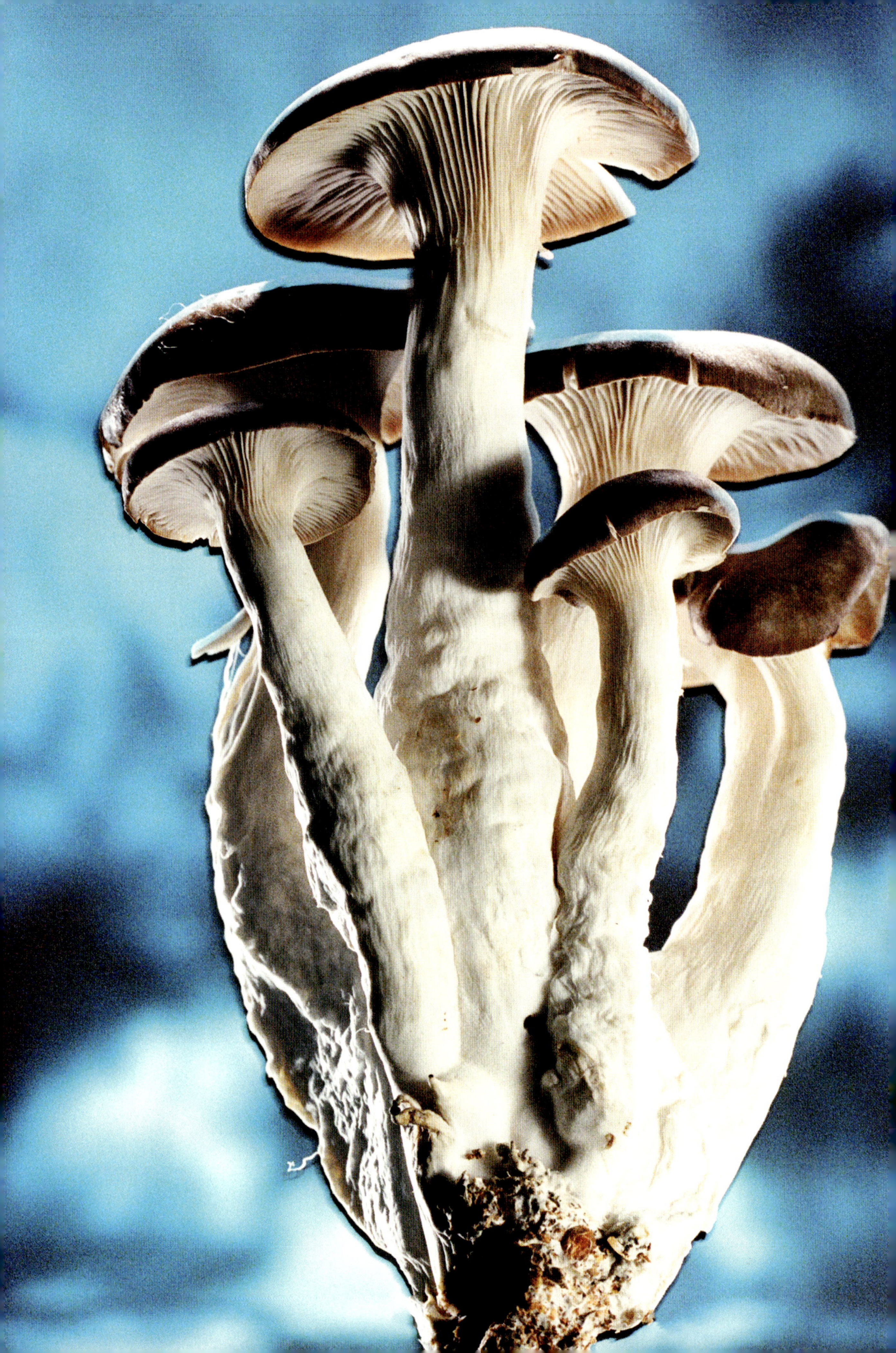

Foreword

by **Jeremy Lee**

PAGE XIII **Bobby Doherty**, *Untitled,* 2025, PAGE XIV **Takeshi Homma**, *Fukushima #48,* 2011
OPPOSITE **Bobby Doherty**, from *I Dream About Nothing,* 2023

In 1999, the RHS Chelsea Flower Show, in London, included a kitchen inside a garden pavilion — the Chef's Roof Garden designed by Terence Conran. Metal troughs brimmed with herbs, vegetables and fruits. It was as though a year's worth of harvests — of chard and peas, tomatoes and redcurrants — were burgeoning at once.

To reach the kitchen, there was what one might call a step, but was in fact a cunningly designed transparent box. This box remained unexposed until the judges — who each year are tasked with giving awards to the most impressive garden displays — made their appearance. As the seven roving judges approached, a covering was pulled off the step-box to reveal a patch of soil inside, dotted with tiny little mushrooms that miraculously — as if in an animated film — began to grow before our very eyes, sunlight working its magic. It was just the sort of trick that sparks the imagination and wins a gold medal at Chelsea. It did both.

Mushrooms are mysterious. More than once, I have seen them appear where one would swear there were none a moment ago. Be they porcini, morels or chanterelles, fungi materialise in front of eager foragers as they lean down and cut, filling a basket with practised ease before you can utter the word "omelette". Impermanence is indeed part of the mushroom's allure. Since the wild varieties appear so briefly and usually but once a year, enraptured cooks and gourmands will go to extraordinary lengths and dig into very deep pockets to acquire these rare beauties.

Antonio Carluccio, a wise owl of a cook, made fungi of all sorts famous at his Neal Street Restaurant, which he owned with his wife Priscilla. As I write, beside me is a reissue of Antonio's famed mushroom book *A Passion for Mushrooms,* celebrating 25 years since publication. Alongside that sits Roger Phillips' seminal book on mushrooms — titled simply *Mushrooms* — and another, *The Mushroom Feast* by Jane Grigson. There are more, all of a certain age. These wonderful guides instructed a public at large — and this cook in particular — not to live in mortal fear of eating mushrooms gathered in the wild, bolstering much confidence to explore the forest floor with due caution. I can still conjure Antonio and Priscilla at the helm of their restaurant, with a white truffle under glass and a great basket of porcini destined for the menu.

The best lesson learned when cooking wild mushrooms is that freshness and simplicity reveal the ephemeral flavour and texture. Cleaned exquisitely of any trace of woodland, the mushrooms are coarsely sliced, fried lightly in olive oil, and finished with a nut of butter, a whisper of garlic, a smattering of finely chopped shallot, and perhaps some parsley and a few drops of lemon juice.

I was the cook in residence that day at the flower show, but the opportunity to prepair the little button mushrooms never arose. Being kept under glass, they were to be admired only. Yet all these years later I still recall those enchanting white caps.

In this third volume from *The Gourmand* celebrating ingredients of influence, we meet an extensive and varied crop of unforgettable mushrooms, which have taken their rightful place under the spotlight to sprout, grow and amaze us with their presence.

OPPOSITE
Takeshi Homma, *Fukushima #43*, 2011

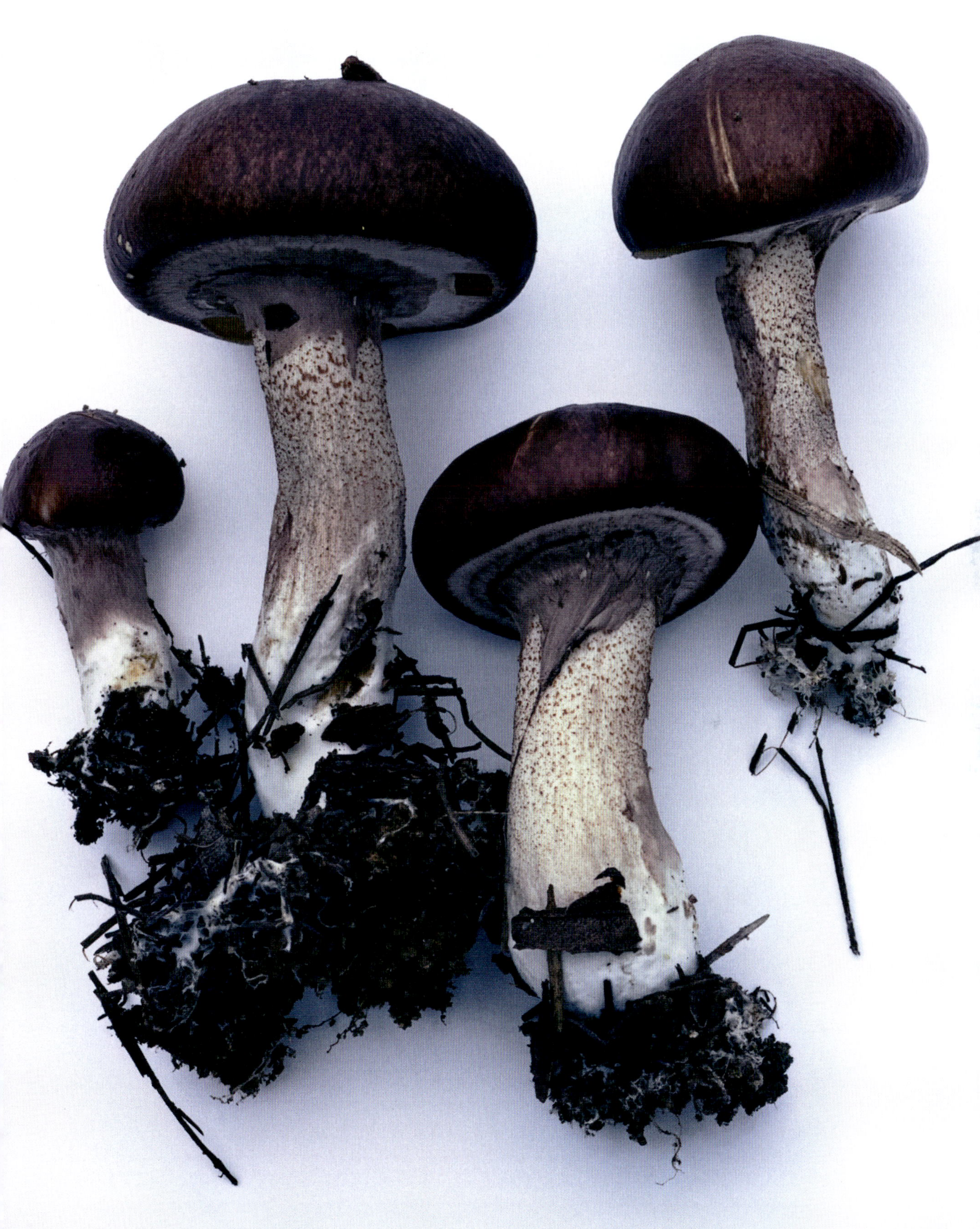

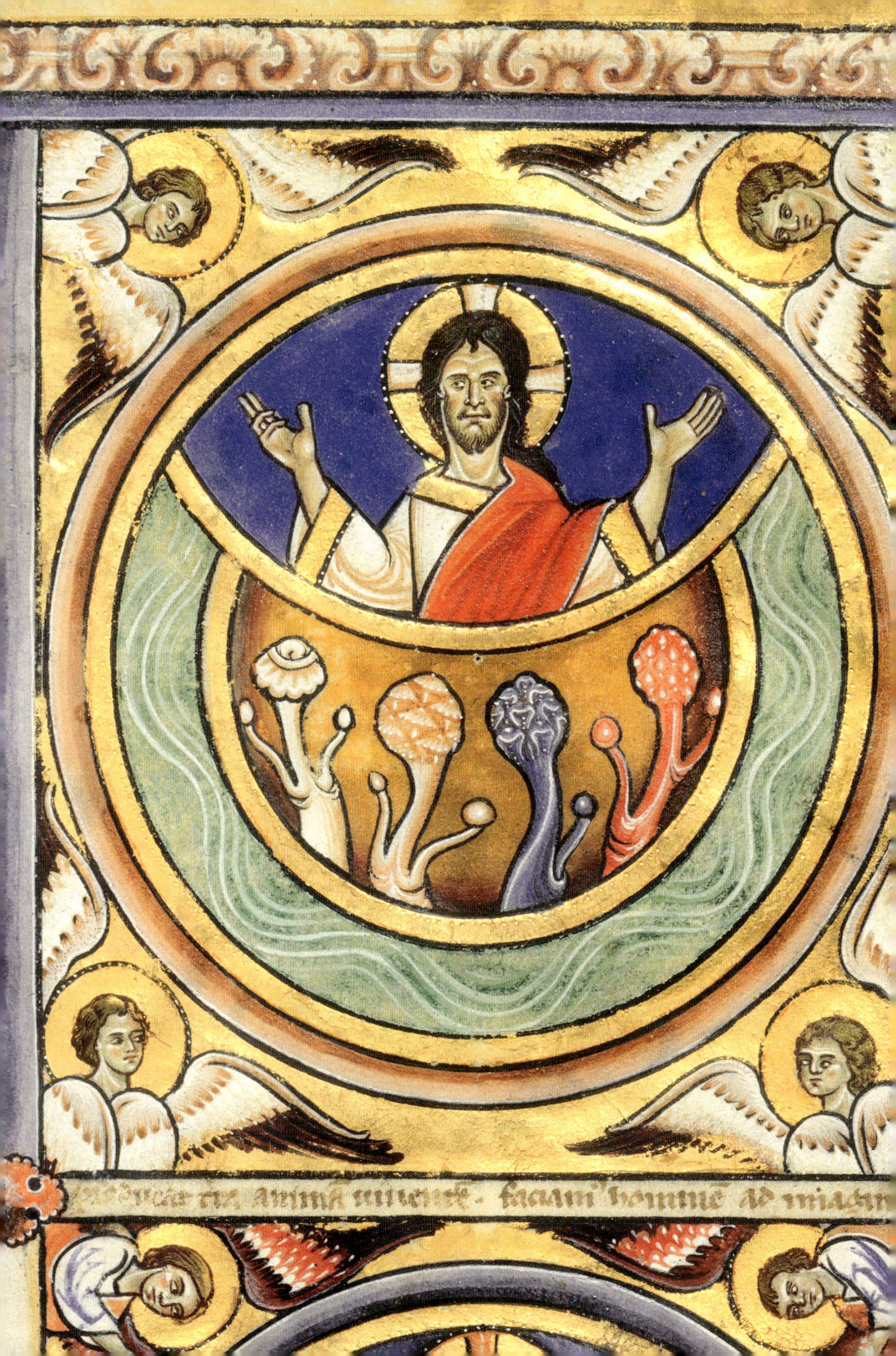

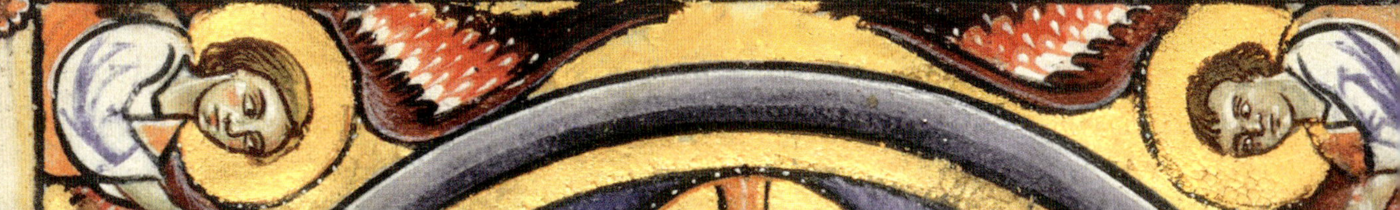

Introduction: Mushrooms are Magic

by **Jennifer Higgie**

OPPOSITE
God Creates Plants, Great Canterbury Psalter, c.1200–1340

Spawning apparently from nowhere, mushrooms are the mysterious spore-carrying bodies of fungi, which are neither plant nor animal (page 34). The influence of mushrooms on both palates and imaginations defies their often modest size. Despite their unprepossessing appearance, for millennia the mushroom has variously been a nourishing foodstuff, a folk medicine, a mind-altering, magical substance, a status symbol, a poison, and a shape-shifting subject for artists and writers.

Mushrooms have appeared in rock paintings and in images at burial sites, been venerated in sculptures for their psychoactive properties and graced still life paintings that honour the sanctity of the kitchen.

In the 20th century, the shape of the mushroom was emblematic of nuclear devastation, and in the 21st century, studies of mycelium – the web-like structure from which mushrooms emerge – have inspired new thinking about art, design, architecture and communication (studies show that mushrooms talk to each other).

Arguably the first representation of a mushroom in Western art is Hieronymus Bosch's *Haywain Triptych* (c.1512–15) – but you need sharp eyes to spot it. At once a study of the pilgrimage of life and a vision of hell on Earth, peer closely at the large painting and you'll see an angel metamorphosing into a monster, while elsewhere men slit throats, rat-like winged creatures loom, a pedlar defends himself against a vicious dog, and a deer on its hind legs leads a fragile man to his doom.

At the centre of the three panels is the wagon or haywain. Seated atop it, a man plays a lute, a couple embrace and another man prays. To its right, a mob surges forwards as if to mount the wooden vehicle – despite the fact that it's being driven by the devil. A crag-like platform above the crowd is crowned by a curious object: an enormous mushroom. A minor detail in a very busy painting, it's easy to overlook, which is a curious inversion given its strange significance.

It's not known if Bosch used hallucinogens to inspire his wild visions. However, there would

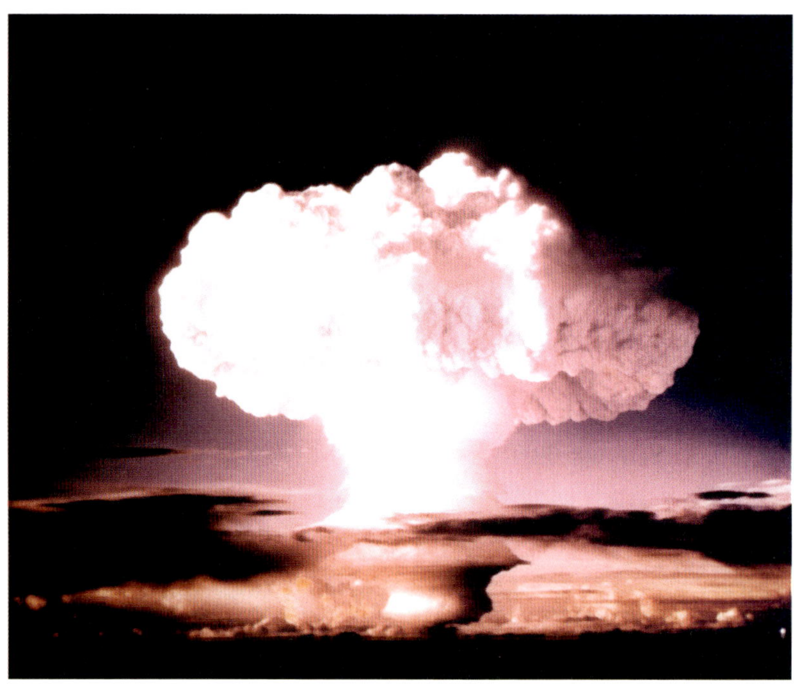

Operation Ivy, detonation on Enewetak Atoll, 1952
OPPOSITE **Hieronymus Bosch**, *Haywain Triptych*, c.1510–15 (detail)

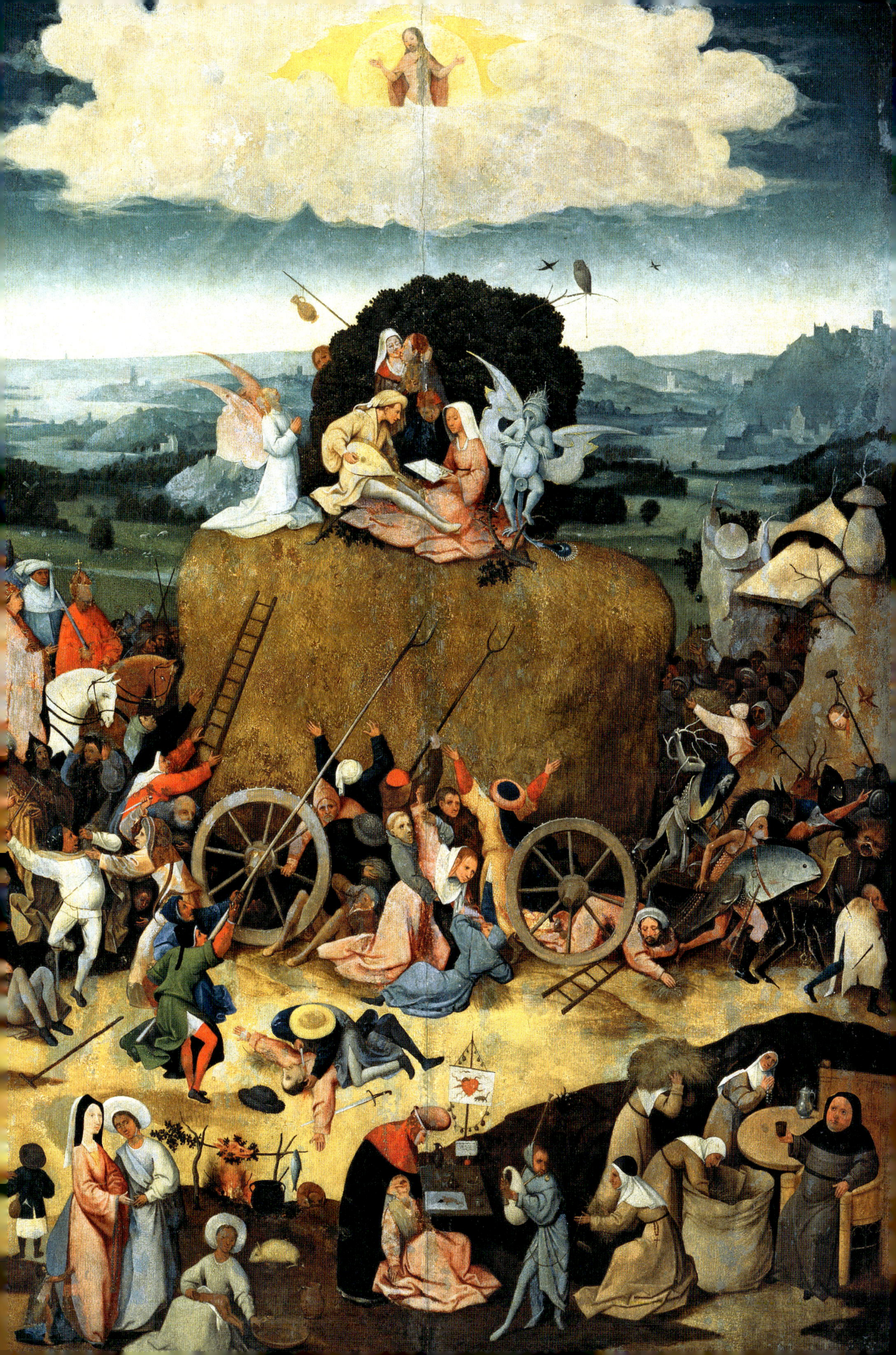

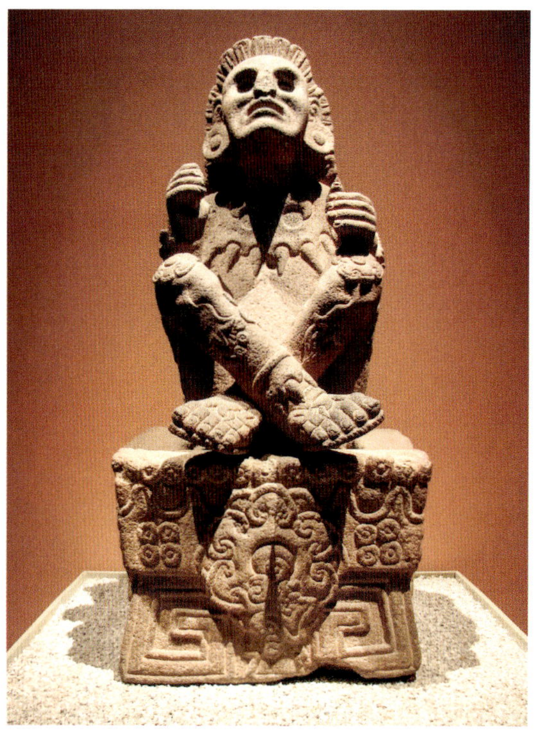

have been dozens of species of mushrooms — edible, poisonous, psychotropic and otherwise — in the forests surrounding the painter's home in 's-Hertogenbosch in the Netherlands. It's possible that Bosch's inclusion of the mushroom in his painting was a nod to their hallucinatory and revelatory effects; the very types of visions that his paintings embodied.

•

Long before Bosch's painting, mushrooms featured prominently in art and ritual far beyond Europe's borders, including in prehistoric rock paintings in the Kimberley region of Australia, the Sandawe rock art of eastern Tanzania, and the cave paintings of Tassili n'Ajjer in Algeria. At the Kudakkallu Parambu burial site in the Kerala region of India, a group of megalithic, mysterious mushroom-shaped monuments were created between 2000 BCE and 500 CE, and in Central and South America, archaeologists have unearthed so-called mushroom stones, which were carved around the same time as the Indian burial monuments; these were possibly used in psychoactive rituals across the ancient civilizations of Mesoamerica and beyond.

In the National Museum of Anthropology in Mexico City sits a statue of Xochipilli, Aztec god of art, games, dance, flowers and song, who instructed both mortals and deities in the uses of *teonanacatl*, "flesh of the gods", psychoactive mushrooms of the genus *Psilocybe* that grow throughout Mexico. Carved by an unknown artist between the 12th and 15th centuries, Xochipilli sits on a patterned plinth, cross-legged and tense-jawed, his hands and face raised to the sky as if frozen in a trance state. His body is decorated with various psychotropic plants, including *teonanacatl* mushrooms on his knees and earlobes. Clusters of mushrooms emerge alongside a curvaceous, stylized bloom on the plinth that supports him.

Statue of Xochipilli, 12th–15th century
OPPOSITE **Tomoyuki**, ivory netsuke of a woman with matsutake mushroom, c.1865

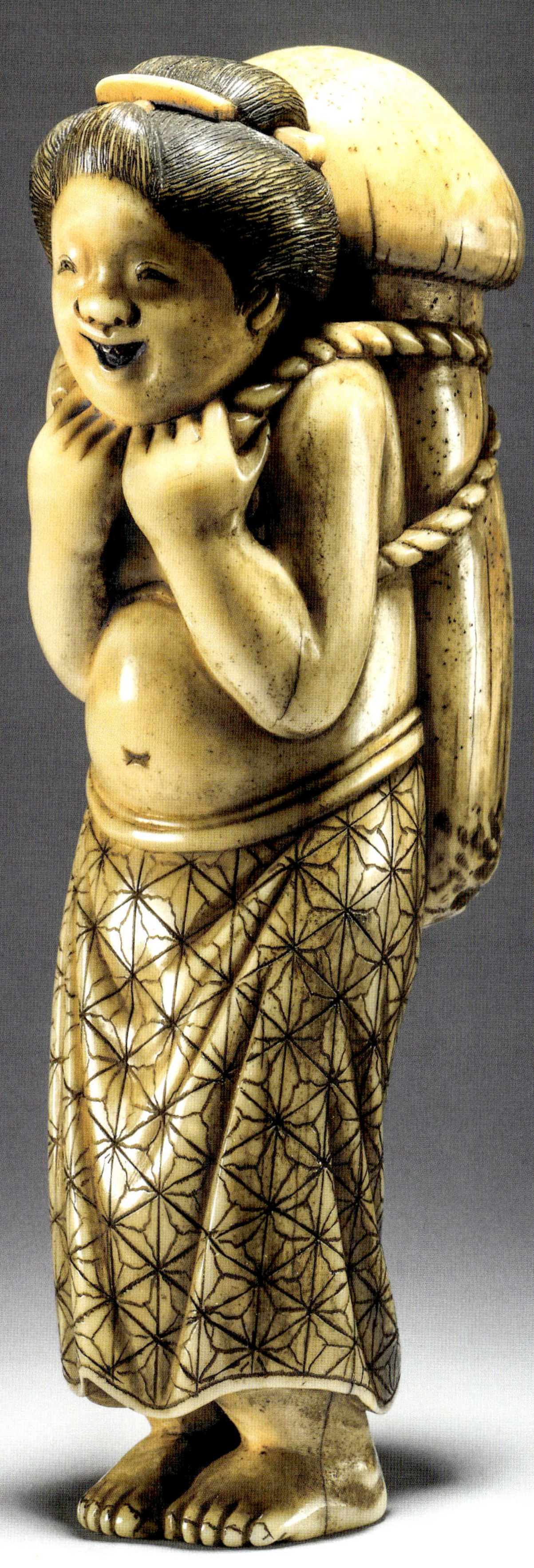

Considered plants of immortality, in ancient Egypt mushrooms were believed to be a gift to humanity from the god Osiris, and deemed so precious they could only be served to royalty; commoners were not even permitted to touch them. Depictions of mushrooms can be found on hieroglyphic tablets and in wall paintings; a frieze at the Temple of Hathor (c.50 BCE) shows a woman holding a basket in the shape of a mushroom, and the design of many of the country's temple pillars seems to be inspired by mushrooms as well. Fringe theories have it that the shape of the Pharaoh's crowns was inspired by *Psilocybe cubensis* — commonly known today as magic mushrooms (though this variety has never been known to grow in Egypt).

While mushrooms are less prevalent in Greek and Roman art, images of them were included in mosaics, frescos and pottery; a beautiful example is the 5th-century BCE wall plaque currently housed in the Louvre, *Exultation of the Flower*, from Pharsalia in Northern Greece. In his 1960 book *Food for Centaurs*, the classicist Robert Graves interpreted the relief as an image of Demeter and Persephone exchanging psychoactive mushrooms as part of the rituals known as the Eleusinian Mysteries, which for more than a thousand years took place in Eleusis, or Elefsina, every autumn. Details of what happened during these ceremonies dedicated to Demeter, goddess of the harvest, and Persephone, queen of the underworld, are scarce: revealing its secrets was punishable by death.

Only members of the nobility in Japan were permitted to eat the rare matsutake mushrooms, which were often gifted to visiting dignitaries, though this changed with matsutake farming in the 17th century, and the growing popularity of the mushroom was even reflected in fashion. From the 17th to the 19th centuries, netsuke were all the rage: these small decorative objects made of ivory, bone or wood acted as weights at the end of cords

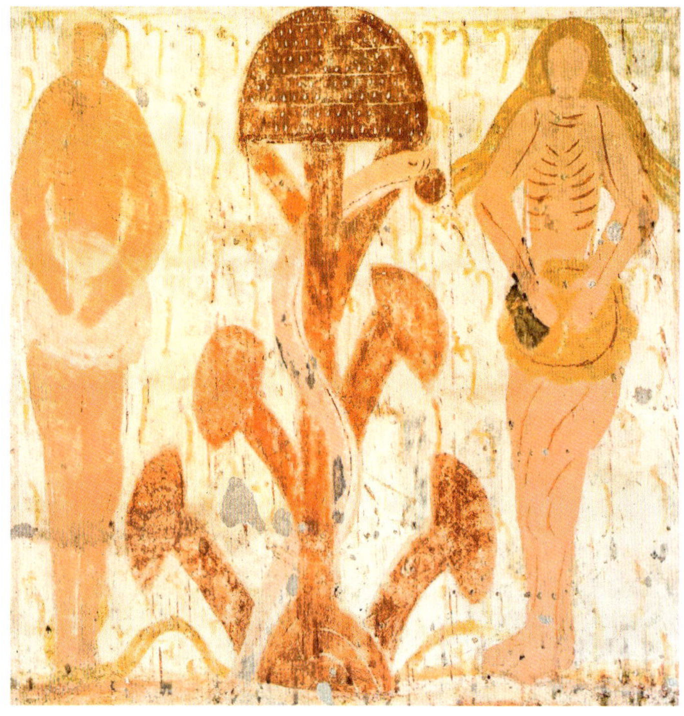

Temptation in the Garden of Eden,
Chapel of Plaincourault, Indre, Central France, c.129

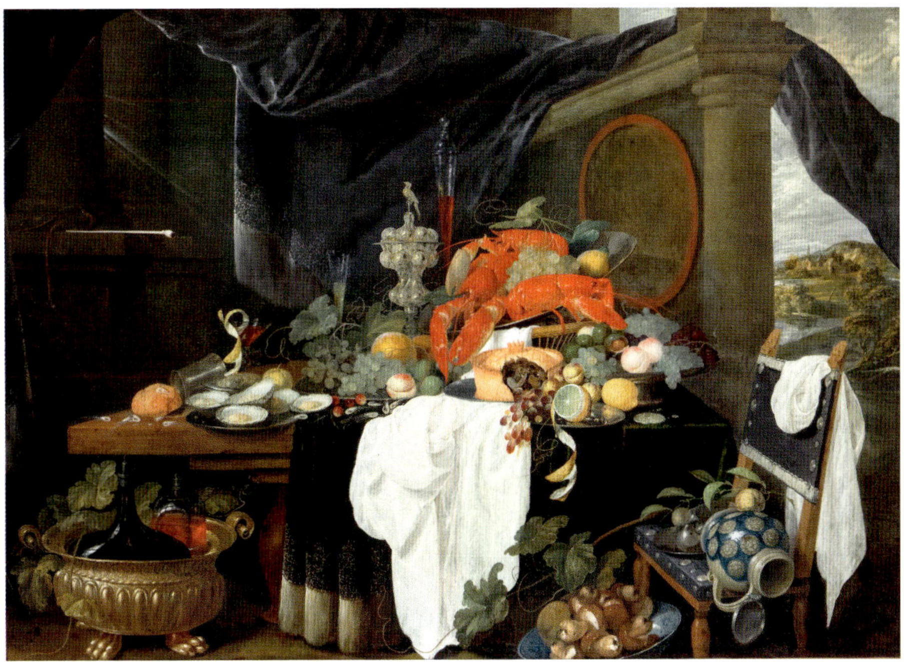

looped through a kimono belt and attached to a pouch. Netsuke came in all shapes – from plants and people to abstract shapes – and many of them depict mushrooms. One especially ribald netsuke, created around 1865 by the artist known as Tomoyuki, depicts a grinning woman, naked from the waist up and carrying a huge phallic matsutake mushroom on her back.

•

After Bosch's inclusion of a mushroom in *The Haywain Triptych*, images of them rapidly spread across Europe. In the Flemish Baroque (c.1600–1750), the golden age of still life, mushrooms are included in many luscious paintings of edible spreads. In Andries Benedetti's sumptuous still life from the 1640s, a table groans beneath the weight of lobsters, oysters, peaches and lemons; in the shadows beneath the table is a basket of mushrooms (possibly *Boletus edulis* – also called the penny bun mushroom because it looks like a bread roll). In a mid-17th-century painting by Otto Marseus van Schrieck (page 52), *Still Life with Mushrooms, Lizard and Insects*, the table is transformed into a fantastical landscape, where fleshy mushrooms and lichen indicate a threatening underworld. Equally fantastic is the German painter Franz Werner Tamm's *Still Life with Flowers, Dead Birds and Pieces of Ruins* (1712) in which large mushrooms catch the light in the midst of a voluptuous carnage of animals and overblown blooms.

The 19th century was a time not only of great advances in scientific discovery but also of shifts in societal attitudes to gender. Women in the West demanded greater access to education, and their voices, in all fields, were starting to make themselves heard. Small groups of talented female artists in Europe and America who were interested in the natural sciences became important botanical illustrators. An even smaller group focused solely on mycology. These included Mary

Andries Benedetti, *Still Life with Fruit, Oysters and Lobsters*, c.1640
FOLLOWING **Jan Josef Horemans the Younger**, *A Kitchen Still Life with Apples*, 1773

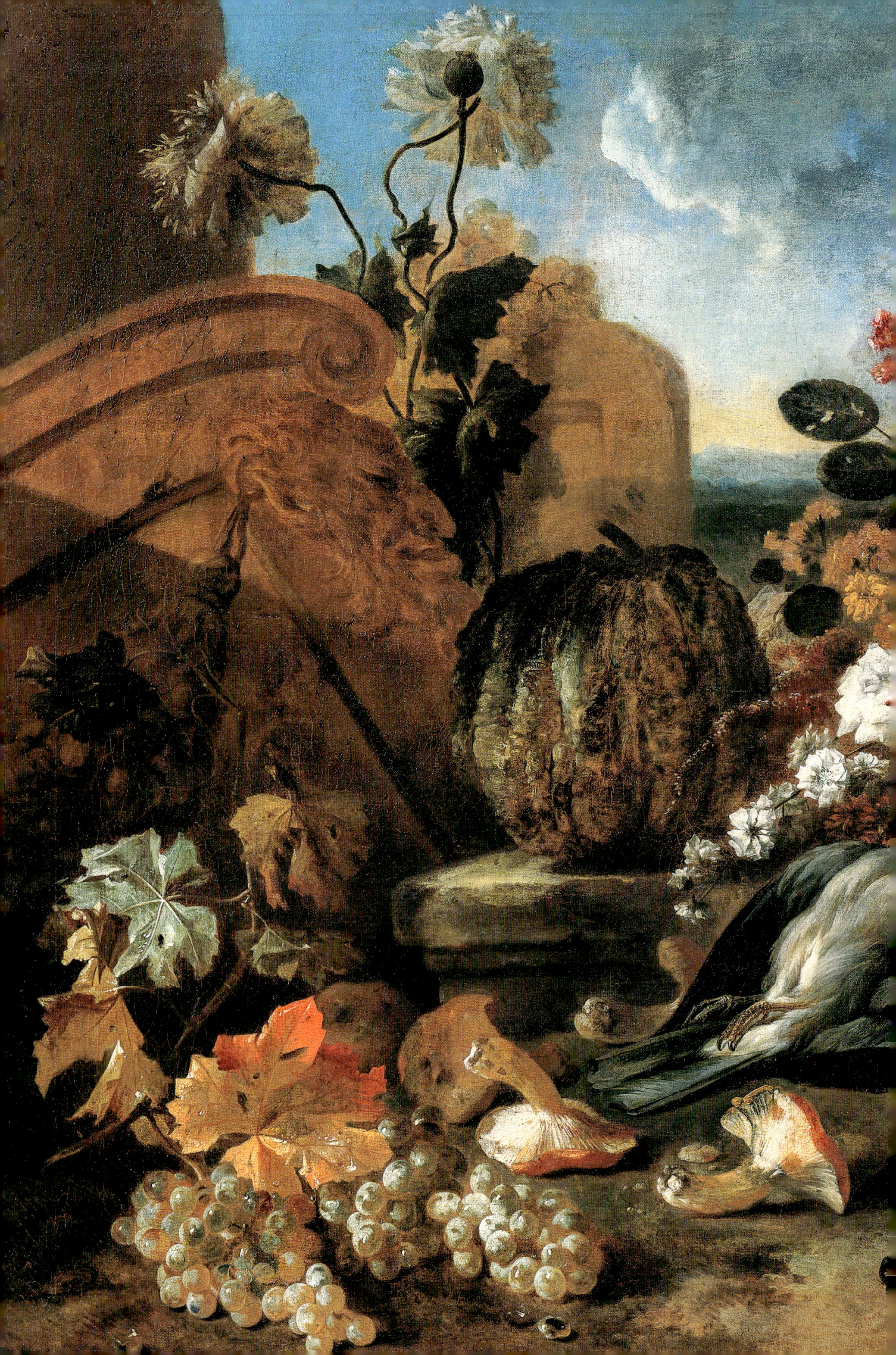

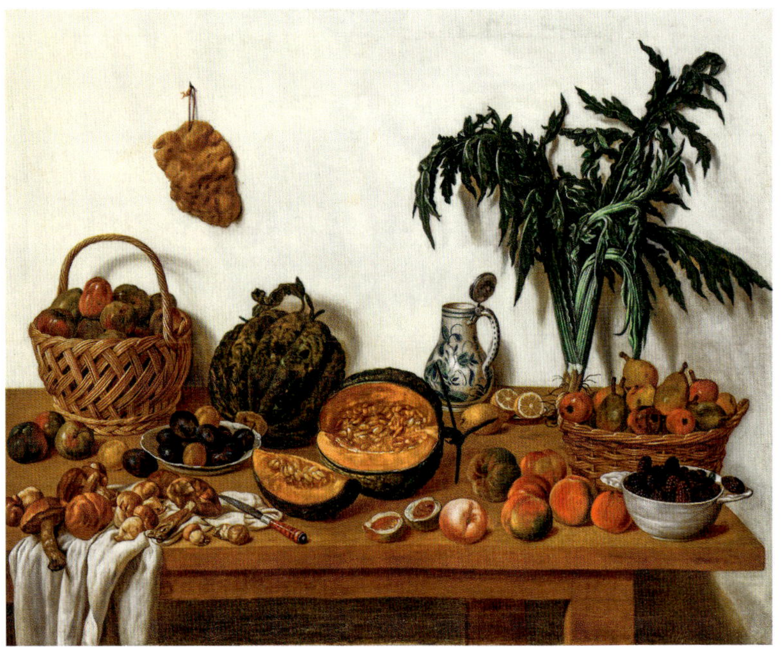

Elizabeth Banning (page 47) — who wrote in 1880 that she had "clean gone mad"[1] for frog-stools — and Anna Maria Hussey (page 47), author of the 1847 book *Illustrations of British Mycology: Containing Figures and Descriptions of the Funguses of Interest and Novelty Indigenous to Britain in Two Volumes.*

Despite the hurdles they faced — as women, they couldn't vote and had little access to formal art training or higher education — many of these illustrators were generous with their knowledge, sharing their detailed botanical drawings with scientists, doctors, herbalists and gardeners.[2]

One of the most renowned mycologist artists was Beatrix Potter (page 62), the English author and illustrator of the *Peter Rabbit* children's books (1902–12). Potter was passionate about fungi, creating over 250 drawings and watercolours of various species. Her biographer, Linda Lear, wrote that Potter was drawn to fungi first by their ephemeral fairy qualities, and then by the variety of their shape and colour, and the challenge they posed to watercolour techniques. Unlike insects or shells or even fossils, mushrooms also invited an autumn foray into fields and forests, where the imagination-rich Potter could go in her pony cart without being encumbered by family.[3]

Although some brave souls ate mushrooms in pre-19th-century England, they were also feared as poisonous and reviled as plants that thrived in dark, moist environments, and were considered if not sinister, then at least uncomfortably mysterious. Several writers referred to mushrooms as "excrements of the earth", and the renowned 17th-century London doctor Stephen Bradwell described them as "a bundle of putrefaction, arising of a cold, moist, viscous matter of the Earth."[4]

In the 19th century, perceptions started to shift. Long associated with magic (despite, or perhaps because of, their shadowy growing habits), mushrooms were frequently depicted by the Victorian fairy painters as symbols of otherworldliness (page 130). The work of Richard Dadd is brimming with mushrooms, including the nocturnal study

Franz Werner Tamm
Still Life with Flowers, Dead Birds and Pieces of Ruins, 1712

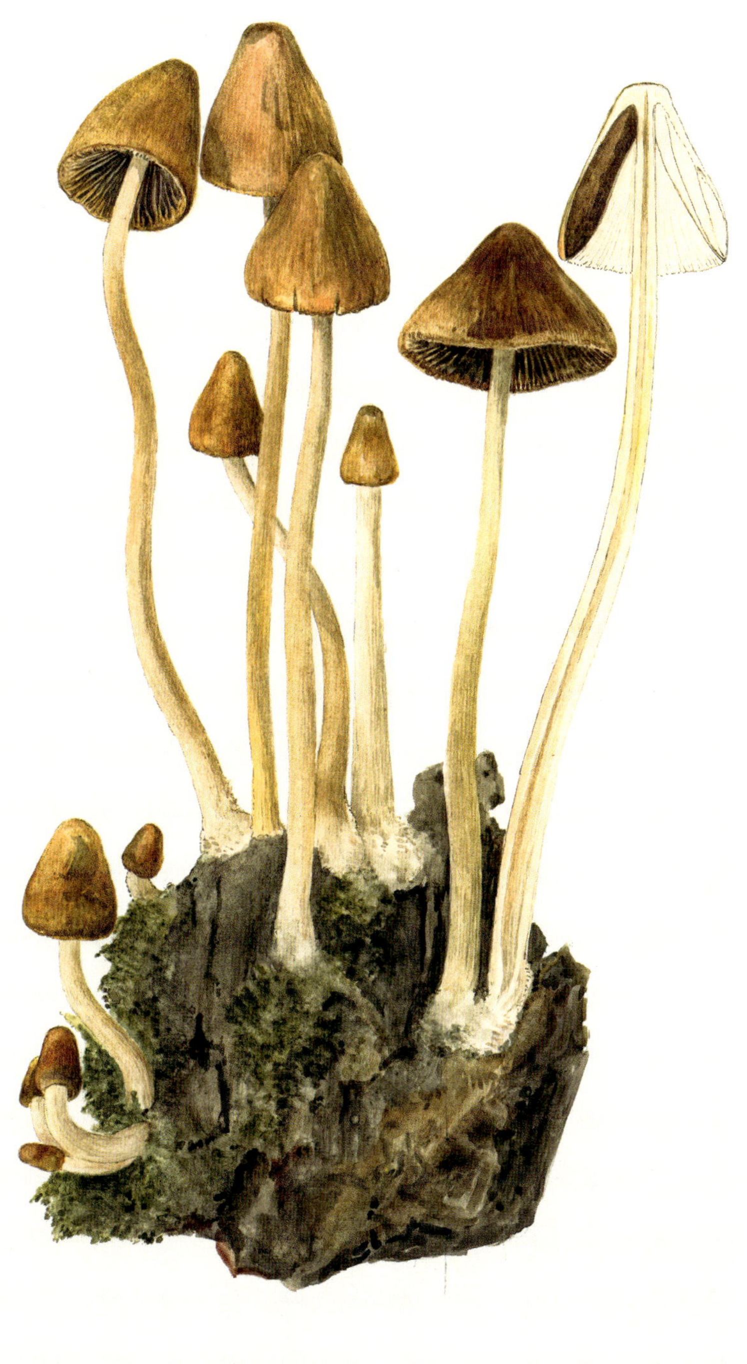

Beatrix Potter, *Psathyrella conopilus*, 1894
FOLLOWING **Anna Maria Hussey**, *Boletus pachypus*, 1864

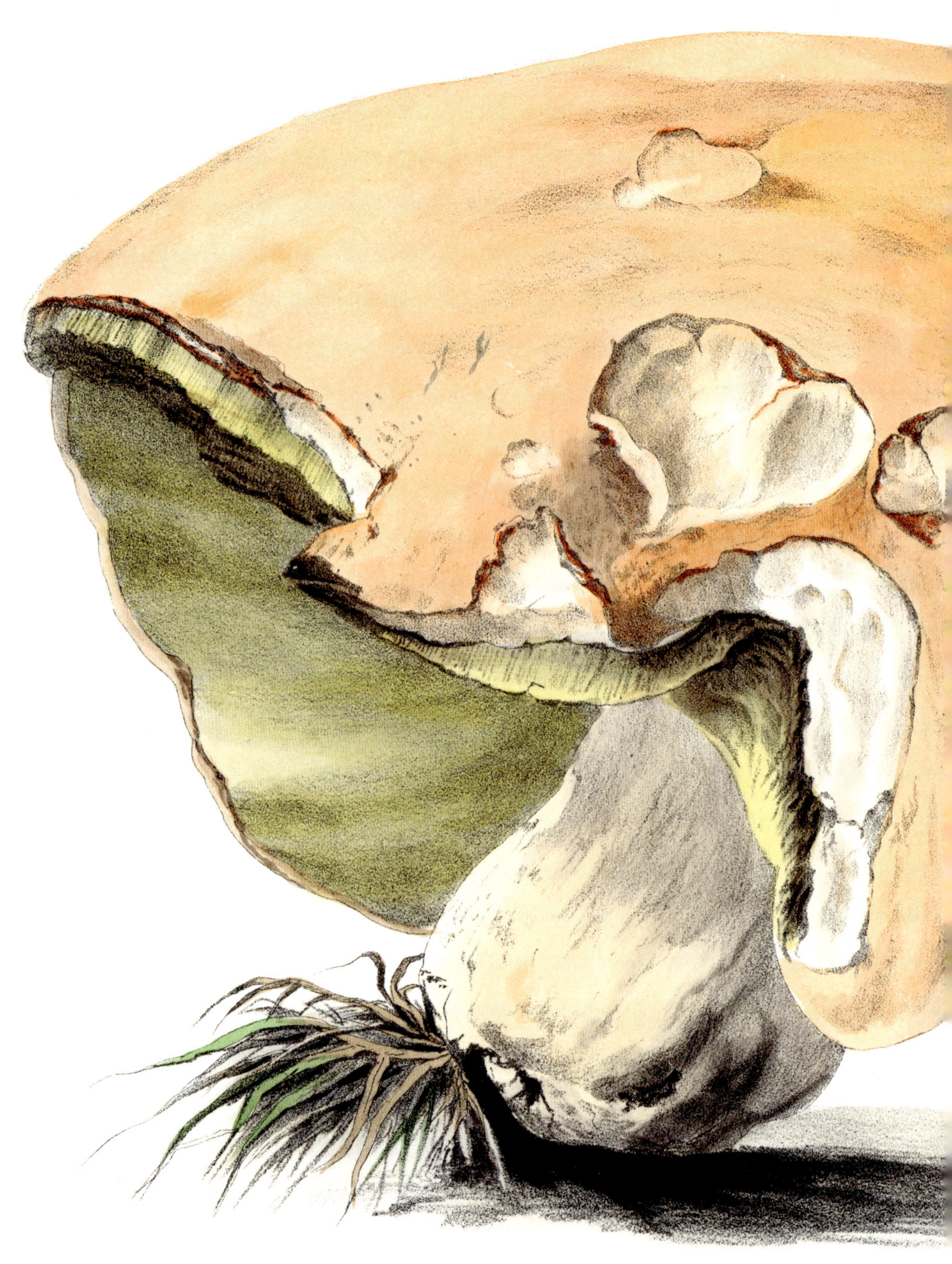

A.M.H. del.

Boletus

Plate XXII.

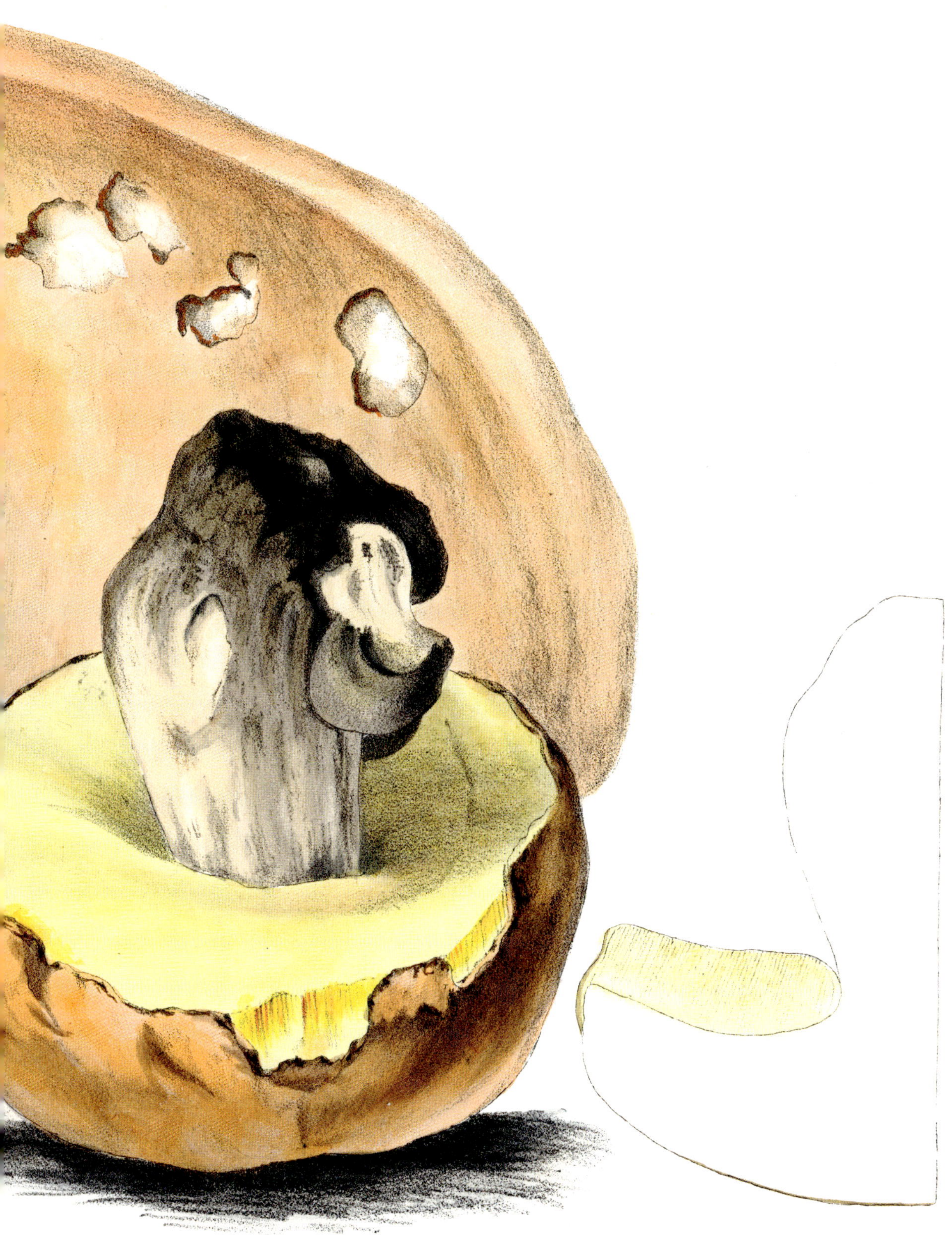

Reeve, Brothers lith. et imp.

, Berk.

Puck (1841), in which the titular naked sprite (or demon) sits atop a giant mushroom with a soft brown cap on a stout white stem as fairies dance around its base. In Dadd's microscopically detailed *Contradiction: Oberon and Titania* (1854–58), the ground is scattered with forest leaves and small pale-brown mushrooms.

Eleanor Vere Boyle's *Fairies Sitting on Two Flowers or White Clitocyboid Mushrooms* (1872) shows sprites lounging on mushrooms as comfortable as sofas, while Lewis Carroll's bestselling 1865 novel *Alice's Adventures in Wonderland* (page 124), famously reiterated their magical properties. In Sir John Tenniel's delicate illustrations, Alice stands on her toes to talk to a caterpillar, who is smoking a hookah and seated on a giant capped mushroom (routinely stylised by artists in the decades to come as the red-and-white hallucinogenic fly agaric). The caterpillar encourages Alice to bite the mushroom, and taking his advice, its psychotropic properties help shape her journey through the upside-down Wonderland.

The late-19th-century artistic turn to realism—in tandem with a greater appreciation of fungi as food—saw artists depicting mushroom pickers as idealised symbols of country life. In the 1860s, the English artist James R Edgar, clearly in thrall to the nature-exalting Pre-Raphaelite Brotherhood, painted *The Mushroom Gatherer*, a romantic portrait of a placid young woman in a striped peasant's dress, sitting in a woodland with a basket of mushrooms beside her. Following this, Danish painter Peter Ilsted made the sensitive portrait *A Young Girl Preparing Chantarelles* (1892), the yellow of the subject's dress echoed in the flesh of the fungi. In 1895, on the other side of the world,

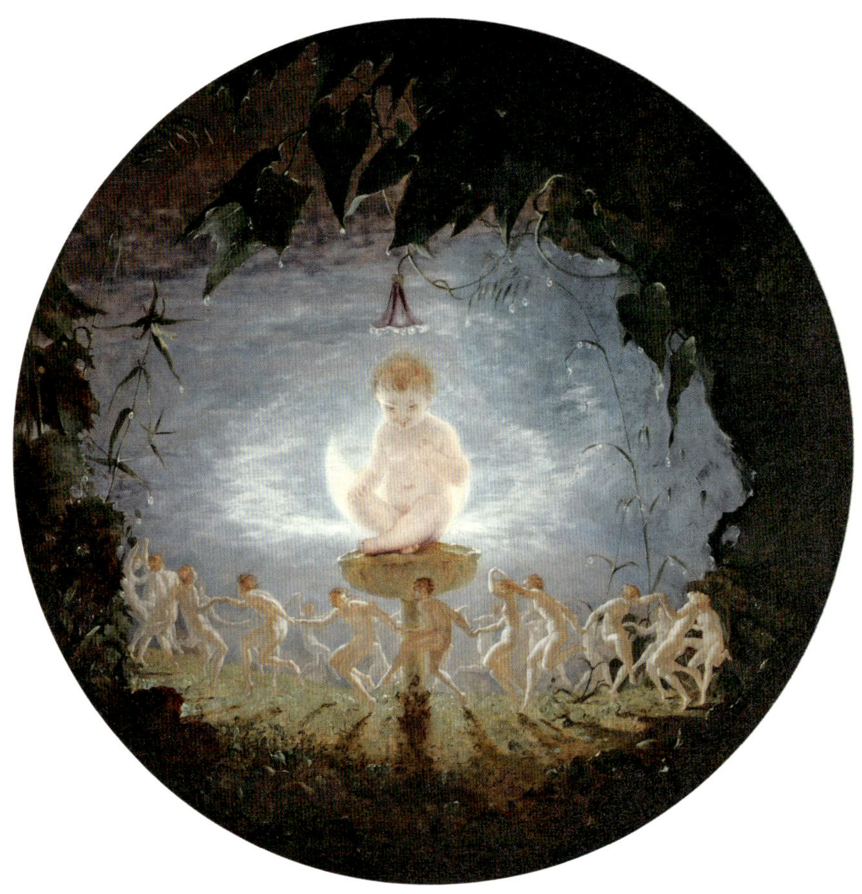

Richard Dadd
Puck, 1841

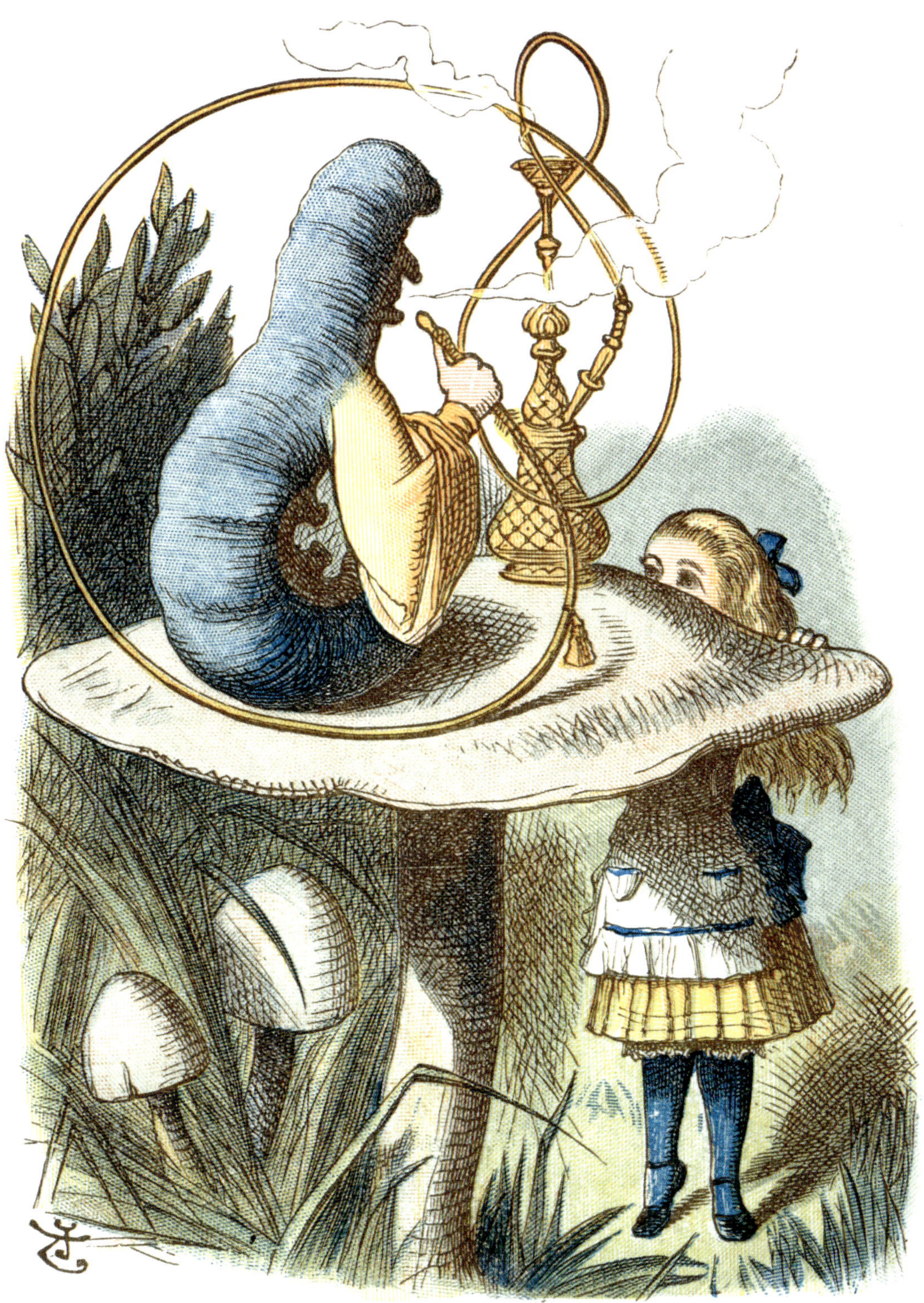

Sir John Tenniel
The Caterpillar, from *Alice's Adventures in Wonderland* by Lewis Carroll, 1865

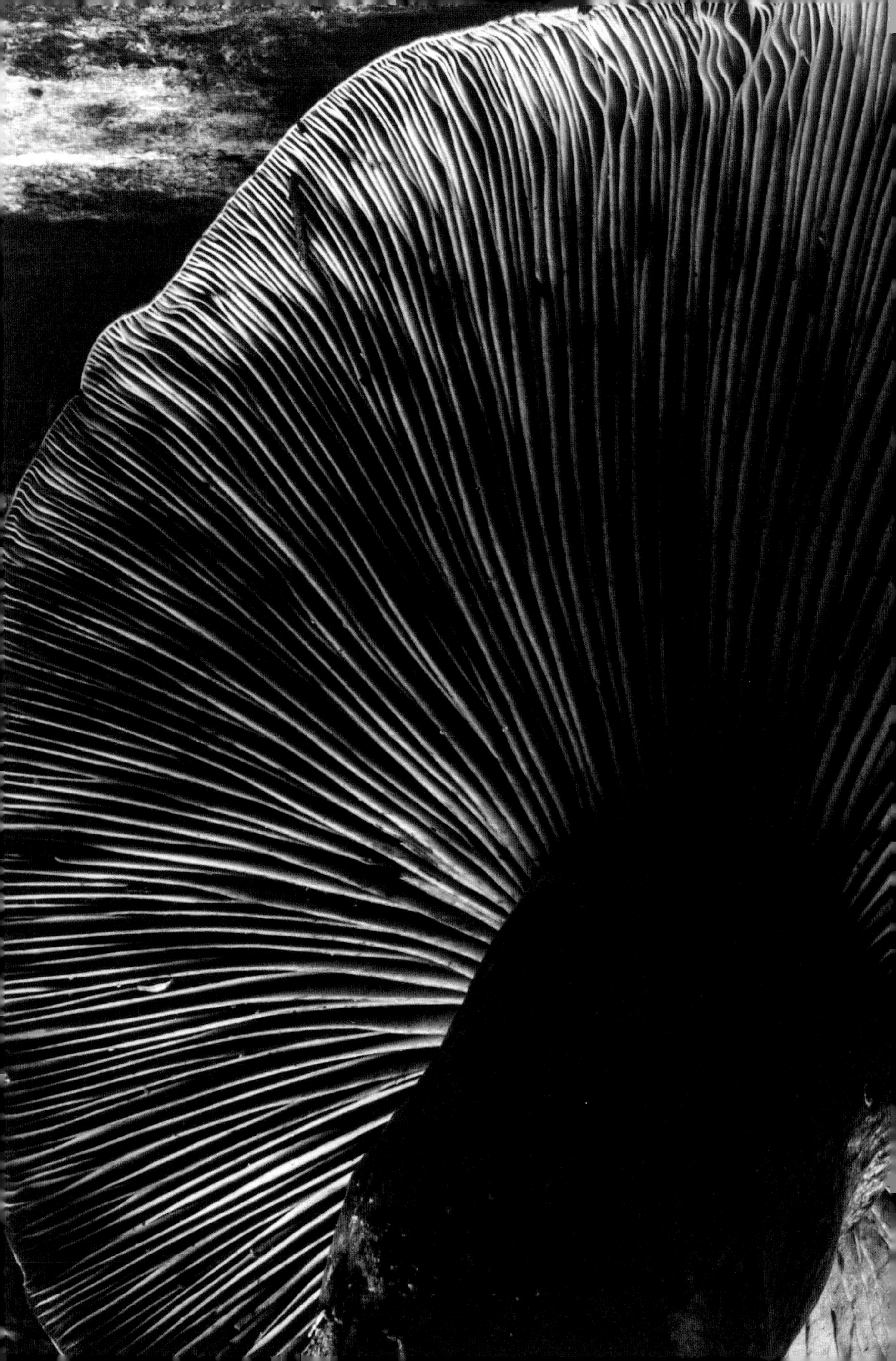

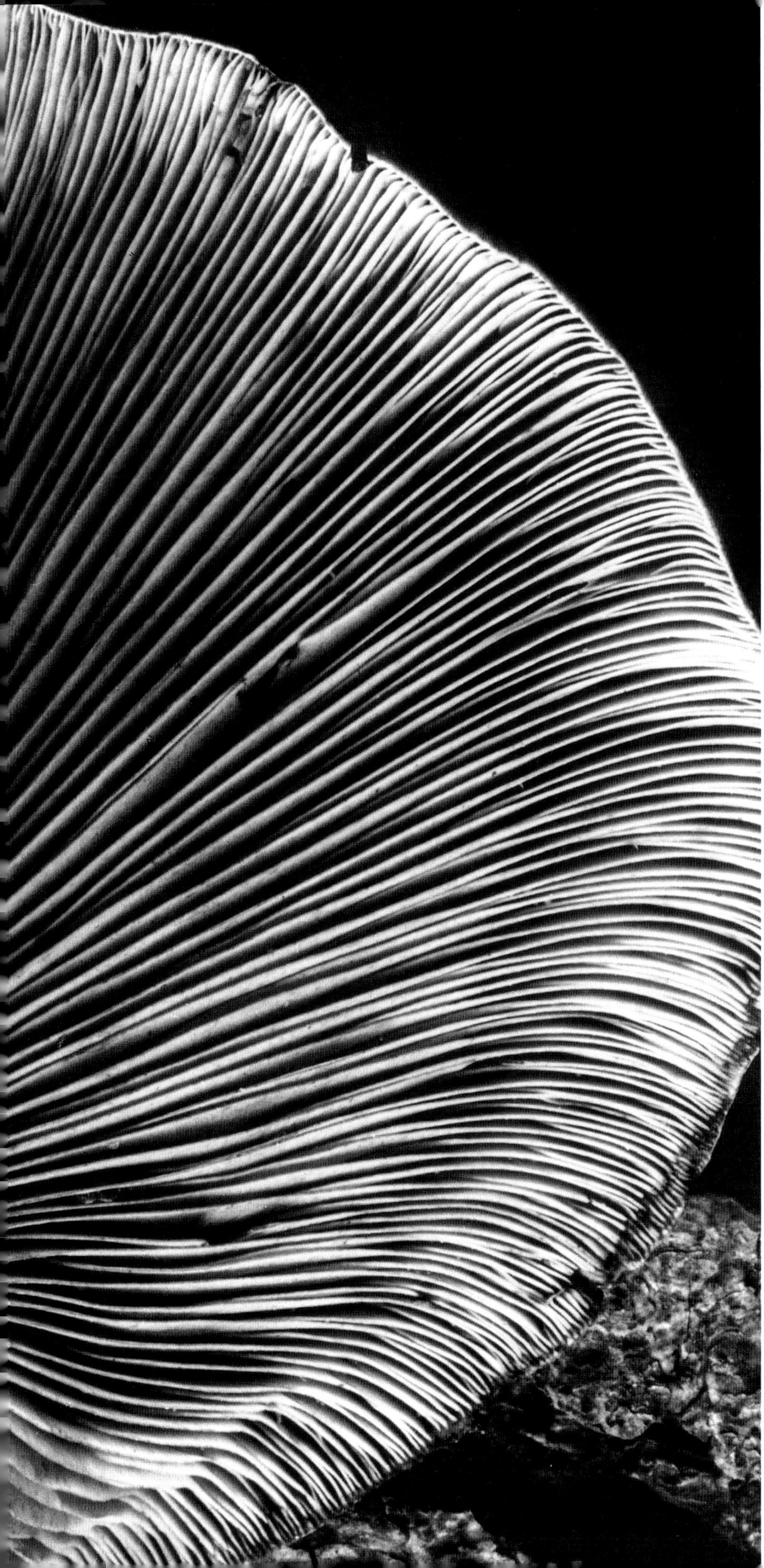

Edward Weston, *Mushroom*, 1931

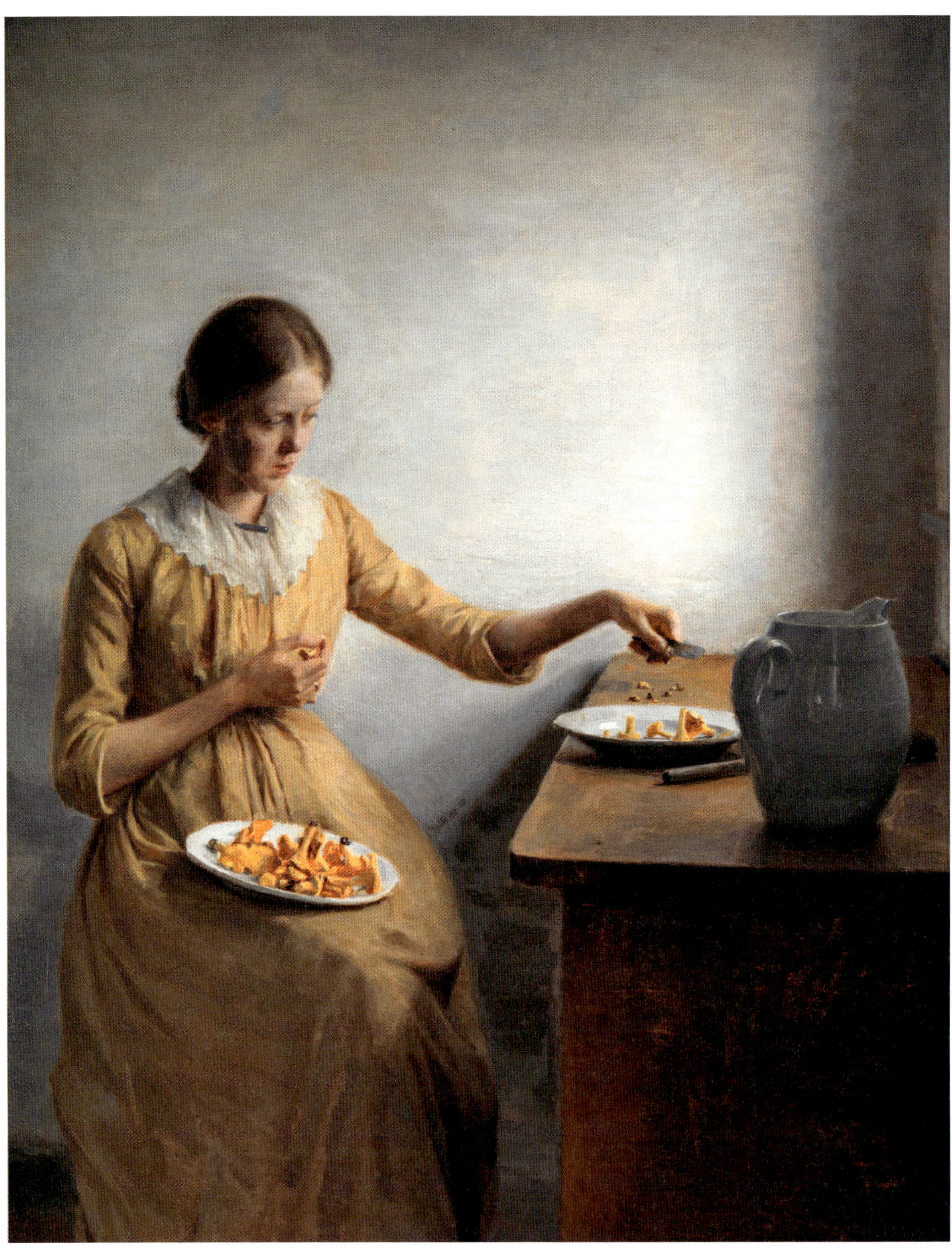

Peter Ilsted
En ung pige, der renser kantareller (A Young Girl Preparing Chanterelles), 1892

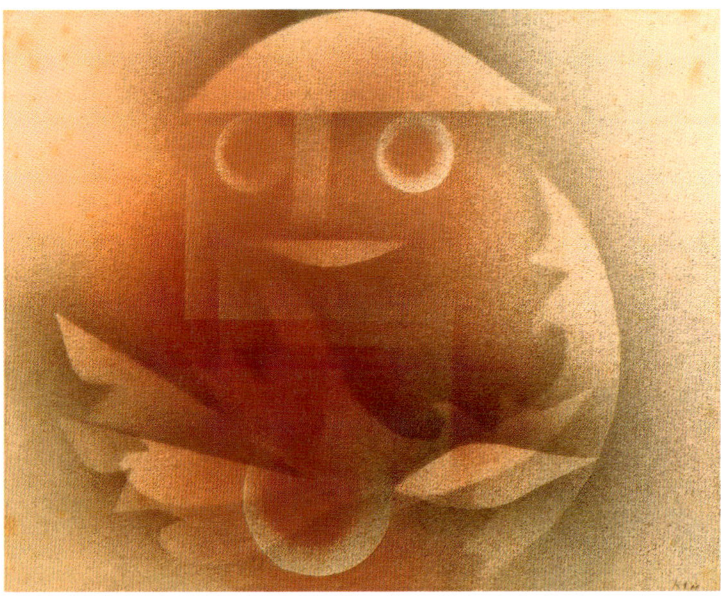

Jane Sutherland, one of the few female Australian Impressionists, painted *The Mushroom Gatherers,* a gorgeously dreamy study of women piling mushrooms into their aprons while standing in a vast lilac-inflected field.

•

Modernity saw artists employing mushrooms for myriad reasons — subjects for still lifes, inspiration for biomorphic sculptures and indicators of altered states, to name a few. In 1915, Russian artist Ilya Mashkov painted a still life with mushrooms that, while in debt to the great 17th-century still lifes of Holland, anticipated new artistic languages with its bold brushstrokes, skewed perspective and vivid palette. Five years later, the German American poet, philosopher, editor and photographer Ernst Fuhrmann shot a sensual, long-stemmed mushroom (its caps remarkably like ear buds) for his book *The Plant as a Living Creature* (1930). Another five years on, the Swiss-born German artist Paul Klee painted an ephemeral, almost cartoon-like mushroom morphing into a human face, its eyes like moons.

Photographer Edward Weston's dramatic black-and-white study from 1940 reveals the underside of a mushroom fanning out like ripples in water and, in 1944, Wassily Kandinsky, the great innovator of abstract painting, made his final artwork: a watercolour of patterned mushrooms, floating in a pale void like strange ships.

As the 20th century progressed, the mushroom continued to appear in various incarnations. Abstracting the everyday and inspired by the natural world, American sculptor Alexander Calder repeatedly employed the sensual curves of the mushroom as a motif. The artist and filmmaker Bruce Conner's first colour movie, the psychedelic *Looking for Mushrooms* (1959–67) comprises footage he shot travelling with his wife Jean and countercultural leader Timothy Leary across Mexico on a quest for magic mushrooms. Their journey wasn't an unusual one at the time for many — sourcing and consuming magic mushrooms was a way of rejecting the constraints of tradition and rigid thinking. It was inevitable that mushrooms, especially the psychedelic kind, would make their way into avant-garde movements.

Paul Klee
The Mushroom (der Pilz), 1925

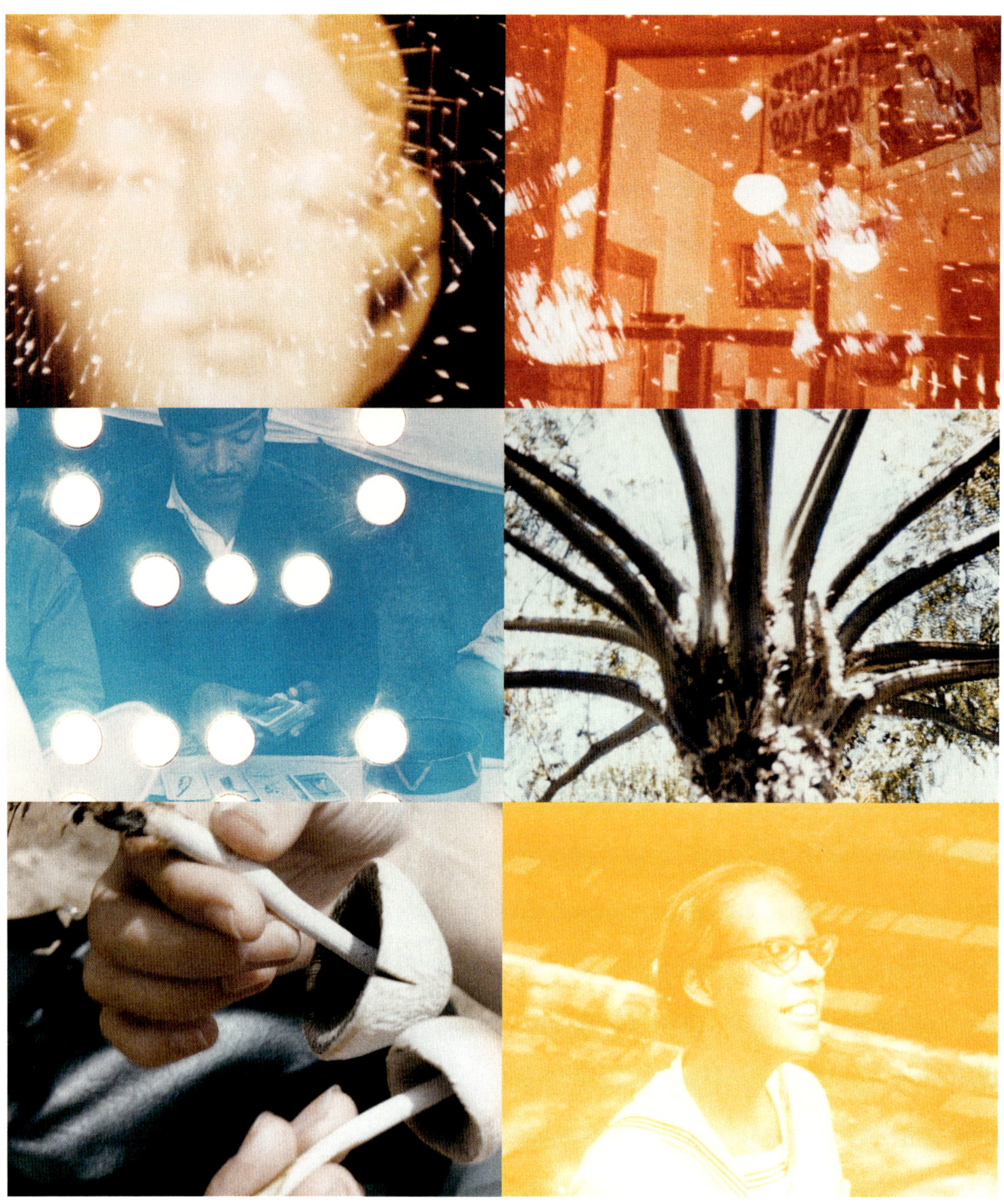

Bruce Conner
Looking for Mushrooms, 1959–67 (film stills)

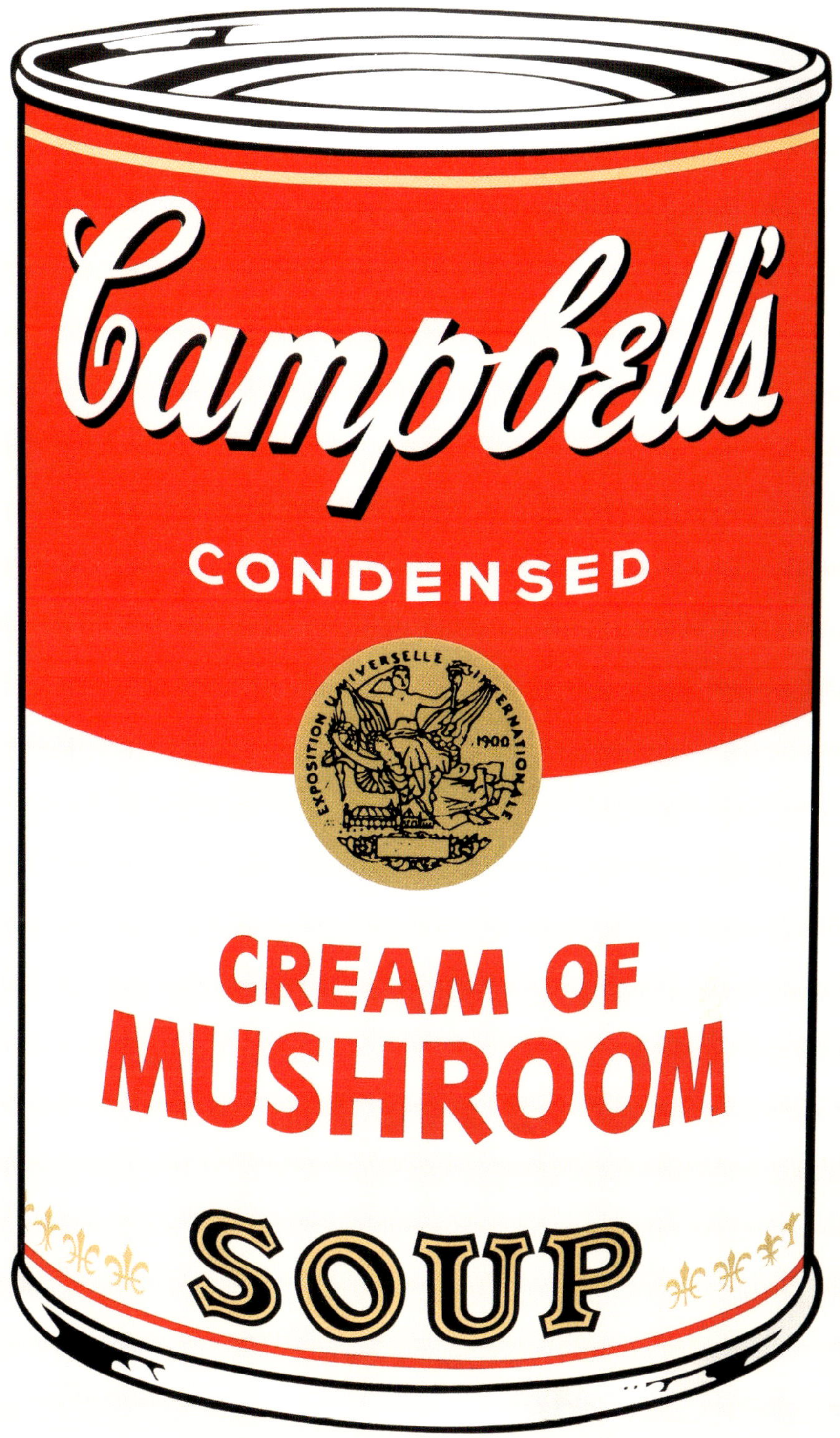

Andy Warhol
Campbell's Soup I: Cream of Mushroom, 1968

The first image of a fungus represented not by its form but by its commercial distribution was created in 1968 in New York by Andy Warhol, who made a screenprint of Campbell's cream of mushroom soup. In 1974, Cy Twombly — a close friend of the composer John Cage (page 50), whose love for mycology knew no bounds — completed a suite of ten lithographs titled *Natural History, Part I, Mushrooms*. This enigmatic work juxtaposes Twombly's loose, lyrical sketches of fungi with found photographs and drawings that reference the Roman author and commander Pliny the Elder's *Natural History* (77–79 CE).

Perhaps one of the strangest mushroom-inspired works was created in 1976, when artist Salvador Dalí and filmmaker José Montes-Baquer made *Impressions of Upper Mongolia (Homage to Raymond Roussel)*, a fake documentary dedicated to the outlier French writer of the title on an expedition to Mongolia in search of giant hallucinogenic mushrooms. The film is a melding of absurdity and sincerity that honours the power of the unconscious to create radically new ways of representing the world.

Nearly twenty years later, Kiki Smith, the German-born American feminist artist who has long been interested in the relationship between the female body, nature and mysticism created *Arm with Mushrooms* (1994), a delicate cast of an arm sprouting mushrooms; in the same year, she cast *Mushroom Head*, a sculpture that evokes the sense of flesh becoming one with nature. Four years after that, Smith created *Fairy Rings (Mushrooms)*, after the naturally occurring circles of mushrooms (page 130), whose genesis has long been the subject of much hypothesizing. She created her own ring of small bronze mushrooms, which appear to be growing from a wall, transforming the white gallery space into a forest glade.

By contrast, the Swiss artist Sylvie Fleury's enormous, brightly glazed sculptures of fungi reference not only fairy tales and altered states but — via their highly polished surface — sports cars. In 2008, she created the 2.6-metre *Mushroom Autowave Rich-Gold Petzold silber F14*, coated in gold, highly reflective car paint. The effect is disorientation: the natural world colliding with a world of masculine excess.

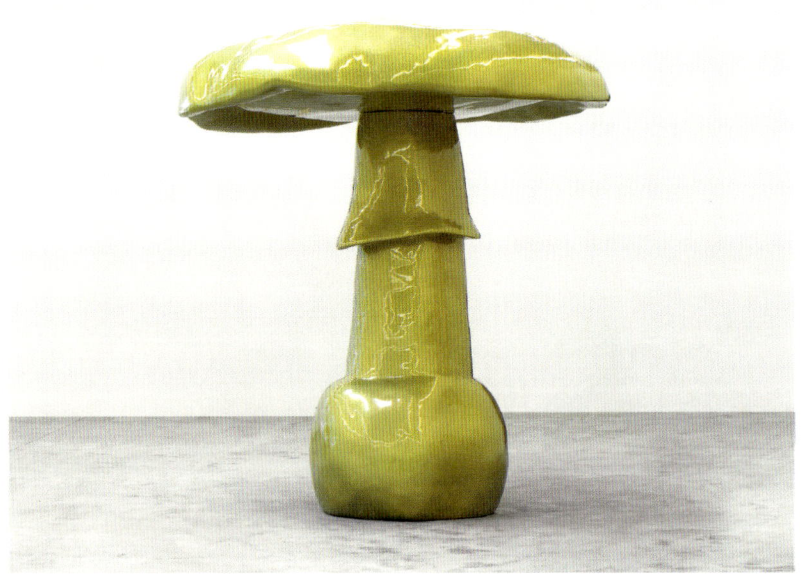

Sylvie Fleury *Mushroom Autowave Rich-Gold Petzold silber F14*, 2008
OPPOSITE **Cy Twombly**, *Natural History Mushrooms Part I / No. X*, 1974

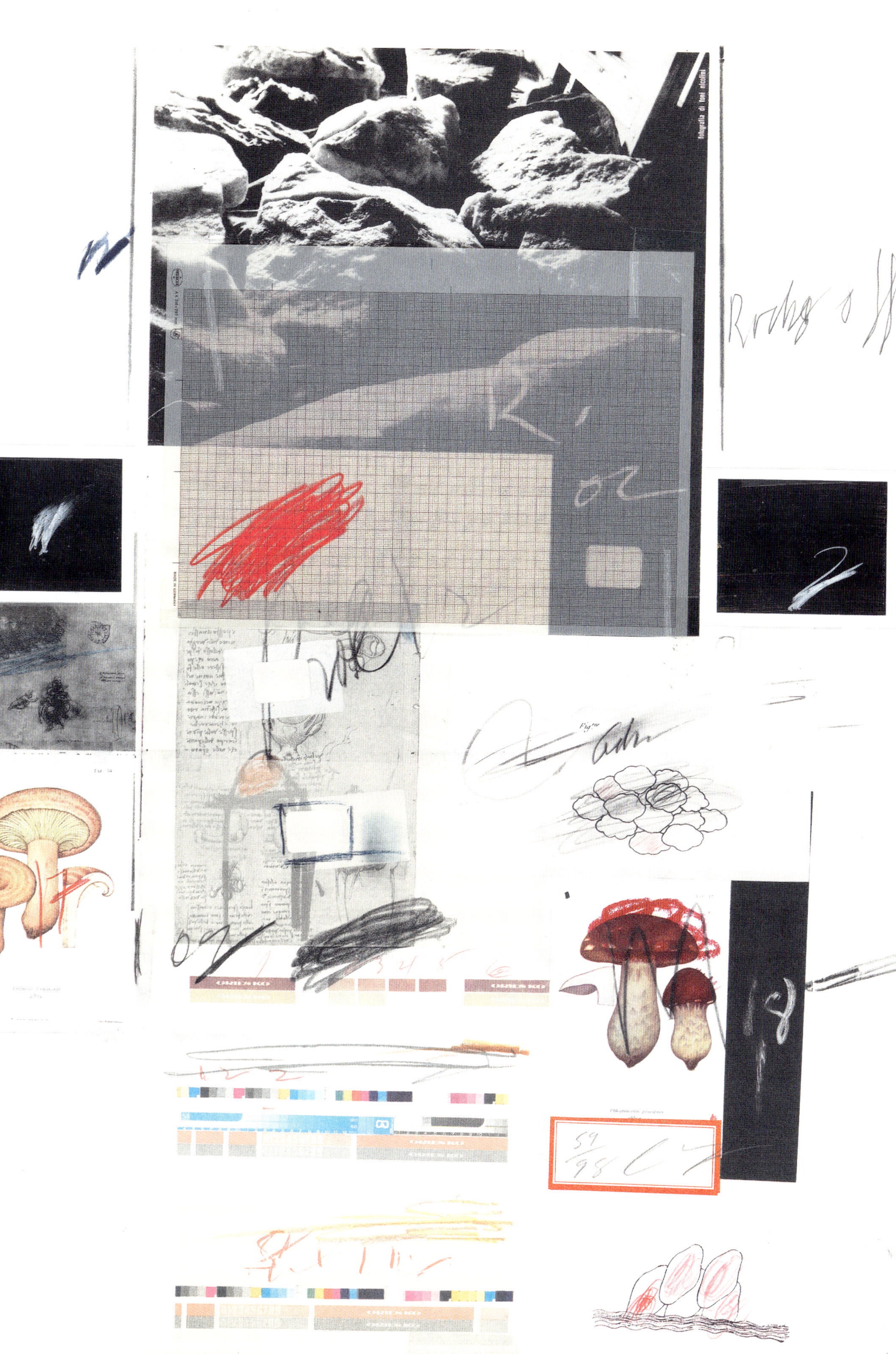
fotografia di toni nicolini
Rocks o ff
MADE IN GERMANY

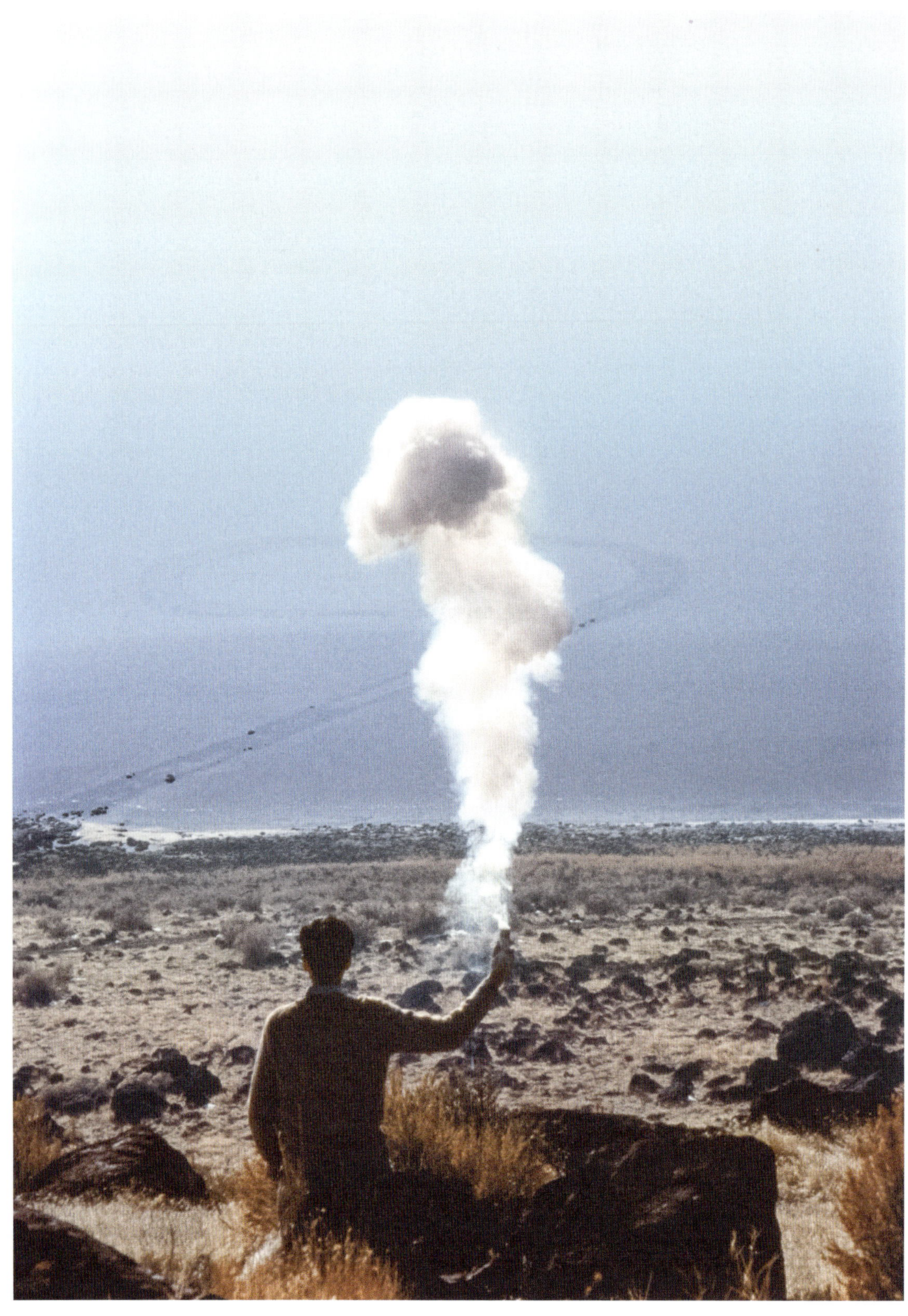

Cai Guo-Qiang, *The Century with Mushroom Clouds: Project for the 20th Century*
Realized at the site of Robert Smithson's *Spiral Jetty,* February 15, 1996

At times, the mushroom has been employed as a symbol of devastation. The most well-known instance is probably the aftermath of the atomic bomb: a mushroom cloud. In Japanese artist Takashi Murakami's *Super Nova* (1999) and *Mushroom Bomb* (2001), the mushroom is both a cheerful cartoon and an intimation of this horror (page 96). In 1995–96, the Chinese artist Cai Guo-Qiang made a 20-page folding album, *Drawing for the Century with Mushroom Clouds: Project for the 20th Century*, from gunpowder, ink and dried lingzhi mushrooms on paper — an intermingling of the mushroom's association with nuclear devastation and its healing powers, (the lingzhi mushroom has long been used to promote health and longevity) (page 132).

Similarly, *The Glacier Series* (1999) by Icelandic Danish artist Olafur Eliasson explores the intersection of nature and culture, despair and hope. Alongside photographs of glaciers — which are, of course, under threat because of global warming — and a waterfall with real water, Eliasson filled the galleries of the Guggenheim with *Lentinula edodes* mushrooms — shiitakes — growing on tree trunks. Eliasson then responded to Peter Zumthor's architecture for Kunsthaus Bregenz in Austria with an indoor landscape titled *The Mediated Motion* (2001). It spanned all four levels of the museum and included a pond with floating duckweed. On the ground floor, Eliasson once again assembled logs sprouting shiitake mushrooms — artworks created by nature that resist the stasis of an enclosed environment.

•

The 21st century has seen a boom in the use of mushrooms by artists working in the emerging field of bioart, a conceptually vast scientific approach to art that uses organic or living materials to explore the relationship between humans, biology and nature. Some of these artists were included in the exhibition Mushrooms: The Art, Design and Future of Fungi, which the writer and curator Francesca Gavin organised at London's Somerset House in 2020. It presented over 40 artists who use bacteria and other organisms "as active collaborators,"[5] to explore "fungi's colourful cultural legacy, as well as the promise it

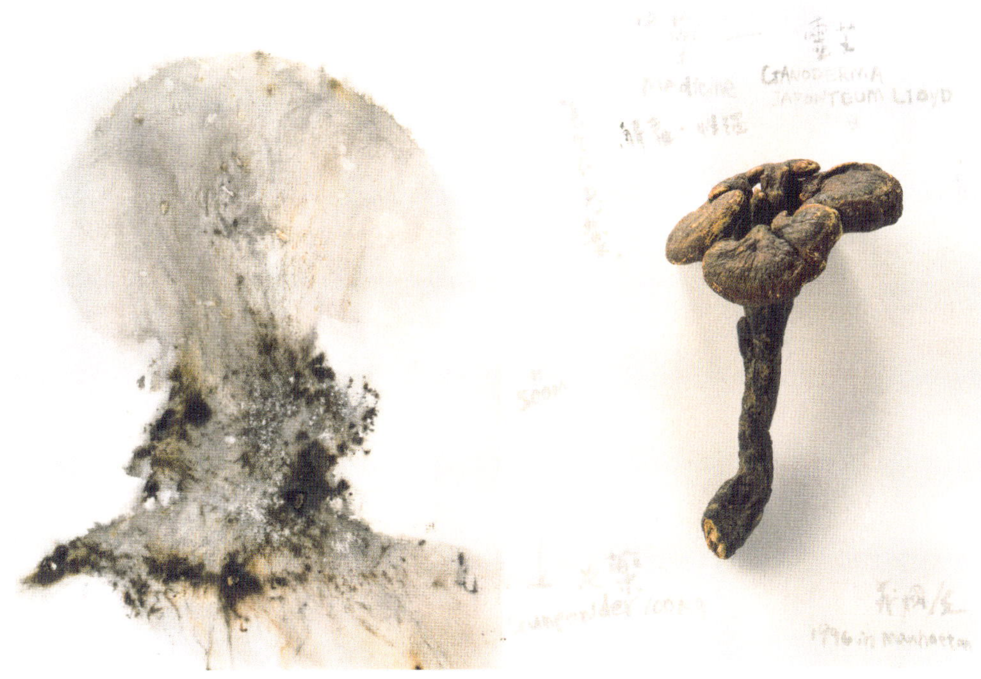

Cai Guo-Qiang
Drawing for The Century with Mushroom Clouds: Project for the 20th Century, 1995–96

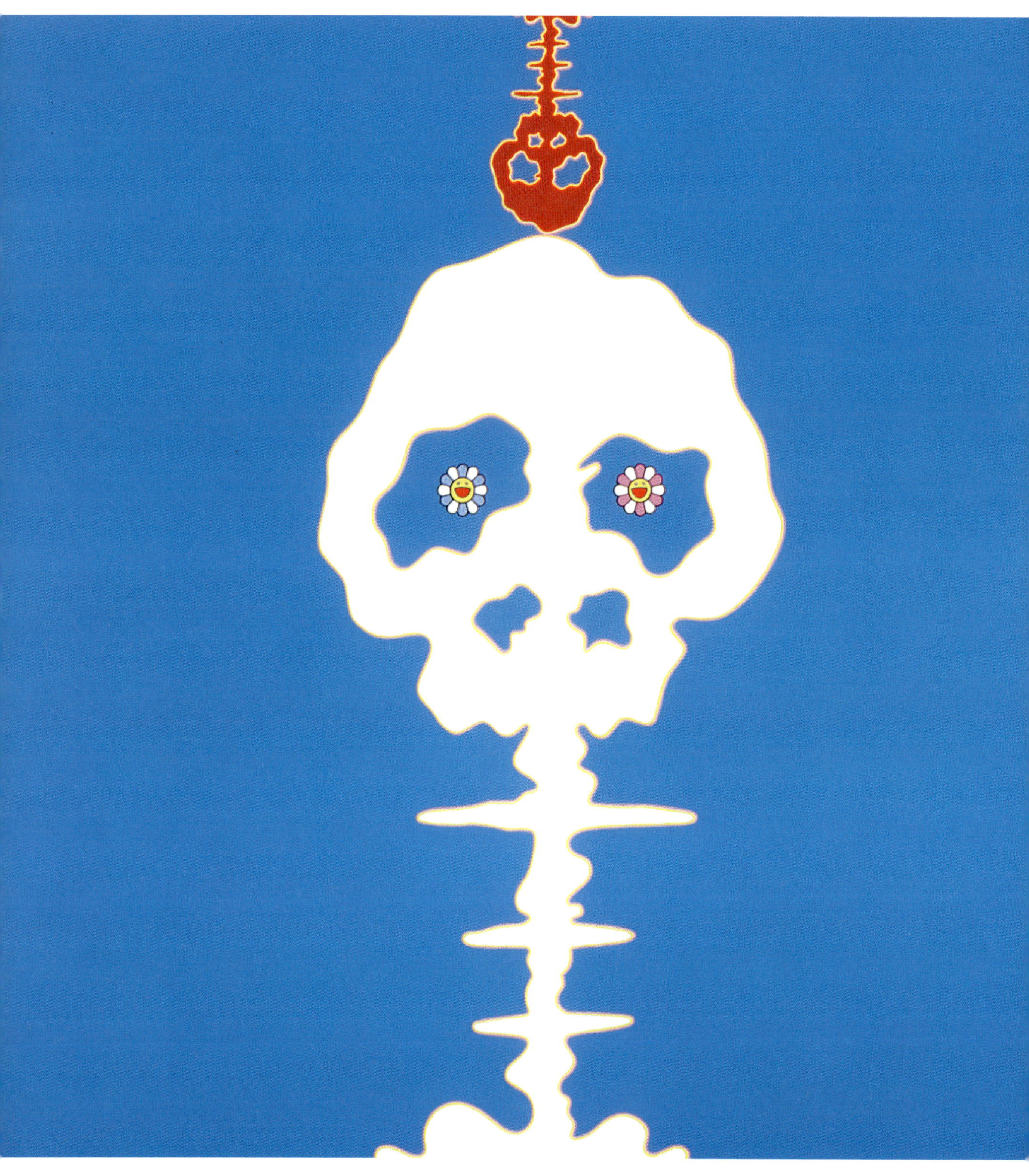

Takashi Murakami
Dokuro Blue, 2000

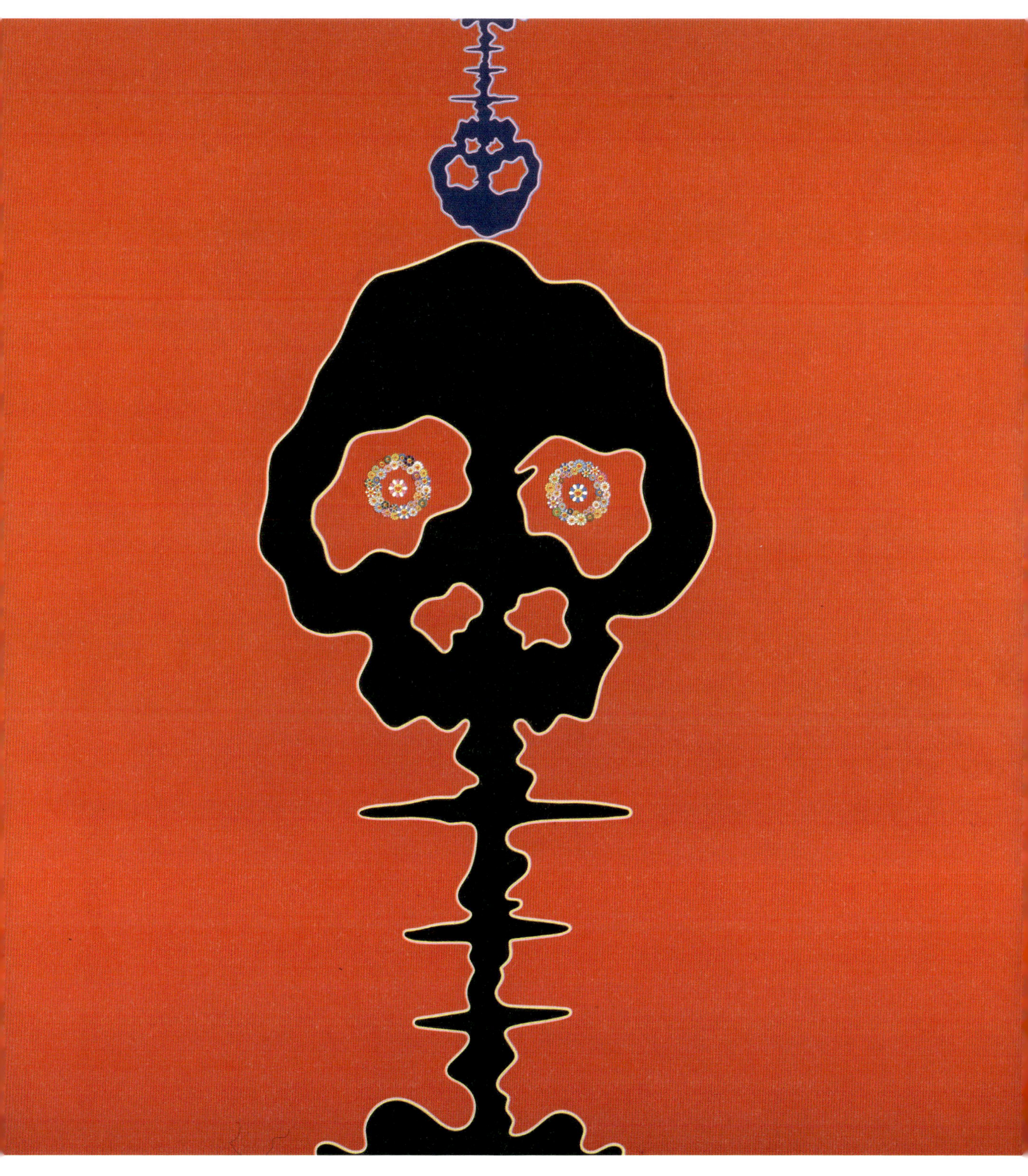

Takashi Murakami
Time Bokan — Red, 2001

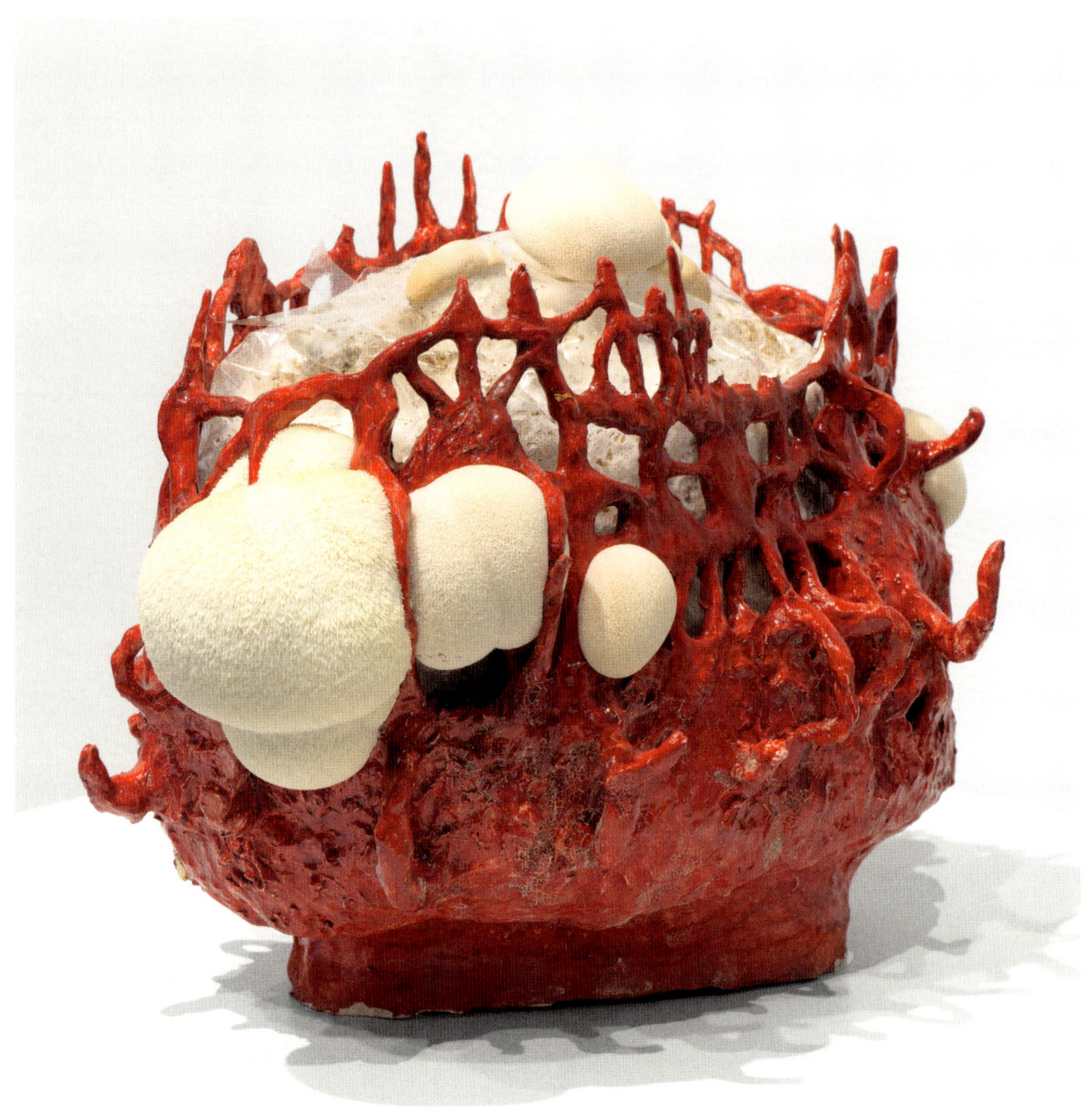

Candice Lin
Memory (Study #2), 2016 (detail)

offers to reimagine our relationship with the planet"[6] — referring to the many ways that mushrooms are being used, including for design (page 102), clothes(page 110), mental health (page 81) and space travel (page 148).

The American artist Candice Lin highlighted the co-dependent qualities of art, people and nature in her interactive sculpture *Memory (Study #2)* (2016). It comprises lion's mane mushrooms — which, if ingested, can apparently improve memory — growing in a coral-like, bright red ceramic vessel and wrapped in plastic. When it's displayed, staff members are required to mist the fungus from a brass sprayer filled with their urine — an insistence on the reciprocity of human and non-human realms. The work was included in a major show at MIT in 2022, titled Symbionts: Contemporary Artists and the Biosphere, featuring more than a dozen international artists whose work engages with living entities, including fungi and bacteria. Also in the show was *Reproductive Logistics* (2020) by the Lebanese American artist Nour Mobarak, who considers the mycelium to be her assistant and collaborator.[7] The work is an abstracted portrait of a past lover that recalls a small patch of blasted landscape; it includes hair, sperm and mycelium.

Three years later, Mobarak staged an "interspecies performance installation" called *Dafne Phono* at the Municipal Theatre of Piraeus, Greece. It was based on the first ever opera, Jacopo Peri and Ottavio Rinuccini's *La Dafne* (1598) — which in turn was based on Daphne in Ovid's *Metamorphoses* (about 8 CE). In Mobarak's interpretation, the characters of Dafne, Apollo, Venus, Cupid, Ovid, Python and the Chorus are "performed" by a group of 15 giant mycelium sculptures that "sing" the tale in four of the most phonetically complex languages through speakers embedded in their "bodies".

Mobarak's opera posits that fungi, which are so deeply linked to ideas of metamorphosis, are an apt metaphor for human communication. The more you delve into them, the richer and more mysterious they become. As John Cage famously observed: "It's useless to pretend to know mushrooms. They escape your erudition."[8]

1. Helt A. M. (2023) "The Fungi-Mad Ladies of Long Ago.".
2. Helt A. M. (2023).
3. Popova M. (2015) "Beatrix Potter, Mycologist: The Beloved Children's Book Author's Little-Known Scientific Studies and Illustrations of Mushrooms." *The Marginalian.*
4. Walkden M. (2019) "'Excrements of the earth': Mushrooms in early modern England." *Folger Shakespeare Library.*
5. Gavin F. (2021) "The Artists Building a Future out of Mushrooms." *Frieze*, No. 128.
6. Somerset House (2020) "Mushrooms: The art, design and future of fungi."
7. de Brugerolle M. (2021) "Nour Mobarak: Movements of Spheres for a Hybrid Economy of Desire." *Flash Art*, No. 336.
8. Marshall C. (2017) "John Cage Had a Surprising Mushroom Obsession (Which Began with His Poverty in the Depression)." *Open Culture.*

FOLLOWING
Dale M Reid, *Oyster Mushroom 55*, 2021

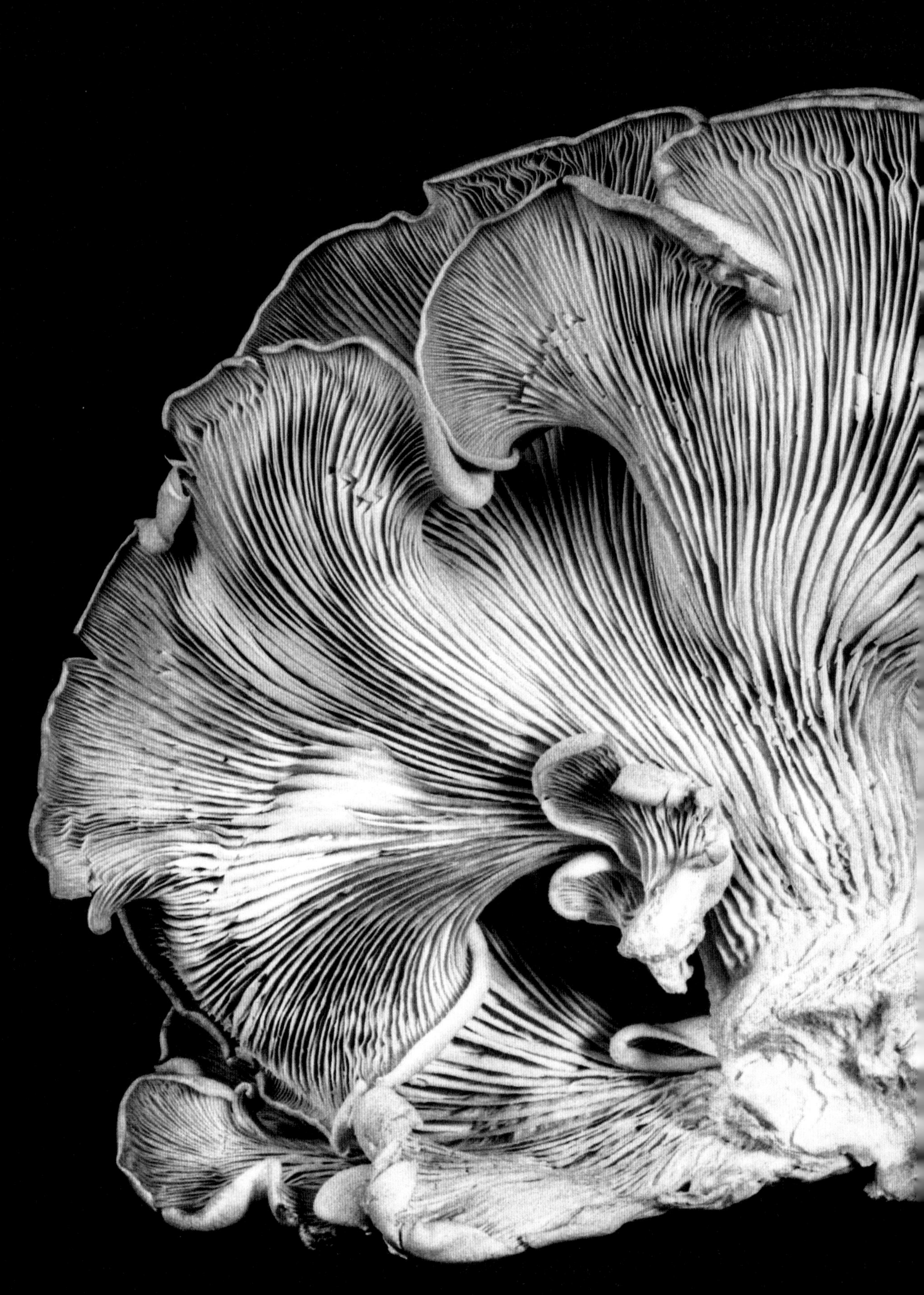

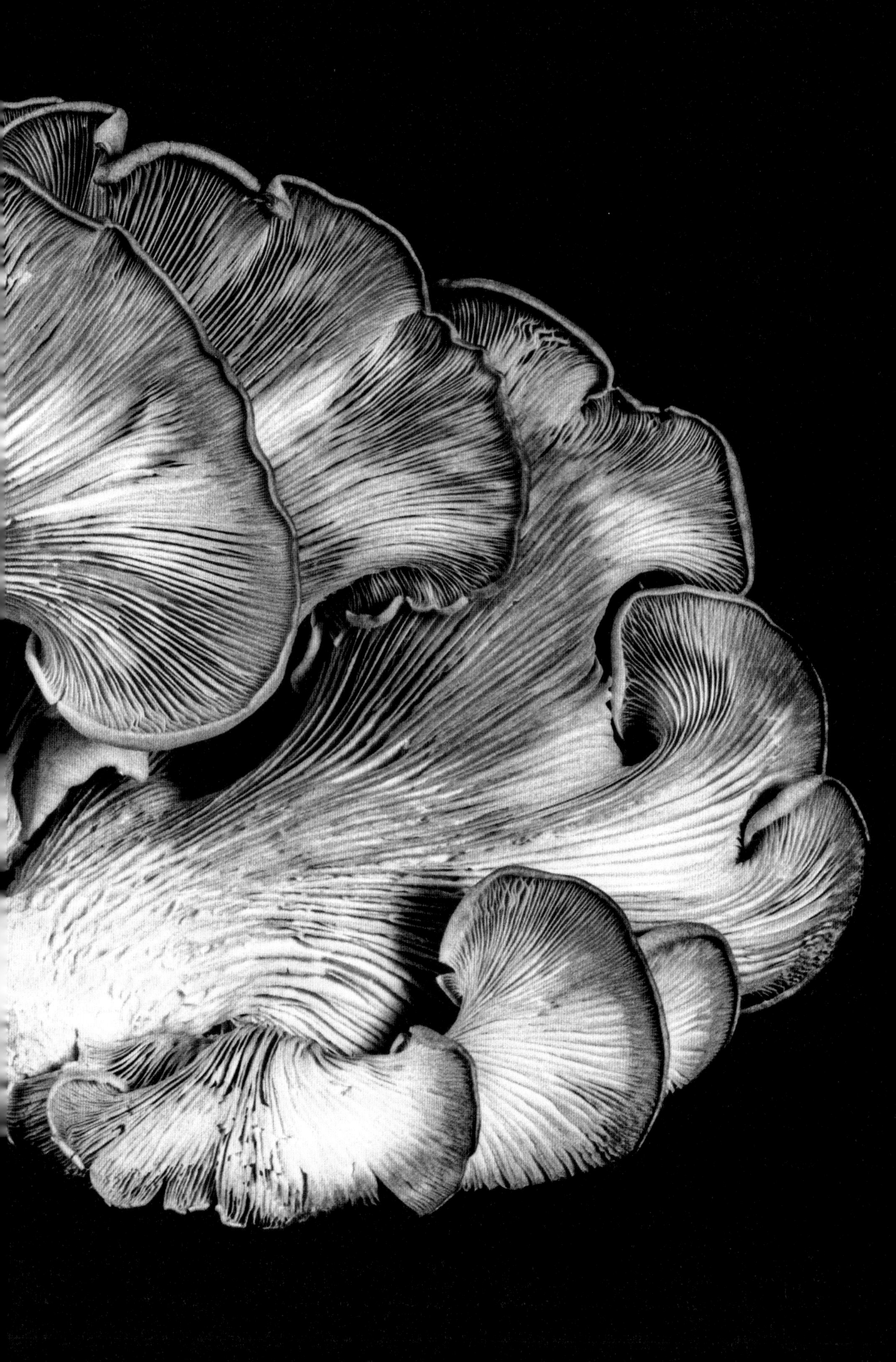

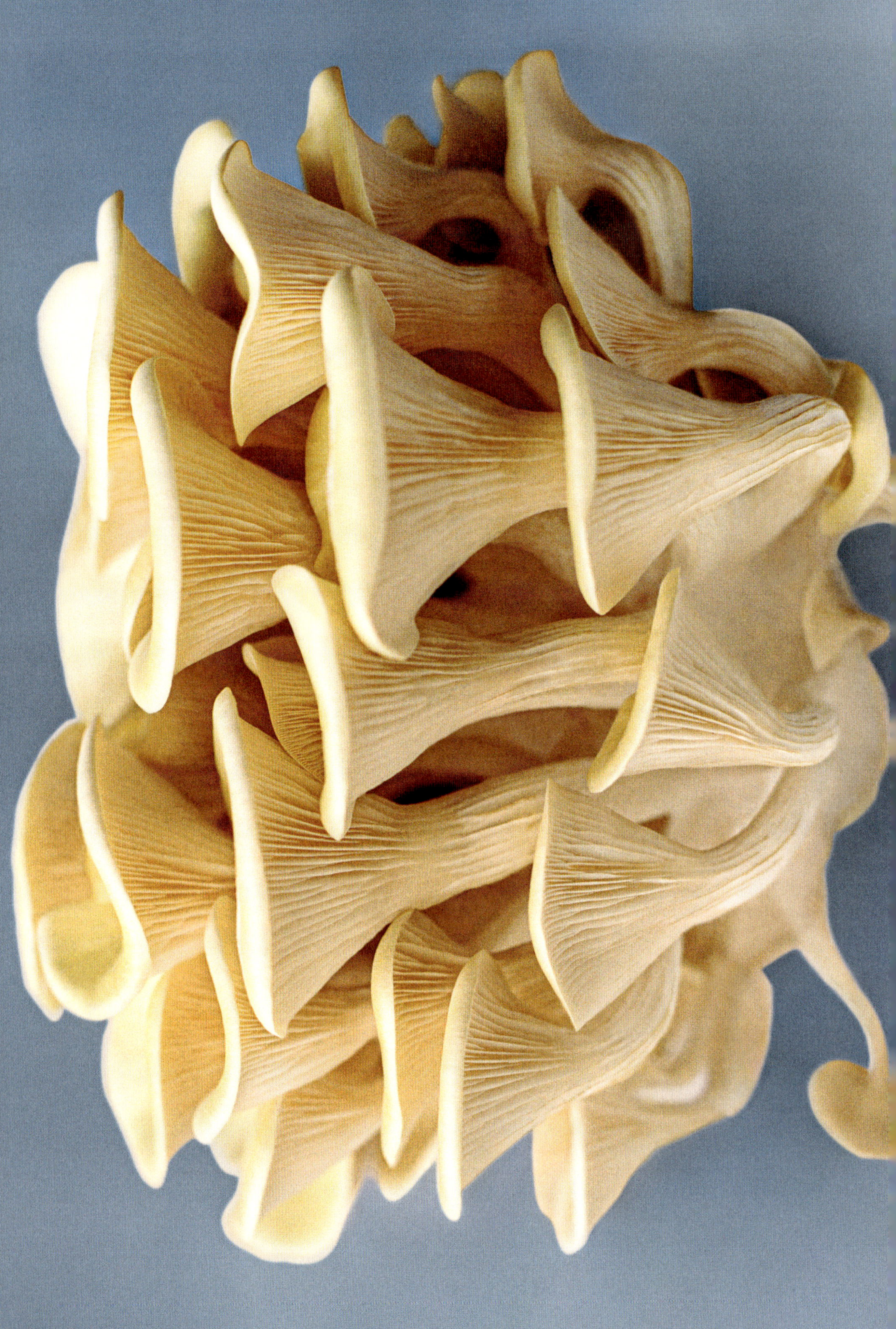

Stories

OPPOSITE
Ben Toms, *Untitled*, 2021

Rhizomatic Roots

A Deeper Understanding of Mushrooms and Mortals

Alongside moulds and yeasts, mushrooms are proud subjects of the kingdom of fungi — and infinitely more enticing to hungry mammals, birds and insects than their fuzz-and-ferment cousins. Eschewing reductive characterization, mushrooms share upwards of 50% of their genes with humans (thanks to a common ancestor dating back over a billion years), and they also share an amino acid with meat, which gives them that oh-so-savoury umami taste. But despite their multitudinous personalities, whether you're wandering through a wild forest or strolling down a supermarket aisle, mushrooms are easy to clock. Identifiable by shared basic features — a jaunty cap, delicately sliced gills, and a stem of various lengths and girths — they may be solitary or huddle together in packs, a little misshapen, speckled with dirt.

Ecologically speaking, mushrooms thrive where different zones overlap; where forest transitions into meadow, earth into water, grassland into shrubland. Here in these marginal spaces, mushrooms form symbiotic relationships with the range of flora around them. And while the bridging tendencies of the mushroom are observable as growth above ground, its more fecund imaginary, like our own unconscious, lies deep below, darkly pulsing and gestating. Mushrooms are just the visible bodies of a much larger organism. Beneath the surface lies the mycelium, a vast, dense underground network made up of tiny, thread-like fungal filaments, called hyphae, which spread through soil, wood and decaying matter, absorbing nutrients and water to sustain the whole system. This is where things really get interesting.

Mycelia secrete enzymes that decompose complex organic compounds into simpler molecules, recycling nutrients back into the ecosystem, and widely sharing these nutrients with other organisms to support new growth. Some even form symbiotic relationships with plants to mutually enhance nutrient absorption for both parties, undergirding an ethics of cooperation and interdependence in the name of survival on this planet.

When conditions are agreeable — cool temperatures, high humidity, the right mix of nutrients — the hyphae cluster together, forming dense structures that grow upward to become mushrooms,

OPPOSITE
Ernst Haeckel, Basidiomycetes fungi, from his book *Kunstformen der Natur*, 1904

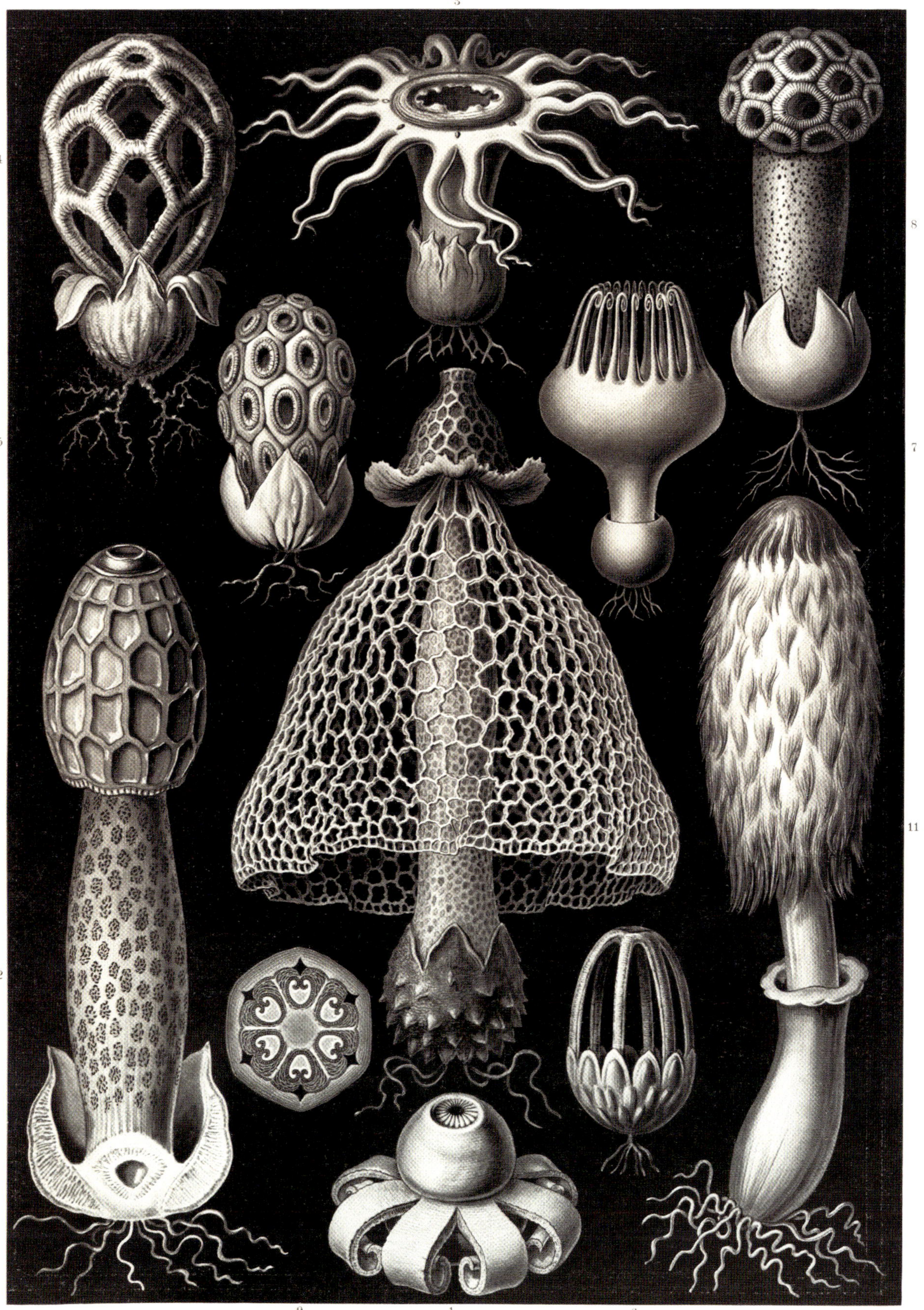

Basimycetes. — Schwammpilze.

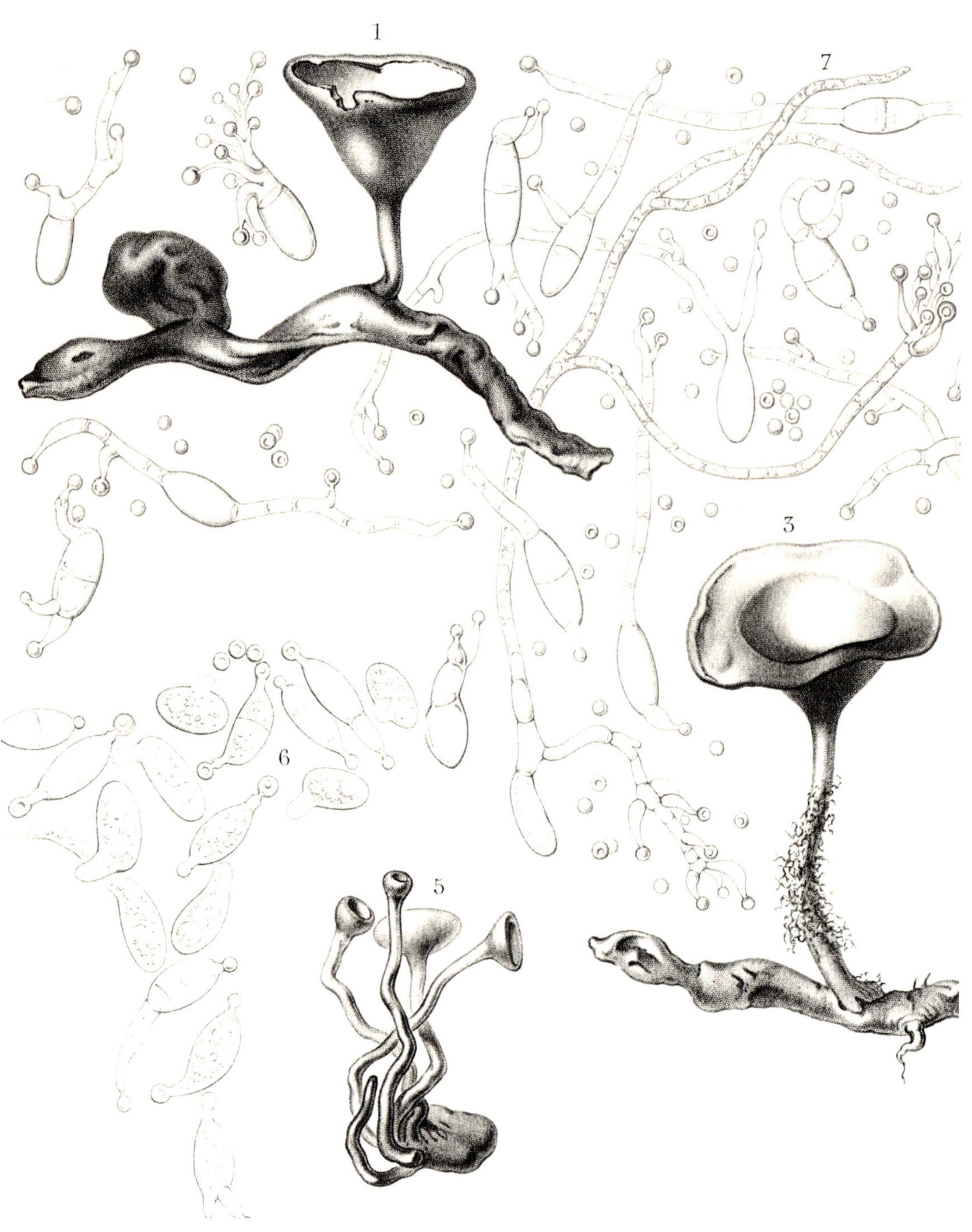

Louis René and Charles Tulasne
Peziza tuberosa, from *Selecta Fungorum Carpologia* (Selected Fungal Carpology), 1865

which release spores and continue the life cycle. New hyphae are formed, kickstarting the growth of mycelium that can eventually merge with the one that birthed it, becoming a larger, interconnected organism that exchanges nutrients, water, and chemical signals across its vast network.

In theory, this cycle could go on forever, mycelium growing ever larger, as new networks emerge and branch outward, fuse with others, forming an ever-expanding, living web underground. Circle of life indeed! But much more awe-inspiring when you consider the magnitudes of time and space under consideration.

Take the "humongous fungus" in Malheur National Forest in Oregon, for example, the mycelium of a honey fungus (*Armillaria ostoyae*) that covers approximately 1,000 hectares (around 1,800 football fields), weighs aproximately 30,000 tonnes, and is estimated to be between 2,000 and 8,650 years old. Although hard to verify this makes it the largest and oldest living organism on Earth, but one that is mostly invisible, thriving underground except when fruiting in autumn, when it produces honey mushrooms in brown clumps at the base of trees.

Despite their awesome capabilities, mushrooms can sometimes give us the heebie-jeebies. One of the reasons they are feared as much as they are revered is their potential to be deadly poison (though only 30 species are estimated to contain deadly toxins, such as amanitin, which is fatal to humans when ingested). But this is a simplification. The mushroom's reality is far more complex. Its process of decomposition and regeneration, of dissemination and symbiosis, of integration and proliferation reflects a cyclical existence that troubles the strict, essentialist duality we impose on it as either life-giver or death-bringer. In fact, the mushroom is neither, because it is always both: simultaneously an agent of creation and destruction, where life and death, or growth and decay, can never be truly distinguished — and are instead woven together in an ever-evolving tapestry of becoming.

Seeing the mushroom for the complex organism that it is — beyond a facile saviour/destroyer dichotomy — leads to a profound philosophico-anatomical understanding that's readable in the very way that mushrooms proliferate. To grasp this, we turn to 1980's hugely influential (and near impenetrable) *A Thousand Plateaus: Capitalism and Schizophrenia*, Gilles Deleuze and Félix Guattari's critique of traditional Western thought. In the hefty tome, these rogue philosophers contrast two fundamentally different approaches to understanding, organizing and navigating knowledge and relationships: the "arborescent" and the "rhizomatic".

An arborescent system is like a tree structure, with a clear top-down organization. Imagine a tree with the trunk representing a main source of knowledge or authority, and branches representing subcategories or concepts — as you would find in a traditional biology textbook, for example. The animal kingdom might be the trunk, with branches like mammals, reptiles and birds, which are then divided further into smaller biological categories of family, genera, species, etc. In an arborescent system, everything flows in a linear, predetermined path from the trunk to each branch — similar to how a company's organizational chart is structured from the CEO down to entry-level employees.

Arborescence demands strict categories for control and clarity. It's premised on binary exclusion; objects, thoughts, people or concepts are slotted into distinct, either/or classifications. You're either a mammal or a reptile, a chief financial officer or an HR manager, but never both. While structured and stable, this approach is rigid and deterministic, with fixed pathways that create hardened, exclusionary boundaries. Arborescence may shut out ideas or identities that don't fit neatly into the established categories, for example.

In contrast, a rhizomatic system is modelled after the underground stems of plants like ginger, bamboo and certain grasses, called "rhizomes". As they grow, rhizomes spread horizontally beneath the soil, producing new roots and shoots from multiple points at once. This growth pattern creates a network without a singular beginning or end, connecting different organisms and environments in unpredictable, non-linear ways.

Flexible, decentralized and multidirectional, rhizomatic systems resemble this root-like web. Rather than policing categories through a central

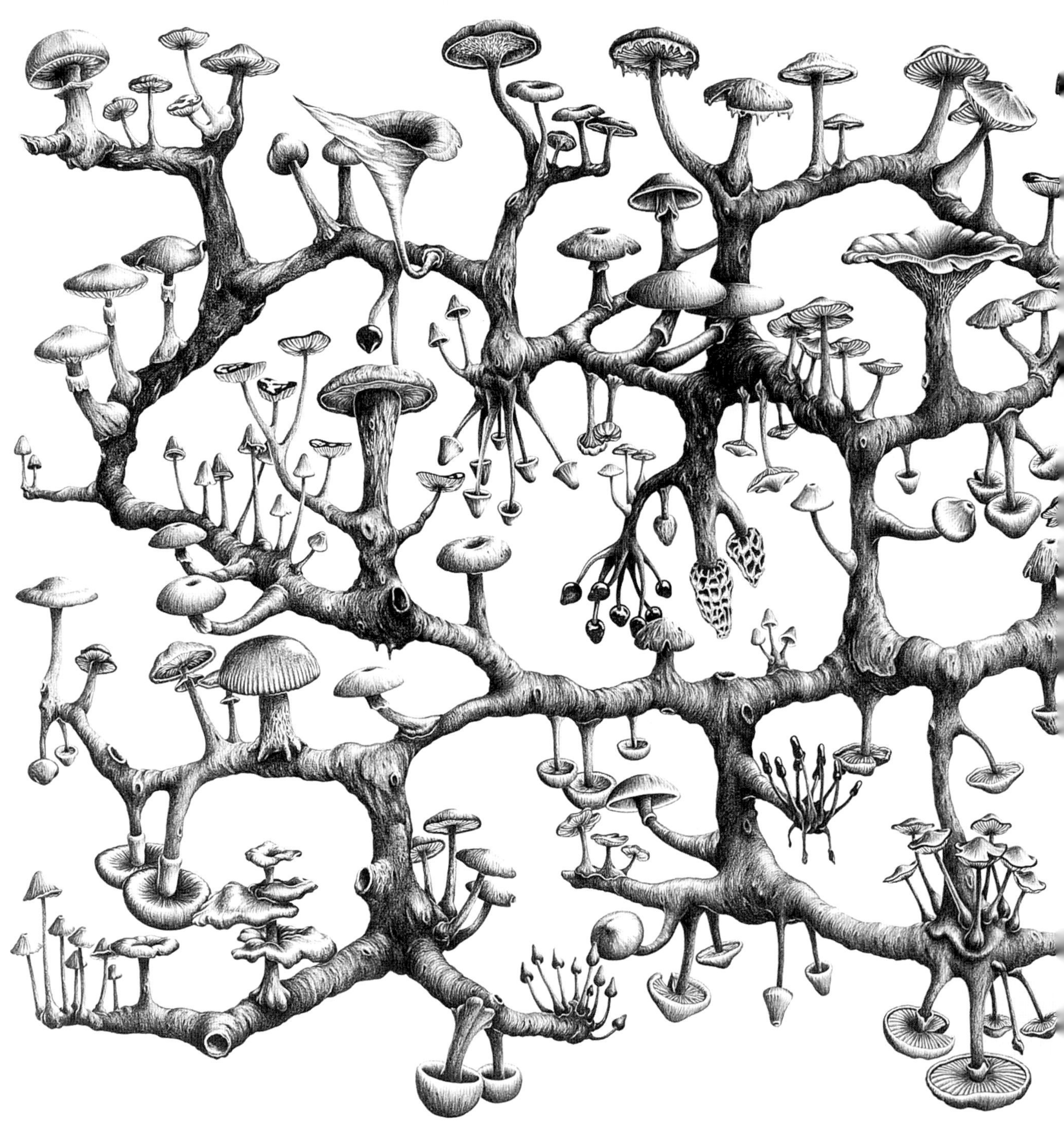

Richard Giblett
Mycelium Rhizome, 2008

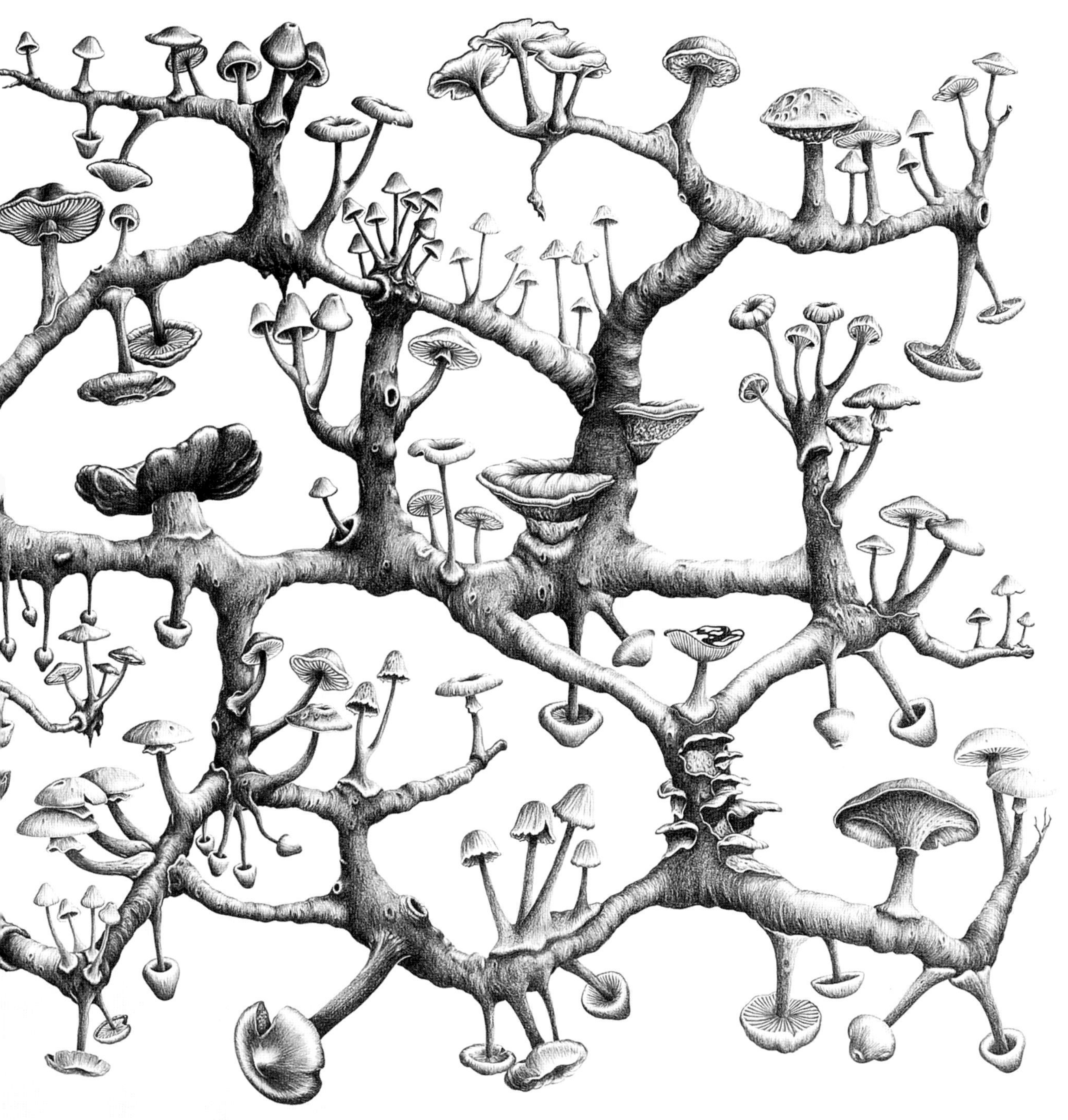

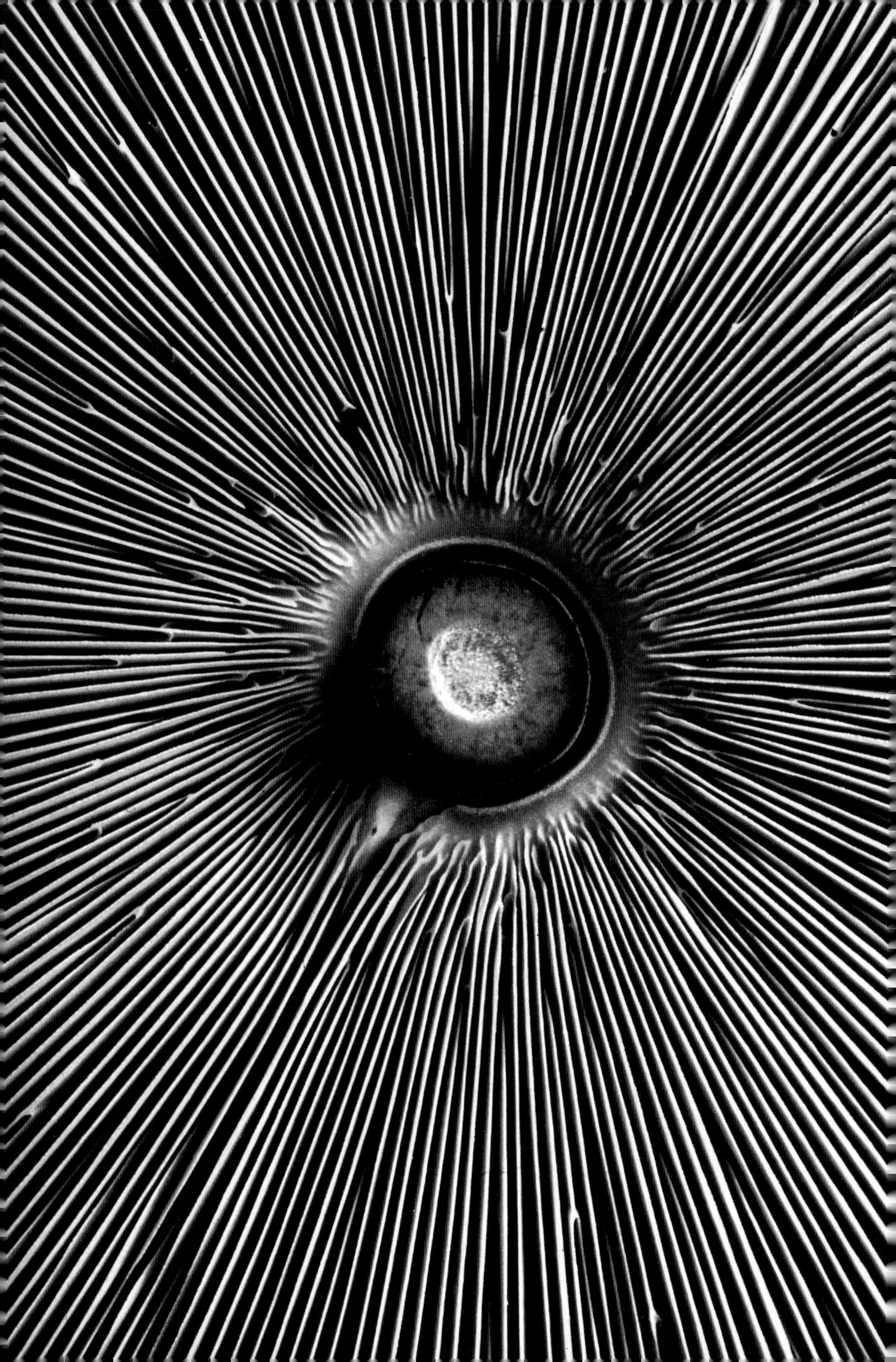

structure, they reject rigid hierarchies and binary categories: any idea, object or person can link with any other, even if they seem unrelated. The result is a system that embraces multiplicity and inclusivity, where countless elements coexist and interact across overlapping, non-hierarchical networks. This openness allows for a rich diversity of voices and viewpoints; it supports continuous adaptation and innovation. Rhizomatic systems are dynamic, fertile ground where ideas and relationships grow organically without being boxed in by fixed pathways or static rules.

Deleuze and Guattari advocate that rhizomatic systems are more reflective of the complexities of reality, where change is constant, connections are not always predictable, and thought is always already non-hierarchical and non-linear, allowing for richer, more diverse, more authentic interactions with the world. Social movements spread organically; many cities grow through informal networks, not just by top-down design; languages evolve through everyday use alongside formal rules; creative trends emerge from remix culture rather than elite institutions; innovation often comes from unexpected crossovers rather than through linear R&D pipelines; and new genres of music and art often emerge out of the margins, not from the centre.

Does this sound like the ramblings of a couple of French philosophical hippies? For sure. But Deleuze and Guattari were onto something. Think how much we rely on arborescent systems to structure the world — not just biological classifications or corporate hierarchies but family trees, military ranks, literary genres, historical periodization, government systems, file directory hierarchies, legal systems, project management structures, religious hierarchies, library classification systems, evolutionary trees, supply chains, financial systems, political structures, education frameworks — the list really does go on. All of these systems use arborescent categorization: clearly hierarchical and tree-like, creating a top-down organization.

Where do mushrooms come in? Well, fungal structures are not actually plant stems, but mycelial growth patterns are rhizomatic through and through. A mycelium is in fact a perfect biological representation of a rhizomatic system, growing in a decentralized, web-like network of hyphae that branch out horizontally in multiple directions. This non-hierarchical structure enables interactions and relationships with different plants, fungi, microorganisms and ecosystems, without rigid boundaries or centralized control.

Deleuze and Guattari say, "The tree imposes the verb 'to be' but the fabric of the rhizome is the conjunction, 'and... and... and...'" Mushrooms, our DNA brethren, might offer us a completely new — and more accurate — way to view the world in which we already live: they present us with a non-linear, ever-branching rhizomatic truth.

The rhizome poses a challenge — and an opportunity, not just to our understanding of the mushroom itself, but of ourselves. It invites us to see beyond the surface and into the rich, dark soil of the soul, to appreciate the complex web of relationships that sustain life and thought, culture and society, and to embrace the transformative power of becoming — of change rooted in the here and now.

In doing so, mushrooms are radically always *more than,* existing beyond their assigned status as fungi, food or dangerous organisms. A mushroom is a perfect symbol of life's inherent complexity and continual transformation. In other words, totems of us, solitary or huddling together in packs, a little misshapen, speckled with dirt.

OPPOSITE
Albert Renger-Patzsch, *Lepiota procera*, c.1930

ME Descourtilz
Atlas des Champignons, 1827

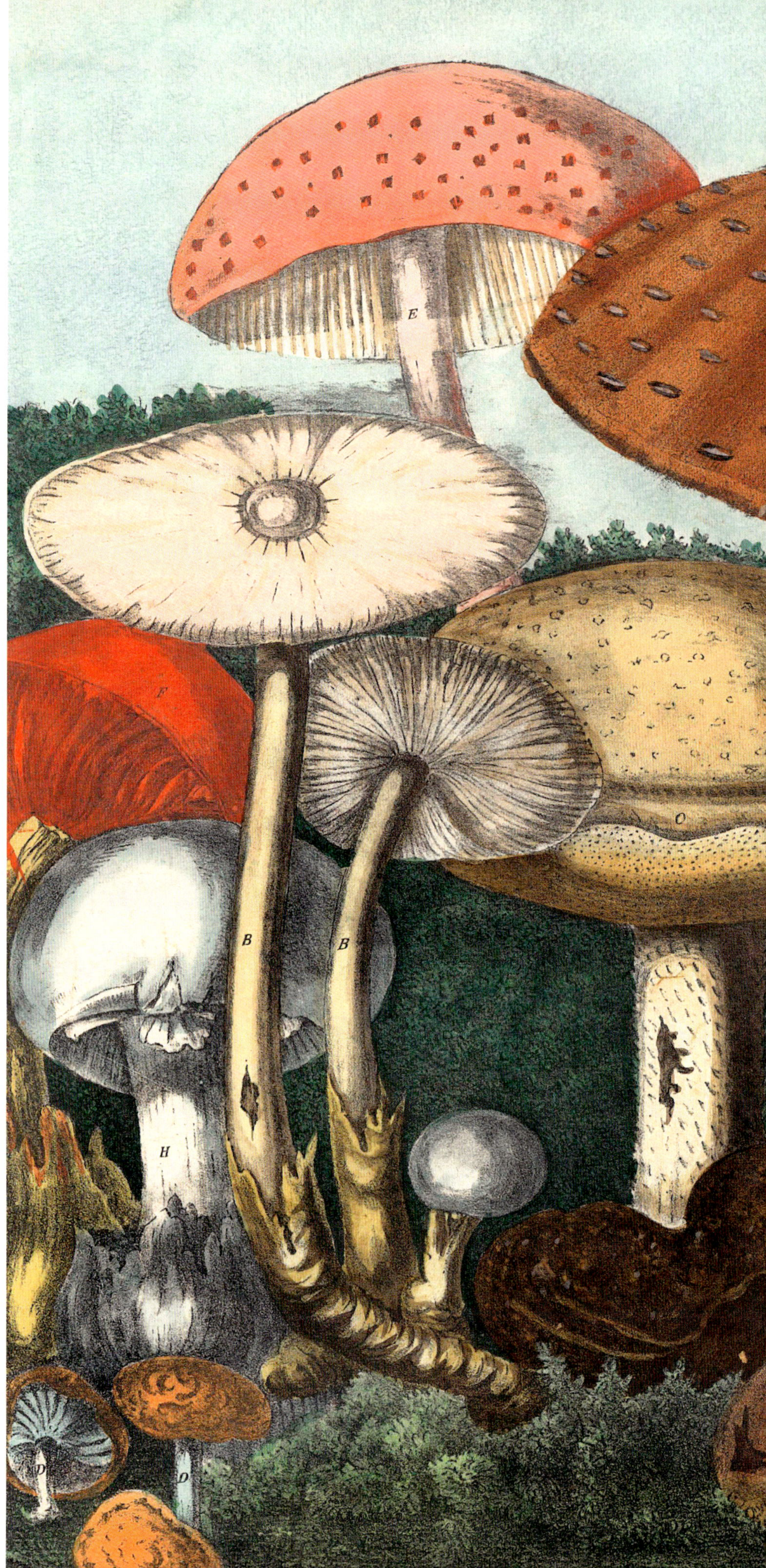

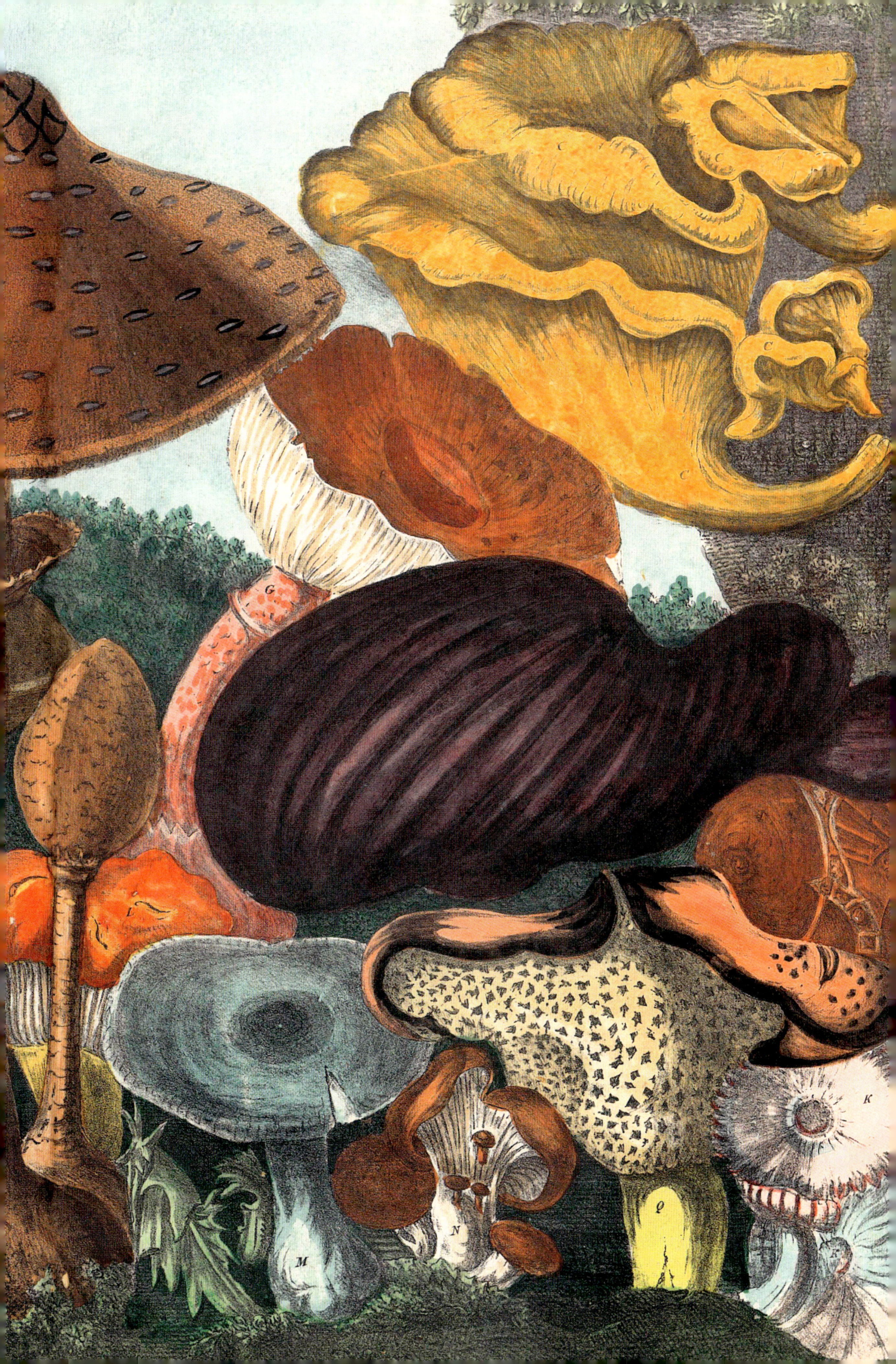
C
C
C
C
G
L
K
Q
N
M

Earthly Etchings

Mycological Illustration from the 15th-Century to John Cage

As any amateur mycologist will tell you, the essential tool for safe mushroom hunting is an authoritative illustrated guide — even more than a trusty knife, brush or basket. Today, no one in their right mind would set out into the woods without pictures — preferably detailed photographs — of the unfamiliar fungi they might encounter. Many mushrooms look similar, and without a clear indication of which are safe to eat, a pleasant day of mushroom hunting could turn deadly. But for centuries, such guides did not exist.

The first printed image of a mushroom is a rather small, rudimentary woodcut in the encyclopaedia of natural history *Ortus sanitatis*, published in Mainz, Germany, in 1491. The round caps depicted in the image are scarcely identifiable as mushrooms, let alone their species. *Ortus sanitatis* translates as "The Garden of Health", and this large book was the most comprehensive of its kind, encompassing not just botany and mycology but also zoology and medicine, alongside fictionalized and mythical species including mandrakes, harpies and dragons.

Another lifetime would pass before the arrival of the first printed image of a discernible mushroom genus. Pietro Andrea Mattioli was an Italian physician and herbalist who served at the pleasure of Emperor Maximilian II of Austria. Mattioli's herbal, *Commentarii secundo aucti, in libros sex Pedacii Dioscoridis* (Commentary on the Six Books of Pedanius Dioscorides), was originally published in 1544, but it was in a subsequent 1560 edition that there appeared a captioned illustration of two trees, their trunks covered in "agaricum" fungi. (In the 16th century, *agaricum* referred to tree fungi; in the 18th century, the Swedish biologist Carl Linnaeus defined the genus *Agaricus* broadly to include many large-gilled mushrooms, such as the famous fly agaric.)

Despite advances in printing technology in the 16th century, woodblock prints remained an imprecise medium. Instead, botanists and mycologists looked for superior means of capturing the intricate physiognomy of mushrooms. Charles de l'Ecluse (Latinized as Carolus Clusius) was a fastidious Flemish scientist, who late in life compiled his research into the multi-volume *Rariorum plantarum historia* (History of Rare Plants, 1601), the first publication to devote a section exclusively to fungi. De l'Ecluse advised the artist who was producing a series of exquisite watercolours, which were misplaced by the printer and resurfaced centuries later in a 1900 facsimile edition.

The invention of the compound microscope transformed science. The full title of a book published in 1665 by the renowned British scientist Robert Hooke was *Micrographia, or, Some physiological descriptions of minute bodies made by magnifying glass: with observations and inquiries thereupon*. Its detailed illustrations were unlike any

OPPOSITE
James Klosty, John Cage at the Hollander Workshop, 1972

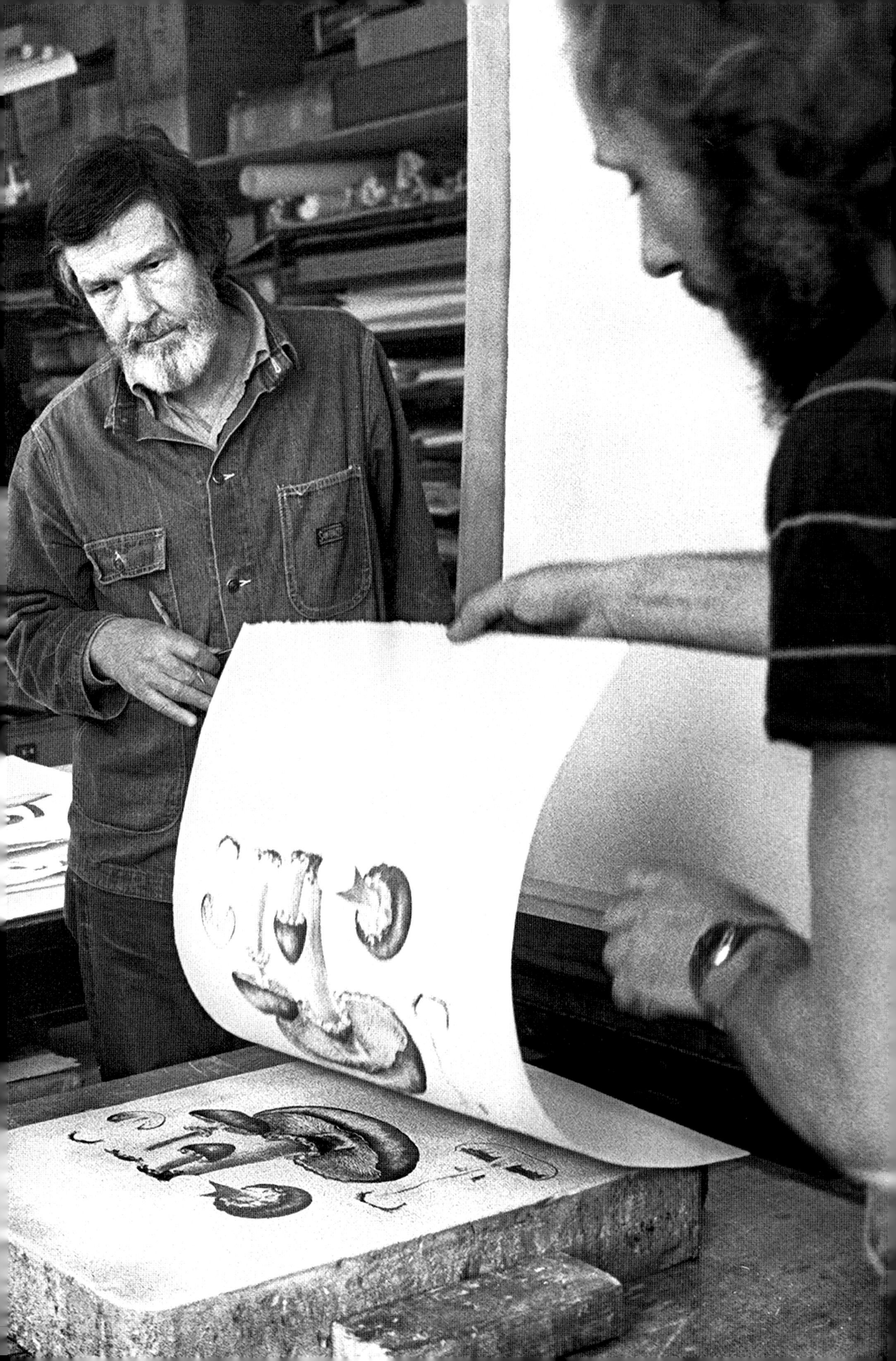

images of plants and fungi that had existed before, depicting their internal structures as well as their outward appearance.

Around this time, copperplate engraving became more widespread in book illustrations, all but eclipsing the woodcut by the end of the century. The first copperplate engraving of fungi appeared in Franciscus van Sterbeeck's *Theatrum fungorum oft het Tooneel der Campernoelien* (The Theatre of Fungi, or the Stage of Campenoelian Mushrooms, 1675), though it is thought that most of the drawings were copied from de l'Ecluse. Hand-coloured engravings were, at first, reserved for only the most lavish books, but in 1737 the first mycological illustrations in colour were published by Johann Wilhelm Weinmann, whose printer used a new mezzotint technique. Now, mushroom hunters could more readily identify specimens by their relative shades of brown, grey, or even bright red with white spots.

Throughout the 18th and 19th centuries, mycological illustration became less decorative and more analytical, the often visually unappealing fungal excrescences sliced open to reveal their inner workings. The field was dominated by patrician scientists such as Louis René Tulasne, whose laboratory research into obscure corners of mycological activity greatly expanded European and, later, American understanding of fungi.

Many important figures in mycological illustration were enthusiasts working at the peripheries of science ("scientist", after all, was not yet a professional occupation). French-born Jean Jacques Paulet, author of the influential, hand-coloured *Traité des champignons* (Treatise on Mushrooms, 1775) was a doctor. Lewis David von Schweinitz, born in Pennsylvania in 1780, was a theologian as well as mycologist. He described hundreds of previously unrecorded fungi, and has been referred to as the father of North American mycology.

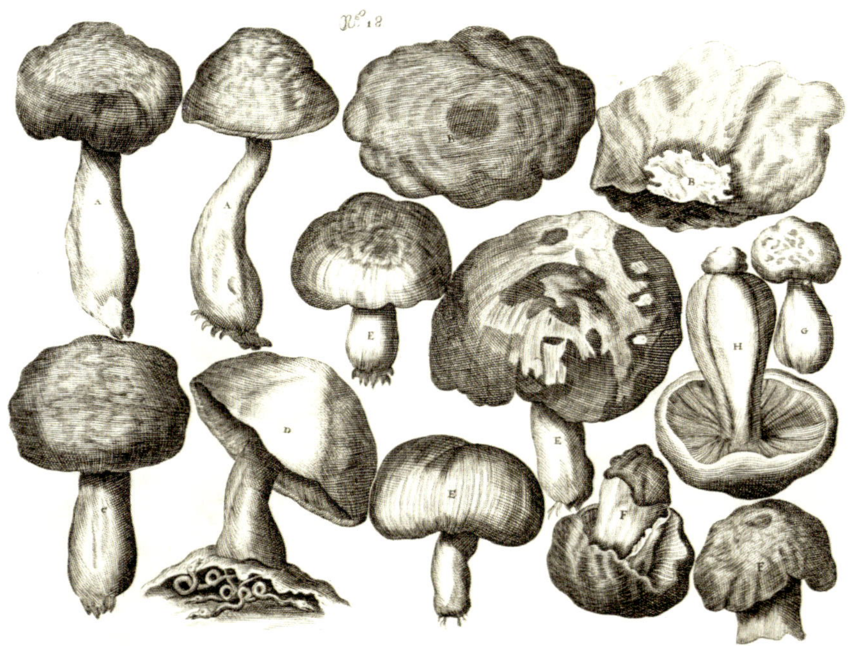

Peeter van Sickeleers
Plate from Franciscus van Sterbeeck's book
Theatrum fungorum oft het Tooneel der Campernoelien, 1675

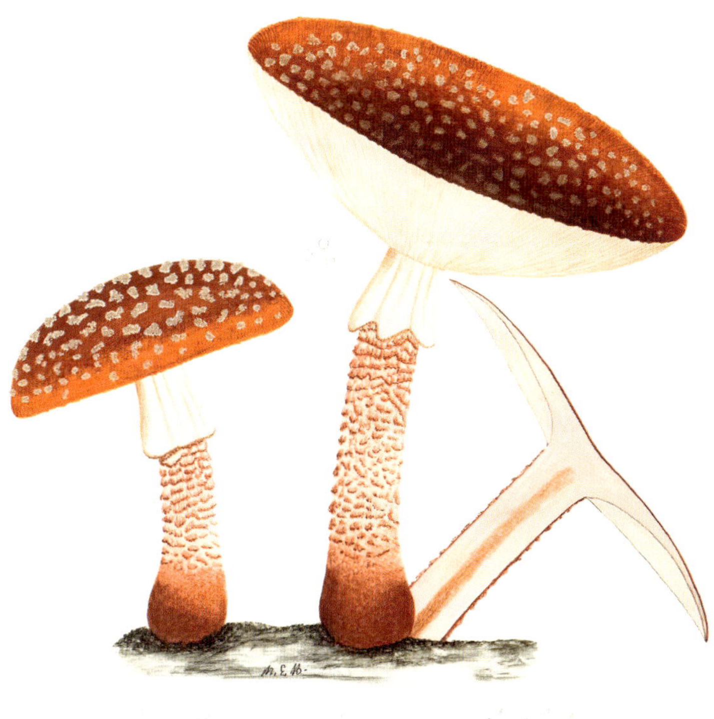

Jacob Sturm was not formally educated but learnt the art of engraving from his father. He compiled his diligent observations of German flora in an affordable pocket guide, complaining of the "large and splendid publications which often even the lover of botany does not get a chance of seeing once in a lifetime". His copperplate engravings helped usher in an era of amateur appreciation of fungi, even as their scientific study was becoming more elevated and exclusive, due to the growth of universities and the establishment of research institutes and scientific societies.

In the late 18th and 19th centuries, painting flowers was a popular pastime for many middle- and upper-class women, some of whom pursued the activity with a scholarly zeal. Botanical and mycological observation was a way for women to contribute to the male-dominated realm of scientific research. The British mycologist Anna Maria Hussey was the daughter of a clergyman who likely educated his daughters at home. In 1831, Hussey married a rector who also happened to be an amateur astronomer and scientist. Resenting her wifely duties, she struck up learned correspondences with various mycologists and scientists, including Charles Darwin. With her sister Frances, an artist, she produced a two-volume guide to British fungi, which not only included fine lithographed illustrations but Hussey's conversational notes about mushroom habitats, foraging and her own recipes.

Little is known about the amateur mycologist Sarah Price, other than that she was born in Shropshire, England, and that, like Hussey, she was probably home-schooled. In 1864, she published a guide, with lithographed colour illustrations, titled *Illustrations of the Fungi of Our Fields and Woods: Drawn from Natural Specimens*, which became a respected reference for mushrooms in her region. In the United States, Mary Elizabeth Banning was a single woman who lived with her sister and their sickly mother in Maryland.

ABOVE **Mary Banning**
Agaricus rubescens Fr., from *Fungi of Maryland*, 1870

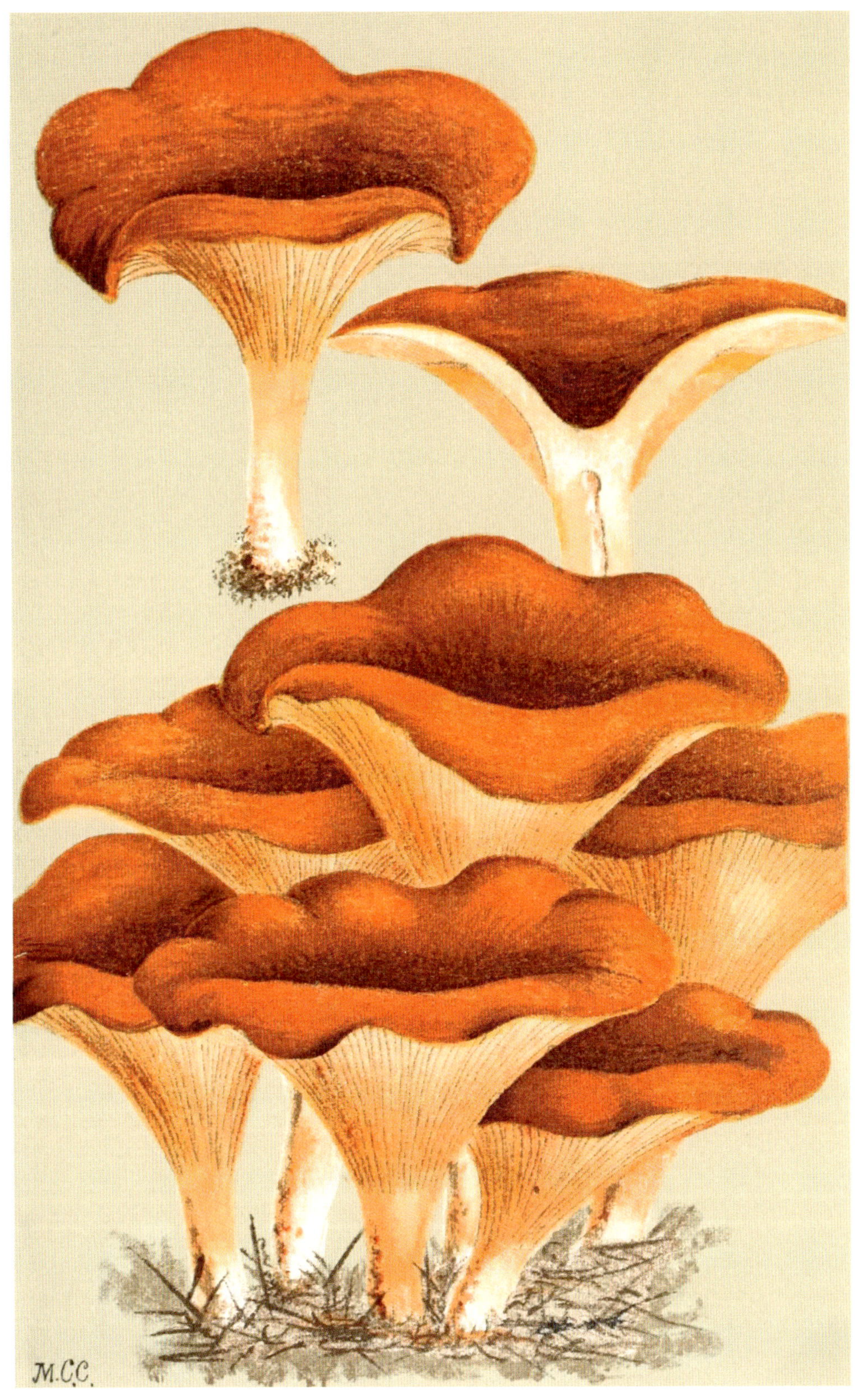

Plate showing *Agaricus lobatus*
from Mordecai Cooke's *Handbook of British Fungi*, 1871

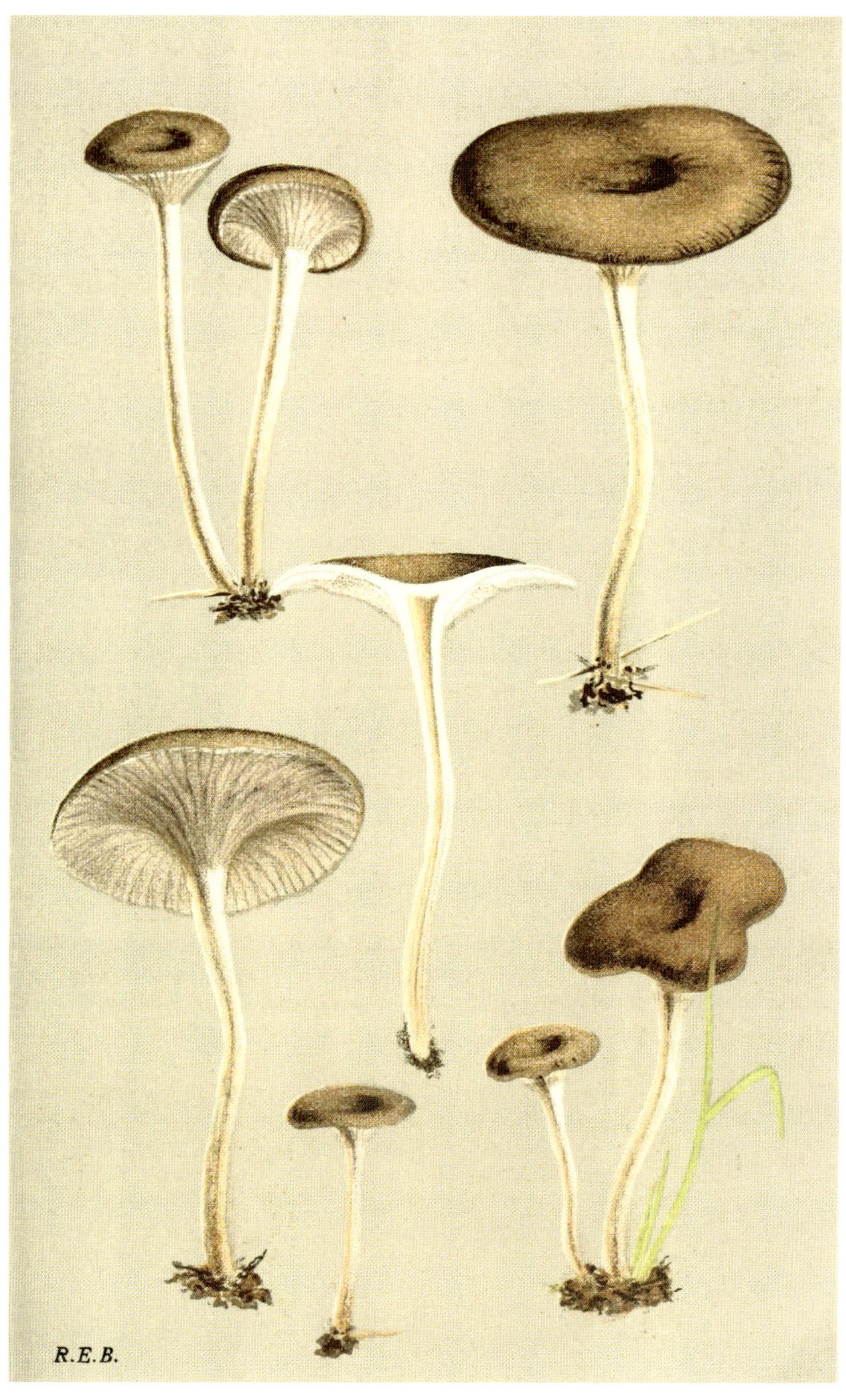

Plate showing *Agaricus expallens*
from Mordecai Cooke's *Handbook of British Fungi*, 1871

In an endeavour that took her over 20 years, she compiled a series of exquisite watercolours, appended with handwritten reflections on faith and morality, for a book she called *The Fungi of Maryland*. It was the most comprehensive study of the region's fungi at that time and included documentation of 23 new species. in 1890 she sent her manuscript to the New York State Museum, but despite its obvious merit, it went unpublished — even as male mycologists had their own books published in the years after her groundbreaking research.

Such experiences were not uncommon for women scholars. Beatrix Potter, later celebrated as the author and illustrator of the Peter Rabbit books, in early life was an accomplished naturalist who excelled in the study and illustration of mushrooms. "Now of all hopeless things to draw," she once joked, "I should think the very worst is a fine fat fungus." On the contrary, Potter's observations were not hopeless but conscientious and revelatory. She used a microscope to investigate the germination of fungal spores, which she cultivated, and was the first to record the parasitic *Tremella* fungus. When she submitted a research paper to the Linnean Society in 1897, it was "well received", she reported to a friend, but deemed to require more work before being printed. No paper was ever published. It seems Potter was affronted by the scepticism of the exclusively male society. She soon diverted her considerable gifts to writing a book about a certain talking bunny rabbit.

Around the same time as *The Tale of Peter Rabbit* appeared in bookstores, so too did the first books containing photographs of mushrooms. Nina Lovering Marshall's *The Mushroom Book* was published by Doubleday, Page & Co. in 1903, replete with hand-coloured photographs of mushrooms, some in their natural habitats. Photography — which could be grainy or out-of-focus or poorly exposed — did not immediately make mycological illustrations obsolete, however; hand-drawn colour lithographs persisted for many decades, as artists could more clearly depict the attributes of the mushrooms they were describing.

When the quality of cameras and colour printing improved in the second half of the 20th century, mycological illustration more or less fizzled out, with hand-drawn plates in mushroom books becoming a luxury embellishment rather than a practical necessity. Today, books are often replaced in the field by smartphone identification apps. But there was a brief modernist coda to the tradition, when the avant-garde musician John Cage was absorbed by mushroom hunting after he moved upstate to Stony Point, New York, in the late 1950s. Referring to his most famous work, *4'33"*, a composition consisting entirely of ambient, incidental sounds, Cage wrote in 1954: "I have spent many pleasant hours in the woods conducting performances of my silent piece, transcriptions, that is, for an audience of myself."

Cage, a student of Zen Buddhism, believed that "the responsibility of the artist is to imitate nature in her manner of operation" (an idea he adopted from the philosopher Ananda Coomaraswamy). Chance, therefore, played an important role in the composition of his work. In 1972, he published *Mushroom Book*, with the illustrator Lois Long, and Alexander Smith, president of the Mycological Society of North America. The small-edition, loose-leaved work contained lithographs of Long's accurate drawings of 20 species of mushroom, accompanied by — on separate, translucent sheets of Japanese paper — Smith's classificatory statements about each one. Picture and caption, therefore, could easily become muddled.

Also printed on the Japanese paper are Cage's diaristic asides and anecdotes — recalling Mary Elizabeth Banning or Anna Maria Hussey's conversational style — and, on other sheets, more of his handwritten notes, scattered like leaves on the forest floor. Refuting the didactic and practical style of nearly all prior mushroom guides, Cage explained that "ideas are to be found in the same way that you find wild mushrooms in the forest, by just looking". Mushrooms, for Cage, were not just specimens to be collected and classified, but wise teachers with many lessons of their own.

OPPOSITE
John Cage, page from *Mushroom Book*, © 1971–72.

PALISADES INTERSTATE

Kosmos is on the move—it goes as well to Tsing Hua (Fuller & China) as to Dharma. Had it not moved, we could have stayed with expertise (Bowles, for example). Just by touching, love indicates. But now that touch must be true [illegible]. Fuller noticed his [illegible] was beautiful.

Last year the last three [illegible] August the woods [illegible] musty scent [illegible] But this year [illegible] very few [illegible] not notice [illegible] and have [illegible] at all [illegible] more susceptible to [illegible] toads ...

At the Shanghai Heavy Building Plant there is a 12,000-ton hydraulic forging [illegible] of the largest. This press is [illegible] than 10,000-ton capacity largely because it was constructed with hollow columns. This [illegible] the solid rods (columns) [illegible] presses, a "struggle" [illegible] the Cultural Revolution. [illegible] day, the oldest concept is [illegible] Education in China is no [illegible] competitive, and is no longer [illegible] personal advancement and [illegible]. Work in factories [illegible] become an [illegible] every child's educational experience.

Route 202

Route 210

any sense ... Mind is not mind (in the [illegible], yet it is not no-mind.

(4) "On the end every law disappears" p. 295. A consummation devoutly to be wished by all good Christians, Nietzscheans and [illegible]

The Snuffelaer

Otto Marseus van Schrieck

In the mid-17th century, acquaintances of the Dutch painter Otto Marseus van Schrieck often noted their friend's eccentric propensity for getting down on hands and knees and peering at his subjects from ground level. Snakes, lizards, toads, bugs, mosses and mushrooms all entranced him, and he rendered them devotedly in dramatic tableaux. His unusual paintings belonged to no established genre of the time but have come to be classified by the Italian term *sottobosco*, meaning "under the woods". His nickname "Snuffelaer" can be translated as ferret, or ferreter, or sniffer, and each term amounts to the same thing: Marseus was as much a creature of the forest floor as he was an upright mammal.

The title of one of his best-known paintings, *Forest Floor with Mushrooms, Snakes, Toad and Lizard* (1662), actually undersells the cornucopia of flora and fauna it depicts. Out of the painting's crepuscular gloom emerges not only three species of snake and various kinds of fungus but also detailed flies, a snail, a dragonfly, a grasshopper, butterflies and a large, wilting tulip. As with the celebrated Dutch flower paintings of the period, life and death, beauty and decay, are compressed here into a single scene. During the Dutch Golden Age, Marseus's elevation of the lowest of the low was not only against convention — it was against God. The hierarchy of all natural things was laid out clearly in the Great Chain of Being, a philosophical model in which God presided at the top, and minerals lay at the very bottom. In between, angels, humans, animals, plants — including fungi — all assumed their rightful positions.

The hierarchy of painting followed a similar pattern: "history painting" lorded over portraiture, which was superior to "genre painting" — that is, scenes of everyday life. Still-life painting was the very lowliest genre, beneath even landscape. Marseus's careful and fond depictions of crawlers and fungi may have been confounding to the general public, but they were embraced by a learned few. Notably the young Florentine Prince Cosimo de' Medici, who travelled to Amsterdam in 1667 and hastened directly to Marseus's studio outside the city's walls. On a parcel of wetland beside his house, Marseus had a pen in which he raised the snakes, lizards, toads and other animals that featured in his pictures. Impressed, the prince purchased three paintings for 500 guilders; the Medici family was one of Marseus's most loyal patrons.

New advances in scientific study bolstered niche-popularity magnifying lenses that allowed for fantastically detailed visions of organic matter. Indeed, Marseus himself contributed to the corpus of zoological understanding through his own close observations, playing a small role in the way that once-despised creatures would come to be acknowledged as part of a holistic (and holy) natural system.

Fungi, one of Marseus's favourite subjects, have complex reproductive systems that were only just beginning to be understood, along with their invaluable role in decomposition and regeneration. In *Forest Floor with Mushrooms, Snakes, Toad and Lizard,* Marseus signs his name on the stem of a mushroom, aligning his artistic identity with fungus that, since antiquity, has symbolized the theoretical phenomenon of spontaneous generation. This is a fitting move for the singular mind behind the marvellous paintings that demonstrated to 17th-century viewers that seemingly foul and rotting matter, slime and mould, mushrooms and lichen were all essential parts of a miraculous ecosystem of growth — of death and new life.

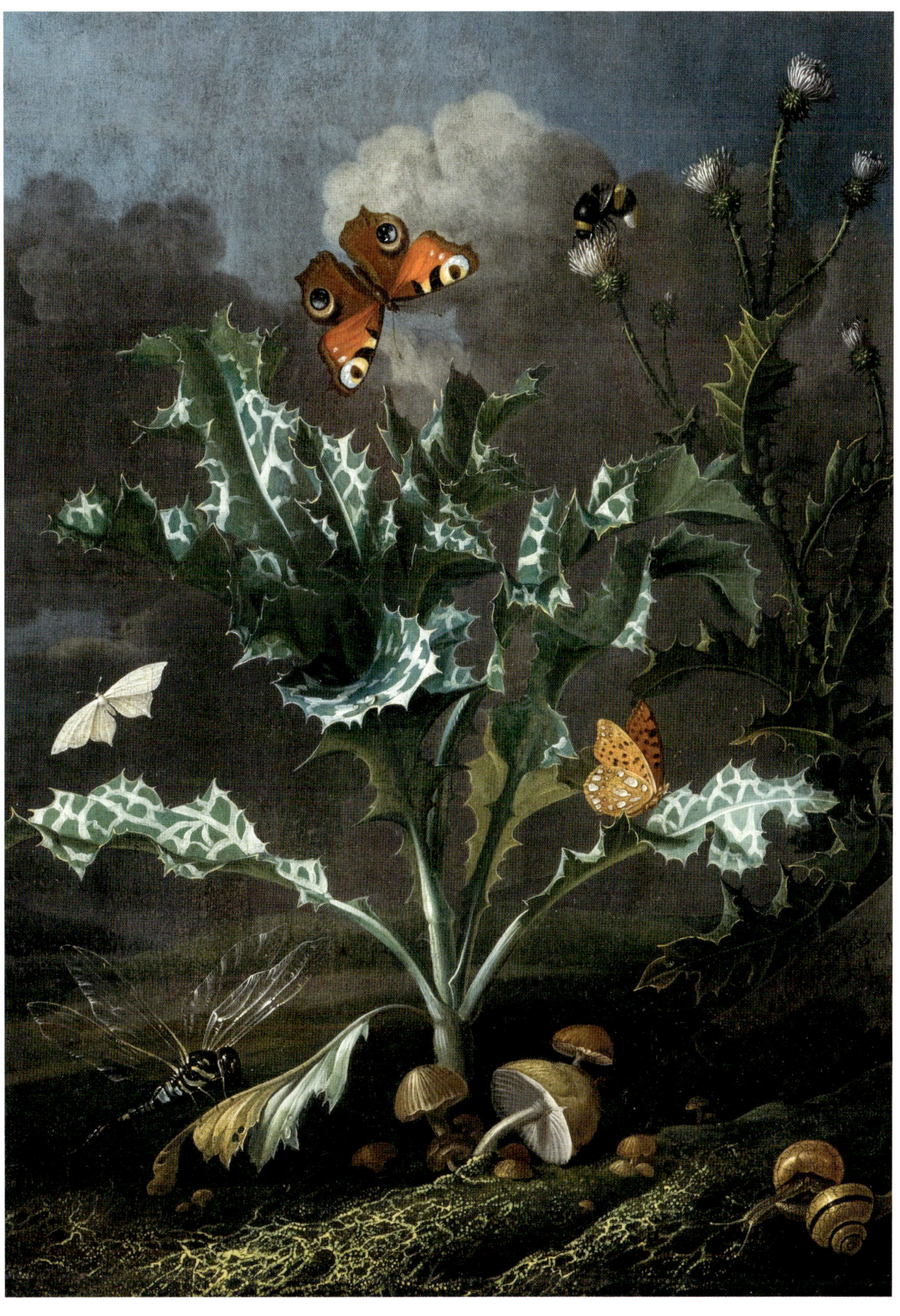

Otto Marseus van Schrieck
Thistles and Butterflies, c.1660

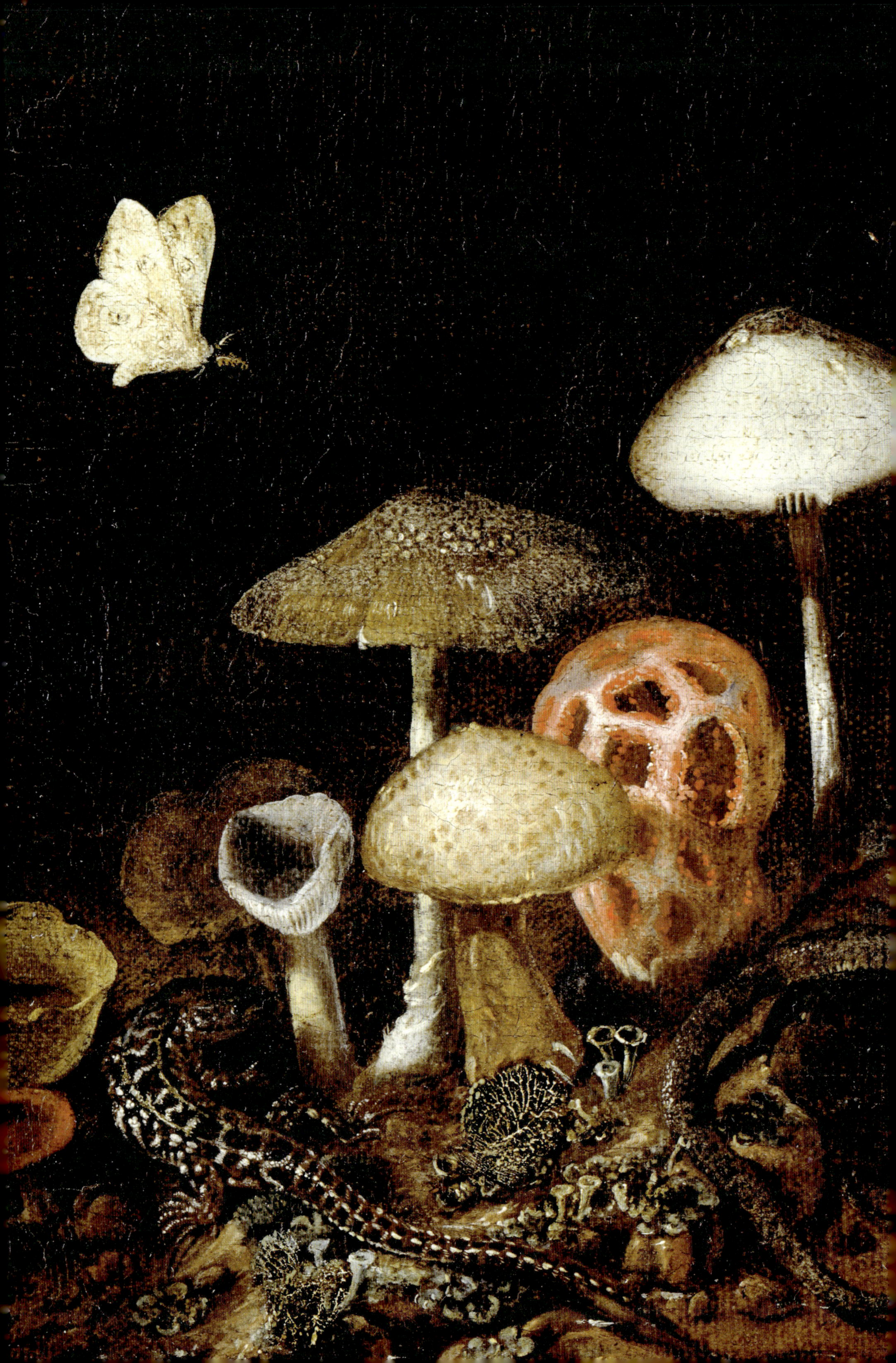

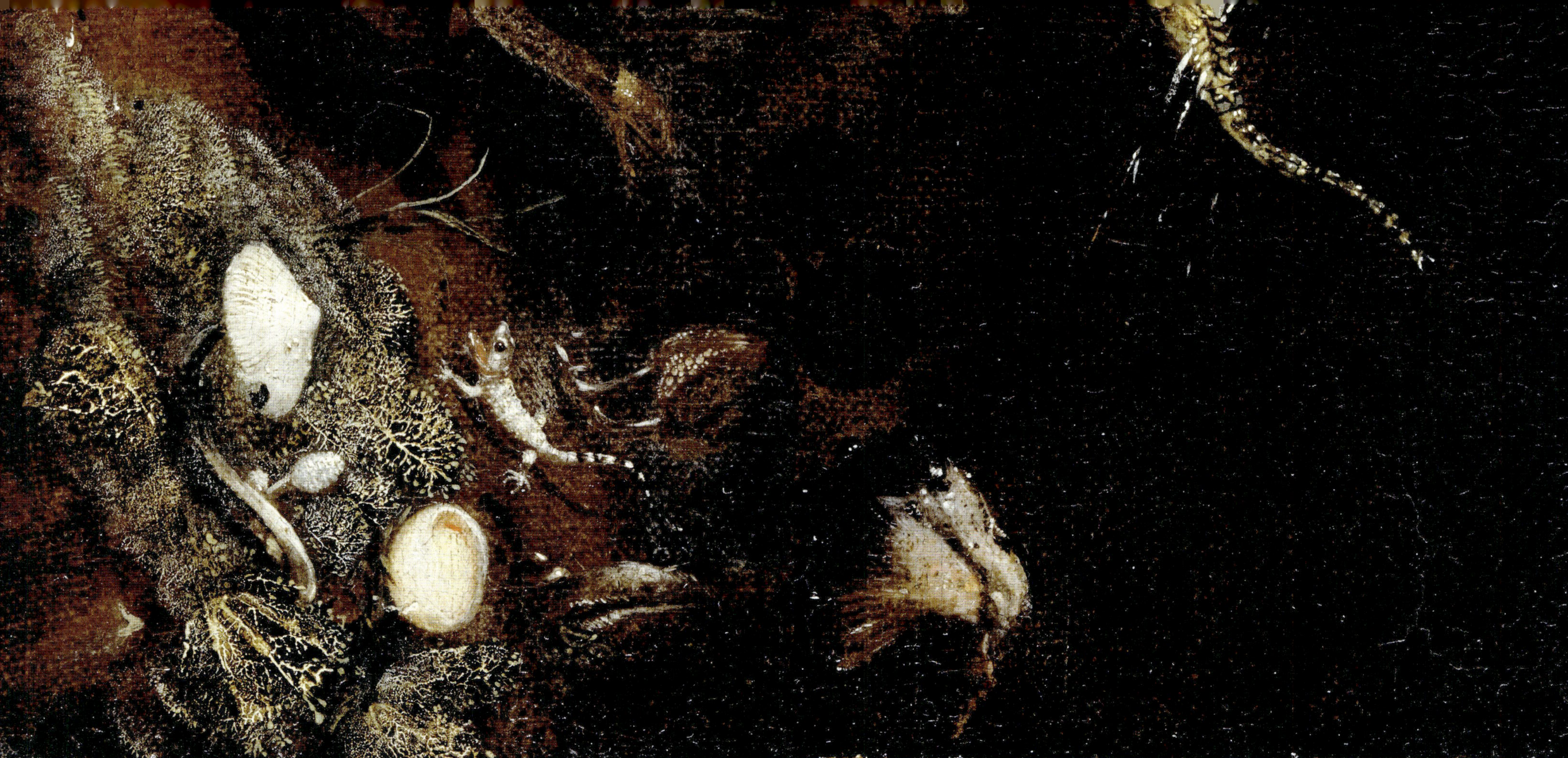

Otto Marseus van Schrieck
Reptiles, Mushrooms and Butterflies, c.1660

Mushroom Masters

A Brief History of Notable Mycologists

Victorian clergyman and trailblazer in plant pathology Miles Berkeley is generally credited with coining the term "mycology", and "mycologist" for fungi fanatics like himself. He was also notorious for the seemingly outrageous claim that the Irish potato blight of 1845 wasn't caused by static electricity from locomotives, or divine punishment from God (as some theories had it), but by a water mould. He was eventually proved right.

But the study of mushrooms had been progressing for millennia before the flowing-haired English reverend christened it. The Red Lady of El Mirón, the 19,000-year-old skeleton of an Ice Age hunter-gatherer, was found to have fungal spores in her teeth; cave art in Algeria's Tassili n'Ajjer national park dating back 9,000 years depicts shaman-like figures holding handfuls of what some scholars believe are psilocybe mushrooms; and in Eastern Spain's Selva Pascuala rock shelter, Stone Age artists appear to have painted 13 fungoid figures with bell-shaped caps about 8,000 years ago. Ötzi the Iceman, a naturally mummified Copper Age man discovered in the Alps, was carrying a bracket fungus (birch polypore) when he was prematurely killed by an arrow in the back. That particular mushroom has a history of medicinal use, suggesting the ill-fated Ötzi had an early understanding of its therapeutic potential.

Berkeley's term "mycology" sprouts from the Greek word for fungus, *mykós*, and it was the Greeks who were among the first to really record their mushroom explorations, if not always accurately; in the mid-fourth century BC, Aristotle's *Natural Histories* classified mushrooms as plants with invisible seeds. Meanwhile, Ancient Greeks imagined Zeus hurled mushrooms to Earth on lightning bolts, which explained their sudden appearance in the wake of thunderstorms, and their moniker, "sons of the gods"; while Greek physician and botanist Dioscorides included fungi in his seminal pharmacopoeia *De Materia Medica* (On Medical Substances, between 50 and 70 CE), particularly highlighting the poisonous varieties.

The hedge witches or healing folk of medieval Europe might be described as early mycologists — they certainly would have known the difference between a delicious and a deadly mushroom. Many included fungi in their plant-based brews. According to Inquisition documents, the wise women of the Basque Country used puffball mushrooms in their potions. Many of them were branded witches, persecuted and burned at the stake, and yet the scientific study of mushrooms was arguably founded on their shoulders. *Rariorum plantarum historia* (History of Rare Plants) by Dutch botanist Charles de l'Ecluse — the first book largely devoted to fungi, published in 1601 — likely grew out of his conversations with such healers.

But it was the classification-loving Victorians who were key to bringing scientific order to the mysterious world of fungi by systematically categorizing them and making the study of mycology official. Naturalists, including Mordecai Cubitt Cooke, co-founder of the British Mycological Society, and author of the classic 1860 tome on psychoactive plants *The Seven Sisters of Sleep*, kept

OPPOSITE
Robert Valentine, illustrations from *Lancashire Fungi* (edited by Miles Joseph), 1872–85

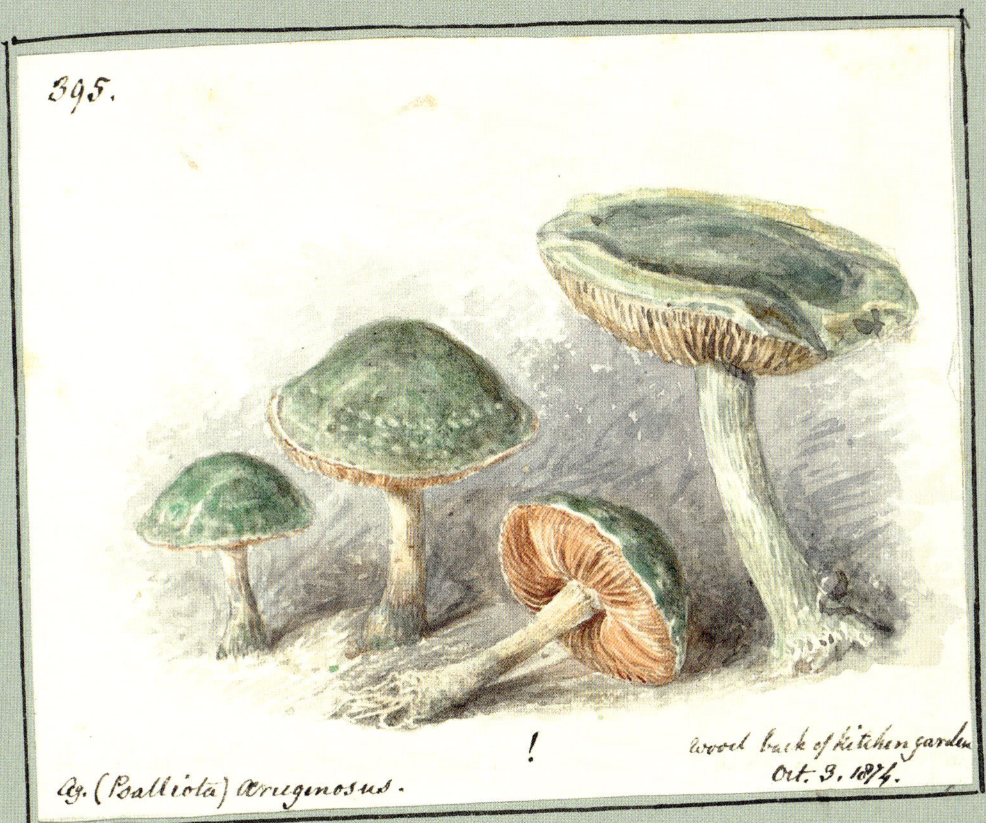

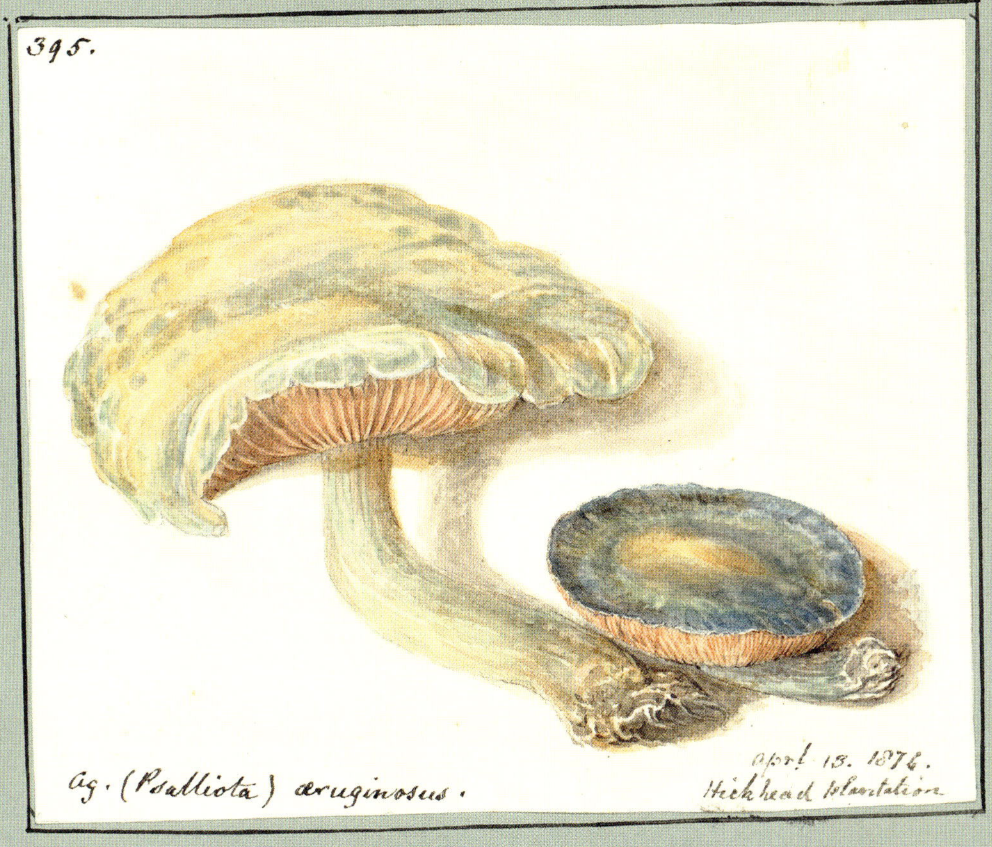

Stropharia aeruginosa

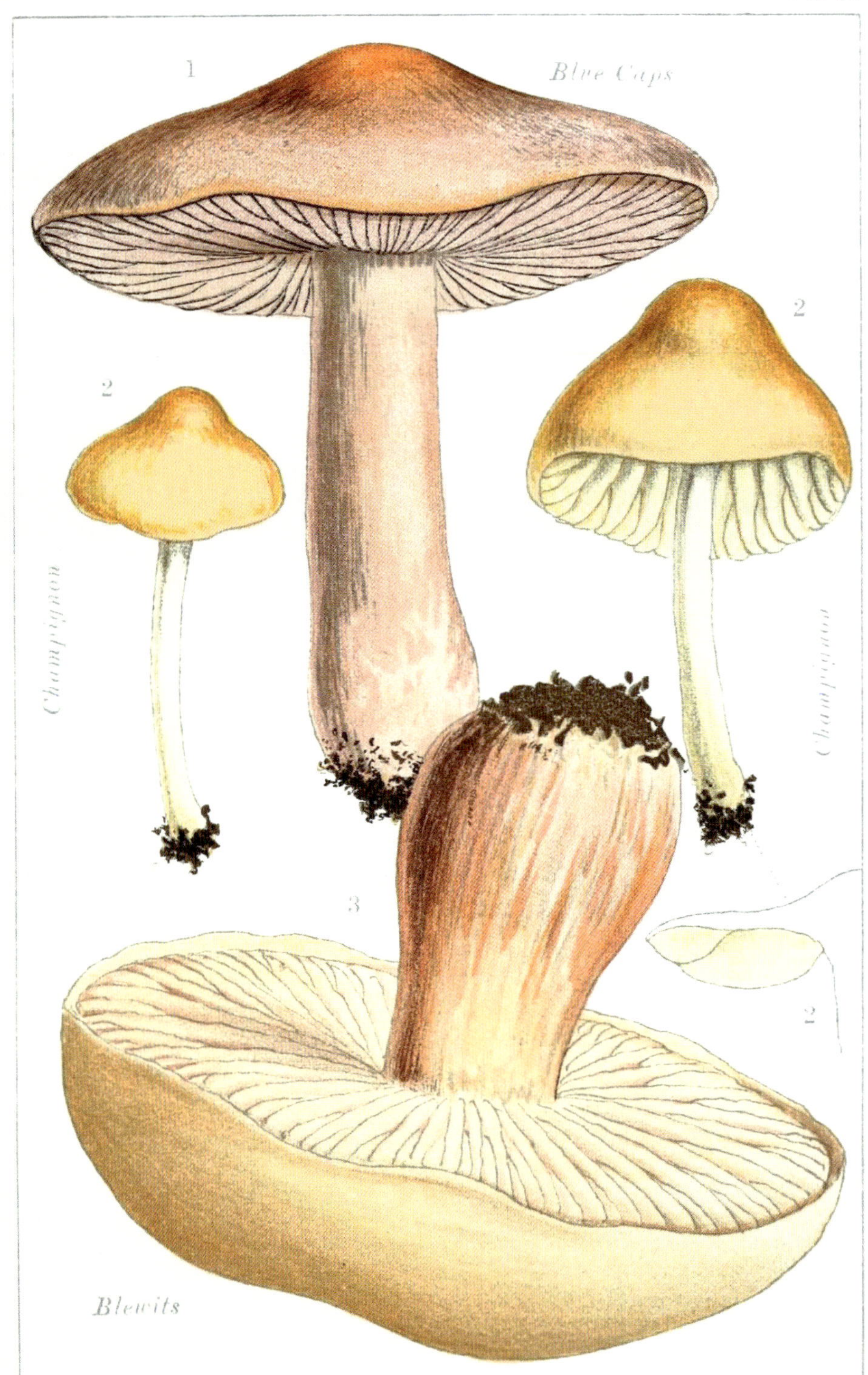

Plate from Mordecai Cooke's book
Edible and Poisonous Mushrooms, 1894

up lively correspondence about their mushroom observations, spurred on by the era's dramatically improved microscopes.

Berkeley's friend Anna Maria Hussey was a rare Victorian woman in the field of mycology—Berkeley named one genus, *Husseia*, after her. Hussey's elegant, minutely detailed drawings—her favourite subjects were morels and puffballs—were accompanied by spirited personal anecdotes and published in her two-volume *Illustrations of British Mycology* (1847 and 1855). (The second volume had to be published posthumously, after Hussey's early death from a stroke brought on by alcoholism.) Yet, as rigorous as Victorian mycologists could be, they always lumped fungi in with the plant world. That assumption continued for generations until the pivotal year of 1969, when fungi were officially recognized as distinct from plants and animals, thanks to differences in cellular structure, reproduction methods and metabolic processes.

Around the time of fungi's ascension to a kingdom of their own, mycologist Gary Lincoff was getting into fungi sideways while researching a novel whose protagonist hides out in New York's Central Park to avoid the Vietnam War draft. The puzzle of what his character might survive on led him to research edible plants and fungi. Gripped by a contagious enthusiasm, he went on to author what is often considered the most comprehensive field guide to North American mushrooms, lead expeditions to Siberia and the Amazon, write poems and songs dedicated to fungi, and co-found the Telluride Mushroom Festival, an eccentric gathering in the Rocky Mountains that brings together scientists and keen amateurs at a mushroom-themed parade climaxing in a communal drum circle. (The August festival has attracted the likes of director Jim Jarmusch, whose near-death experience from eating a wild mushroom propelled him to become an amateur mycologist himself.)

Logger turned mycological entrepreneur Paul Stamets was hooked on mushrooms after a psilocybin trip cured him of a teenage stutter. He's the founder of Fungi Perfecti, a company that sells mycelium-based products and researches the use of fungi to protect bees from extinction and remove toxic substances from the natural environment (fungi can be trained to eat used nappies,

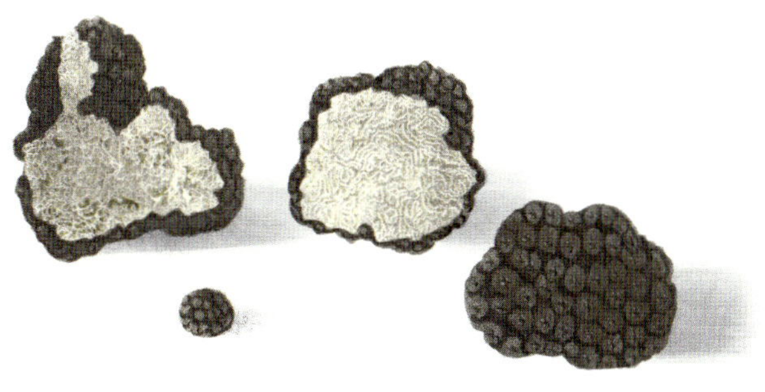

Anna Maria Hussey
Tuber cibarium (black truffle), from her book *Illustrations of British Mycology*, 1847–55

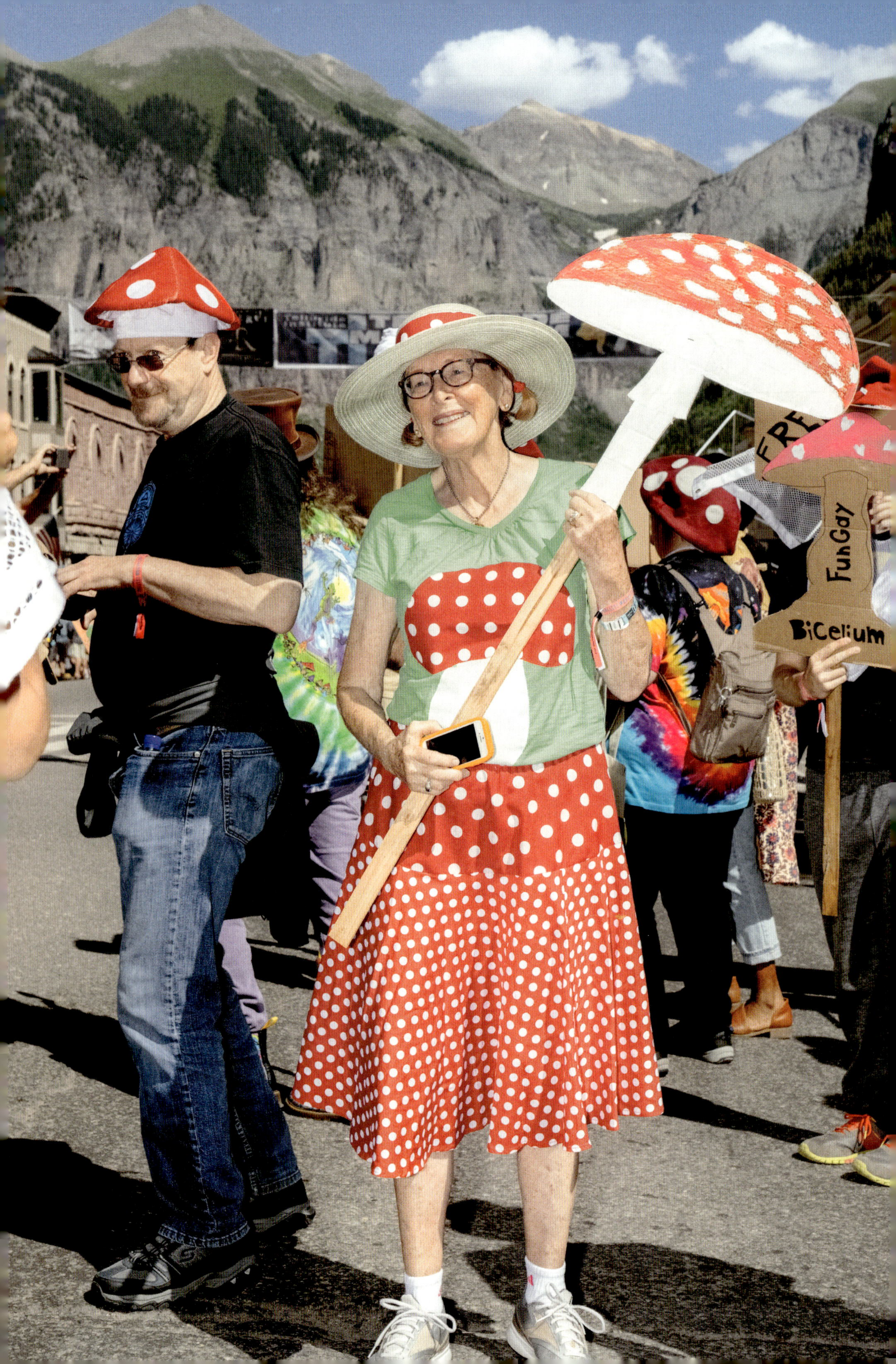
FunGay
BiCelium

cigarette butts and even oil spills). Stamets spends much of his time exploring old-growth forests, in a hat made from the amadou mushroom. "I see the mycelium as the earth's natural internet," he says, "a consciousness with which we might be able to communicate." In the small pool of celebrity mycologists, Stamets is so notorious that a fictional "astromycologist" in *Star Trek: Discovery* is named after him: Lieutenant Commander Stamets of the USS Discovery.

Stamets isn't the only fictional character to have been inspired by a mushroom lover. Laura Palmer's wayward therapist, Dr Jacoby, in David Lynch's cult 1990s TV series *Twin Peaks* is almost certainly based on ethnobiologist, counterculture guru and one-time hashish smuggler Terence McKenna. At least, they certainly share a love of Hawaiian shirts, colourful glasses, unruly hair and even more unruly ideas. McKenna focused mostly on the psychotropic qualities of the mushroom and had the honour of being named the "Timothy Leary of the 90s" by Leary himself. A Jung-reading child who first became interested in mushrooms through R. Gordon Wasson's 1957 *Life* magazine story "Seeking the Magic Mushroom", McKenna brought back spores from the Colombian Amazon and devised an innovative method for growing magic mushrooms at home using kitchen appliances and a rye substrate, sharing his innovations in a handbook that inspired many a student of psycho-mycology.

McKenna advocated magic mushrooms for everyone — preferably five grams taken alone on an empty stomach "in silent darkness". (He was ahead of his time — microdosing mushrooms has now gone mainstream.) He was a wellspring of far-out ideas, including that magic mushroom spores were blown across the cosmos to Earth from other planets.

But his most famous is the "stoned ape" theory, which posits psychedelic mushrooms as the missing link in human evolution — a catalyst that shook loose early man's imagination. Psilocybin, he believed, had transformative effects on early *Homo sapiens*, laying the basis for language, religion and culture: "we ate our way to higher consciousness", he writes in 1992's *Food of the Gods*. (For those with more religious than evolutionary leanings, McKenna also suggested Adam and Eve's watershed moment in the Garden of Eden didn't come via a tempting-looking apple but via a mushroom, the fly agaric. There's a 13th-century fresco of the scene in a French chapel in the village of Mérigny that seems to back him up.)

McKenna's ideas about the evolutionary riddle of our collective cognitive leap were often dismissed, but he took the long view from his jungle retreat in Hawaii, considering his book as a kind of Trojan horse "left on the doorstep of anthropology". If he was considered a fringe figure during his lifetime, today some devotees of the mushroom might be said to have entered the spotlight — that's the case at least of mycologist Merlin Sheldrake, whose 2023 IMAX documentary *Fungi: Web of Life* was narrated by admirer Björk. Sheldrake has taken up the task of challenging our assumptions about fungi and sharing the wonder and ingenuity of the mycorrhizal networks operating under our feet.

He writes in *Entangled Life* (2020) that fungi can be found everywhere — in the soil and on ocean floors, along coral reefs, inside living and dead plants and animals, as well as in rubbish dumps, carpets, floorboards, old books, household dust and even the materials of old paintings in museums. The book recounts some mind-boggling details, from the 30,000-tonne, ten-square-kilometre fungus that lives underground in Oregon to the discovery that some mushrooms can metabolize radiation. Sheldrake celebrated his book's release by seeding the paperback with oyster mushroom spores that slowly transformed the pages into white mycelium, which he then ate. He's also been known to cut mycorrhizal spores into lines and snort them.

Sheldrake name-checks pioneering activist, Giuliana Furci, Chile's first female field mycologist and discoverer of several new species of fungi. She founded the world's first NGO dedicated to the protection of fungi, as an inspiration to today's mycological community. But with untold ecological challenges ahead and 2.5 million species yet to be discovered according to the Royal Botanic Gardens at Kew, the field is wide open for aspiring mushroom experts to join the fray.

OPPOSITE
Caroline Tompkins, Telluride Mushroom Festival, 2019

Beatrix Potter

And the Little Tiny Fungus People

One spring evening in 1897, a group of top-hatted, tail-coated naturalists gathered at London's Linnean Society, the world's oldest institution devoted to natural history. An item on the agenda that night was a scientific paper submitted by Helen B Potter, "On the Germination of the Spores of Agaricineae", accompanied by some meticulously detailed, and exceptionally beautiful illustrations of fungi. Its author was conspicuously absent — being a woman, she wasn't allowed membership or even access to the Linnean Society's Palladian Piccadilly headquarters. Potterhad previously approached the head of Kew Gardens, William Turner Thiselton-Dyer, with her theories — he had dismissed them as "mares' nests". Similarly, the gathering of Fellows at the Linnean showed little interest in a paper submitted by an amateur — and worse, a woman. But mycology's loss was literature's gain. Faced with these intransigent Victorian gatekeepers of botany, Potter turned her curious mind to children's books, lighting up imaginations across the globe with mischievous radish thief Peter Rabbit and a menagerie of other crafty, spirited animals, from Mrs Tiggy-Winkle to Mr Jeremy Fisher to Jemima Puddle-Duck.

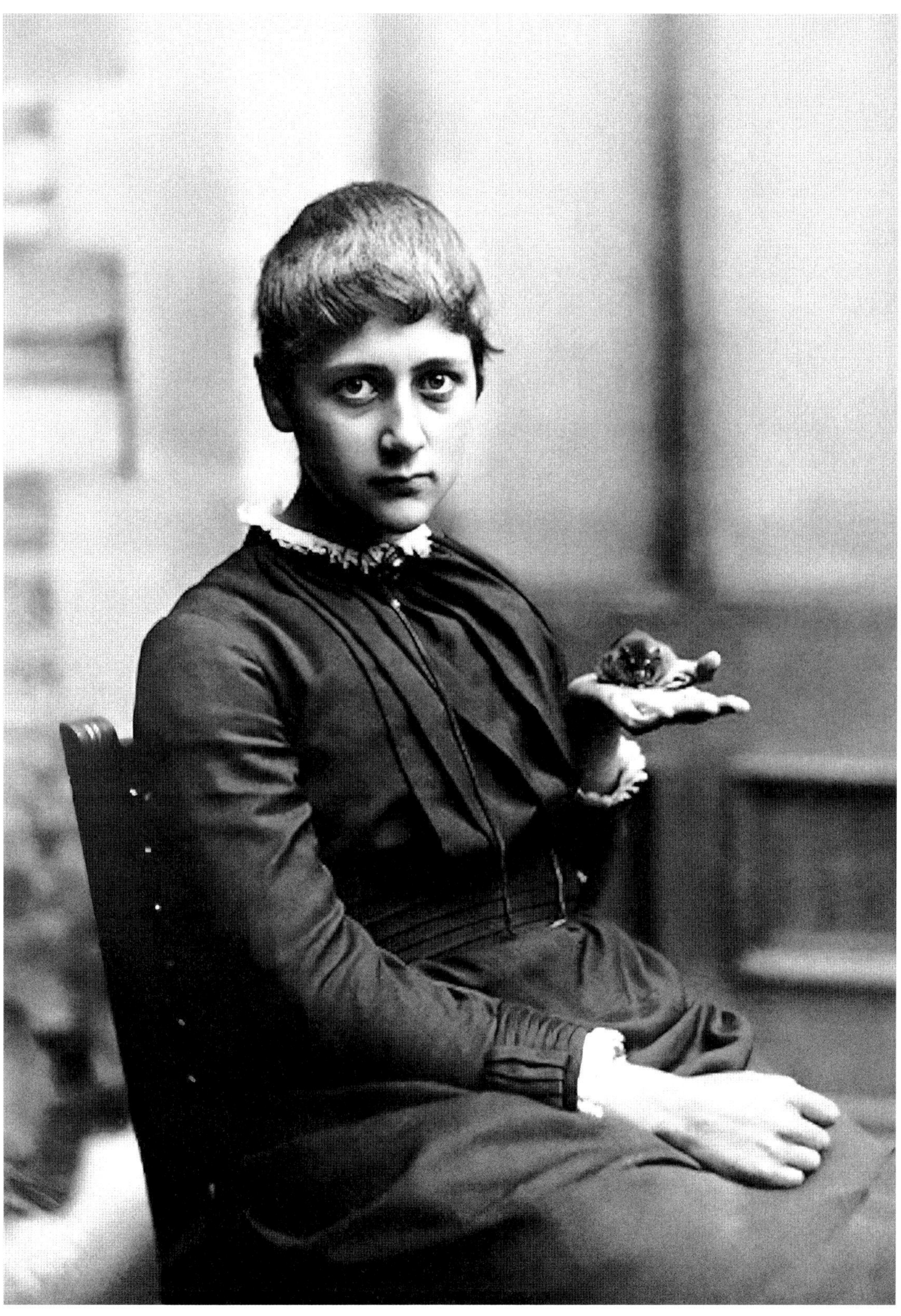

Beatrix Potter with her pet mouse Xarifa, 1885

Born in South Kensington in west London to a wealthy family of cotton merchants and shipbuilders, Potter was educated at home by a governess in a third-floor schoolroom. It was an isolated and emotionally chilly childhood that she brightened up with numerous pets brought home in paper bags: hedgehogs, newts, salamanders, guinea pigs, rabbits, snakes, even bats. She drew them all, and many became the prototypes for the newspaper-reading frogs, impertinent squirrels and busy dormice that later peppered her books.

Potter's fascination with flora and fauna developed amid a widespread Victorian enthusiasm for identifying and cataloguing the natural world — from her window, she had a clear view of the newly built Natural History Museum, where wooden drawers brimmed with pickled fungi, fossils, bird's eggs and butterflies. At home, Potter created a miniature museum of her own, full of plants and animals both alive and dead. Potter had a scientist's lack of sentimentality — when her pets died, their skeletons were boiled, and their bones carefully measured and labelled. (Her children's books were equally un-syrupy and never forgot nature's tooth and claw: the gruesome spectacle of Tom Kitten or the lumpy minced-mouse pie accidentally eaten by Duchess the Pomeranian still elicits a shiver.)

But there was only so much London could offer by way of nature; Potter longed for the freedom of the summer holidays, when the family swapped the city smog for Scotland or the Lake District. Exploring local woods and country lanes, she filled her journals (written in a code broken only after her death) with observations on flora and fauna. Mushrooms, in particular, had a whimsical,

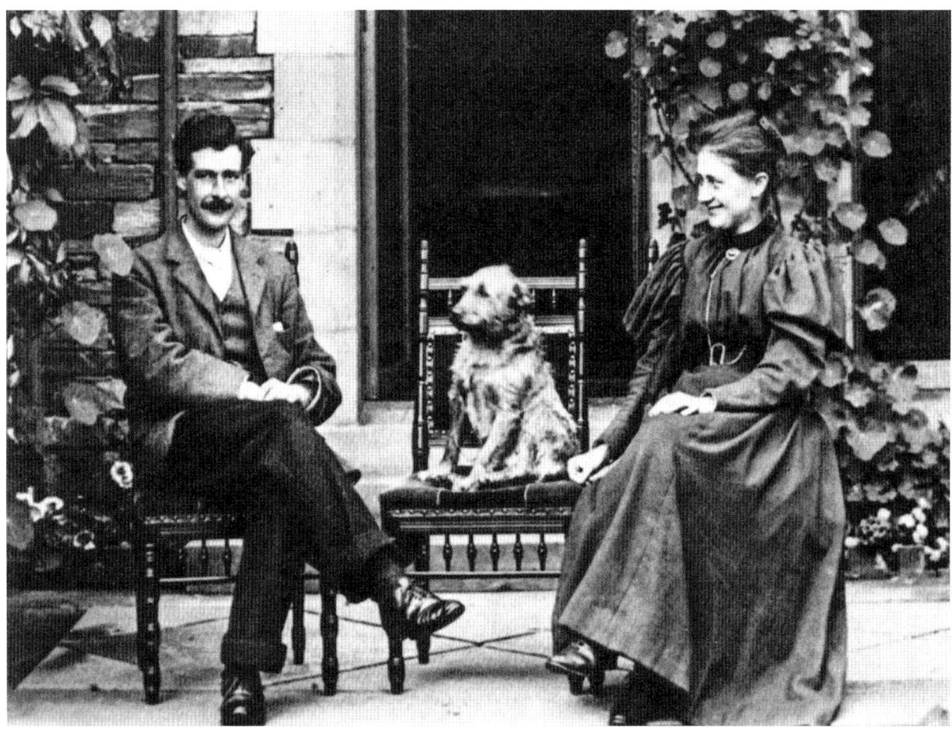

Beatrix Potter and her brother Bertram, 1898

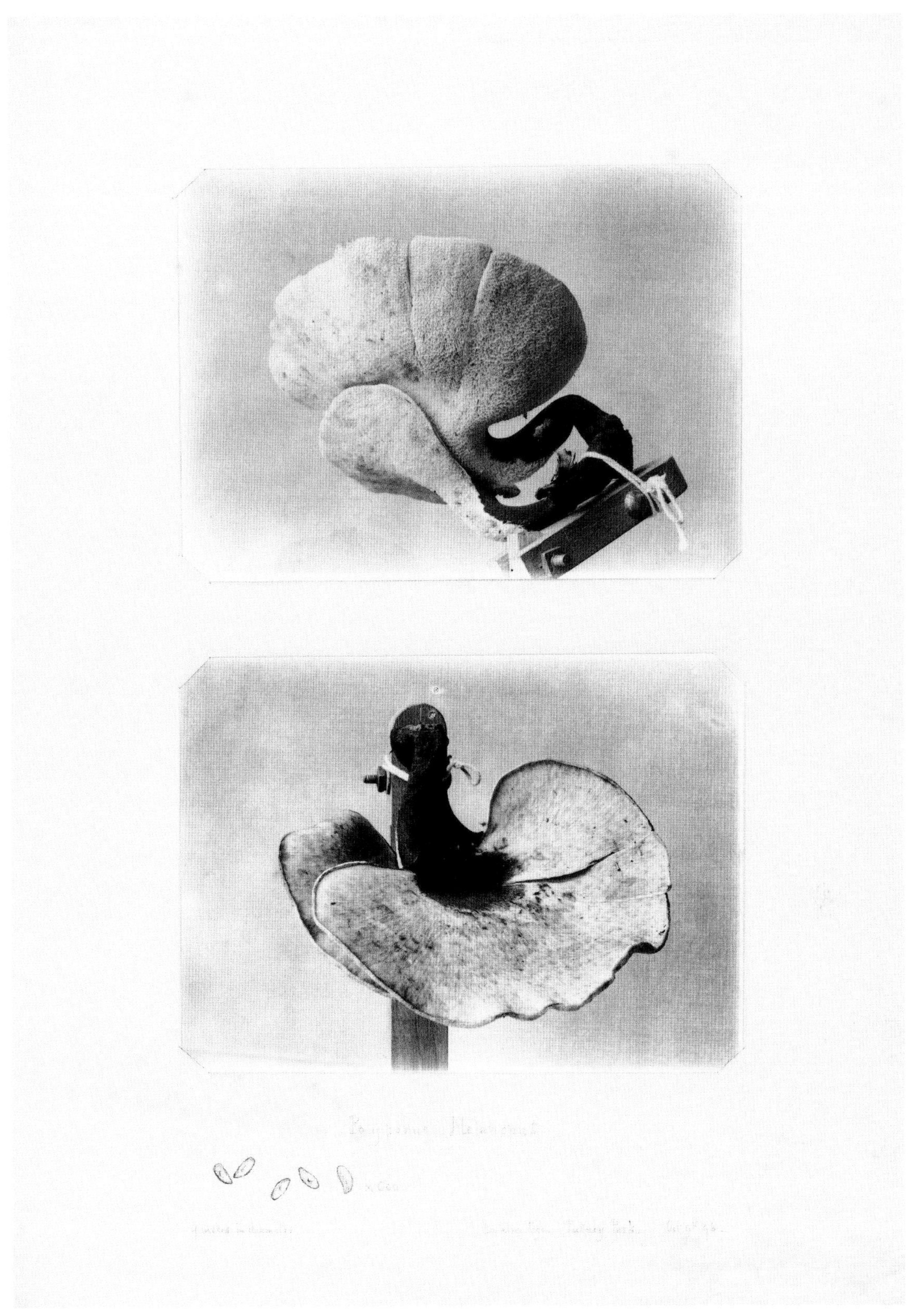

Beatrix Potter
Photographs of polypore fungi, with notes and sketches of spores, 1896

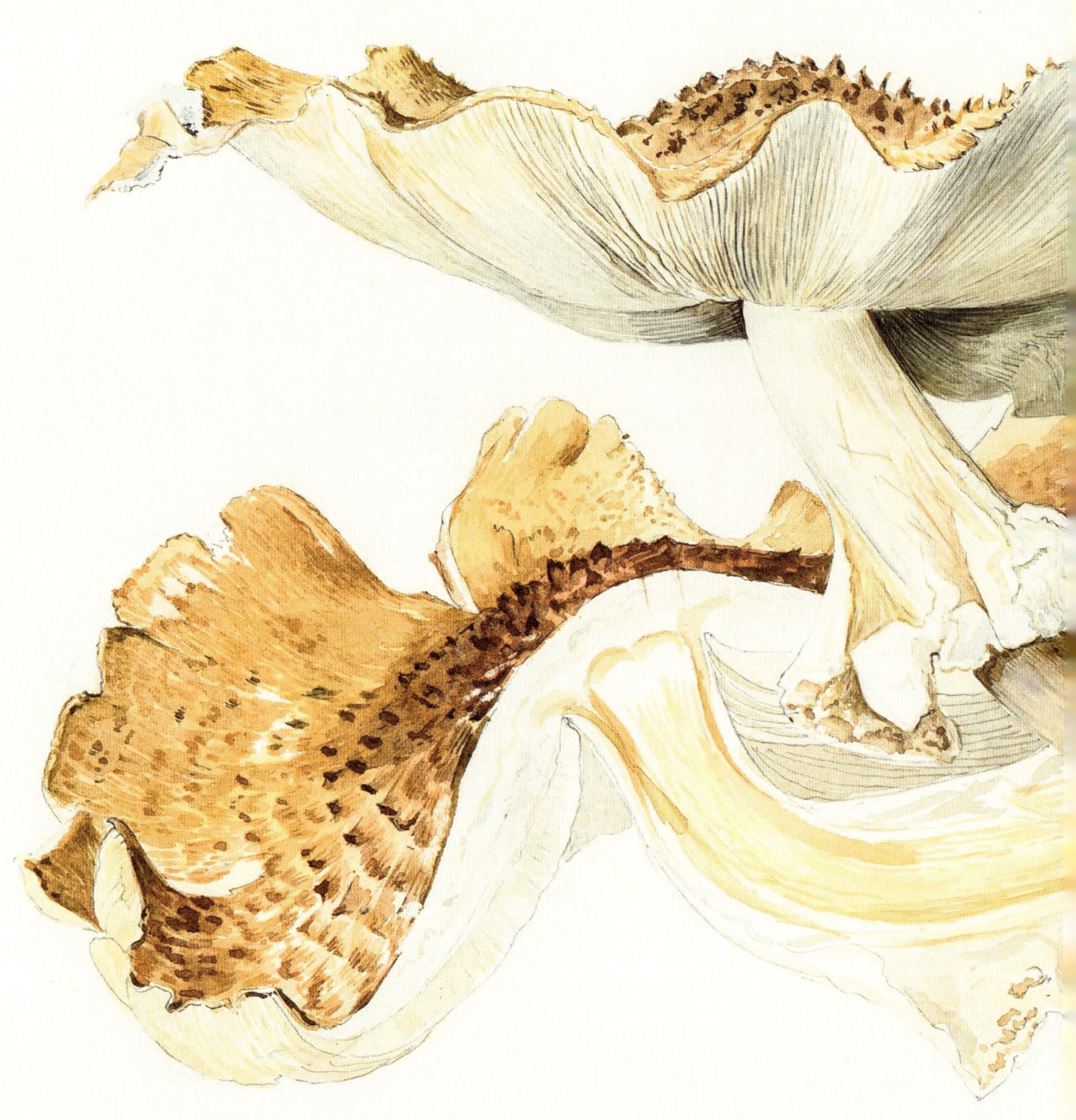

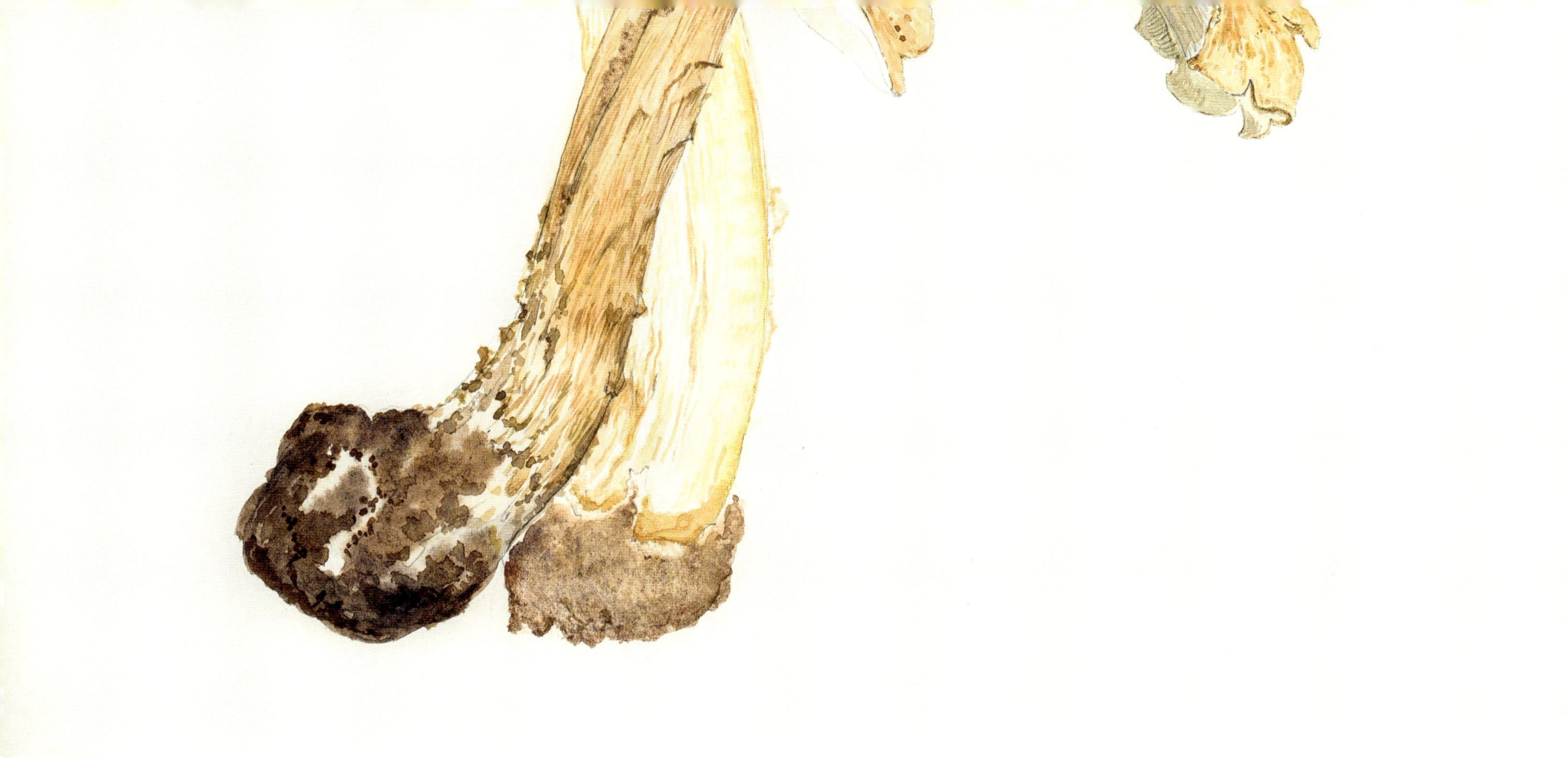

Beatrix Potter, *Lepiota friesii*, 1895

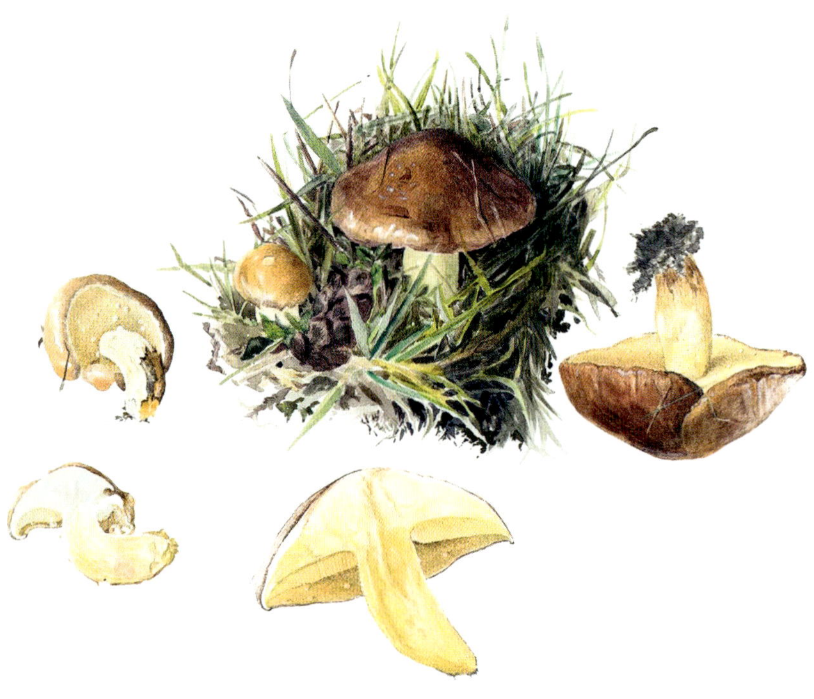

anthropomorphic quality that appealed to the nascent author: "the little tiny fungus people singing and bobbing and dancing in the grass and under the leaves all down below," she wrote in 1896. "I cannot tell what possesses me with the fancy that they laugh and clap their hands, especially the little ones that grow in troops amongst the dead leaves in the woods."

It was on holiday in Scotland when Potter was a child that she first met the postal worker, musician and self-taught naturalist Charles McIntosh, a singular character who had lost the fingers of one hand in a sawmill accident. A tall, generously bearded figure — many theorize he was the inspiration for Peter Rabbit's nemesis, Mr McGregor — he used his daily rounds as a country postman to study sprouting fungi, later identifying four entirely new species. As Potter's passion for the botanical grew in her mid-20s, the pair began to exchange flurries of letters and mycological theories, with McIntosh mailing Potter dried specimens, and Potter replying with vivid illustrations of them. With her new mentor's encouragement, she rendered fungi in incredible scientific detail, depicting cross-sections and different stages of development.

Voyaging in the kind of warm, wet weather that brought mushrooms out in crowds, Potter endured multiple tick bites to make more than 350 illustrations, including rare species like old man of the woods (*Strobilomyces strobilaceus*) and witches' butter (*Exidia glandulosa*). In between the job of managing her parents' affairs, she also began growing spores on glass plates — including larch canker and dry rot, which she hid under a stone in the garden — fearing her parents might

Beatrix Potter
Boletus granulatus, 1895

object to fungi in the house. Studying specimens through a microscope, she began to posit theories about germination, culminating in that ill-fated scientific paper, presented at the Linnean Society when she was 30 years old. Although its quality can't be judged – the paper is long lost – 100 years after its reading the society issued a posthumous apology to Potter, acknowledging she had been "treated scurvily".

"Time has been far kinder to Beatrix's scientific efforts than her contemporaries were," writes Linda Lear in her 2006 book *Beatrix Potter: A Life in Nature*. "When she tied up her portfolios of fungi paintings with ribbons many years later, she could not have known that her conclusions about the symbiotic nature of lichens and the hybridization of fungi would later be proved and accepted. Nor could she imagine that her watercolours are considered so accurate that modern mycologists refer to them still to identify fungi."

Perhaps it's unsurprising that those watercolours were not bequeathed to Kew Gardens or the Linnean Society. Anyone wishing to study them today must travel to the diminutive Armitt Museum and Library in Ambleside, a small town in Potter's beloved Lake District. In 1905, the writer and illustrator bought Hill Top Farm in the area with the considerable money she'd made from her books – more than 250 million copies have sold worldwide today. Aged 39 and finally free of the dark, stiffly formal house in Kensington, Potter went on to raise award-winning sheep. On her death in 1943, she left her entire estate – 4,000 acres of land and 15 farms – to the National Trust.

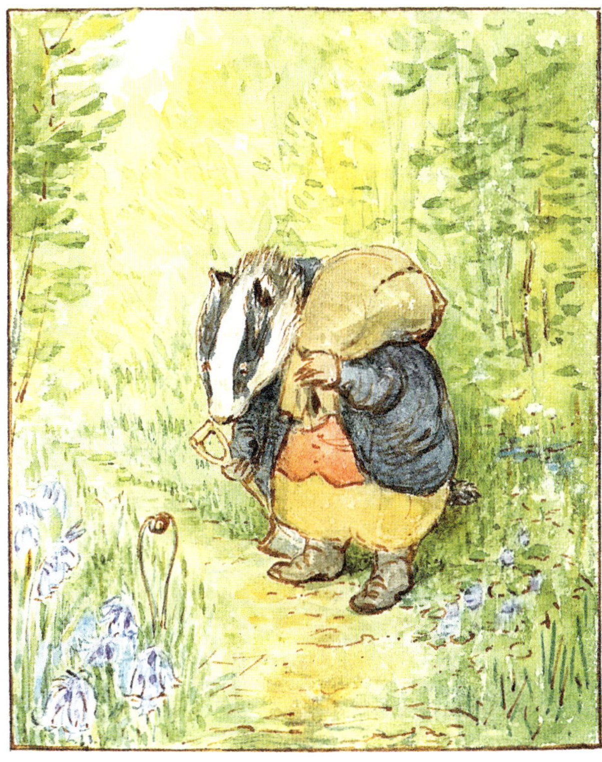

Beatrix Potter
Tommy Brock, from her book *The Tale of Mr Todd*, 1912

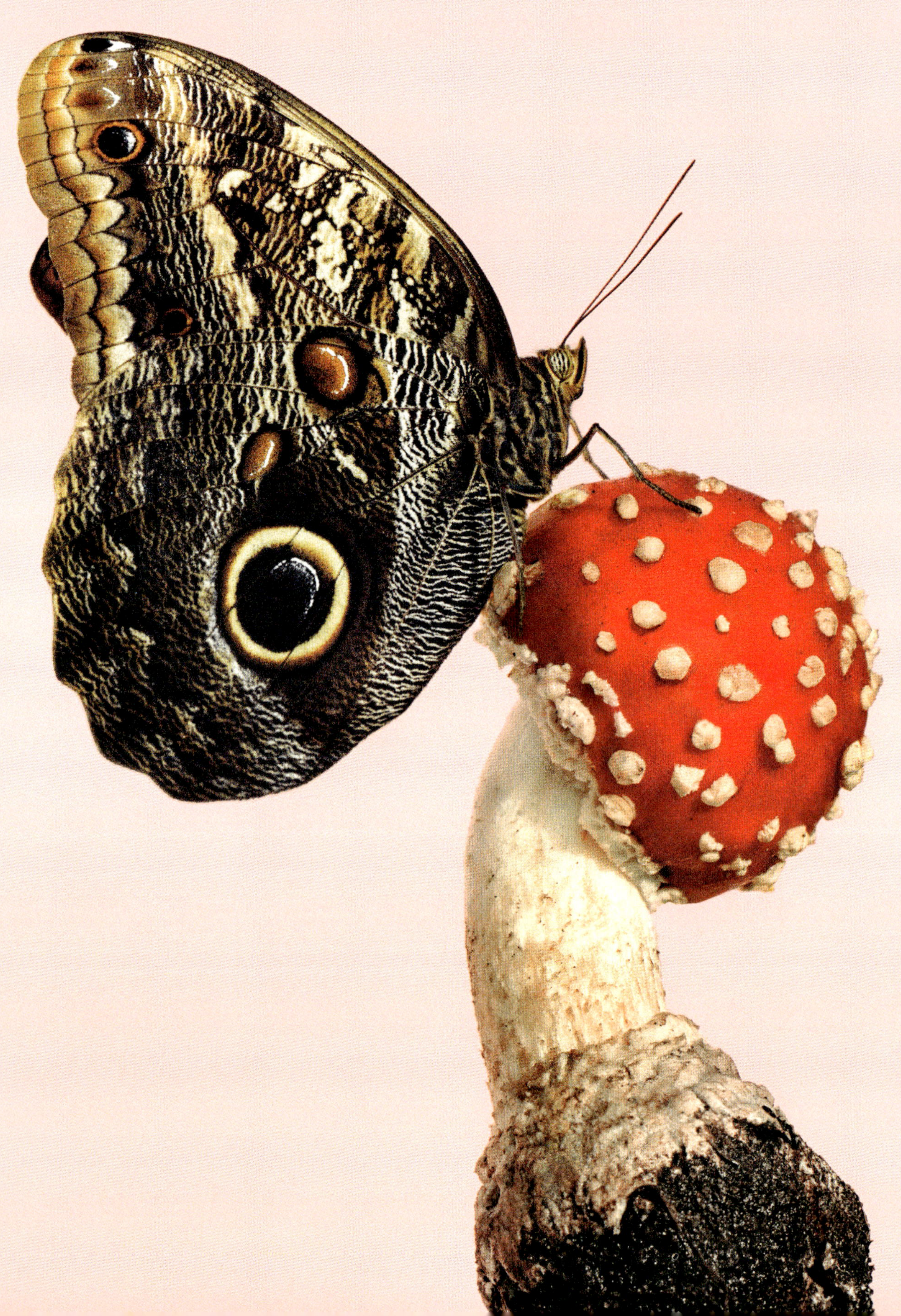

A Spotty History of Fly Agaric

In Vézelay Abbey, a monastery overlooking the charming department of Yonne in the Bourgogne-Franche-Comté region of France, the customarily terrifying Antichrist cuts a curious jib. Gaze up at the columns supporting the barrel-vaulted, 12th-century roof, and you'll discover a trove of biblical themes chiselled into the limestone. There's over a hundred Old Testament parables to be seen, and one notable anomaly. A single column features a minstrel blasting his horn inches from the Devil's flaming hair and uncharacteristically ballooning, cock-eyed face (the countenance of a court jester, or a stoned teenager). The outrageous claim of this tableau is that a mere mortal musician has turned the sly Prince of Darkness into a slack-jawed dullard with his song.

In between the minstrel and his oafish companion, a plant emerges with a long stem, a bulbous dome and several clusters of spots that bears a remarkable resemblance to *Amanita muscaria*, more commonly known as the fly agaric mushroom. This narcotic fungus induces powerful hallucinations, and might be responsible for the Devil's dopey expression.

Fly agarics are the iconic red-capped toadstools with white-spotted warts found throughout the Northern Hemisphere, often hunted for their psychoactive effects. Over centuries they have attracted a motley pantheon of devotees — from the bard Shakespeare to the painter Hieronymus Bosch, to witches and shaman, the inhabitants of Wonderland, Satan and Super Mario.

Folklore, pop culture and Burning Man anecdotes all express similar cautionary tales about these psychoactive trips. Those who partake of fly agaric may experience a smorgasbord of reported effects, including perceptual distortions, synaesthesia, euphoria, visions of sacred geometry, fits of paranoia and ego death. A mixed existential bag to be sure. These psychedelic consequences can be explained away as chemical interactions, but many belief systems hold the fly agaric's effects as sacred, even divine.

For the Uralic and Paleo peoples of Western Siberia and the Russian Far East, fly agarics were reserved for shamans, who used them to achieve a trance state. The Kamchatka Peninsula, which juts into the northwest Pacific, is home to the Koryak people, who have a myth dedicated to the divine origins of the fly agaric. The tale begins when the deity Vahiyinin (Existence) spits on the earth, and his gob transforms into *wapaq* (fly agaric). Enter Big Raven, the shaman god and progenitor of humankind, who gobbles up the *wapaq*, and is thus granted the strength to carry a stranded whale back to its home. After experiencing the power of the *wapaq* firsthand, Big Raven is so exhilarated that he instructs it to grow forever on the earth so that humanity can experience its powers as well.

Then there's the ancient Siberian origins of the Santa Claus legend. Unsurprisingly, fly agaric is rare in the frozen tundra, which may have led to tribespeople sharing mushroom-infused urine to pass along its magical properties. Supposedly, this psychoactive piddle was sought by the native reindeer — perhaps for the same trippy reasons the tribespeople liked to indulge in laced wee. Once combined and extrapolated, the wintery landscape, the reindeer and the red-and-white colour scheme of the fly agaric can be seen as Old Saint Nick's origin story. In this telling, Father Christmas is a personification of the mushroom, bestowing otherworldly favours onto mortals. Thankfully, the bit about drinking urine didn't stick as a holiday custom.

OPPOSITE
Ben Toms, from *Evolution*, 2023–24

The Death Cap

Mushroom Toxicity and Poisoning

Corsets, planking and tapeworm diets are all examples of tales as old as time: when something dangerous trends, bandwagoners perish. With mushrooms enjoying a cultural moment over the last few years — moving from forests and kitchens and into laboratories and outer space — poisonings are on the rise, with amateur foragers frying up just about any old fungi they can find. As one fungal expert at a poison centre bluntly put it, "We do have adults that maybe think they know what they're doing foraging... but we see they don't."

Depending on the type of mushroom, adverse effects of poisoning range from mild gastrointestinal symptoms to organ failure and death. Even the most iconic of all mushrooms, the fly agaric (*Amanita muscaria*), with its cute li'l red cap and white dots, will have you hallucinating on the toilet. And never, ever be fooled by the unassuming appearance of the fittingly named death cap (*Amanita phalloides*). Its woefully unhip, chartreuse-tinged bowler hat belies its status as the world's most toxic mushroom, responsible for about 90% of all mushroom-related deaths.

More broadly, recent global estimates suggest mushrooms cause about 10,000 illnesses and 100 deaths annually. However, with symptoms delayed and often misdiagnosed, fungus poisonings are notoriously difficult to track, a challenge compounded by our still-limited understanding of the mycological world. Estimates of known mushroom species range widely, from tens of thousands to well over 100,000, and the number of poisonous species varies from around 100 to over 600. These wide ranges represent only a fraction of the total number of unidentified mushroom species that experts assume exist but have yet to be identified.

While a good rule of thumb is that roughly 1–3 per cent of all mushroom species are likely poisonous (with some 30 truly lethal), confusing matters is that many common edible varieties, like morels, contain toxins that are only harmful if not cooked properly or consumed in large quantities. Raw shiitakes, for instance, can cause flagellate dermatitis, a rash that looks like whip marks. Despite having a supervillains' gallery of damning names such as train wrecker (*Neolentinus lepideus*), poison pie (*Hebeloma crustuliniforme*) and destroying angel (*Amanita virosa*), poisonous mushrooms can be difficult to identify, whether in the wild by a hapless forager or on the plate of an unsuspecting victim.

OPPOSITE
Bobby Doherty *Untitled*, 2025

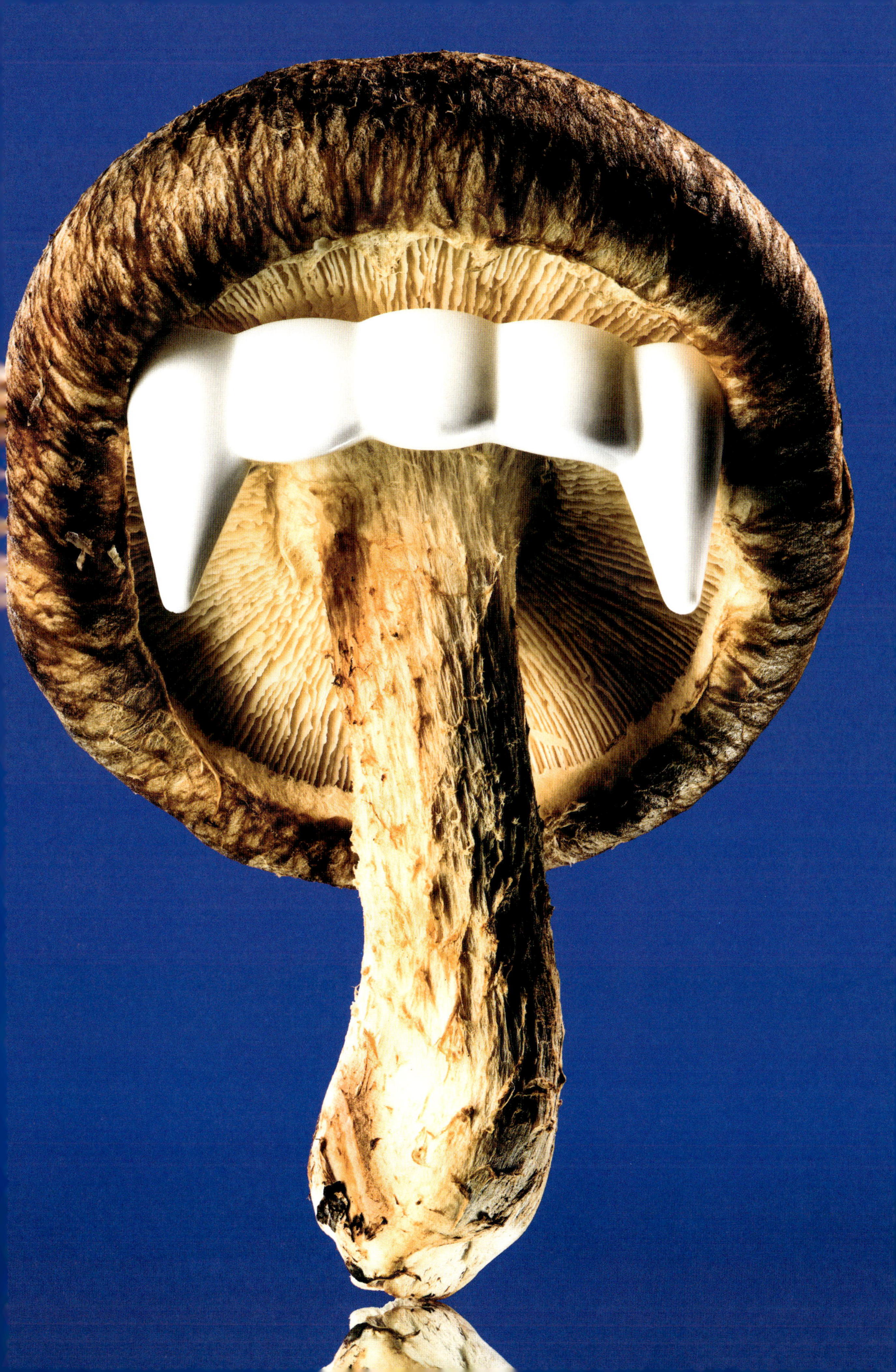

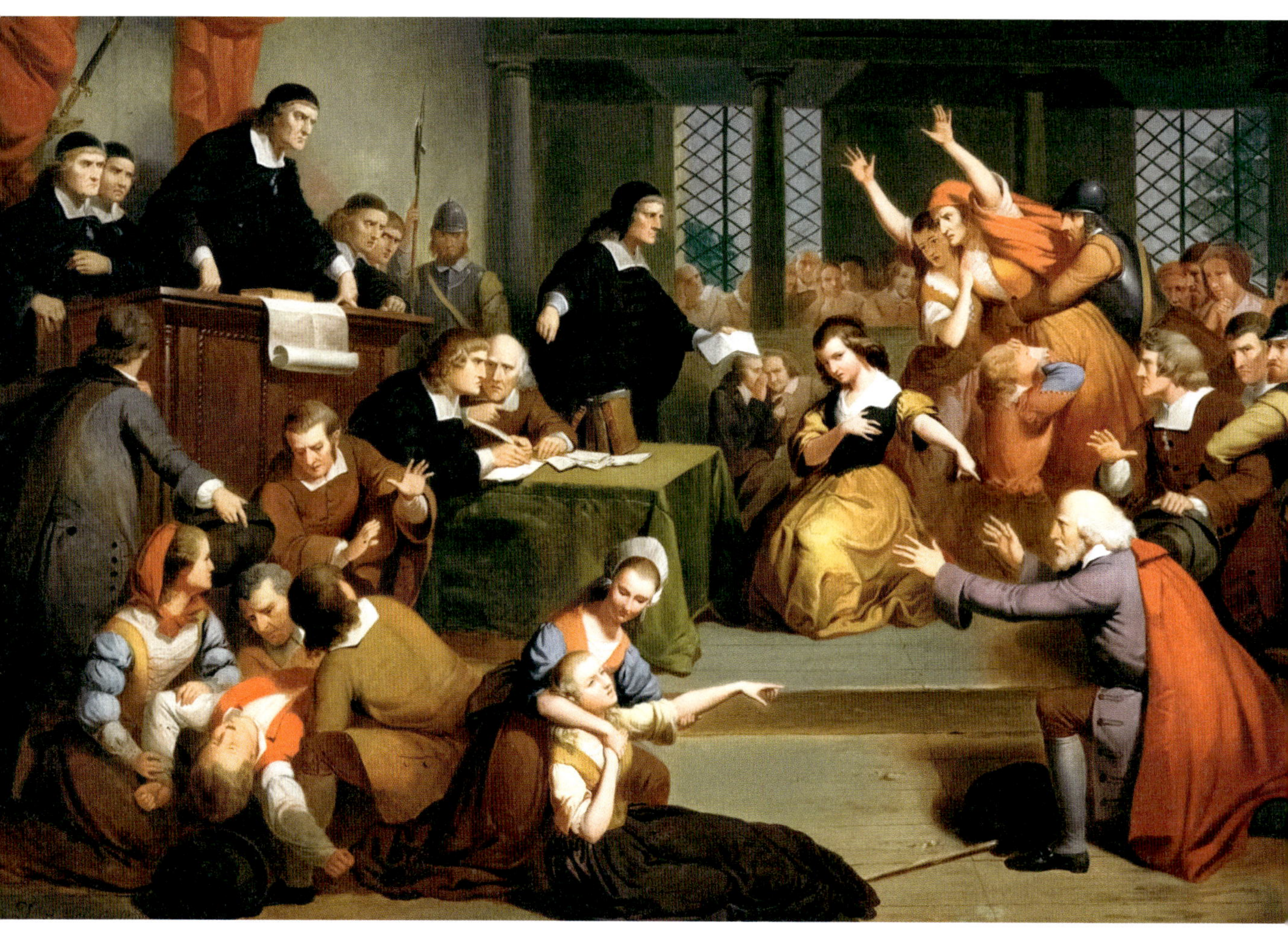

Thompkins H Matteson
The Trial of George Jacobs, 1855

Just ask Nicholas Evans, author of international bestseller *The Horse Whisperer* (1995), who, along with his wife, required a kidney transplant after consuming foraged deadly webcap mushrooms (*Cortinarius rubellus*) he misidentified as edible. Or Emperor Claudius, who in 54 CE was purposefully fed poisonous mushrooms by his fourth wife, Agrippina, thus securing the throne for her soon-to-be-notorious son, Nero. Or the four in-laws of infamous Australian Erin Patterson, aka the Mushroom Murderer, who in 2023 cooked up a nice beef wellington for members of her estranged husband's family—which happened to be made with death caps, and sent four to the hospital, where two of them died.

Back in 1767, German composer and unwitting mass murderer Johann Schobert died alongside his wife, one of their children, a maidservant and several others after eating poisonous mushrooms he insisted were edible, despite warnings from chefs at two restaurants that they were not. Even the Buddha was said to have died from mushroom poisoning. Indeed, from Roman emperors to scheming Aussies, stubborn composers to enlightened beings, toxic mushrooms like Satan's bolete (*Rubroboletus satanas*) and the man on horseback (*Tricholoma equestre*) do not discriminate in death, leaving behind a lethal legacy: a fear of poisoning that still taints Western views of fungi.

The toxic or hallucinogenic properties of mushrooms contributed to their association with the supernatural, and, in medieval Europe, they were often linked to witchcraft and magical rituals. Their fearful reputation meant that simple village healers, usually women employing fungi for medicinal purposes, were suspected of being conspiring, malevolent witches brewing deadly magical potions to kill or seduce, further intertwining mushrooms with themes of death and deception. Fear shapes language, suspicion worms into taxonomy, and what we dread, we label accordingly, giving us the poison fire coral (*Trichoderma cornu-damae*), the fool's webcap (*Cortinarius orellanus*) and the false morel (*Gyromitra esculenta*).

But fungal poisoning isn't always the result of mistaken identity or malicious intent. While not a mushroom, ergot (*Claviceps purpurea*) is a highly toxic fungus, capable of infecting rye and other grains if not properly treated after a cold winter and damp growing season. Inadvertently ground up and consumed, the poisoned grain can have severe and sometimes fatal effects. Convulsive ergotism is characterized by hallucinations and convulsions, while gangrenous ergotism causes a vasoconstriction that can lead to limb loss.

Ergot outbreaks were common in the Middle Ages, especially in Europe, fuelling superstitions and religious fervour. Sufferers often claimed that their symptoms was the work of divine punishment, supernatural forces or witchcraft. There is speculation that the mass hysteria leading to the 1692 Salem Witch Trials might have been caused by ergot poisoning. Rye was prominent in the colonial Massachusetts diet, while weather records for that year indicate conditions conducive to ergot infection; the convulsions and hallucinations described in the trial as symptoms of bewitchment are consistent with ergotism.

Much like witches, the mushroom's wrongly maligned reputation has undergone a long-overdue detox of late, as knowledge of its ecological and medicinal value grows. The fear and suspicion that once surrounded mushrooms are receding, as modern mycology highlights their importance in advancing medical science and sustaining ecosystem health.

Mushrooms are profoundly complex organisms, and so much more than their body count. Thriving in decaying environments, decomposing organic materials, recycling nutrients, supporting new plant growth and (when picked wisely) providing us with sustenance, they are agents of mortality and rebirth. Holding this power to give life and to take it away, mushrooms can be seen as a bridge between beginnings and endings, a poetic reminder that we humans, like all other living things on Earth, will eventually get our angel's wings (*Pleurocybella porrigens*).

Mind Over Mushroom

María Sabina, Psilocybin and the CIA

Psilocybin is a chemical compound found in certain types of mushrooms that, when ingested, induces hallucinogenic effects, promotes neuroplasticity and, in some, produces an inexplicable love of jam bands. For millennia, these “magic mushrooms” have been directly integrated into the cultural, spiritual and medicinal practices of many societies, including religious ceremonies, rites of passage, divination, psychotherapeutic uses, and whatever occasion your hippie aunt Linda used the contents of her “medicine” box for.

Around the world, cave drawings and folkloric myths depicting the healing and mind-opening powers of mushrooms hint at their wide-reaching and longstanding significance. However, during the modern period — roughly the 16th century onwards — alongside maths, hygiene, roads, central heating, libraries, philosophy and the roundness of the earth, the power of magic mushrooms was largely dismissed or forgotten by northern Europeans and, later, pretty much their entire diaspora across the global North.

Today, there’s growing interest and research into the use of psychedelic mushrooms, particularly psilocybin, for mental health treatment. Recent clinical studies confirm psilocybin’s potential to significantly improve conditions like depression, anxiety, PTSD and addiction, often with just a few doses. Such promising and prominent research is shifting public perception and policy, leading some governments to redraw regulatory frameworks for its recreational and medicinal use. But to arrive at this cultural shift, the“rediscovery” of the magic mushroom in North America in the 20th century first had to emerge from shadows that might seem likely to some: the CIA’s foray into mind control.

Alarmed by rumours that Soviet Communists were conducting brainwashing experiments, the CIA initiated top-secret Project Bluebird in 1950 to explore the dark arts of coercive persuasion. Given the outlandish nature of the mission, who better to lead Bluebird than one Sidney Gottlieb: American, spy, chemist, environmental activist, Orthodox Jew, Zen Buddhist and poet, who lived off-grid in a remote cabin with his goats. In postwar Germany, Gottlieb took over leadership of Bluebird, working at secret sites where his off-the-books team of freelance ex-Nazis would dose — or overdose — Axis POWs using the recently discovered lysergic acid diethylamide (LSD) to probe the inner workings of their minds. Not content to experiment on unwitting subjects overseas, Gottlieb returned to the US and rebranded Bluebird as MKUltra, expanding its mind control research by purchasing the entire known world’s supply of LSD. Literally. He had a soft spot for the synthetic hallucinogen himself, claiming to have dropped acid at least 200 times.

Some of MKUltra’s so-called experiments, like Operation Midnight Climax, where Gottlieb opened brothels in New York and California, employing sex workers to dose unsuspecting johns with LSD, were left in the shadows. Other jobs, like the purposeful dosing of CIA colleague Frank Olson (and subject of the 2017 Errol Morris

OPPOSITE
Bobby Doherty, *Untitled*, 2025

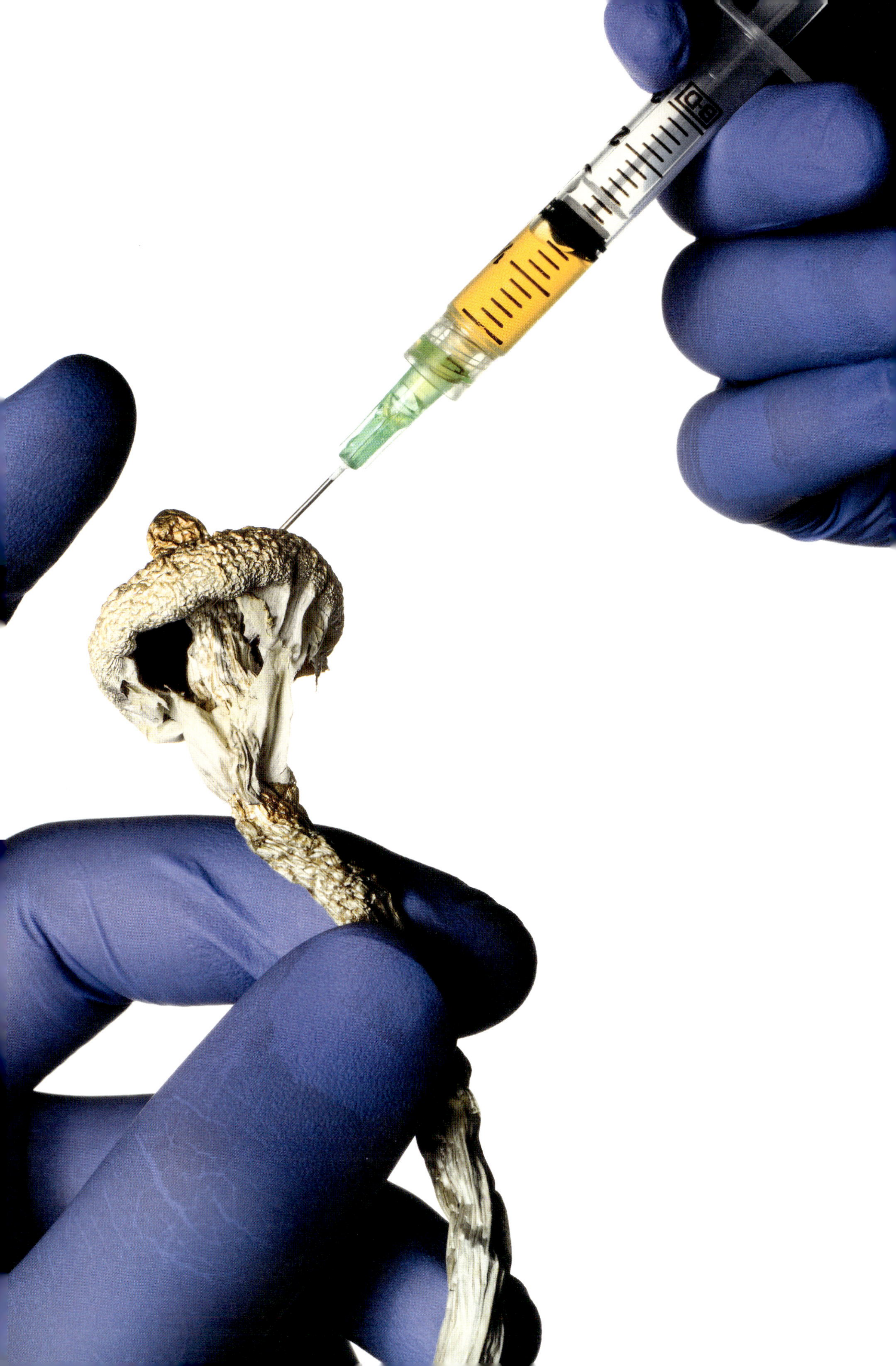
BD

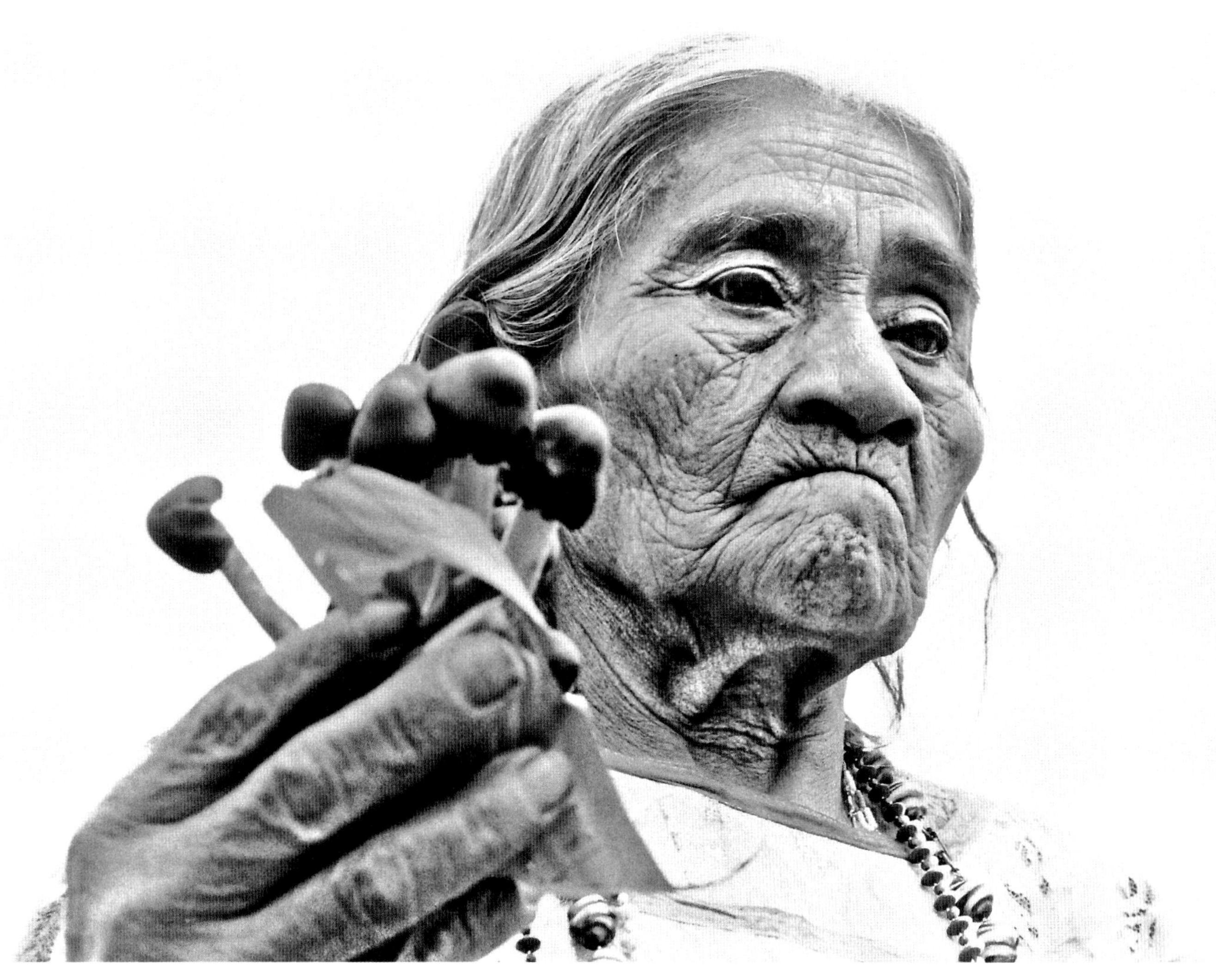

Gusmano Cesaretti
María Sabina with mushrooms, Huautla de Jimenez, 1982

docuseries *Wormwood*), who then died under mysterious circumstances, were more public. With this incident, Gottlieb's approach to mind control had crossed the one uncrossable line for the CIA: public scrutiny. It was time for a rethink.

Enter mushrooms. Inspired by the death of Roman Emperor Claudius, who was killed by a poisonous mushroom, a CIA officer penned a memo in the early 1950s suggesting the agency invest in the "technology of assassinations" by exploring mushrooms for their lethal potential. Gottlieb wasted no time in dispatching operatives across the globe to find new kinds of discrete poison. Assigned to forage the Mexican countryside for potentially lethal mushrooms, one CIA officer learned of their use in spiritual practices. But what piqued his superiors' curiosity was that some shamans were known to use certain narcotizing mushrooms to elicit confessions — or, seen from the CIA's perspective, enhance interrogations. MKUltra immediately hired chemist James Moore to further investigate what very much sounded like the mind control potential of mushrooms.

While Moore would eventually denounce MKUltra as a zealous group of "mad individuals", he first recruited eccentric banker and passionate amateur mycologist Robert Gordon Wasson, whose previous claim to fame was whitewashing his boss JP Morgan's war profiteering. Robert's lifelong mycological fascination had been sparked on a forest walk during his Catskills honeymoon, when he and his Russian wife Valentina found some edible wild mushrooms.

Struck by the stark cultural differences between their native countries regarding fungi, the Wassons embarked on a decades-long investigation of mushrooms and their uses. Field research into Indigenous mushroom use eventually led Robert to venture into the mountains of Mexico. And, in 1955, in the remote town of Huautla de Jiménez in Oaxaca state, Wasson ingested psychedelic mushrooms for the first time, after joining a local Mazatec ceremony led by a certain shaman called María Sabina Magdalena García.

María Sabina had allowed Wasson to participate in the ceremony and subsequently instructed him in the use and effects of psychedelic mushrooms — but only because he had deceived her. The ritual was traditionally enacted to find missing persons or items, and Wasson lied about not knowing his son's whereabouts. Back in New York, Wasson touted that he was the first White person to ever participate in an Indigenous ritual involving psychedelic mushrooms, catching the ear of CIA chemist Moore. Operating undercover, Moore offered to fund Wasson's ethnomycological studies in exchange for Wasson leading a research trip back to Oaxaca. Wasson agreed, not knowing that he was now part of a CIA intelligence operation, one that covertly provided him with the equivalent of around $23,000 today, disguised as a grant from the Geschickter Fund for Medical Research (named after the pathologist Charles Freeman Geschickter, who took millions from the CIA for decades to perform unethical experiments on unknowing human subjects, and who also has a type of malignant tumour named after him).

In late 1956, chaperoned by Wasson, Moore travelled to Huautla and participated in a sacred Mazatec ritual involving psychedelic mushrooms. While Moore reportedly had a bad trip, his CIA taskmasters were more than pleased when he returned with an impressive haul of 'shrooms for experimentation. Still oblivious to being funded by the CIA, the Wassons' amateur mycological work began to attract significant international attention. In 1957, the couple published *Mushrooms, Russia, and History*, a hefty tome illustrating the cultural differences between how Russia and the US view mushrooms, while Valentina wrote a detailed account of their research for the popular *This Week* magazine. But what truly exposed the quiet, localized use of psilocybin was "Seeking the Magic Mushroom", a 17-page photo-essay in *Life* magazine, a title that regularly reached an audience of 20–30 million people. The feature was Robert's account of his time with María Sabina, replete with mystical descriptions of the magic mushrooms' revelatory powers and staged, self-mythologizing photos that cast him as an intrepid explorer. The essay marked a pivotal moment that introduced psychedelic mushrooms to a global audience, sparking widespread interest in their spiritual and mental health benefits.

Inspired after reading Wasson's findings, one mild-mannered Harvard psychologist named

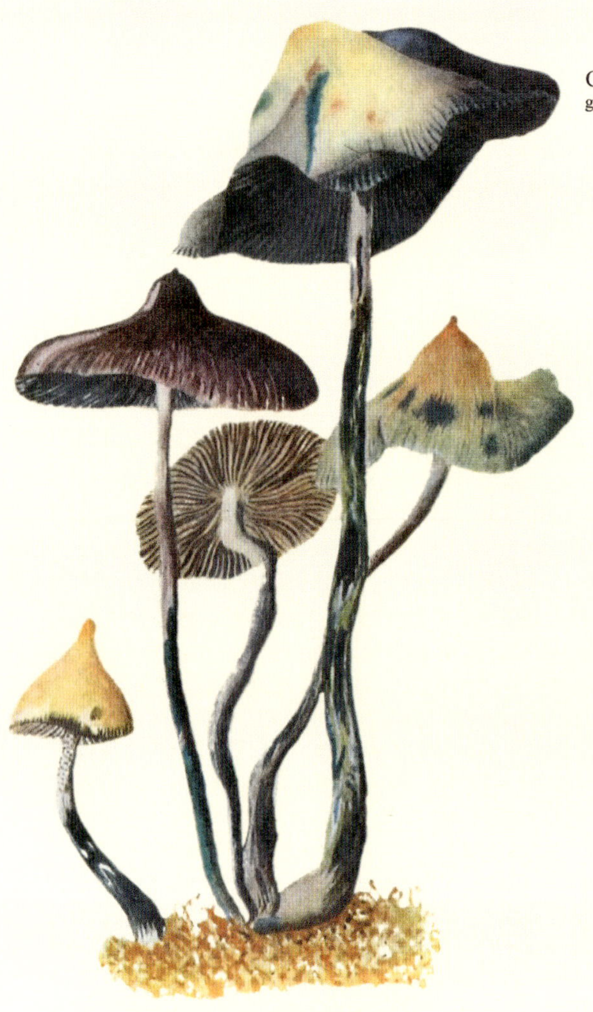

CROWN of Thorns," *Psilocybe Zapotecorum* Heim *(left)* grows in marshy ground. It was first found in 1955.

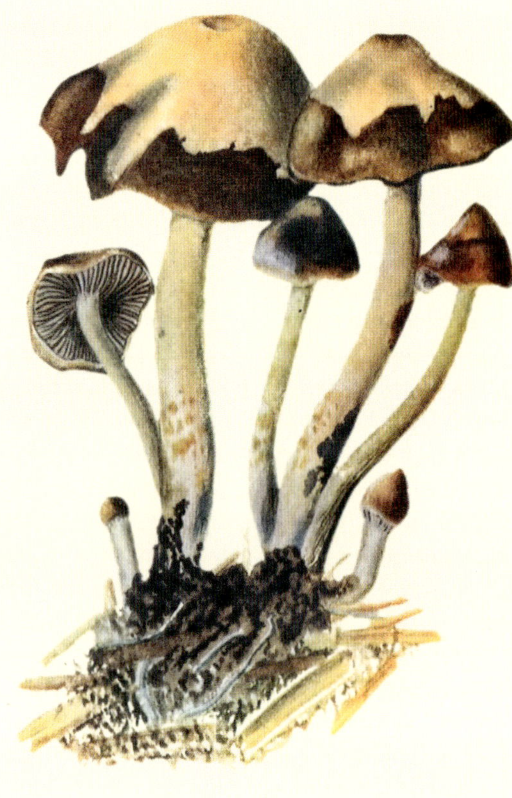

LANDSLIDE" mushroom, *Psilocybe caerulescens* Murrill, var. *Mazetecorum* Heim, grows on sugar cane residue.

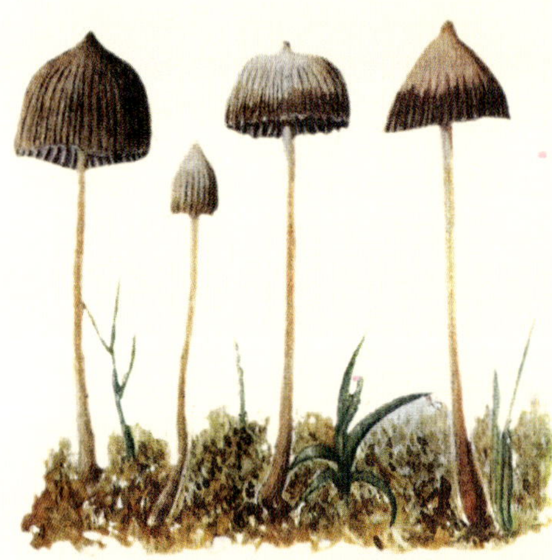

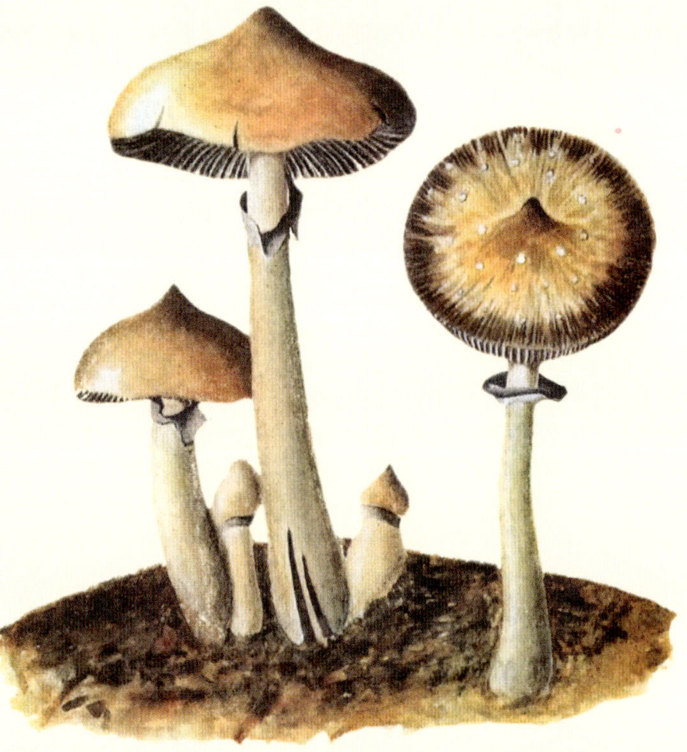

MOST PRIZED by Indians and most widespread of these fungi, *Psilocybe mexicana* Heim grows in pastures.

MUSHROOM of Superior Reason," *Psilocybe caerulescens* Murrill var. *nigripes* Heim *(left),* grows near Juquila.

FIRST DISCOVERED in Cuba in June 1904, *Stropharia cubensis* Earle (*right*) grows on cow dung in pastures.

Dr Timothy Francis Leary journeyed to Mexico in 1960, where he ate magic mushrooms. Leary described this first-ever experimenting with psychedelics as the transformative event of his life, claiming he learned more about how the brain functions during five hours of hallucinations than he had in 15 years of academic research. Returning to Harvard, Leary assumed the mantle of the high priest of getting high, extolling the benefits of such psychedelics, conducting experiments with mushrooms, and encouraging beat poets Allen Ginsberg and Jack Kerouac to explore them. Cue Jefferson Airplane's warpy single "White Rabbit" and the meteoric rise of the American psychedelic movement that dramatically shifted 1960s culture.

Following leadership changes, the failed assassination attempts of two presidents (Castro and Lumumba), and the realization that mind control wasn't as easy as it looked, MKUltra and its controversial experiments gradually wound down, but not before *One Flew Over the Cuckoo's Nest* author Ken Kesey, and Robert Hunter, lyricist for the Grateful Dead, were heavily dosed in its so-called "acid tests" — experimental sessions exploring the effects of psychedelics on human consciousness. After their quick ascendancy in the 1960s, psychoactive drugs were criminalized in many countries by the early 1970s, influenced by the broader cultural and political reactions to the counterculture and hippie movements (probably after one-too-many parties ruined by whispery acoustic ballads).

Near the end of his CIA career, Gottlieb funded research into psychic spying. By 1973, the man who had earned the moniker "poisoner-in-chief" and the reputation as "the most prolific torturer of his generation" had retired from the CIA to briefly manage a leper colony in India and become a speech pathologist. Others did not enjoy such an easy exit. Following Wasson's *Life* essay and Leary's proselytization, the village of Huautla was overrun by hippies, eager to participate in psychedelic rituals with the now-famous shaman María Sabina, foisting spring-break levels of debauchery, disturbances and disrespect on the small town. The angry locals ostracized Sabina for bringing unwanted attention and wafts of patchouli to their quiet town and its religious practices, leaving her to die, penniless, in 1985.

Fast-forward decades later, and magic mushrooms have gotten a glow-up, making their way back into the medicinal and recreational mainstream with enough momentum to be swarmed by wellness start-ups and Silicon Valley tech bros who market microdosing as a tool for productivity, creativity and mental-health optimization. As part of this reconciliation, magic mushrooms are slowly entering a legal grey area where possession is enforced much less frequently, and a quick internet search will help you source them in all variety of forms. Meanwhile, the town of Huautla has embraced its psychedelic heritage and returned María Sabina to her vaunted status, celebrating her with murals and turning her former home into a museum.

OPPOSITE **Roger Heim**, illustrations from "Seeking the Magic Mushroom" by Robert Gordon Wasson and Roger Heim in *Life* magazine, 1957

Melodic Mushrooms

Music For, About and By Fungi

Pink disco, lemon disco, midnight disco and, most memorably, hairy nuts disco are all common names for species of fungi. But the mushroom isn't solely associated with a four-on-the-floor beat. The bonnet mould has been described as "punk rock" by mycologist Tom Volk, for its spiky mass of pins, or sporangiophores, that resembles Sex Pistols singer John Lydon.

If any of these evocatively named mushrooms were to make their own music, it might sound something like Czech composer Vaclav Hálek's playful compositions. In 1980, Hálek was mushroom hunting in the woods around Prague when he came across *Tarzetta cupularis*, a species that's something of an unusual find. According to Hálek, music began to emanate from the fungus: harps, flutes and a harpsichord. He wrote a full symphony when he returned home. Since that fateful day, the prolific composer has produced more than 2,000 mushroom melodies, ranging from melancholy to majestic, several gathered in his book *The Musical Atlas of Mushrooms* (2003). It's unclear whether Hálek has a kind of fungi synaesthesia or a more mysterious extrasensory power, but he gives himself little creative credit for his oeuvre, saying simply, "I record music that mushrooms sing to me."

The mushroom as a musical muse has a long tradition. As avant-garde composer John Cage pointed out, the words are adjacent to each other in the dictionary—with references that tend to conjure the psychedelic or the nuclear, or both. Kate Bush's 1980 synth-fuelled single "Breathing" came out with doomy cover art featuring a fragile white mushroom against a deep black night punctuated by the "twinkling" chips of plutonium namechecked in her lyrics. Written from the point of view of a foetus experiencing nuclear fallout, the song's accompanying video ends with Bush dressed in a hazmat suit, sitting among some giant fungi tinged an ominous shade of blue. Equally apocalyptic is Can's "Mushroom Song", from the krautrock band's 1971 album *Tago Mago*, a dark mystic brew recorded over several days in a hulking medieval castle near Cologne. The song's machine-gun drums and vocalist Damo Suzuki's disconnected, haiku-like lyrics evoke a sinister tempest of flaming red skies and post-atom-bomb annihilation.

But if Germany was still grappling with the hangover of world war, the mushroom mood across the Atlantic in the early 1970s was more free-spirited. Southern jam rockers The Allman Brothers Band set the standard for '70s psychedelic album art with the gloriously kitsch gatefold to their 1972 classic *Eat a Peach*. Created by South Carolina artist Flournoy Holmes, it features a magic-markered, mushroom-filled fantasy idyll. As Jay Babcock wrote in *LA Weekly*: "I bought the record for the art... and kept it for the music."

OPPOSITE
Vidar Logi, cover of Bjork's album *Fossora*, 2022

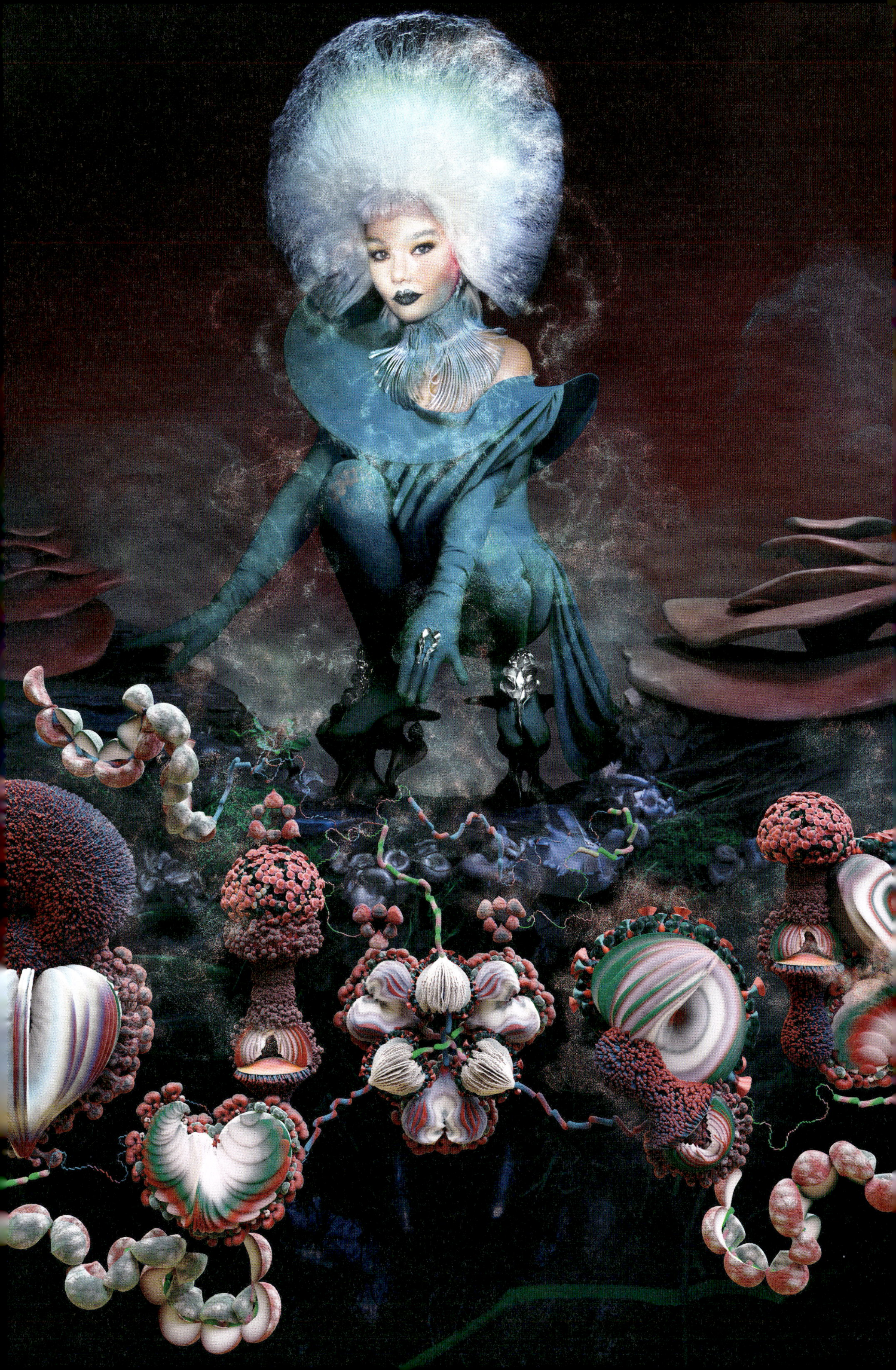

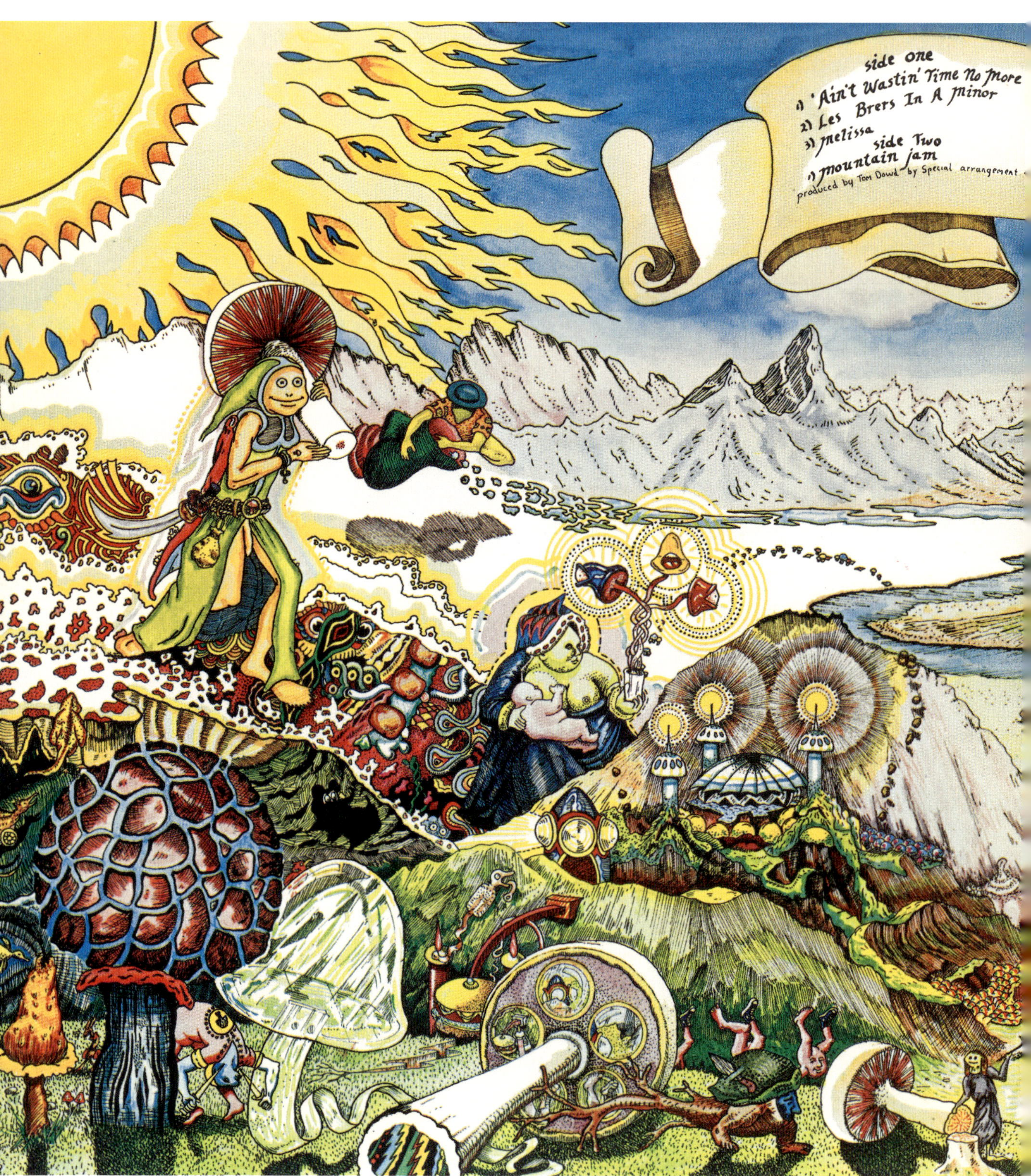

W David Powell and **Flournoy Holmes**
Inner gatefold of *Eat a Peach* by The Allman Brothers Band, 1972

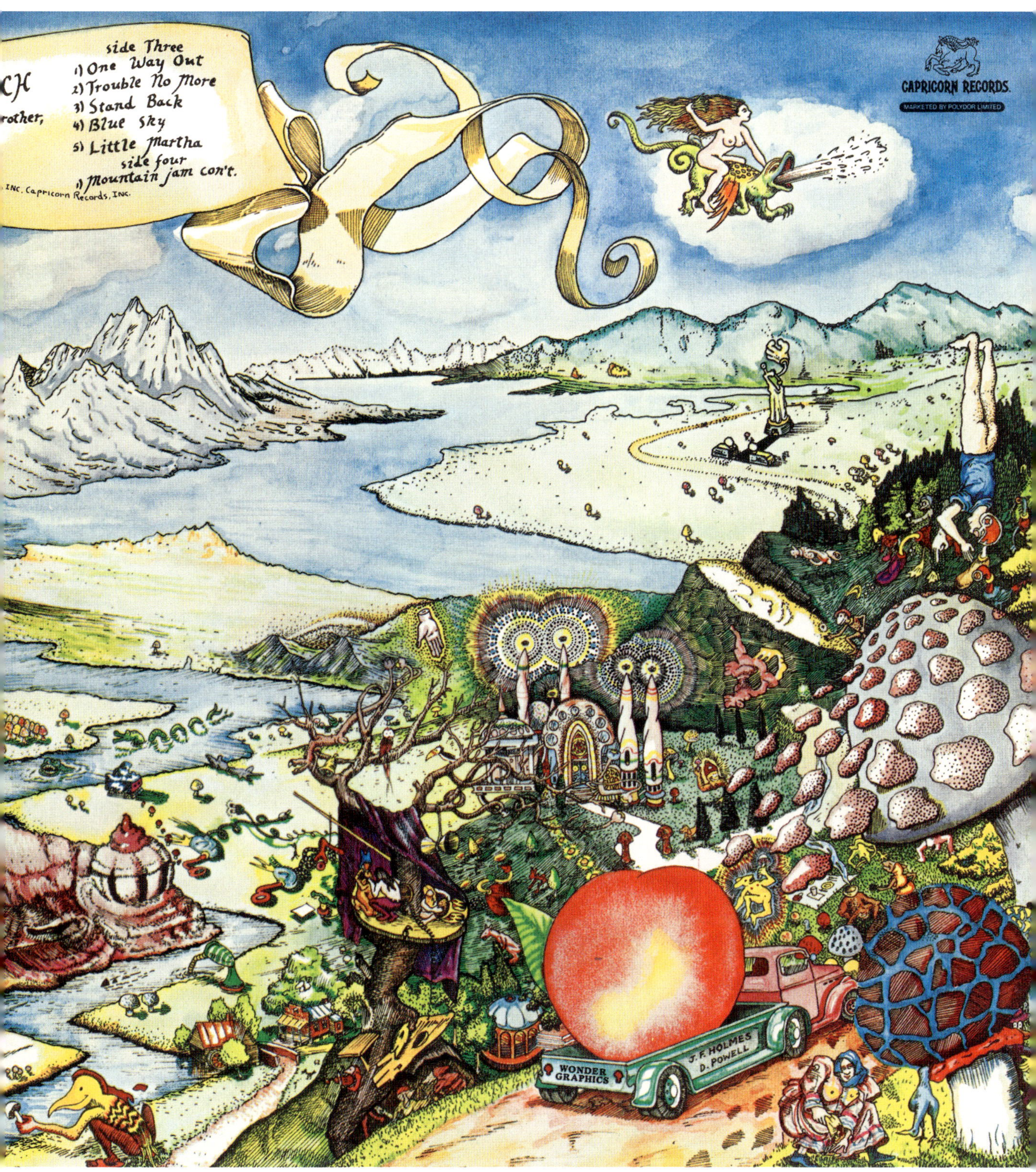
side Three
1) One Way Out
2) Trouble No More
3) Stand Back
4) Blue Sky
5) Little Martha
side four
1) Mountain jam con't.
CH
rother,
INC. Capricorn Records, INC.
CAPRICORN RECORDS.
MARKETED BY POLYDOR LIMITED
WONDER GRAPHICS
J. F. HOLMES
D. POWELL

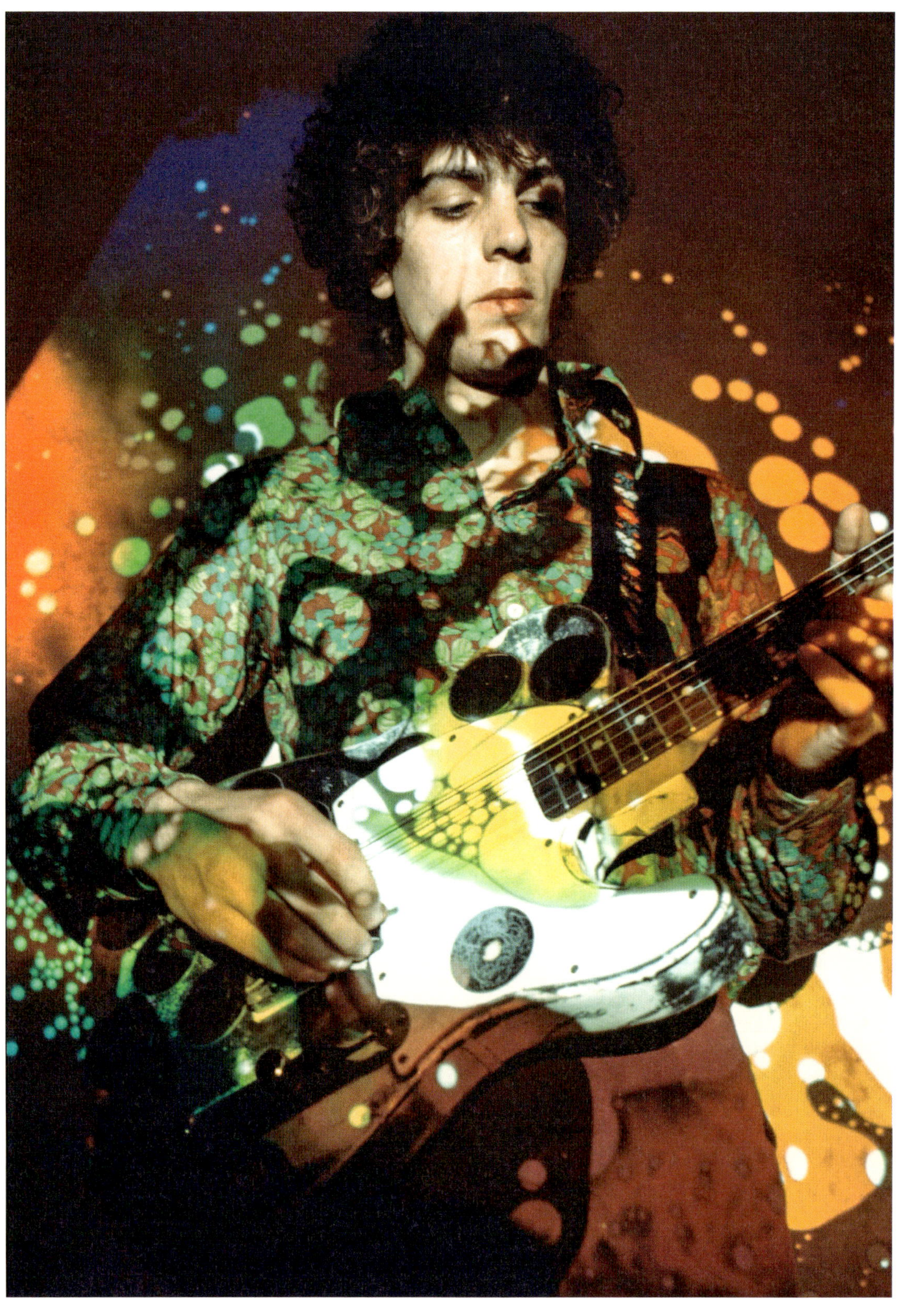

Andrew Whittuck
Syd Barret of Pink Floyd, 1967

The band's spontaneous, lengthy rehearsals were fuelled by "pure psilocybin mushroom extract", as songwriter Gregg Allman recalls in his memoir *My Cross to Bear*. We can probably blame that extract for the album's 33-minute instrumental "Mountain Jam". So dedicated was The Allman Brothers Band to the mushroom, it soon became part of their logo, designed by tattoo artist Lyle Tuttle (tattooer of Janis Joplin, Cher *et al.*), and inked onto the right calf of every member — either during a party in Columbus, Ohio, or a hotel room in San Francisco; no one can seem to remember.

Some counterculture musicians sought out qualified guides for their experiments with magic mushrooms. It's been alleged that John and Yoko, Mick Jagger and Keith Richards all made their way to a town in the mountains of Oaxaca, Mexico, for a psilocybin ceremony presided over by mushroom priestess María Sabina. She called the mushrooms her *niños santos*, or holy children. "She claimed to see the mushrooms as children dancing around her, singing and playing instruments. She translated for them, was their instrument," writes author Chloe Aridjis, who met Sabina as a child, and possesses a collection of her poetry signed with her fingerprint.

But if Sabina supplied enlightenment to many a musical icon, their notoriety only brought her unwelcome attention, angering her neighbours and eventually Sabina herself, who found the stream of visitors beating a path to her door were more interested in hedonism than ancient wisdom and healing. "I realized the young people with long hair didn't need me to eat the little things," she said. "Kids ate them anywhere and anytime, and they didn't respect our customs."

As Sabina well knew, the mushroom's power is not to be underestimated. Its mind-expanding possibilities were famously pursued by Pink Floyd's Syd Barrett, but psychedelics sadly ended up consuming him. Barrett's first ever trip was captured on grainy Super 8 by his friend Nigel Gordon in the summer of 1966, in a short film shot in the wizardy-sounding Gog Magog Hills, a ridge of gentle chalk hills near Cambridge. Barrett roams the landscape, studies his hands with wonder, and at one point, places foraged mushrooms over his eyes and mouth. It was a day that altered the course of the pioneering musician's life and makes for a sobering watch in the knowledge of the integral part psychedelics would come to play in his mental disintegration.

Fungi might have triggered another musical loss many decades later, when Bob Dylan was hospitalized in 1997 with histoplasmosis, contracted from *Histoplasma capsulatum* spores found in bird or bat droppings. (Not to be confused with the fungal spores that like to congregate in the warm, moist environment of the bagpipe — in 2013 pipers across the world were implored to clean their instruments more diligently when a Glaswegian musician fell dangerously ill with a lung infection caused by inhaling the nefarious spores.)

Mouldy woodwind aside, the infinitely mysterious, irrepressible mushroom has most often been celebrated as a life force. Björk's tenth album *Fossora* (from Latin as "she who digs") features the Icelandic pop auteur surrounded by a kaleidoscope of fungal shapes in neon pinks, electric blues and greens. In the record's expansive vision, the mushroom's mycorrhizal networks evoke family, community and regeneration. "I see a lot of hope in mushrooms," she said of her fungal and fruitful musical period. And if Björk found a musical muse in the mushroom, sound artist Brian d'Souza has gone even further, creating what he calls duets with them by capturing the electrical activity of the oyster, reishi, lion's mane and shiitake, and converting them into MIDI notes. His experimental compositions suggest the future might hold additionally rich, as-yet unexplored possibilities for human–mushroom musical collaboration.

Aliens, Spirits & Evil Kings

The Colourful World of Cartoon Mushrooms

Spongiforma squarepantsii, is a bright orange variety of mushroom that lives deep in the rainforests of Borneo. Shaped somewhat like a sea sponge, it was discovered in 2011 and named for its resemblance to cheerful, accident-prone hero SpongeBob SquarePants. The *Mycologia* journal may have grumbled at the name, but the mental leap from mushroom to Nickelodeon prankster wasn't such a stretch — in the world of animation, the mushroom has long been a rich and diverse source of inspiration.

Thanks to their umbrella-like shape, mushrooms have often moonlighted as dinky, hollowed-out shelters for forest creatures. Papa Smurf and his clan created their squat two-storey homes out of clusters of *Amanita muscaria,* adding chimneystacks and fully equipped kitchens for cooking smurfberries. "Les Schtroumpfs", as Belgian creator Peyo originally named them, have grown from 1950s comic book beginnings through 1980s Saturday morning cartoons to multi-million-dollar film reboots. Yet some, including French academic Antoine Bueno, have found all the communal eating, collective labour and currency-free economics of their mushroom idyll suspicious, accusing the Smurfs of glorifying communism — a charge Peyo's son felt was unlikely, given his father's disinterest in politics.

The 1958 Soviet short *Gribok Teremok* (The Mushroom Teremok), on the other hand, was probably extolling the benefits of that ideology. The cartoon by Vladimir Polkovnikov stars an ant that reluctantly shares its mushroom house with other woodland dwellers during a thunderstorm,

OPPOSITE
Hergé, *The Shooting Star* (*The Adventures of Tintin,* Volume 10), 1942

HERGÉ

THE ADVENTURES OF

TINTIN

THE SHOOTING STAR

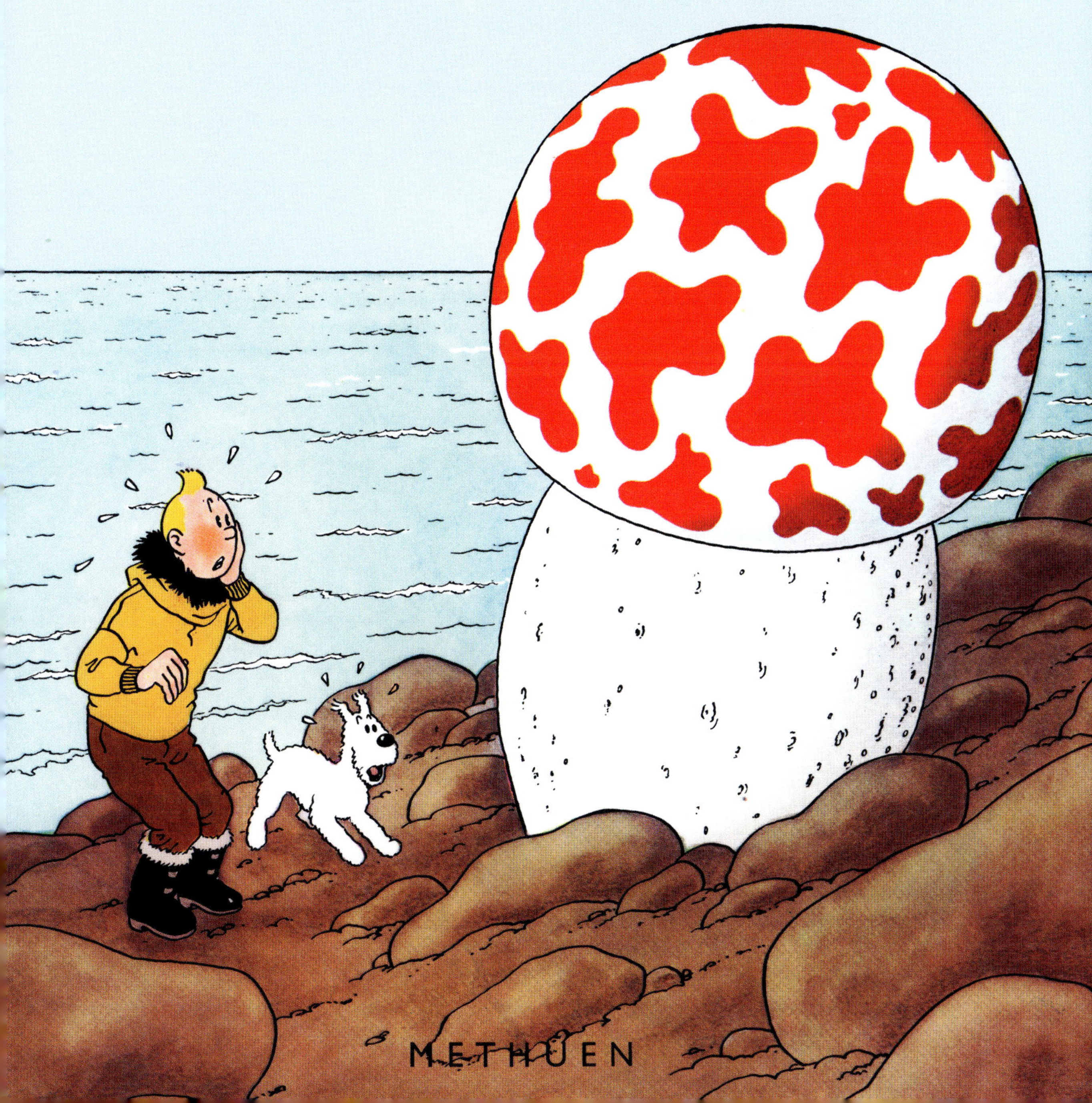

METHUEN

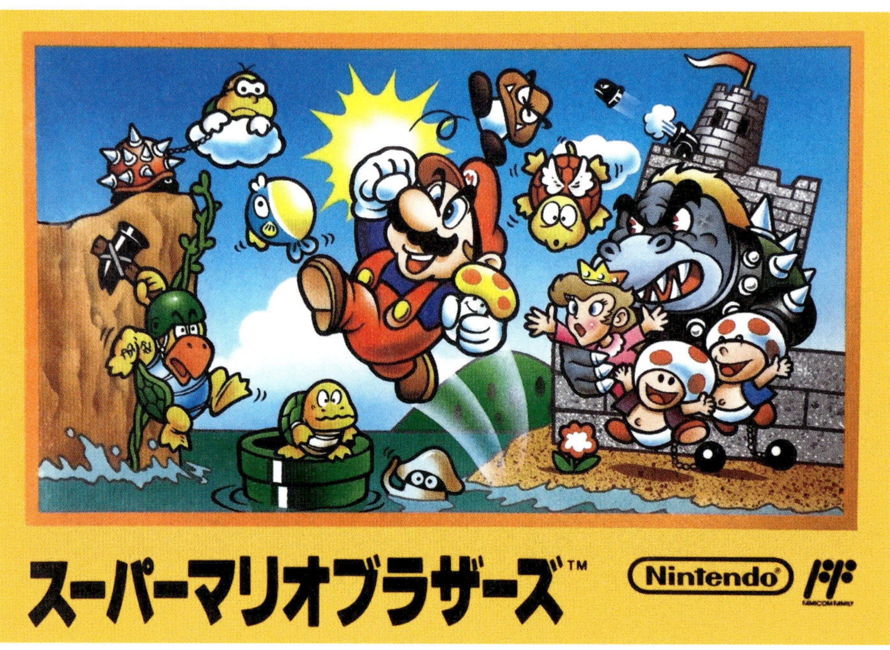

before the mushroom reveals itself to be a wise, snowy-bearded soul with a giant hat and a lesson to impart about the power of collective action.

Perhaps it's those caps — so easily reimagined as headgear — that have made fungi ripe for anthropomorphism. *The Nameko Families* (2013–14), a Japanese cartoon series about the daily escapades of a family of mushrooms and their pet mushroom cat, is an unsettling watch. Nameko is the slimy variety often used in miso soup, and this cartoon fungi family regularly gathers around the table for cannibalistic dinners of the dish.

Also from Japan, the peerless Studio Ghibli reimagined the mushroom as a benign, life-giving presence in anime master Hayao Miyazaki's ravishing environmental fable *Princess Mononoke* (1997). The tale of a monumental struggle between the destructive forces of humans and the natural world, the film's parades of *kodama* — tiny white-and-brown tree spirits that resemble mushrooms — signal the health of their pristine medieval forest. In the closing scenes, after bloody clashes with demon boars, wolf goddesses, samurai and tribes of apes, a single *kodama* standing alone amid the foliage offers a glimmer of hope that nature might regrow and recover.

Elsewhere, fungi have been cast as villains. In the kids TV series *H.R. Pufnstuf* (1969), a puppet gang of malevolent, misshapen mushrooms is led by a muddy-coloured, cigar-smoking, James Cagney-like gangster who transforms anyone who touches him into a mushroom also. In one of the more apocalyptic Tintin adventures, *The Shooting Star* (1941–42), the world very nearly ends via the crash landing of an enormous mushroom meteorite that resembles a fly agaric, with radioactive spores that cause small things — apple cores, spiders, maggots — to grow to gigantic sizes. The indefatigable boy-reporter and his canine sidekick are briefly trapped on an Arctic island with the monstrous meteorite, but happily for humankind it sinks into the icy sea — taking its toxic extraterrestrial spores with it.

The Goombas — little brown mushrooms based on the shiitake, with added fangs and generous eyebrows — are also a nefarious force, if easily stomped on with a satisfying squish, in the bestselling video game *Super Mario Bros* (1985).

Super Mario Bros, 1985

In fact, the whole Mario franchise, brainchild of Nintendo overlord Shigeru Miyamoto, has been loyally mushroom-centric since its inception: the mushroom is of course the famous catalyst for Mario to morph into his Super form, and the moustachioed plumber's Mushroom Kingdom has green hills densely populated with them. In *Super Mario Odyssey* (2017), a "music toad" in the form of a toadstool can be found listening to music on the rooftops of any kingdom, giant headphones fixed to its cap.

Croatia's Milan Blažeković took the animation — and musical — possibilities of the mushroom much further, by giving us perhaps the world's only mushroom rock group — another wicked crew of fungi, this time brandishing instruments including a keytar. In the animator's *The Elm-Chanted Forest* (1986), the first feature-length Croatian animation, there are magical forces at play (as is so often the case where mushrooms are concerned).

The plot centres on a painter who falls asleep under a tree and wakes to find he can communicate with the flora and fauna around him. Soon he's on a mission to save the woodland folk from an evil cactus king. Along the way, he's captured by a band of sentient mushrooms who treat him to a high-energy 1980s-inflected musical set alongside a crew of breakdancing fly agarics, before he's rescued from the din by a pink grizzly bear. Blažeković has been described as Croatia's answer to Disney, though card-playing characters at the Sashay Inn Saloon drink a lot more booze than Mickey Mouse ever did.

Which brings us to the progenitor whose imagination shaped so much of animation history: Walt Disney himself. His 1940 masterwork *Fantasia* truly pushed artistic boundaries with Mickey Mouse as a broom-wielding sorcerer's apprentice, a ballet-dancing hippopotamus and anthropomorphic mushrooms performing a traditional (yet trippy) Chinese folk dance to Tchaikovsky's Nutcracker Suite.

Fantasia was a flop on its release, but in 1969, via a psychedelic ad campaign — a poster of eye-searing pinks, greens and yellows, and a tagline touting "the ultimate experience" — the film finally turned a profit, thanks to the dollars of counterculture college students whose minds had been blown the year before by The Beatles'

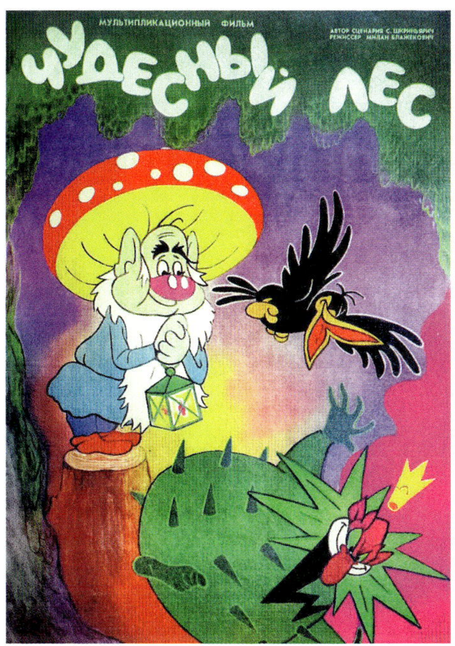

Poster for *The Elm-Chanted Forest*, 1986
FOLLOWING Poster for the *Fantasia* stereophonic re-release in the UK, 1979

HEAR THE PICTUR

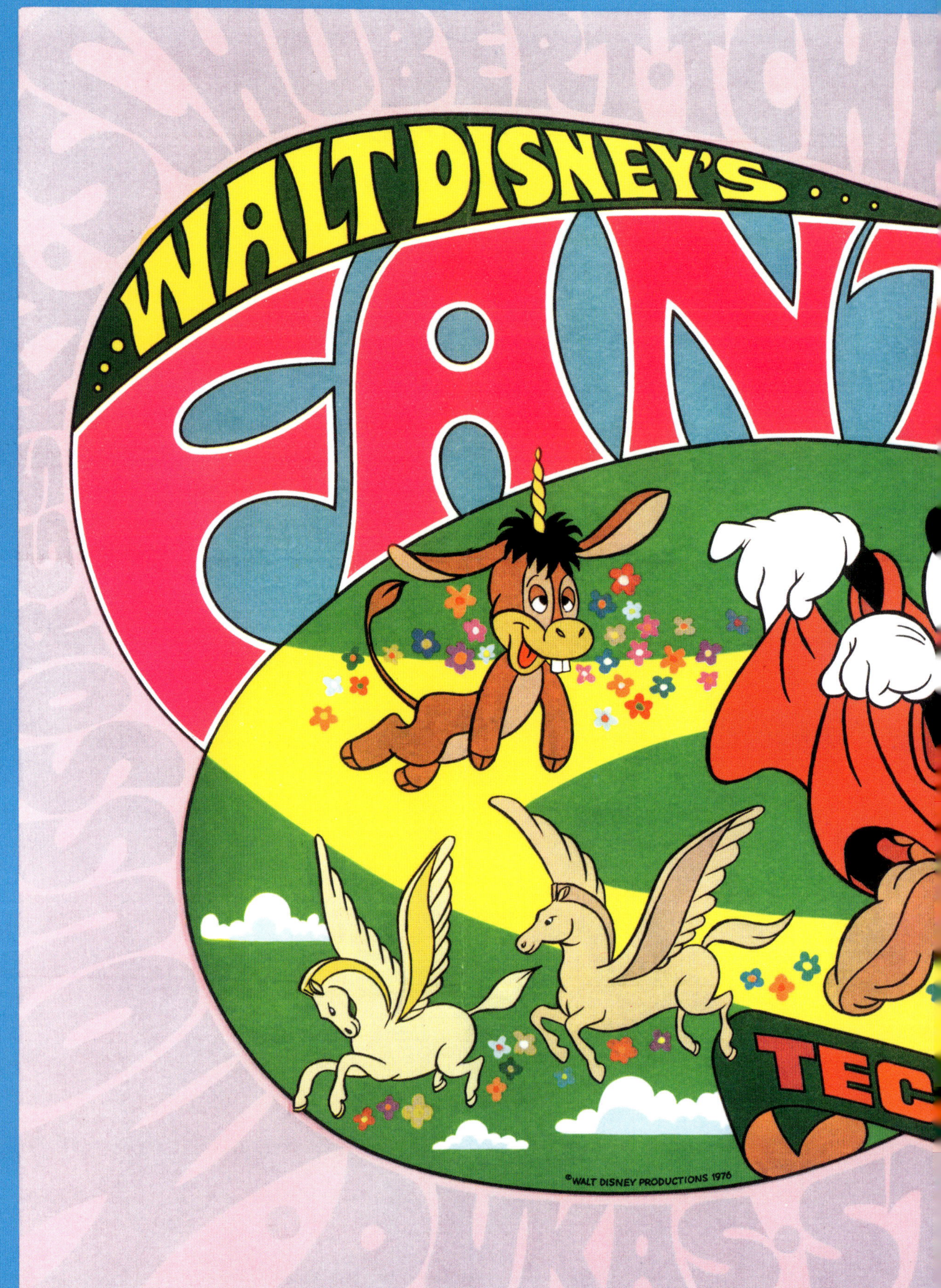

THE ULTIMATE EXPERIENCE–

SEE THE MUSIC!

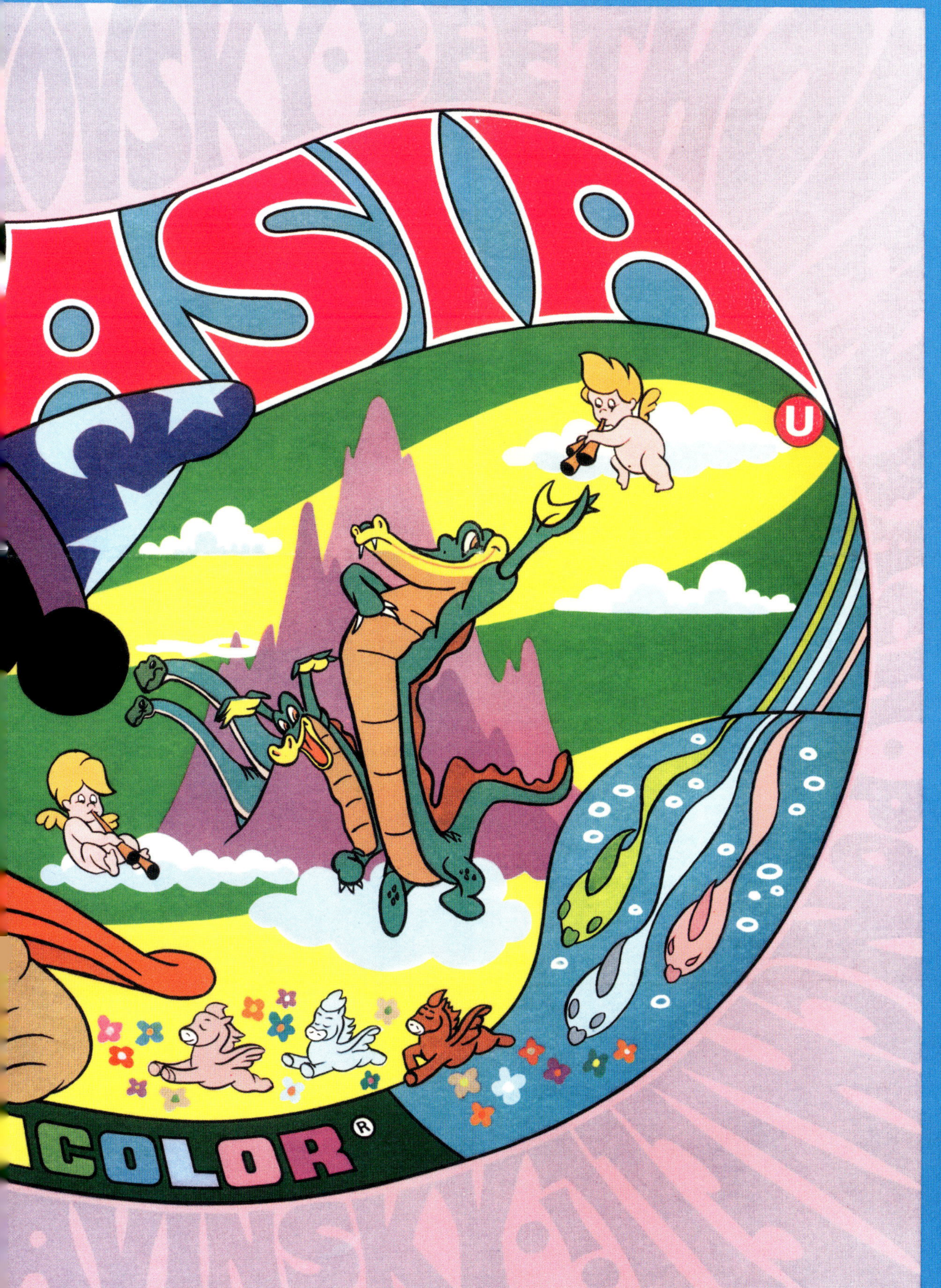

W IN STEREOPHONIC SOUND

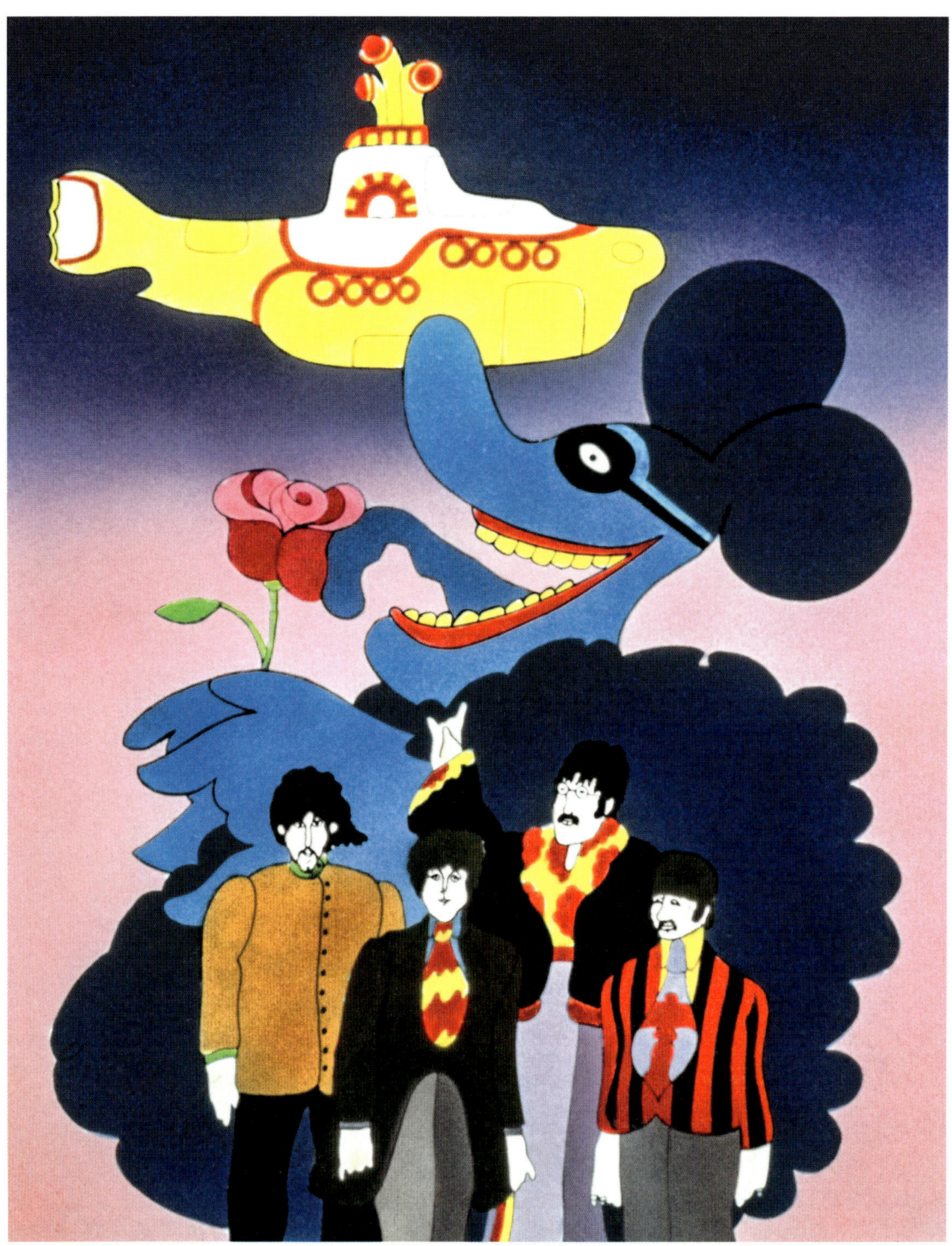

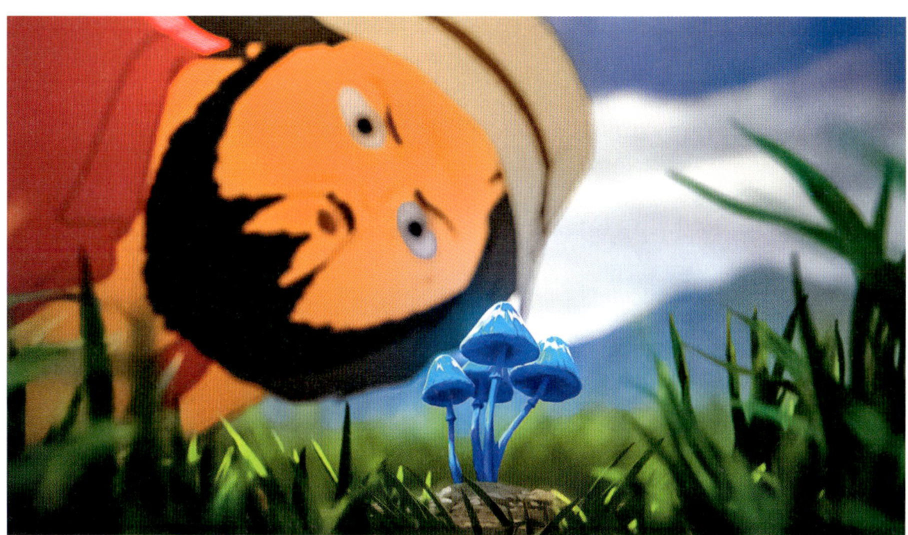

Yellow Submarine. (That film's malignant army of Blue Meanies, incidentally, could reference *Psilocybe cubensis*, a highly hallucinogenic mushroom that turns blue when bruised.)

Fantasia's mushroom dance is part of the "Nutcracker Suite" segment, occurring when a collision of sugarplum fairies scatter glittering dust over a group of mushrooms with red-and-yellow caps. They're animated into a troupe of dancing fungi, with the smallest, Hop Low — part Dopey, part Ugly Duckling — struggling to keep up with its full-sized friends. The scene is a problematic watch today for its racial stereotyping: it's a reinterpretation of the Tchaikovsky ballet's equally problematic "Tea (Chinese dance)" that stylizes the mushroom's caps to look like the traditional *douli* hats historically worn in Asia.

But *Fantasia* wasn't the first time Disney animated mushrooms. 1932's *Flowers and Trees*, part of the *Silly Symphonies* animation series, was the first cartoon he created with the Technicolor process — having invested untold dollars in the technology. Depicting a forest waking at dawn with smiling mushrooms rocking their heads to and fro, the eight-minute film is the story of a romance between two trees and the self-defeating jealousy of one wizened old stump. The year it was released, *Flowers and Trees* became the first cartoon in history to win an Academy Award, putting mushrooms front and centre at Hollywood's biggest night. Almost a century on from Disney's win, mushrooms remain a force in animation. The hero of Adult Swim's critically acclaimed 2024 series about shady Big Pharma, *Common Side Effects*, is the imaginary blue angel mushroom, purported to heal any ailment, including death. Evidently, the mushroom's presence in animation is as enduring as Mickey himself.

Joe Bennett and **Steve Hely** (for Adult Swim), *Common Side Effects*, 2024
OPPOSITE **George Dunning**, *Yellow Submarine*, 1968

Cute & Apocalyptic

The Graphic World of Takashi Murakami

Takashi Murakami's graphic art is simultaneously upbeat and upsetting, and the duality of mushrooms, symbols both of fertility and toxicity — not to mention nuclear annihilation — have been recurrent motifs in his wide-ranging work.

Murakami was born in 1962 in Tokyo, 17 years after the United States dropped atomic bombs on Hiroshima and Nagasaki, and as a child would have been aware of people suffering from illness and injuries related to the blasts. His mother had lived in Kokura, the intended target on the day of the Nagasaki bombing, which was spared due to cloud cover. She often told him, "If the bomb had been dropped in Kokura, you wouldn't be here..."

The huge mushroom clouds that rose over Hiroshima and Nagasaki in August 1945 cast long shadows over Japanese culture in the decades to come. They loomed especially over the country's conflicted relationship with the United States, the victorious superpower whose exports came to dominate global pop culture in the postwar period, comingling with the aesthetic traditions of Japan.

At university, Murakami studied Nihonga, or "Japanese-style" painting, a movement established during the Meiji period (1868–1912) in opposition to the Western modernism that was popular at the time. His ambition, however, was to pursue animation, then — as now — one of the visual–cultural

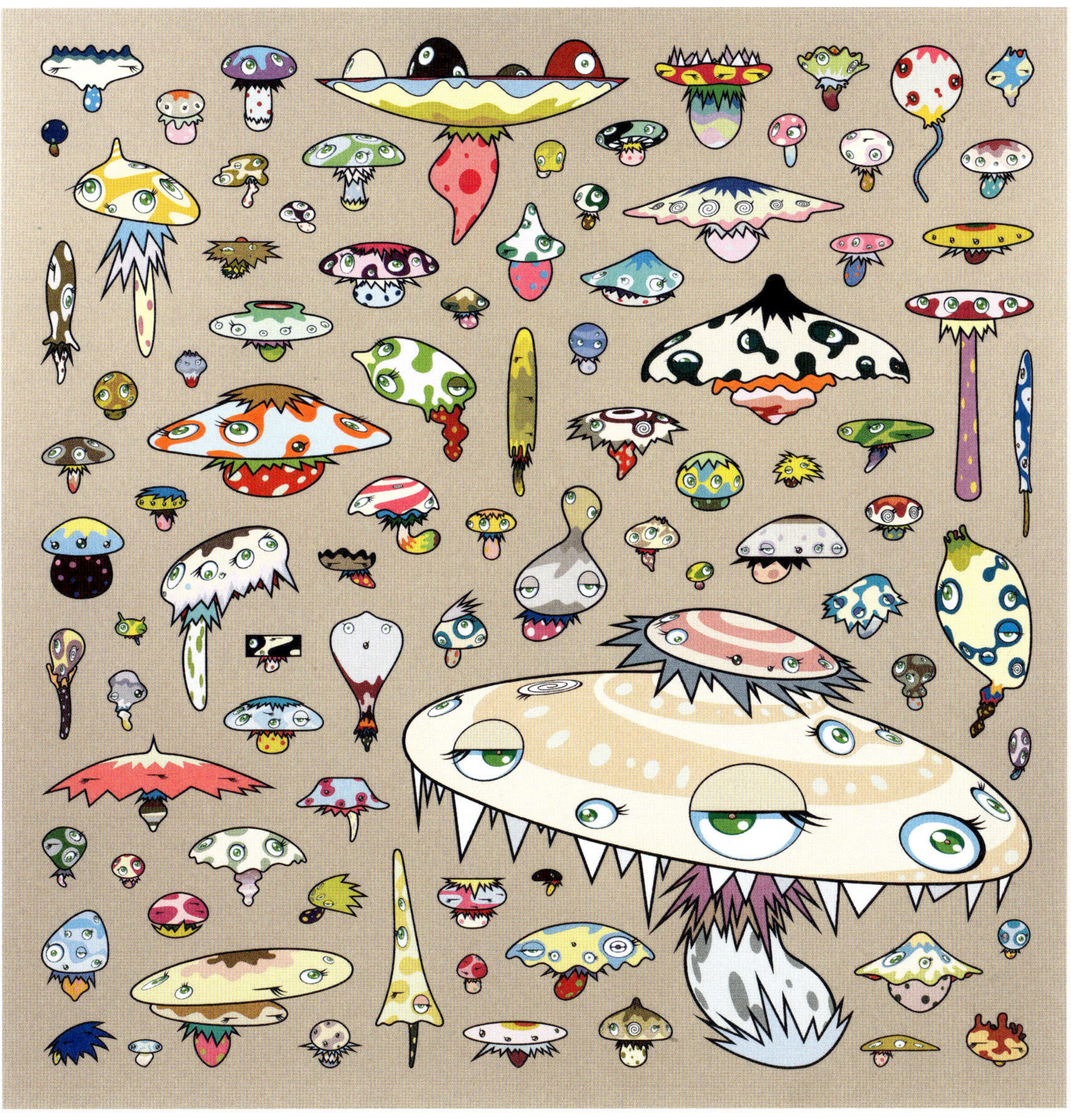

Takashi Murakami
Army of Mushrooms, 2003

exports of Japan. When he later focused on contemporary art, Murakami found his voice by combining the aesthetics of anime, manga and Nihonga. After several years in NewYork, during which time his popularity rapidly grew, Murakami returned to Japan, where he founded a multidisciplinary studio that he named, with a deliberate nod to Andy Warhol, Hiropon Factory. In 2001, he renamed this large studio cum production facility cum business corporation as Kaikai Kiki Co. (translated as "dangerous yet appealing" — another duality), and, under its banner, pursued a seemingly limitless array of commercial and artistic projects.

Murakami never lost focus on the foundational theme in his art: Japan's unresolved traumas, symbolized by the atomic mushroom cloud. In 1999, he completed a seven-panel painting over ten metres in length. *Super Nova* was one of his biggest works to date. Against a flat grey background, the painting features an array of different mushrooms, painted in acid colours and studded with cartoon-style eyes. Murakami coined the term "Superflat" to describe his black-outlined, graphic style and the postmodern art movement he founded. At the Kaikai Kiki Co. studio, a crew of technicians could execute large paintings all at once, copying designs (which Murakami composed on a computer) onto large canvases simply by filling in areas of solid colour. *Super Nova*, the artist said, was influenced by Itō Jakuchū, the Edo-period painter whose *Compendium of Vegetables and Insects* (1790)— a 12-metre-long silk scroll — features a section detailing various species of mushroom that are celebrated in Japanese cuisine.

But Murakami's mushrooms are not as wholesome as Jakuchū's. Their staring eyes and sharp gills evoke genetic mutants, or the hallucinations of a bad psychedelic trip. A painted fibreglass sculpture completed the same year, *DOB in the Strange Forest* (1999), depicts Murakami's signature character "Mr DOB" surrounded by more freaky fungi. As with *Super Nova*, the mushrooms'

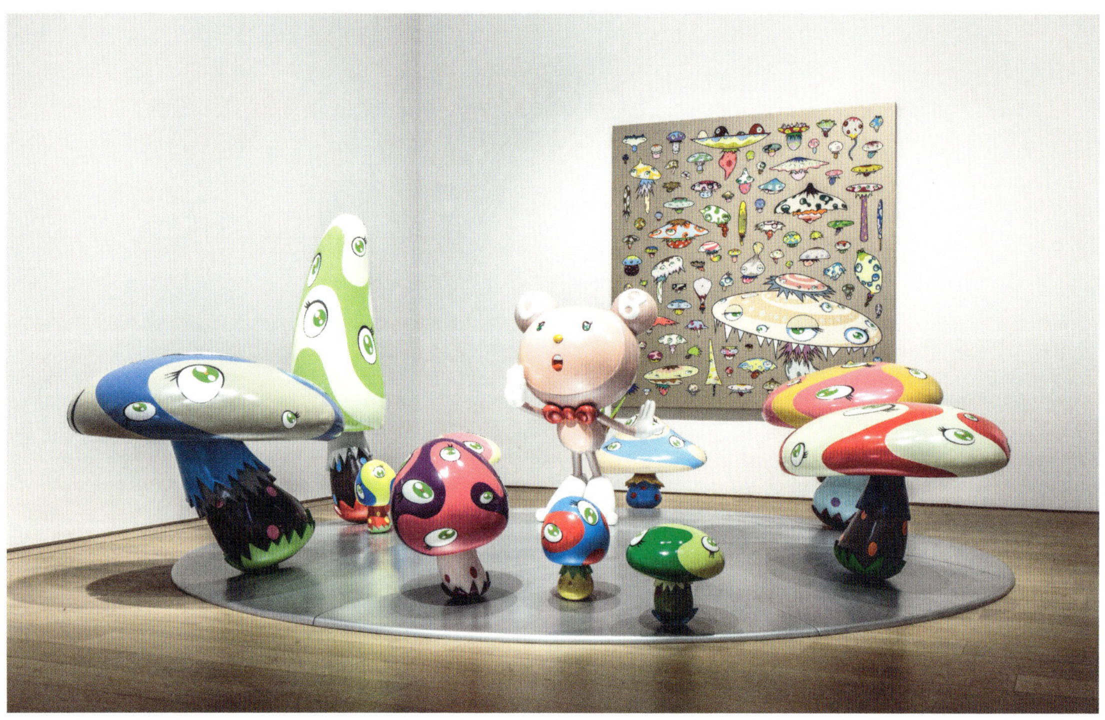

Takashi Murakami
DOB in the Strange Forest, 1999

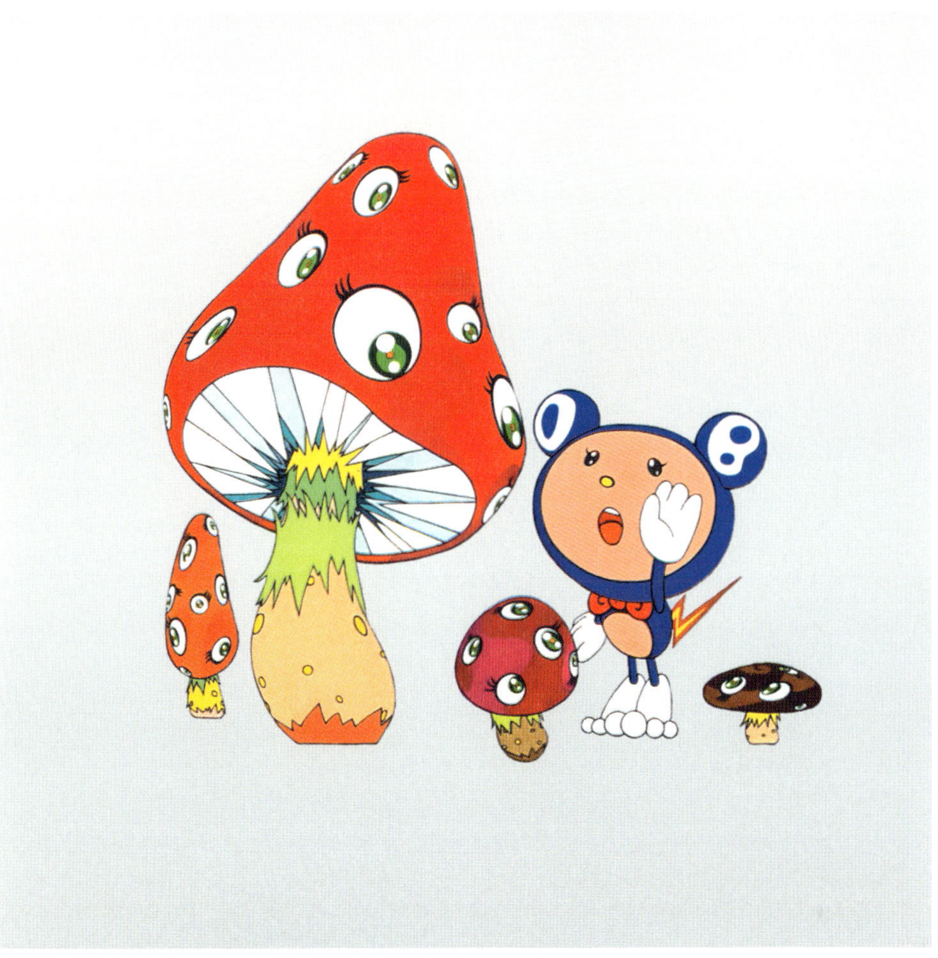

sharp-lashed eyes are neither obviously malevolent nor benign, but their presence alone makes for a discomfiting scene. A subsequent series of paintings, *Time Bokan* (2001), also combines contradictory motifs. Against various colourful backgrounds, silhouettes of a mushroom cloud in the shape of a skeleton each have rings of intricately painted flowers for eyes. In the centre of each tiny flower is a laughing, happy face. "*Time Bokan* describes the fear that good and evil might be two sides of the same coin," Murakami has said. This is the atmosphere that underpins so much of his art: superficial levity layered on deep trauma and dysfunction. Across cultures, the mushroom has long been an ambiguous symbol, but against the context of Japanese history, Murakami brings together associations at once gentle and violent, cute and apocalyptic.

Takashi Murakami
HOYOYO, 1998

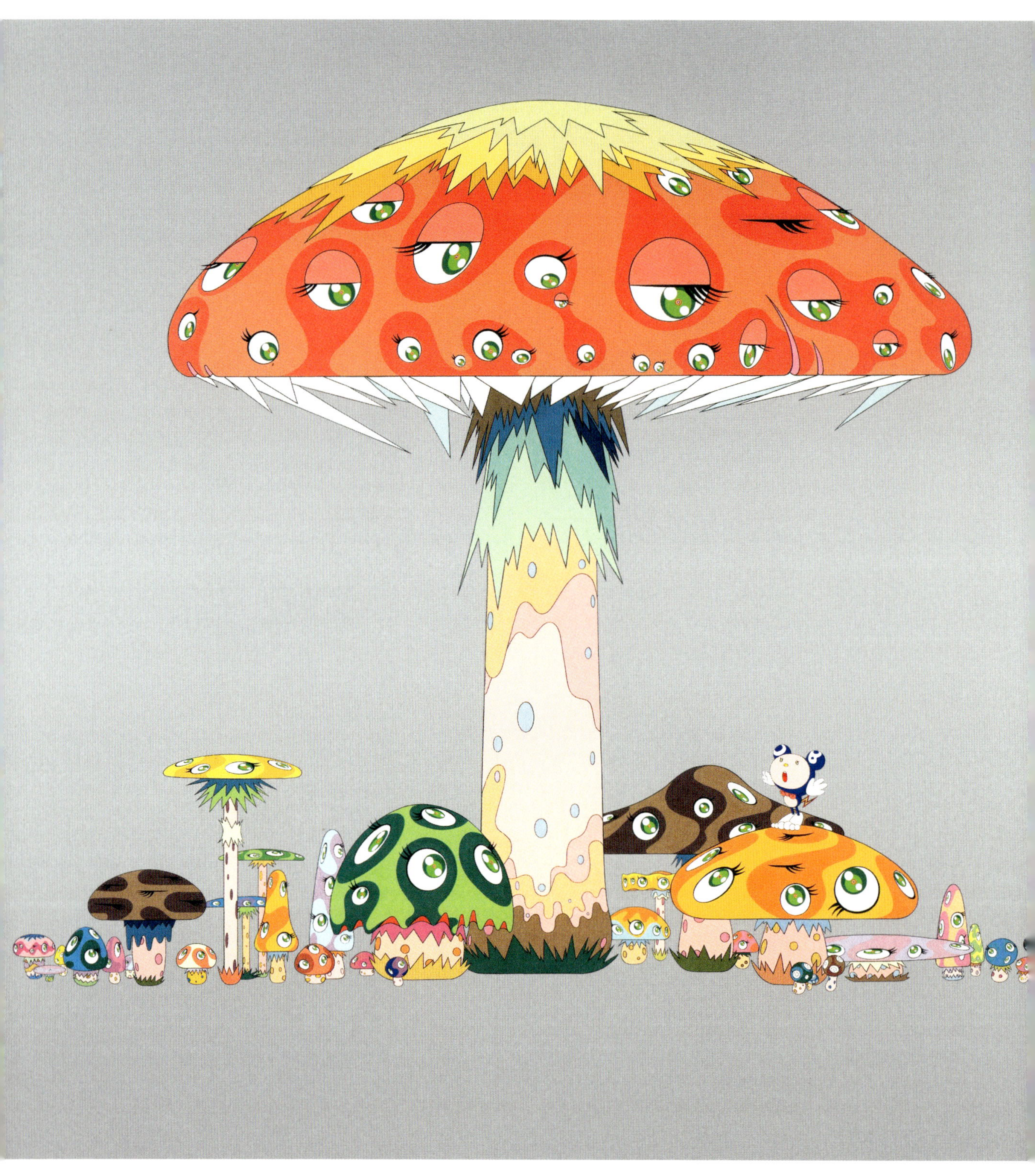

Takashi Murakami
DOB in the Strange Forest, 1999

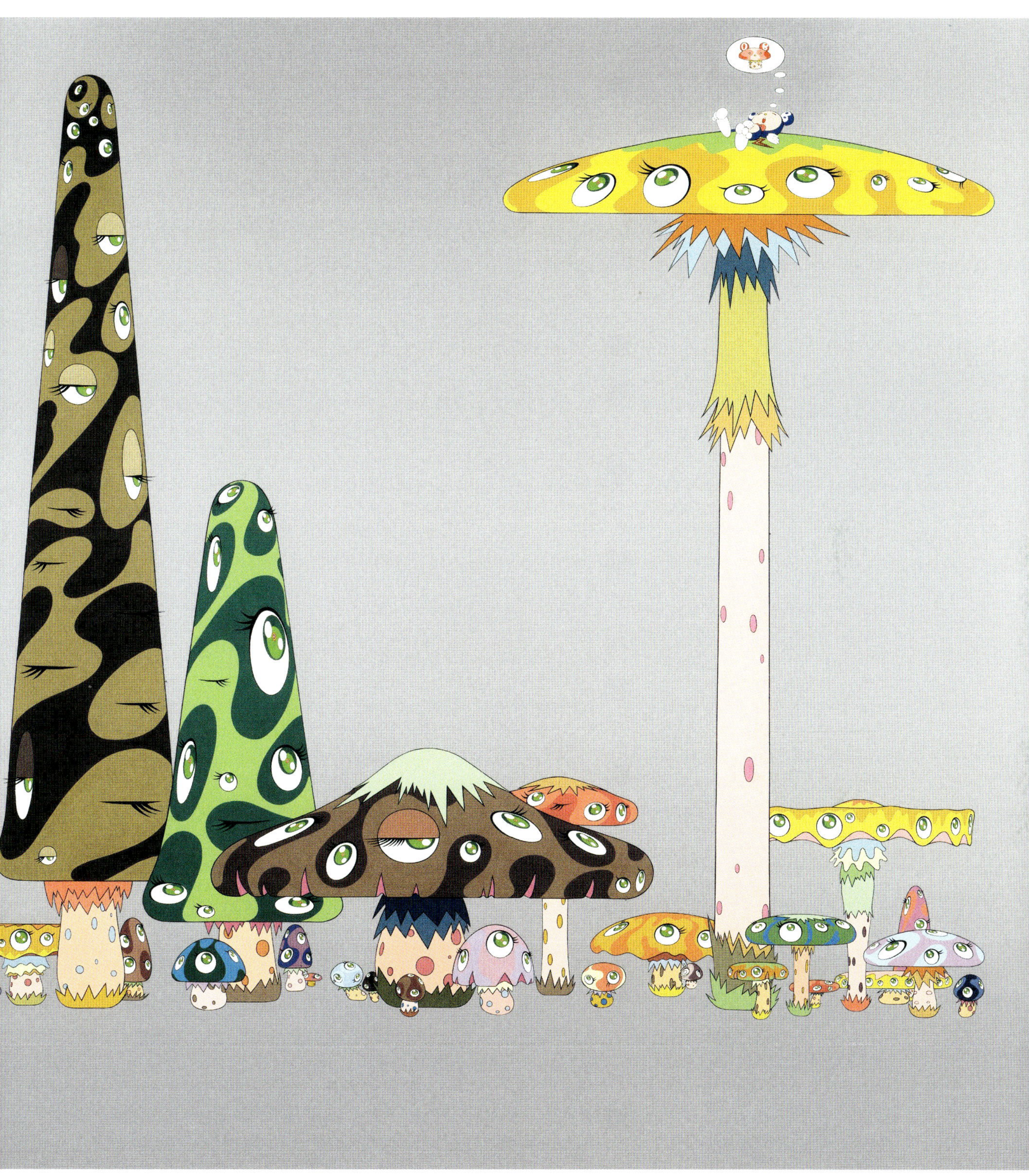

Takashi Murakami
Dream of Opposite World, 1999

Form Follows Fungi

Mushrooms in Design and Architecture

Whether leaning on the structural integrity of a mushroom to decide the shape of a lamp or replicating its contour and patterns for a cheery cookie jar, designers have created some extraordinary, if sometimes kitschy, pieces celebrating this distinctive organism. Over the last couple of centuries, it's usually common mushrooms that have been celebrated in design. The reassuring shapes of ceps, trumpets, criminis, enokis and buttons have been chosen over some of the rarer, more visually complicated varieties — like the spindly yartsa gunbu or the bioluminescent *Filoboletus manipularis,* for example. And the more realistic the mushroom design, the cutesier it seems to get.

Much beloved Portuguese ceramics studio Bordallo Pinheiro, renowned for its biomorphic representations of flora and fauna, introduced a range of mushroom-shaped earthenware jars in 2015 that are hand painted in suitably bosky browns. This modest range of dark-capped, high-gloss storage jars is a down-to-earth addition to the company's lip-smacking line-up of fish, fowl and vegetable-inspired designs. Loosely based on the king oyster's squat stalk and shallow cap, the mushrooms are among some of the brand's most straightforward pieces, compared with the surreal expression of a cabbage tureen topped by a lobster, or the riotous pink of a curvaceous pitaya box.

Looking further into the past of mushroom-inspired kitchen storage, when American retail behemoth Sears, Roebuck and Co. released its Merry Mushrooms in 1970 it bet the farm (and most of the forest) on getting people to put fungi-like objects at the heart of their homes. Merry Mushrooms joined the Bewitching Butterflies range, creating a distinctly outdoorsy collection of kitchen coordinates.

Between their arrival on the kitchen counter and the end of the line in 1987, the firm filled its catalogues with well over 200 mushroom-themed products, the most famous of which are arguably the cookie jars, followed by the napkin holder, spice jars and butter dish. But the range was infinitely vaster, taking in curtain swags, address cards, a bulletin board, a bacon rack, two types of fondue sets, two types of dinner bells and tinkling wind chimes. To Merry Mushrooms collectors, one of the most desirable and hardest to find pieces is the stool/ice cooler, a half-metre-high, two-handled metal tub with a sickly sulphurous yellow exterior, a polystyrene insert and a brown pleather cap.

Some may cry "whimsy!" in their assessments of these irrepressibly chirpy designs, but the inventiveness and joy of this immensely fertile design family has won itself a legion of unwaveringly passionate fans. Since Merry Mushrooms

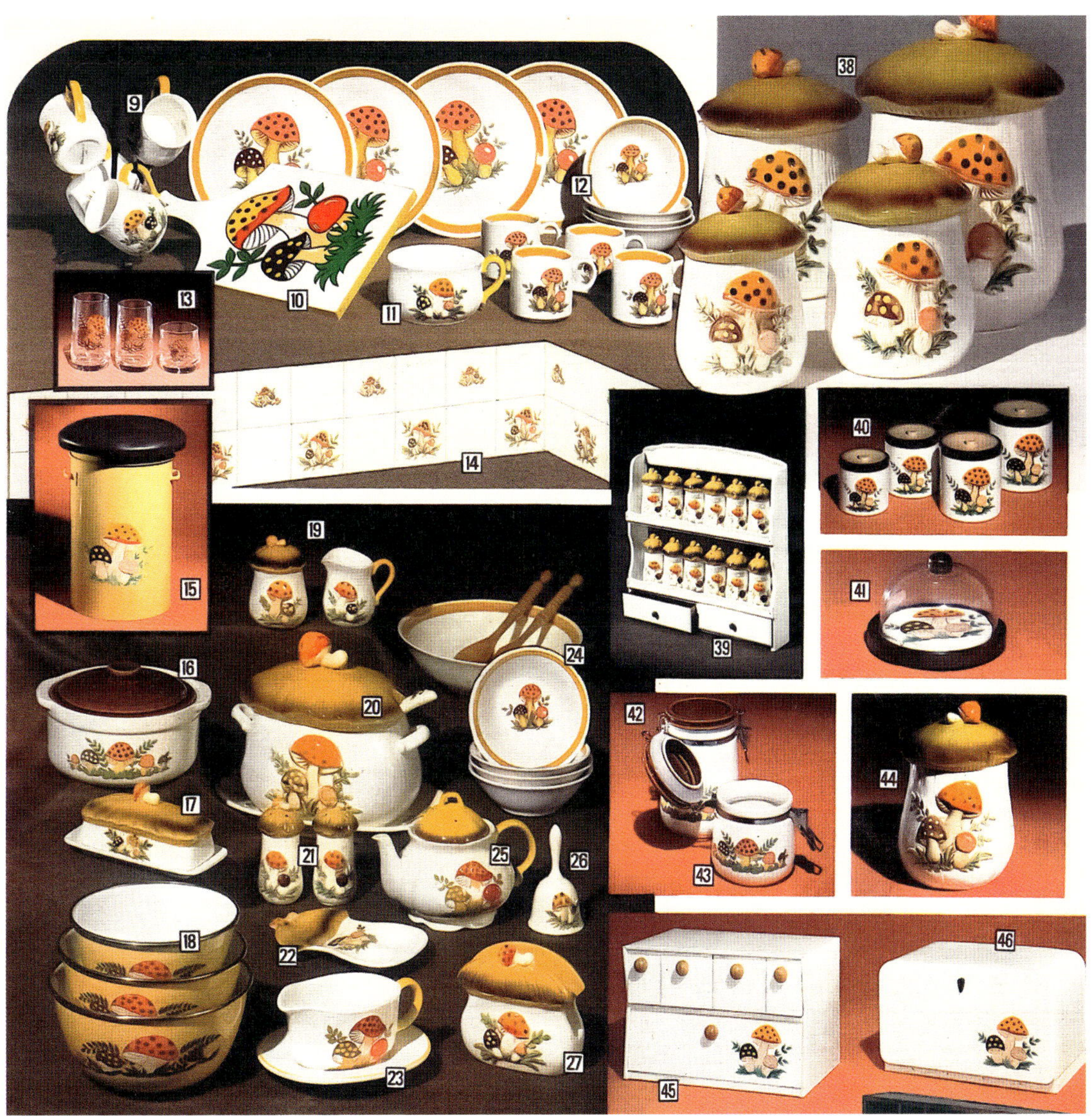

Sears, Roebuck and Co.
Merry Mushroom set catalogue, 1970s

served every imaginable kitchen need — and then some — there is no shortage of scouring, bidding and treasuring to be done at thrift stores and auction sites, especially for the more obscure items.

Mushroom lamps are another mainstay in the world of interiors. Among the most recognizable are the glass ones made by Daum, the products of a workshop in the northeastern French city of Nancy, set up by Jean Daum and eventually run by his sons Auguste and Antonin. Famous for its depiction of plants and animals, and for collaborations with designers and artists including Philippe Starck and Salvador Dalí, the factory produced mushroom-shaped lamps in the late 19th and early 20th centuries. They came in many shapes and designs: some squat and simple, others tall and elaborate, such as a wispy wrought-iron stand with a willowy liberty-cap-inspired topper.

Exquisite illustrative details were painted onto multi-coloured pâte de verre shades using the factory's palette of nearly 70 separate hues. Though Daum mass produced some items, its handmade lamps, especially those produced in the Art Nouveau period, commanded high prices and, as a result, could be found on many a discerning sideboard.

A mushroom's shape is perfect for hiding ugly cabling within the spherical stem, and the umbrella-like cap naturally helps cast light downwards — a duality of purpose not lost on product designers. An archetypal squat-stemmed, cap-domed glass mushroom table lamp produced by mid-century masters Peill & Putzler, manufactured in the 1970s, can now sell for several thousand pounds. The WV339 Glass Wall Lights by Wilhelm Wagenfeld for Lindner, manufactured in 1960, also bear more than a passing resemblance to fungal forms. The question that comes up is whether these and similar objects were consciously designed to resemble mushrooms, or whether they were latterly christened as such to capitalize on novel marketability.

The great Danish architect and designer Verner Panton sometimes used mushroom forms in his designs, both above and below ground. Perhaps best known for his single-piece eponymous chair, debuted in 1967, Panton was a serial innovator whose use of new materials and groundbreaking forms have gained him a place in the pantheon of 20th-century design greats. His own Mushroom Lamp was produced in a very short run, and used Cellidor in its manufacture, a bio-based plastic that most famously appears in the handles of Swiss Army knives. More interesting still is Pantons installation, Visiona II, in which the Mushroom Lamp was first exhibited, on an excursion steamer moored within a short walk of the Cologne Furniture Fair in 1970. In setting out a subterranean, below-deck rabbit warren of looping, undulating structures, Panton's interior layout for the river-borne showroom echoed underground mycelium threads.

But instead of stygian gloom, the exhibition was illuminated with bold hues – a kaleidoscope of purples and greens, mauves and scarlets – typical of maximalist interiors of the time. Rooms had signature colours and accompanying sounds: hooting owls, mellifluous nightingales and lapping waves. And, rising from deep red shagpile at the heart of the show: a pair of Panton's Mushroom Lamps. At one metre high and as white as a common puffball, the design expanded from a tapered base to a wide ellipse – looking rather like an upside down waterdrop.

The hand-thrown, clay-fired mushroom-shaped lamps created in 2021 by lighting and furniture designer Nicholas Bijan Pourfard are far more earthy in their texture compared with Panton's pristine plastic mouldings. His handmade-to-order pieces are a fine example of mushroom design excellence; a ball-joint at the top of the stem allows you to make a jaunty tip-of-the-cap to direct the light wherever you wish.

Arguably, one of the most extraordinary pieces of mushroom-inspired interior design can be found at a house in Holmby Hills, a suburban neighbourhood west of Los Angeles that Frank Sinatra and Elvis Presley once called home. The Smalley House, designed by modernist architect A Quincy Jones, is now owned by a Los Angeles gallerist who has populated its 700 square metres with an eclectic set of artworks from her own collection, including pieces by Naama Tsabar, Kathleen Ryan, Judy Chicago and Lauren Halsey.

Front and centre of this interior, rich in distractions, is a colossal fly agaric mushroom by

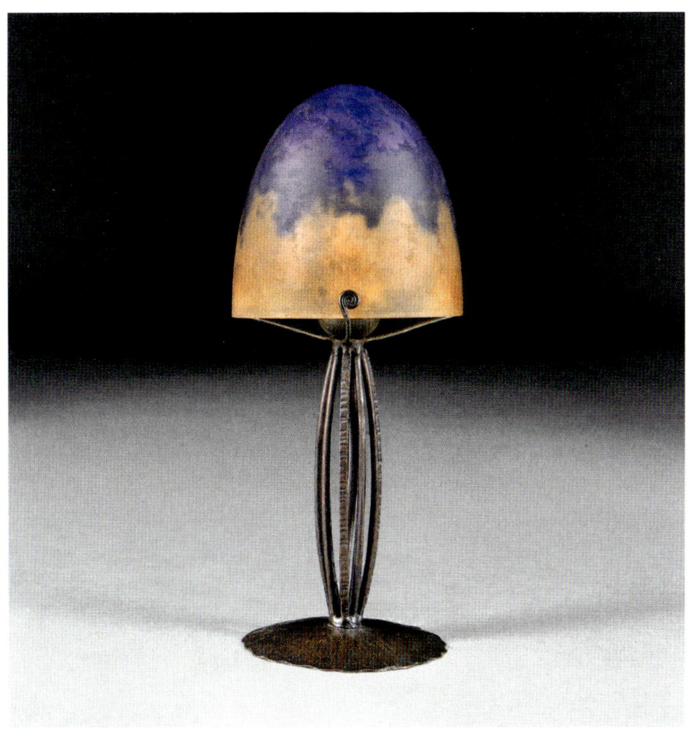

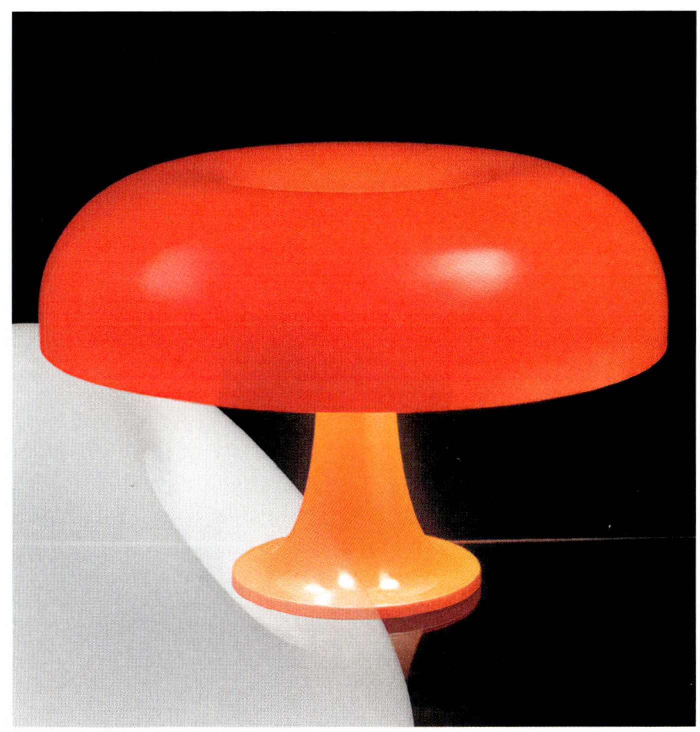

TOP **Daum**, Art Nouveau lamp c.1900
BOTTOM **Giancarlo Mattioli**, Artemide Nesso table lamp, 1960s

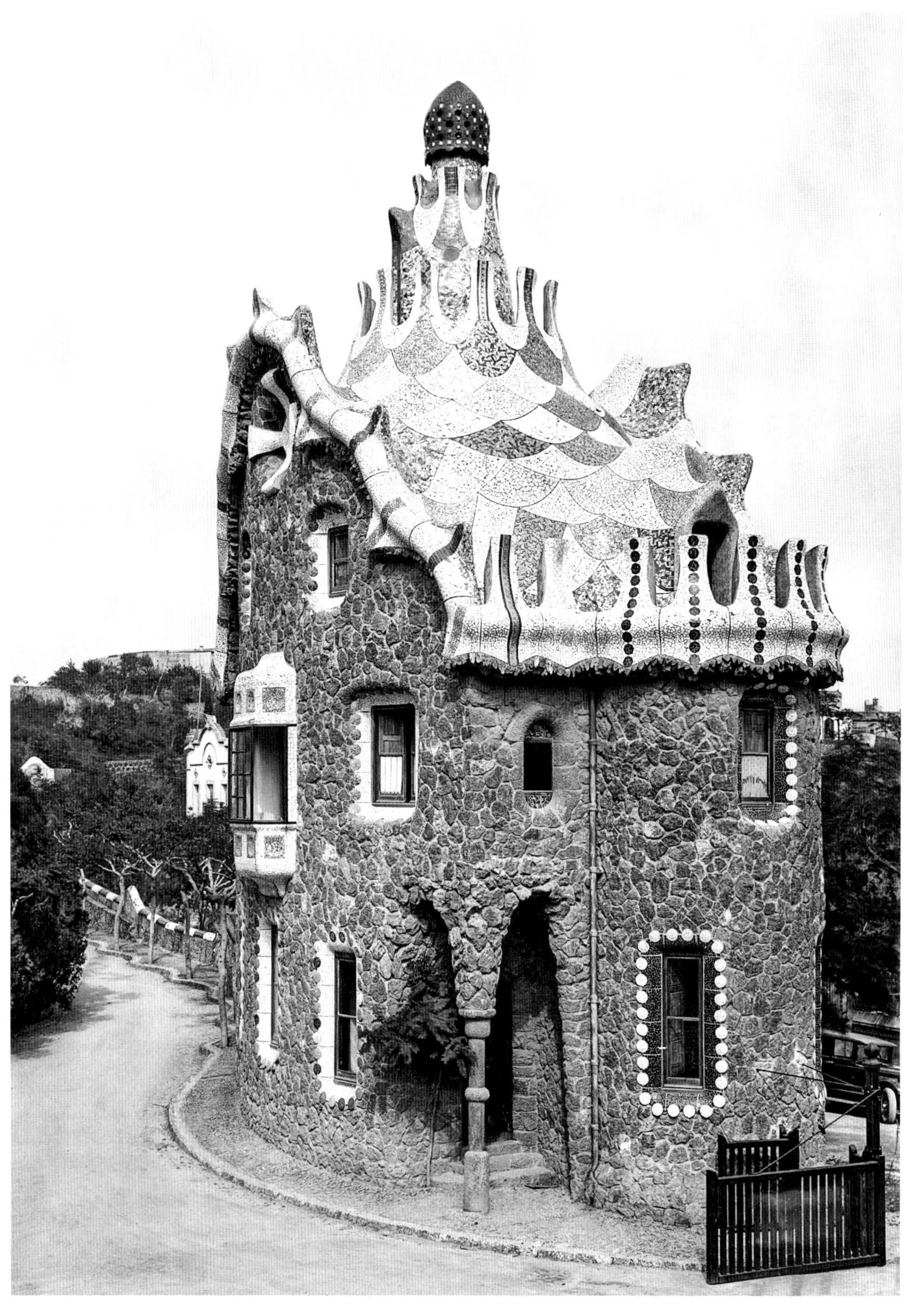

Antoni Gaudí, Casa del Guarda, Parc Güell, Barcelona, 1900–14
OPPOSITE **Antoni Gaudí**, Mosaic tower of Casa del Guarda, Parc Güell, Barcelona, 1900–14

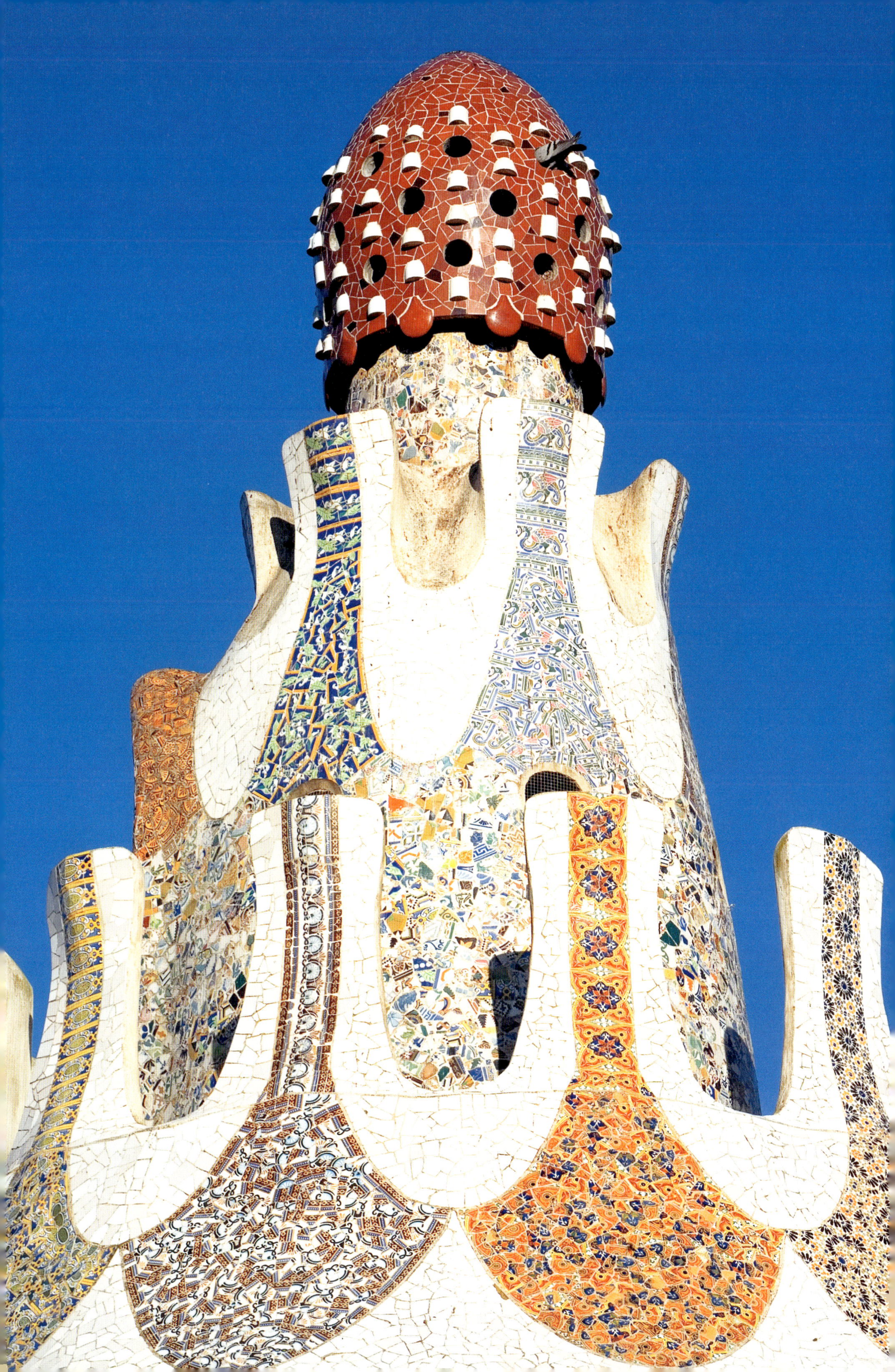

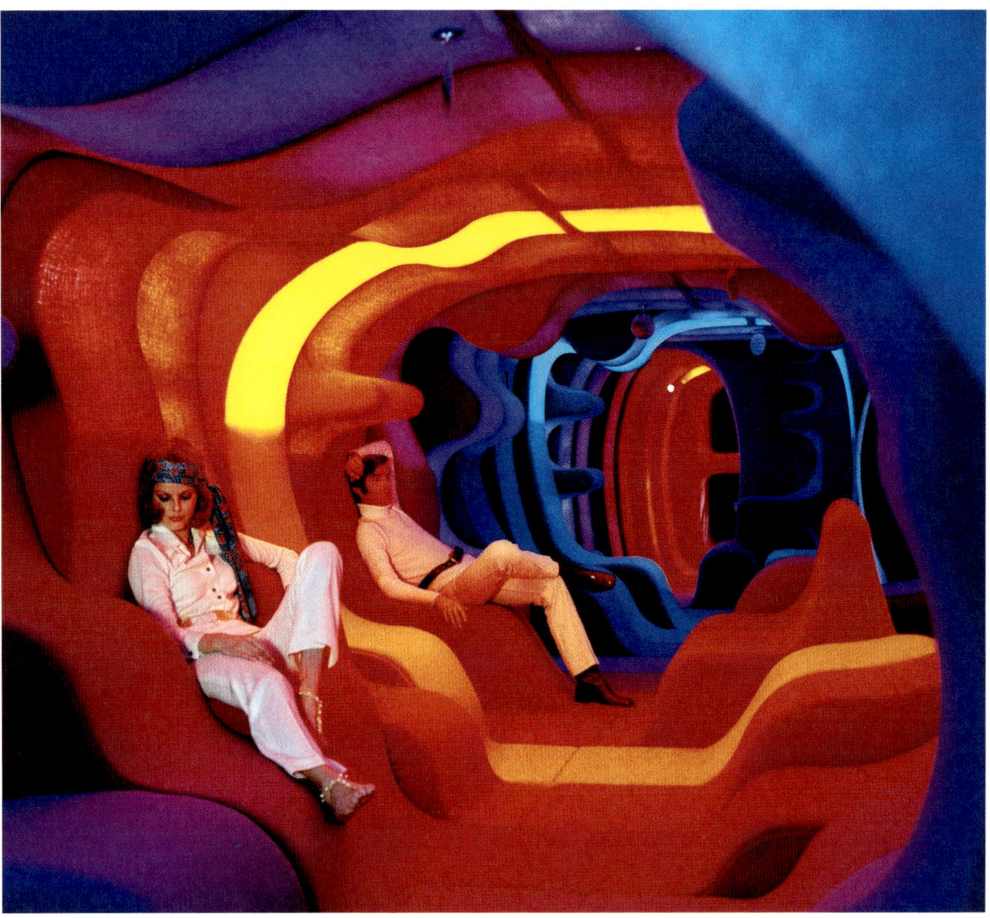

Texan artist twins the Haas Brothers, known for their biomorphic sculptural forms. This towering piece, *Fungus Humungus* (2015), is in line with similar work from the duo's fantastical fungal oeuvre, which includes the royal blue and pink of *Mary Tyler Spore* (2015) and the green and yellow of *Cream of Some Fungi* (2016). *Fungus Humungus* is, in essence, a 2.5-metre-tall reimagining of a fly agaric, with a glistening bronze cast base and a lush red cap woven from many, many thousands of glass beads. Nestled between three low stools, it casts a shadow across a floor embedded with pebbles, overlooking a garden brimming with cacti.

Another attention-grabbing fly agaric can be found in Barcelona's Parc Güell, atop the Casa del Guarda, a gingerbread-house-come-to-life designed by nature-loving architect Antoni Gaudí. The cap of the stout residence's jolly roof boasts the mushroom's familiar red base with white spots, and though Gaudí never name-checked the mushroom in question, the resemblance is undeniable.

But when it comes to a celebration of the mushroom as a permanent exterior structure, it is Earl Young who stands above the forest floor in his evocation of fungus for the look of his signature dwellings. Most of Young's homes can be found in Charlevoix, not far from the shoreline of

Verner Panton, *Fantasy Landscape*, Visiona II exhibition, 1970
(Credit: Design by Verner Panton © Verner Panton Design AG)

Lake Michigan and less than an hour from his birthplace of Mancelona. In his early years, Young developed many strings to his bow. He was a realtor and an insurance agent in the family business, and a self-taught builder and mason.

One of the first houses he designed of the fungal ilk was built in 1918 using rocks and boulders lifted from a nearby lake and surrounds. Young's ambition with 304 Park Avenue, which became his family home, was to meld the house with the landscape, instead of simply placing the building on top of it. The result is a house whose thatched roof droops towards the lawn, centimetres from the backs of Adirondack chairs. This organic form exemplifies Young's ambition to harmonize the built environment with the natural one — a motivation he shared with the illustrious Frank Lloyd Wright. Unlike Wright, however, Young did not complete his formal training as an architect, having left his course at the University of Michigan School of Architecture after just one year. His work in Charlevoix broke rules and eschewed norms, primarily because he didn't stick around to demonstrate his understanding of either; he chose practice over paperwork.

But it would be a house on the corner of Clinton and Grant Streets, practically adjacent to the family home, that would be Young's fungal paean. Out of all Young's buildings, this structure was the one most referenced as The Mushroom House — and it looks like it sprouted from the land itself. The roof in particular presents a very fungus-like outline, achieved in part by setting the shingles nine deep in places to create undulations that ripple across the property; for instance, the lip of the roof seems to reach below the height of the front door. Leaded windows, many of which are welded shut, are said to have come from the dilapidated castle of a Polish lumber baron. Inside, a circular floor plan orbits a central fireplace and chimney breast shaped from slabs of Onaway stone set at a vertiginous 45 degrees. As he told one visitor to his office, "I always build the roof first, and then shove the house under it."

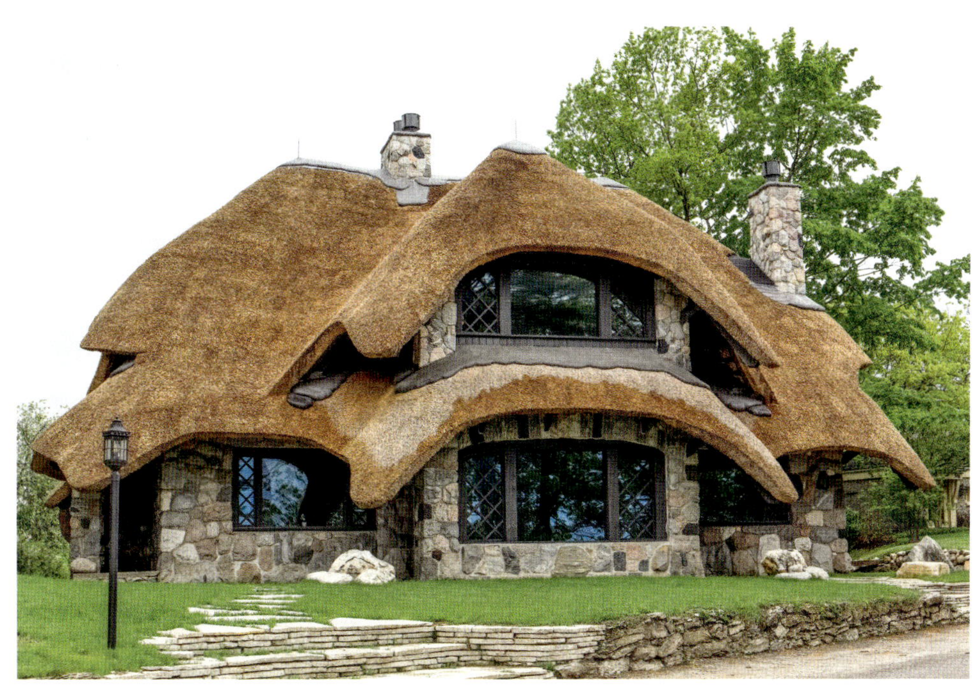

Earl Young
The Mushroom House, Charlevoix, Michigan, 1918

Mushroom à la Mode

Fashion's Enduring Relationship With Fungi

"For about six months we have endured the sight of mushroom shapes in every kind of straw," complained suffragette and author Evelyn Sharp, in a 1907 edition of the *Manchester Guardian*. She continues: "I suppose there was some attraction in the mushroom hat when it was first designed, and I can still see its charms when it is very small and very flexible... worn by somebody in a motor car. But this autumnal growth of large felt fungi deserves nothing but condemnation."

Her stern words did little to diminish the trend, and the mushroom hat remained clamped to female heads throughout that decade and beyond, reaching its pinnacle with Christian Dior's revolutionary New Look collection in 1947, which featured a satellite-dish-sized specimen that balanced out the silhouette's tiny waistline.

But the mushroom's impact on fashion goes deeper than Edwardian headdress, or the kitsch fungi printed across the shirts of Haight-Ashbury free spirits. If fashion is "the mirror of history... rather than mere whimsy", as Louix XIV of France said back in the 17th century, today that means reflecting many customers' increasing interest in the natural world and sustainability. Some designers have taken inspiration from the mushroom to do that, giving fungi sartorial life via patterns, layers of fabric, frills and dangling threads.

The inaugural collection from Milan-based Daniel Del Core's eponymous label was sprouting with mushrooms. His 2021 couture pieces included a crystal-studded patent leather fungi-shaped coat — ideal for a mycological dominatrix — and a tiered silk organza gown replete with glowing green mushroom print — worn by Björk with a matching mushroom mask made in collaboration with Swedish artist David Åberg.

"Fungi are really powerful poster organisms for ecological thinking," mycologist Merlin Sheldrake has said. His book *Entangled Life* (2020) was a key source for Dutch-born Iris van Herpen, an innovative designer who often draws on nature for her futuristic garments and accessories.

Van Herpen showcased a fantastical homage to fungi in her S/S21 haute couture show, a collection that appeared to grow and breathe with 3D gills, expandable lace and twisted straps curling organically around its wearer. The same year, Indian couturier Rahul Mishra's S/S21 collection recognized the marvel of engineering that is the mushroom, tasking his *petites-mains* with hand-embroidering 3D mushrooms onto breathtakingly intricate garments in tulle and silk organza.

In 2022, Sarah Burton at Alexander McQueen sent models down the runway in psychedelic mushroom dresses picked out in red, yellow and acid-green beads, knitwear whose messy, frayed ends mimicked tendrils, and sheer dresses that evoked intricate mycelium webs.

Mycelium, an infinitely renewable tangle of root-like strands that make up the body of a fungus, has emerged in fashion not just as a symbol of interconnectedness and community but also as a material itself: a more ethical, more sustainable

OPPOSITE
Arnaud Lajeunie, *Del Core*, 2021

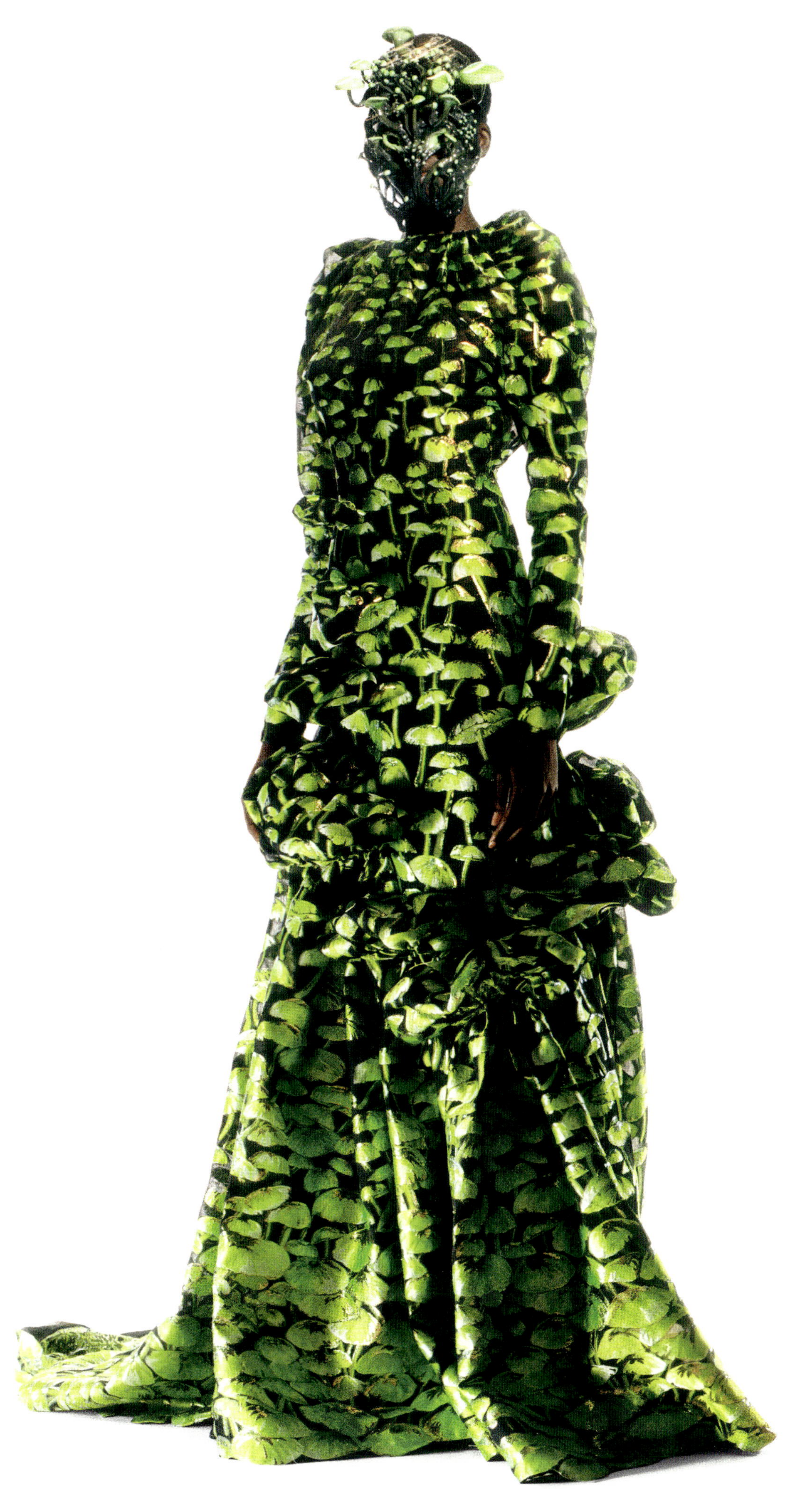

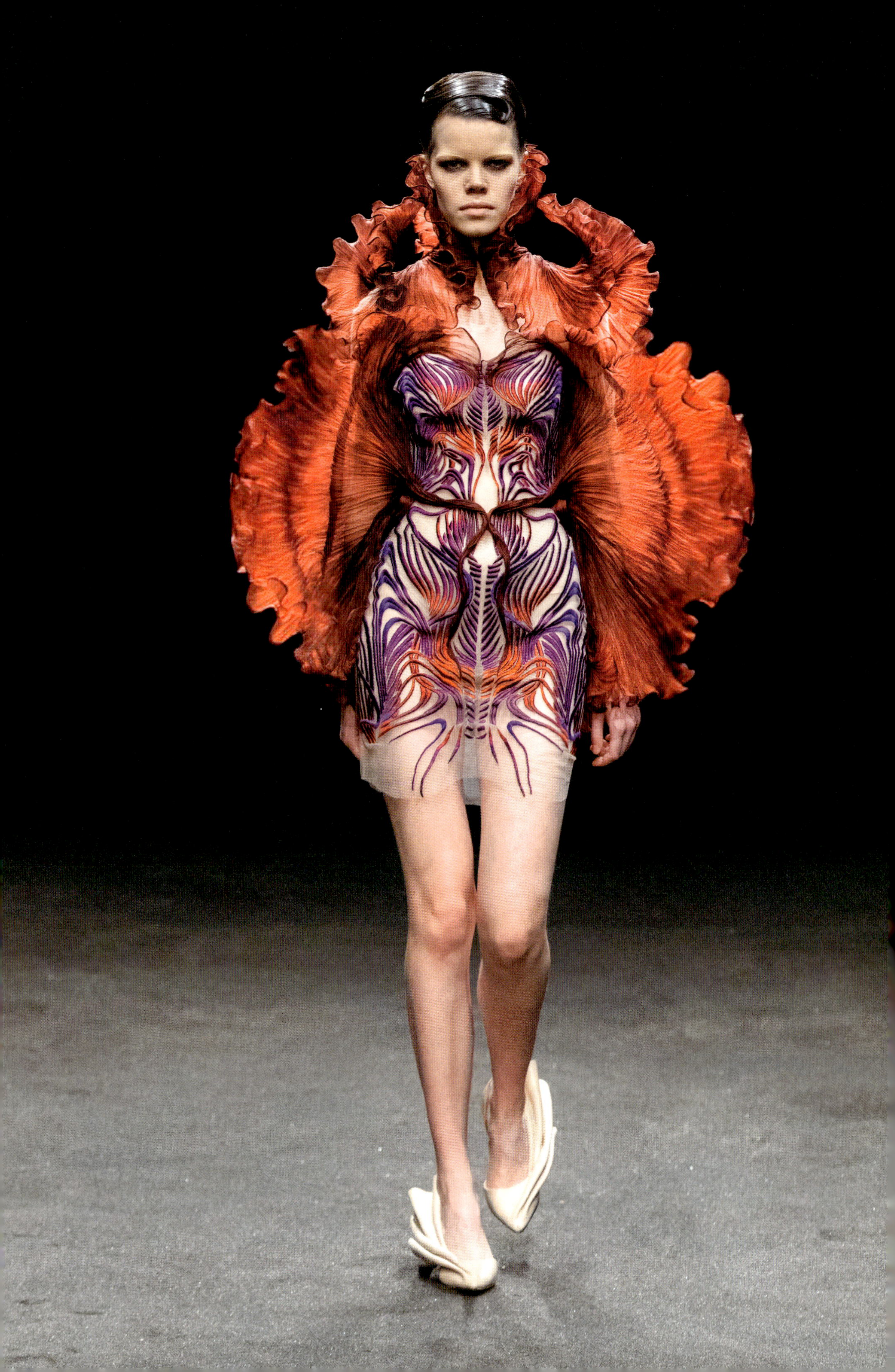

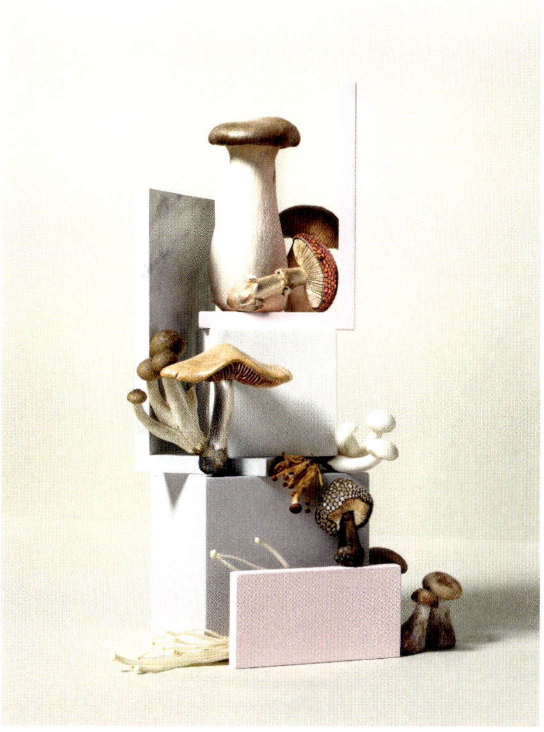

alternative to leather. Stella McCartney offered a glimpse of its potential when she created a prototype bodice and trousers made of Mylo, a mycelium-based material. The garments comprised billions of cells grown in a lab, a vertical farm in the Netherlands, using mulch, air and water. Adidas made a pair of Stan Smiths from the same process. Another venture, Mycoworks, grows the *Ganoderma lucidum* fungus in trays of sawdust, resulting in a strong yet flexible material that was used to produce a luxury handbag with the until-now leather-centric brand Hermès.

Since World War II, that French fashion house has been associated with a signature citrus-orange shade, but in recent times its Kelly and Birkin bag ranges have added a muted "mushroom" hue, joining a widespread trend for forest-floor colours that has taken root in the fashion industry: colour-matching company Pantone crowned its own mushroom colour as a "new classic" in its spring/summer 2024 trend report.

Jewellery and accessories have also had a whimsical mushroom takeover. Haute joaillerie brand Hemmerle, the exacting fourth-generation suppliers to royalty and the Vatican, has often found creative fuel in unexpected flora and fauna — eggplants and cauliflowers included — but arguably its most charming pieces are lifelike mushroom brooches, scattered with diamonds and other precious stones.

Perhaps as we get ever more comfortable wearing fungi, more of us will sign up for that ultimate ensemble: the mushroom death suit. The brainchild of US-based artist Jae Rhim Lee, it's a pair of "ninja pyjamas" impregnated with mushroom spores and other micro-organisms intended to help the body decompose and neutralize whatever toxins we've built up over a lifetime, ensuring our return to the earth is embalming-fluid free. The idea takes mushroom fashion to its logical conclusion, replacing mushroom hats with actual fungi, sprouting straight from our heads.

ABOVE **Thomas Brown**, *Rich Pickings*, from the *The Gourmand,* Issue 07, 2016
OPPOSITE **Gio Staiano**, Iris van Herpen's Roots of Rebirth Spring/Summer collection, 2021

Yayoi Kusama's Obsession

Since the 1950s, Yayoi Kusama's colourful polka-dotted art has spread like a jolly virus across the world. The Japanese artist has printed and painted on nearly every imaginable surface — from standard canvas, paper and fabric to more outlandish materials including inflatable vinyl, mirrors, furniture and mannequins. Even naked humans have been painted with her trademark dots, applied with body paint. Whether executed as fields of tiny speckles or as clumps of fat round blobs, Kusama's dots often emulate both the appearance and the natural accumulation of mushrooms.

Things that resemble mushrooms regularly crop up in Kusama's art, even if she rarely refers to them directly. When she covered huge red inflatable vinyl balls with white spots, the association with the poisonous fly agaric was inescapable. The immersive installation *Dots Obsession* — the red and white edition of an extended series by the same name — implies danger and fantasy, the potential of death or hallucination, but also the promise of transport into another, fantastical realm.

Kusama's art not only looks like mushrooms, but sometimes, through its repetition, it behaves like them, too. As art critic Sir Herbert Read put it in 1964, the artist "creates forms that proliferate like mycelium". But the works that Read had in mind were not, in fact, Kusama's early polka-dot paintings, nor her subsequent paintings of mushrooms and toadstools, but early iterations of her *Accumulation* series (1961–ongoing) of sculptural installations. For these immersive, gallery-filling environments, she affixed plaster-filled fabric — about the size and shape of sweet potatoes — to found objects including a baby carriage, a boat,

OPPOSITE
Yayoi Kusama, *Mushroom*, 1980

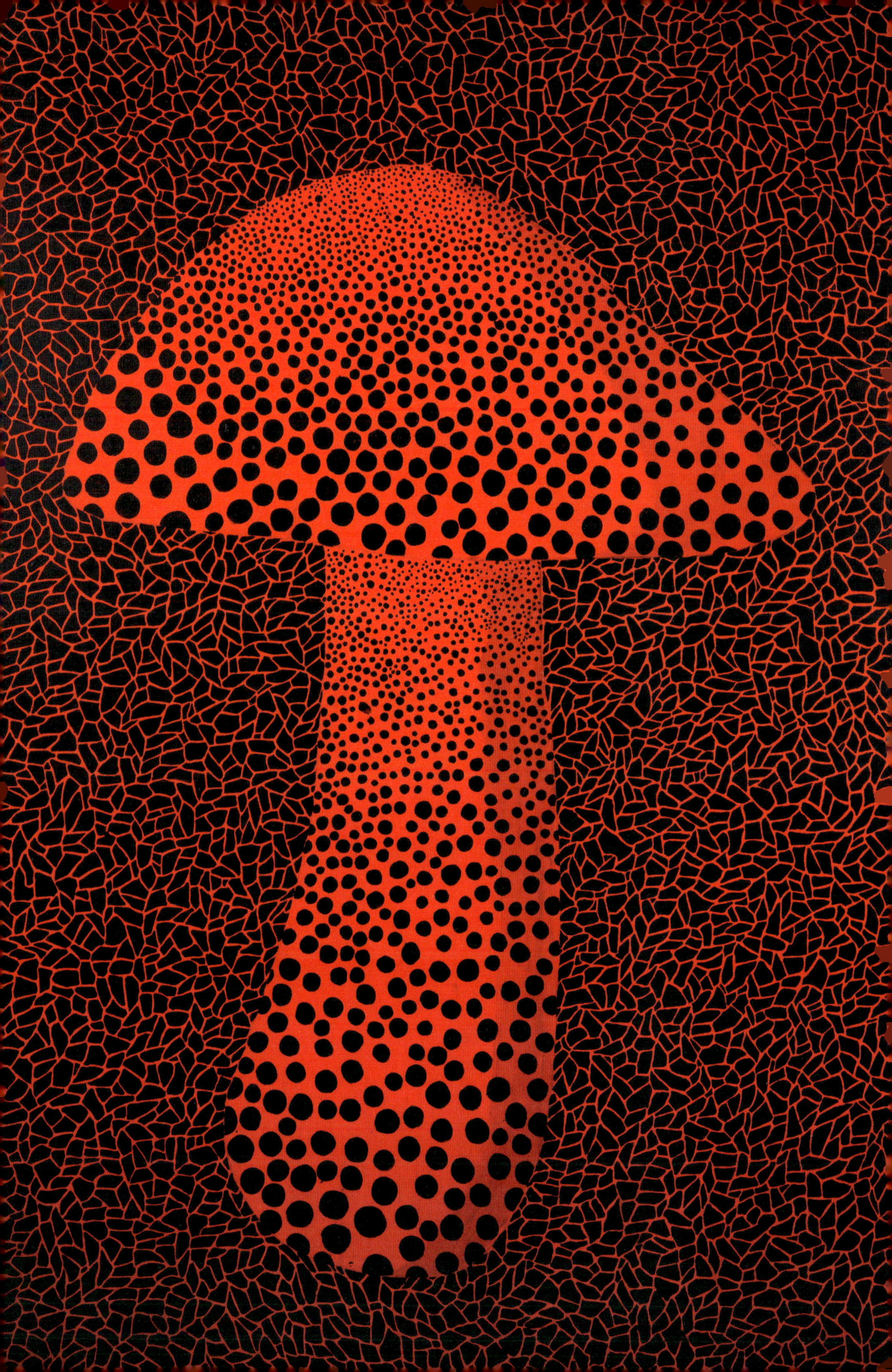

Yayoi Kusama, *Collage*, 1966
(Photo by Hal Reiff of Kusama reclining on *Accumulation #2*, 1962)

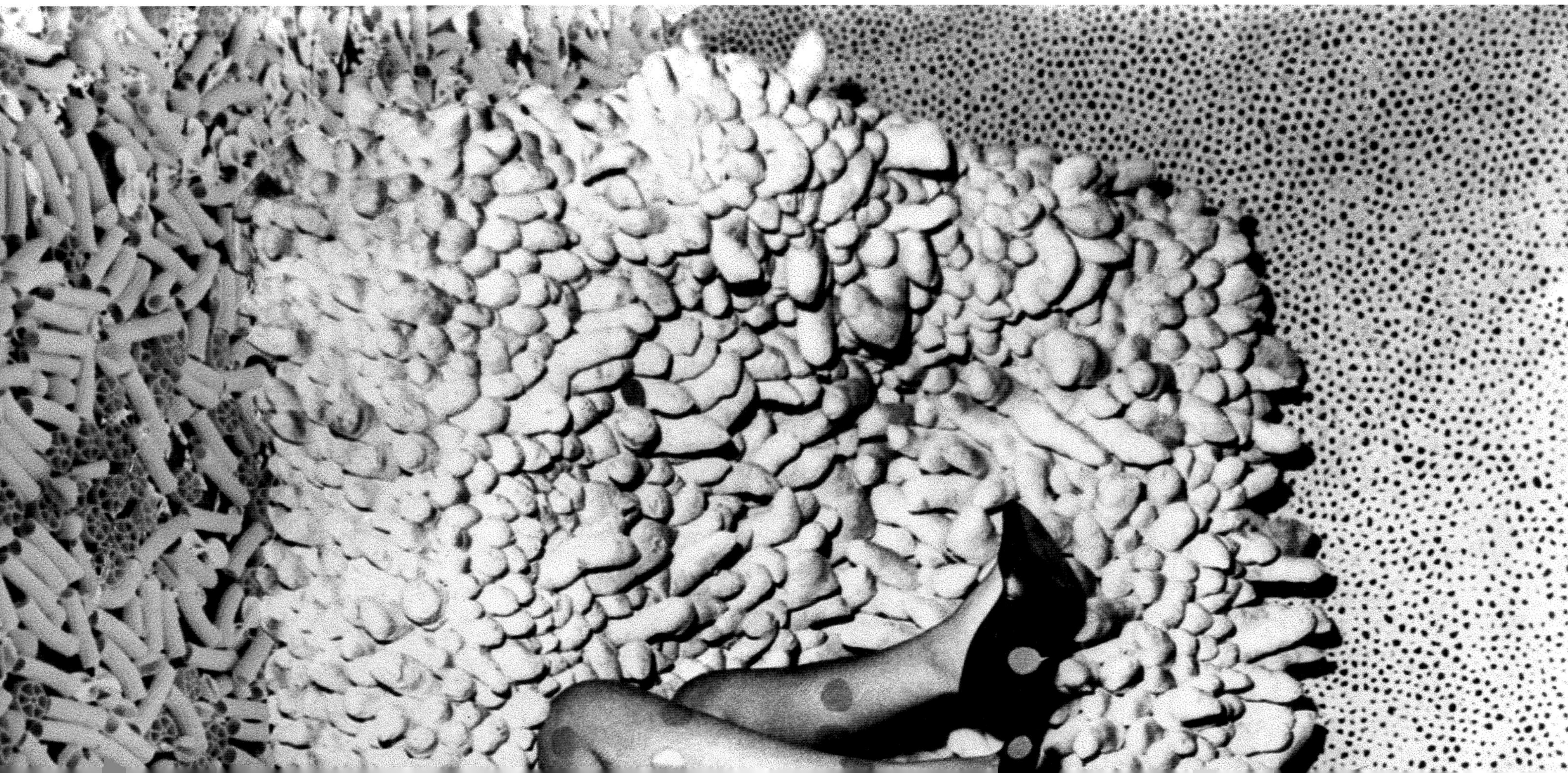

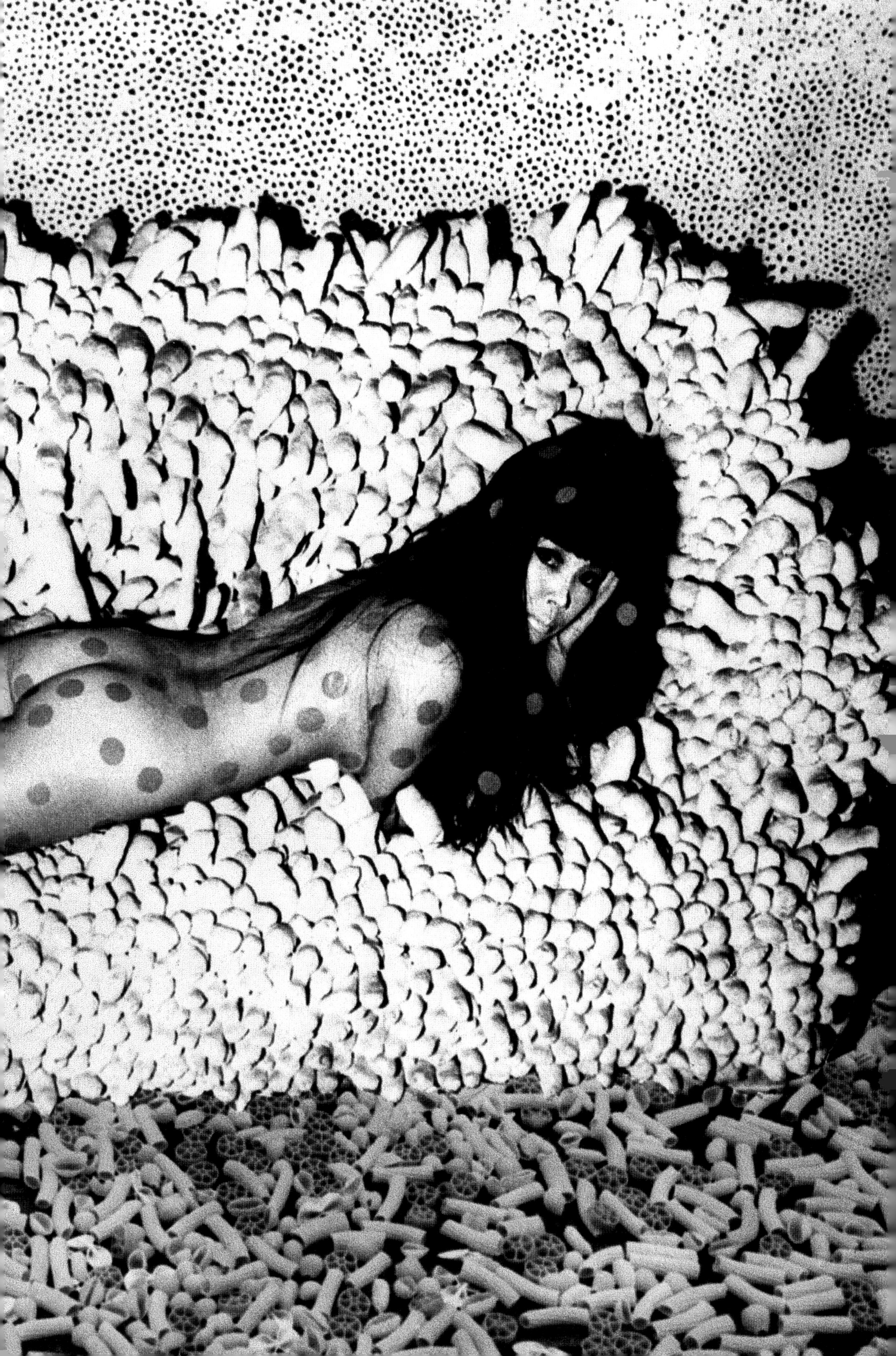

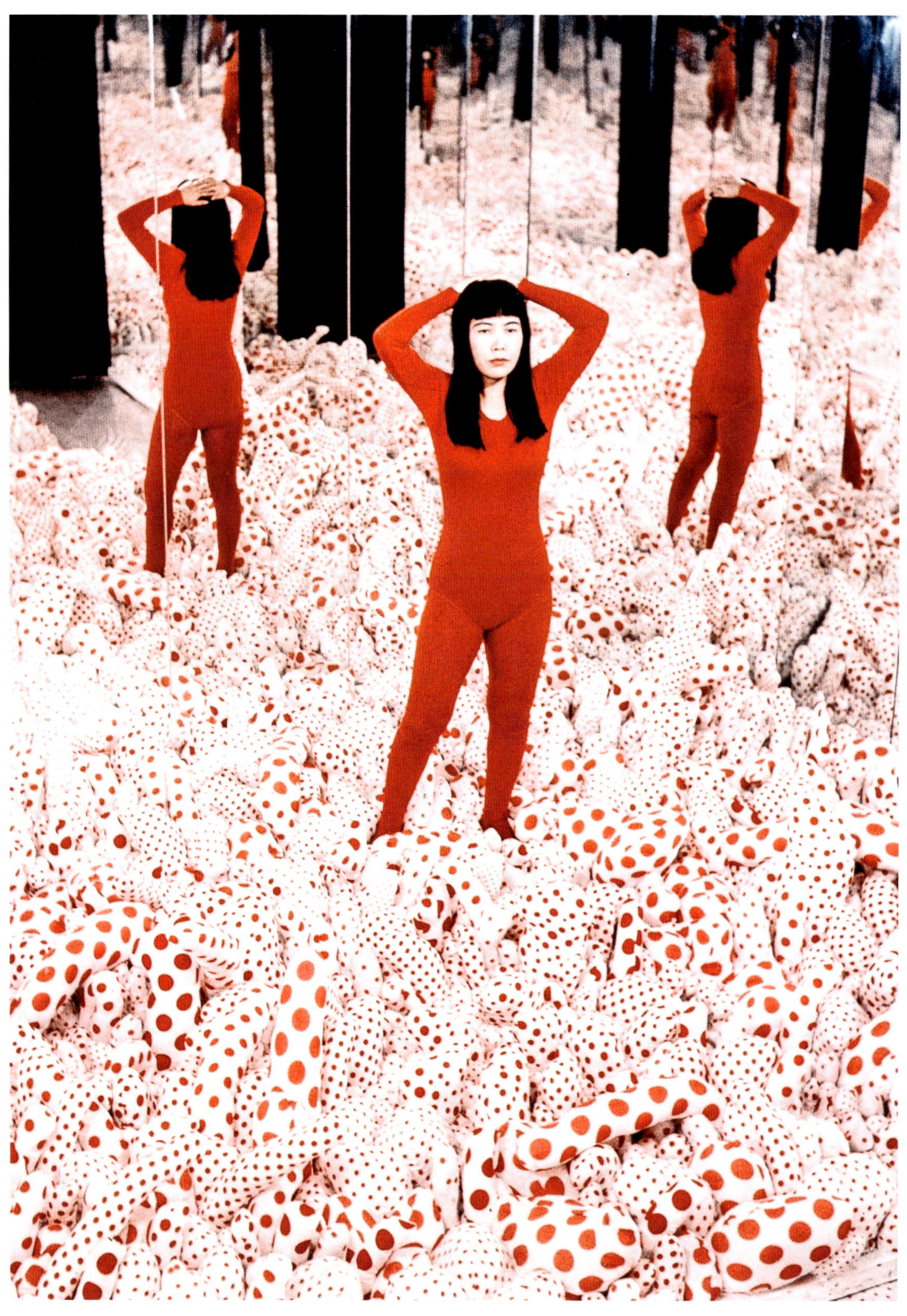

Yayoi Kusama
Infinity Mirror Room — Phalli's Field, 1965

ladders, chairs, and tables. These white growths enveloped the objects beneath in what one critic called "an eerie mould." While these sculptures may have recalled fungi to some, what they looked like most of all was penises. Kusama herself was unabashed in her acknowledgement of the symbolism. She covered surfaces with these phalluses be, she explained, "because I am afraid of them. It is a 'sex obsession.'"

Kusama had a troubled childhood. She was born in 1929 in the Japanese city of Matsumoto, in the mountainous prefecture of Nagano. Her wealthy family owned a nursery and seed farm, propagating plants in hothouses on their land. Her father was a womanizer, and her abusive mother forced her to spy on his affairs. Witnessing him *in flagrante* instilled in Kusama a lifelong abhorrence of physical sexuality. "I began making penises in order to heal my feelings of disgust towards sex," she wrote in her 2002 autobiography, *Infinity Net*. "Reproducing the objects, again and again, was my way of conquering the fear. It was a kind of self-therapy."

Kusama self-therapized for other reasons, too. Since childhood, the artist had been gripped by hallucinations in which auras and dots would appear around objects, flowers from the tablecloth would cover the walls and ceiling of the room, or flowers in the field would start talking to her. Again, attempting to reproduce these experiences in her art was her way of coming to terms with these terrifying episodes. In 1977, she voluntarily took up residence in a psychiatric hospital, where she still resides today. The psychiatric term for the rupture from her identity that Kusama experienced is "depersonalization". While her work is a stylized depiction of her traumatic hallucinations, it is also her attempt to "self-obliterate" through immersion in an infinitely repeating field of pattern. Her popular *Infinity Mirror Rooms* series (1965–present) — mirrored spaces filled with hanging LED lights or paper spheres, or spotted sculptures of pumpkins or phalli, which repeat endlessly — reproduce the hallucinations that beset the young artist.

Relinquishing the ego, becoming one with nature and reconnecting with the universe are ideas that appear in many philosophies, not just Japanese Buddhist traditions. Kusama has declared that she adheres to no religion and has downplayed the influence of Japanese culture on her work. But ego-death is plainly there to be found, and so too is the natural cycle of existence. "Now the theme of my artistic creation is 'death,'" Kusama said in 1975. The irony is unavoidable; she has explored this theme through joyful symbols of aliveness and fertility, from phalli to flowers to pumpkins and mushrooms.

Philip Guston's Mushroom Nail

When he painted *Untitled (Nail)* in 1968, Philip Guston was in spiritual crisis. Not in the evangelical sense, but artistically, as a high priest of modern art who was starting to lose his faith. In the New York of the 1940s and '50s, Guston had established himself as a leading figure of the Abstract Expressionist movement. But by the end of the next decade, his early refusal of representational imagery seemed untenable.

As the title suggests, his now-famous oil painting depicts a nail. A nail that might also be a mushroom. Guston's ambiguous, mushroomy nail is two things at once: a sharp metal spike driven hard into a piece of wood, and a soft, organic efflorescence that has emerged up out of it. As with much of the art that Guston produced from the late 1960s onwards, the work manages to be both gently comical and foreboding — even violent. The "banality of evil" — a phrase coined by philosopher Hannah Arendt in her book about the trial of Nazi Adolf Eichmann — was a theme that occupied Guston throughout his career.

Guston was born Phillip Goldstein in 1913 in Montréal, Canada, the youngest of seven siblings. His parents had fled pogroms in Odessa; his father, Louis, always struggled with depression. In Los Angeles, where the family had moved in search of a better life, Louis got by as a self-employed junkman, driving a horse-drawn cart through the city streets. Aged ten, the young Phillip discovered his father's body hanging from a rafter in a shed. Processing that indelible trauma, he began drawing incessantly, often hiding in a closet illuminated by a single lightbulb.

The family was poor, but Guston's mother was supportive of her son's artistic talents, enrolling him in a correspondence course for cartooning. He was admitted to Manual Arts High School in 1927, where he befriended a similarly artistic classmate named Jackson Pollock. The rebellious duo were expelled for pamphleteering against the presence of military trainers at the school, the conservatism of the English department and an excessive emphasis on sports. Pollock, penitent, was allowed back to graduate; the intractable Guston was not.

It was in 1935 that the young artist started using the name Philip Guston, and a year later he followed Pollock to New York City, where he lived for a time with Pollock's brother. During this

OPPOSITE
Philip Guston, *Untitled (Nail),* 1968 (detail)

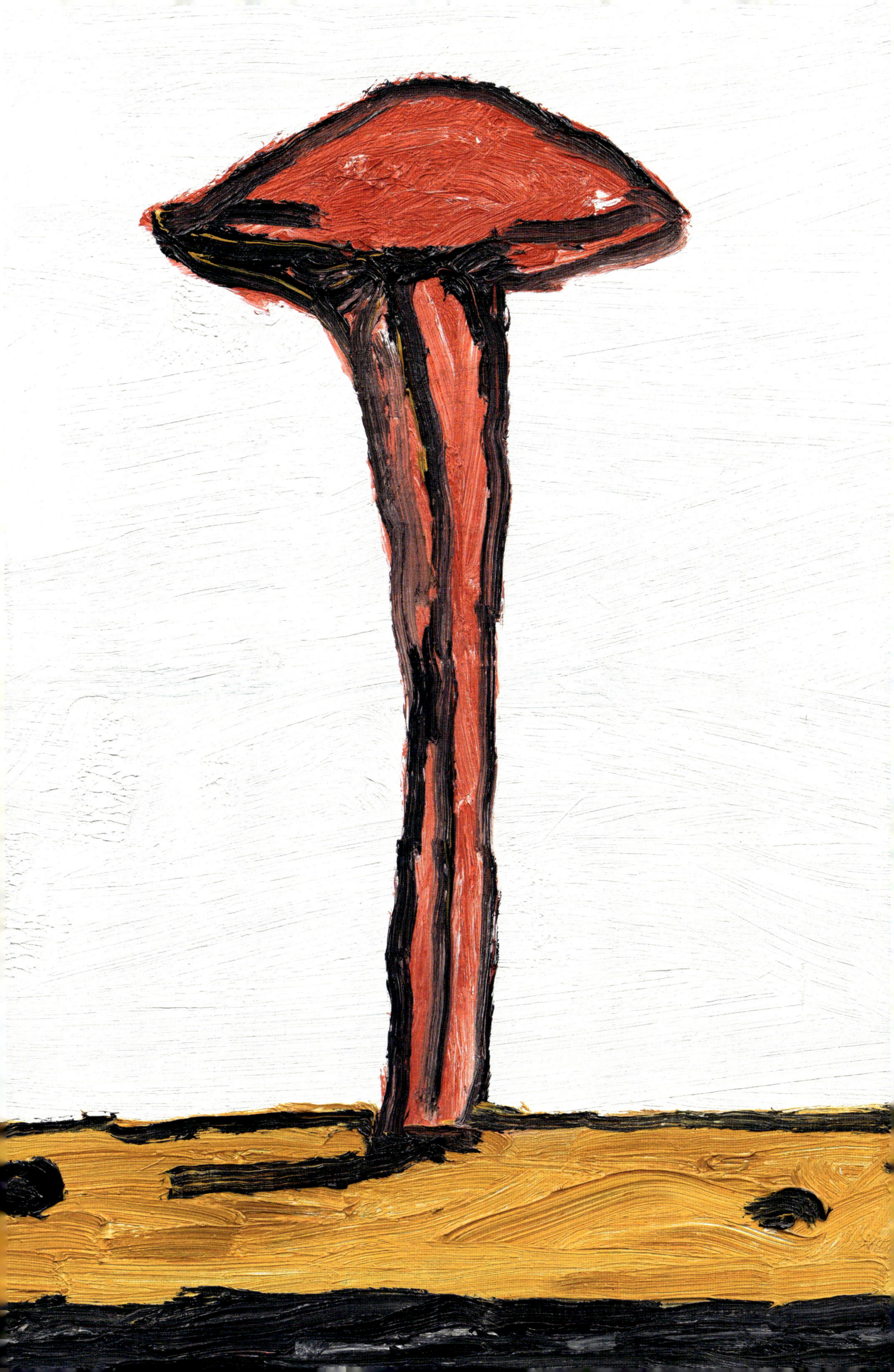

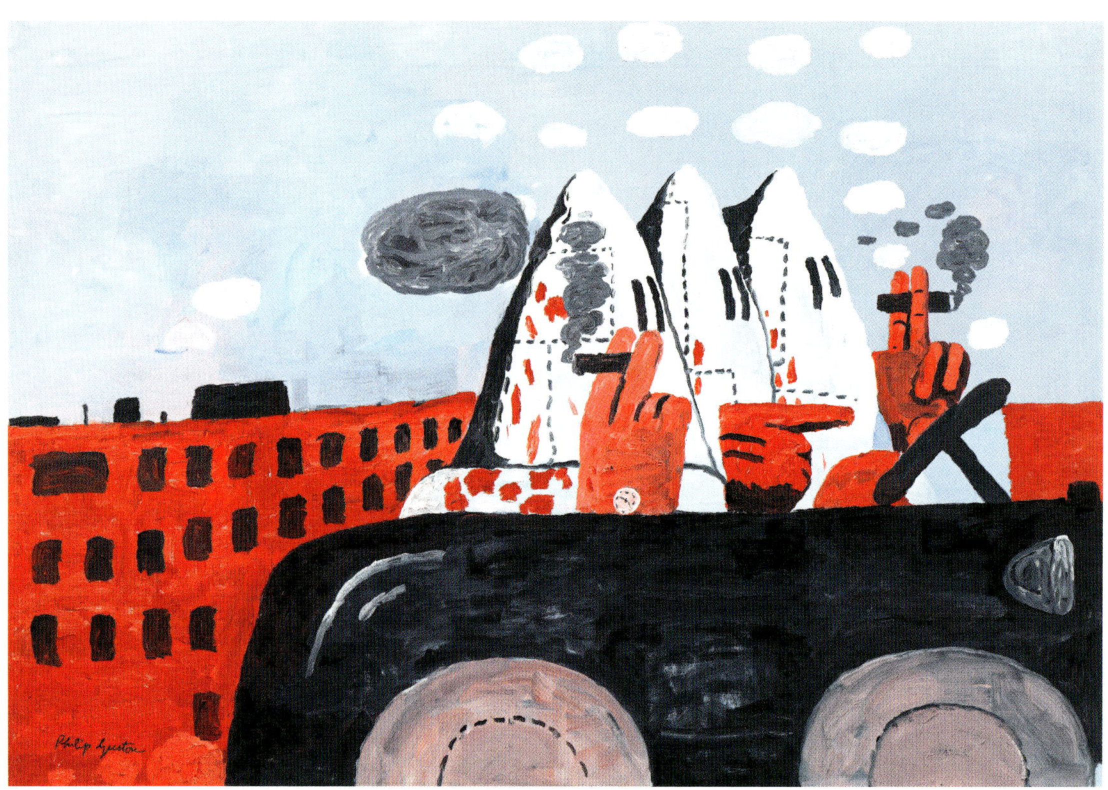

Philip Guston
Riding Around, 1969

period, Guston's art was greatly influenced by the Mexican muralists; he even signed up to paint political murals for the US Government's Depression era Federal Art Project. His graphic, powerful portraits and bold figure paintings — some of which depicted white-hooded members of the Ku Klux Klan — were influenced by his Marxist politics, his commitment to civil rights and his appeal to the struggles of working-class Americans. These works won him prizes and critical accolades, but Guston was uncomfortable with success. He left New York City shortly after World War II, removing himself to the relative isolation of Woodstock in rural upstate New York.

It was here, among the pines and the silver birch, that Guston gradually emptied his art of identifiable subject matter, arriving at a style of abstract painting where clusters of marks accumulated in the middle of the canvas, invoking pictorial space but with no hints of scale, texture or detail. He became friends with the experimental composer and amateur mycologist John Cage, who took him to hear the Zen philosopher DT Suzuki. After this, Guston's paintings became *tabula rasae*, meditations on the substance of nothingness. *White Painting I* (1951), for example, was hardly white at all, but a gathering of tentative marks in greys and pale ochres that imply the dissolution of forms, or even the dissolution of the painting itself. Looked at another way, this organic cluster of stems and cross paths could be said to resemble an underground system of roots (perhaps of a gathering of mushrooms...).

Once again, Guston met with critical success. By the late 1950s, he was one of the most celebrated North American painters alive, and a pillar of the New York School, a group of experimental painters, poets, musicians and choreographers who coalesced in the city. Frustrated by the solitude of Woodstock, Guston rented a studio in Greenwich Village, and was energized by the fervent discussions that took place in the famous artists' bar the Cedar Tavern. By the 1960s, however, the cultural appetite for Abstract Expressionism had waned, while the irreverence and immediacy of Pop Art and Conceptualism were starting to make painters like Guston seem self-absorbed and out of touch: life was happening — often violently — on the streets and in the universities, not to mention in the jungles of Southeast Asia, but abstraction seemed to have little to say about it.

In his Woodstock studio, Guston drew and drew. "They were all over the walls and floors," he later recalled of his drawings. "My strongest sensation at that time was a feeling of needing to start again with the simplest means to clear the decks." Some of his drawings and paintings were pared-back abstractions — a single, elegantly curved line as part of his *Pure Drawing* series (1966–67) — while others depicted quotidian objects: an umbrella, a coffee cup, a book, a lightbulb. And, of course, the mushroom-nail.

In 1970, Guston exhibited his new, cartoony paintings at Marlborough Gallery in New York. Most of these featured dopey, white-hooded Klansmen — smoking; driving in cars; packed into a small room beneath a single, hanging lightbulb; painting at easels. The figures seemed not so much representative of America's scarcely disguised racism as they were ciphers for the artist himself — a privileged White man (albeit a Jew) living in a country founded on racial inequality. They hinted, too, at Guston's perception of his own personal shortcomings; the Klansmen are not ominous or threatening so much as bumbling and clownish. It was as if Guston were inviting condemnation, bringing culpability upon himself. This time around, the work wasn't met with success; it was widely misunderstood, even ridiculed.

Years later, Guston would become a hugely influential figure for younger generations of painters emulating the comic absurdity of his tormented, existential art. Just as fungal life relies on something else dying, and regeneration relies on degeneration, his work from this later period is recognized today for what it is: an improbable growth that sprang up, unbidden and unexpected, on the decaying remains of Modernist abstract painting.

Shady Stories

Mushrooms in Fiction

With his ample beard and pocket watch, Mordecai Cooke looked every bit the Victorian naturalist, yet underneath was a hippie sensibility a century ahead of its time. His defining 1860 book, *The Seven Sisters of Sleep*, was an open-minded survey of narcotics, which also traces the long and failed history of penalizing their use: in the 14th century, Egyptians caught using marijuana had their teeth extracted; 17th-century Russia punished snuff takers by cutting off offenders' noses.

Cooke's chapter on the psychoactive properties of the fly agaric has been singled out as the inspiration for Alice's surreal disappearance down the rabbit hole in Lewis Carroll's enduring children's classic, *Alice's Adventures in Wonderland* (1865). "A day's intoxication may thus be procured at the expense of... one large or two small toadstools, and this intoxication is affirmed to be, not only cheap, which is a consideration, but also remarkably pleasant," Cooke wrote. "Erroneous impressions of size and distance are common occurrences... a straw lying on the road becomes a formidable obstacle to overcome."

Carroll visited the Bodleian Library at Oxford, where Cooke's opus had recently been deposited, before he embarked on his own book — with its magic toadstool that causes Alice to grow as high as the treetops. In Jules Verne's *A Journey to the Centre of the Earth*, published a year before *Alice*, it's the mushrooms that grow to surprising sizes — channelling the "hollow earth" theories still in vogue. Verne's intrepid heroes travel down an Icelandic volcano into a subterranean world of giants, dinosaurs, electrical storms and forests of 12-metre-high mushrooms.

But it was the slippery dream logic of Carroll's story — with its talking rabbits and flamingos moonlighting as croquet mallets — that struck a chord in the 1960s. Most famously, the book provided the inspiration for 1967's "White Rabbit" — trippy rockers Jefferson Airplane's summer-of-love homage to a generation taking their own trips through the looking glass. "And you've just had some kind of mushroom / And your mind is moving low / Go ask Alice / I think she'll know..." sings Grace Slick. She once said parents "read us all these stories where you'd take some kind of chemical and have a great adventure," and was convinced of Carroll's hallucinogenic subtext: "*Alice in Wonderland* is blatant;

OPPOSITE
Peter Blake, *"But isn't it Old!"*, from *Through the Looking-Glass*, 1970

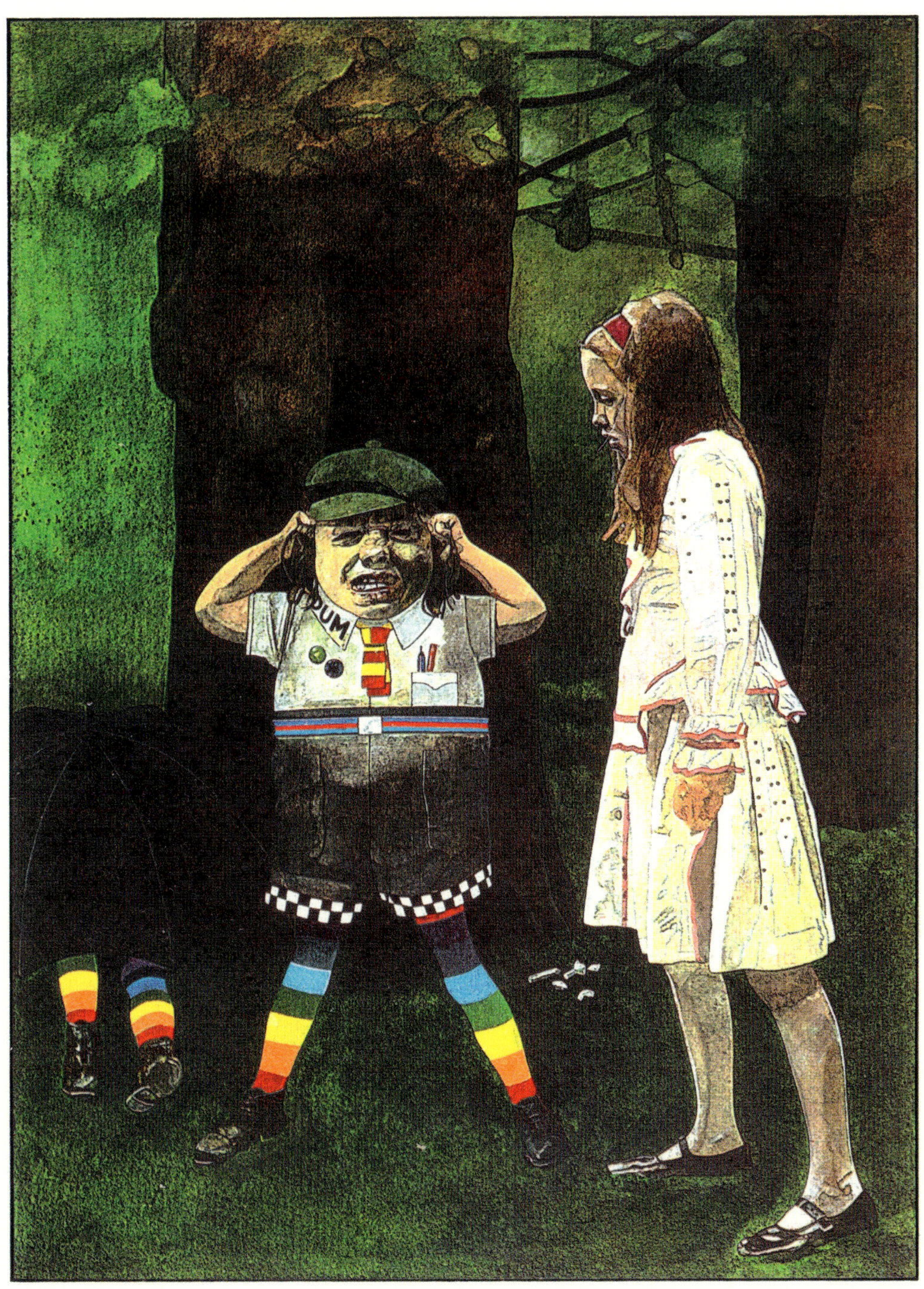

"But it isn't old!" Tweedledum cried, in a greater fury than ever. "It's new, I tell you — I bought it yesterday — my nice NEW RATTLE!" and his voice rose to a perfect scream. A/P Peter Blake

she gets literally high, too big for the room, while the caterpillar sits on a psychedelic mushroom smoking opium. "In *The Wizard of Oz*, they land in a field of opium poppies, wake up and see this Emerald City. *Peter Pan*? Sprinkle some white dust cocaine on your head and you can fly."

Of course, back in Victorian times, drugs like opium, cocaine and cannabis were legal and prescription-free, so perhaps that seemingly uptight era had more in common with hippy counterculture than we think. It might explain the Victorians' affection for fairy paintings, which depict enchanted parallel worlds populated by pixies, sprites, elves — and plentiful mushrooms.

If the fly agaric is often aligned with a liberation of the mind, another mushroom with psychedelic properties, *Psilocybe semilanceata*, was a symbol of casting off more literal chains during the French Revolution. British poet Samuel Taylor Coleridge is considered the first to have nicknamed this small, conical mushroom the "liberty cap" while writing about the unfolding uprising. He spotted the similarity between the mushroom and the "bonnet rouges" — the red, Smurf-like caps adopted by angry mobs storming the Tuileries — writing, "it seems offered by Nature herself as the appropriate emblem of Gallic republicanism".

But where one Romantic poet saw a spirit of freedom and rebellion in the mushroom, another was less beguiled. Percy Bysshe Shelley and his wife Mary were staying in Pisa in the spring of 1820, grieving their young son's recent death. Contemplations of mortality are laced throughout "The Sensitive Plant", a poem he wrote in the Italian city, ostensibly about a garden shifting through the seasons: "And agarics, and fungi, with mildew and mould / Started like mist from the wet ground cold; / Pale, fleshy, as if the decaying dead / With a spirit of growth had been animated!"

Arthur Conan Doyle found similarly doomy associations in fungi: his novel *Sir Nigel* (1905–06), set in England during the Hundred Years' War and against the backdrop of the bubonic plague, uses the mushroom as a harbinger of death: "The fields were spotted with monstrous fungi of a size and colour never matched before — scarlet and mauve and liver and black. It was as though the sick earth had burst into foul pustules; mildew and lichen mottled the walls, and with that filthy crop Death sprang also from the water-soaked earth."

Conan Doyle's ominous vision of the fungi as parasite was taken up by DH Lawrence, who compared the mushroom with male members of the English middle classes in his vitriolic 1917 poem "How Beastly the Bourgeois Is". Written at a time of social and labour unrest in the country (approximately one million working days were lost to strikes the year he wrote it), Lawrence let rip at the entitled few. He writes: "Nicely groomed, like a mushroom / standing there so sleek and erect and eyeable and like a fungus, living on the remains of bygone life / sucking his life out of the dead leaves of greater life / than his own." He goes on, hitting the point home: "What a pity they can't all be kicked over / like sickening toadstools, and left to melt back, swiftly / into the soil of England."

That link with the grotesque, with disease and infection, was picked up in 20th-century sci-fi literature and combined with the mushroom's slightly unsettling, shapeshifting, otherworldly quality. HP Lovecraft harnessed mushroom creepiness to uncanny effect, filling multiple stories with fungoid aliens, starting with his chilling novella *The Whisperer in the Darkness* (1931), in which the creatures infest the Vermont hills and come seeping out of the rivers. They then surgically extract people's brains to store in jars and peel off human faces to plaster over themselves as disguises.

Fungi are also invading extraterrestrials in Ray Bradbury's paranoia-infused sci-fi short story "Come into My Cellar", published in *Galaxy Magazine* in 1962. This time, they invade Earth via the surprising route of mail-order mushroom kits. Something of a Cold War allegory, children begin planting these nefarious jumbo-sized organisms in their basements, unwittingly home-growing a hostile army across America. The story was reportedly based on a lunch Bradbury had with friends: "I was eating steak and mushrooms with a group of editors from a magazine. I said: 'What if these mushrooms are creatures from another world, which landed in the deep south and grew up in a swamp! When we eat them we become monsters, and take over the earth.' They all laughed at the idea, but I thought it was great.

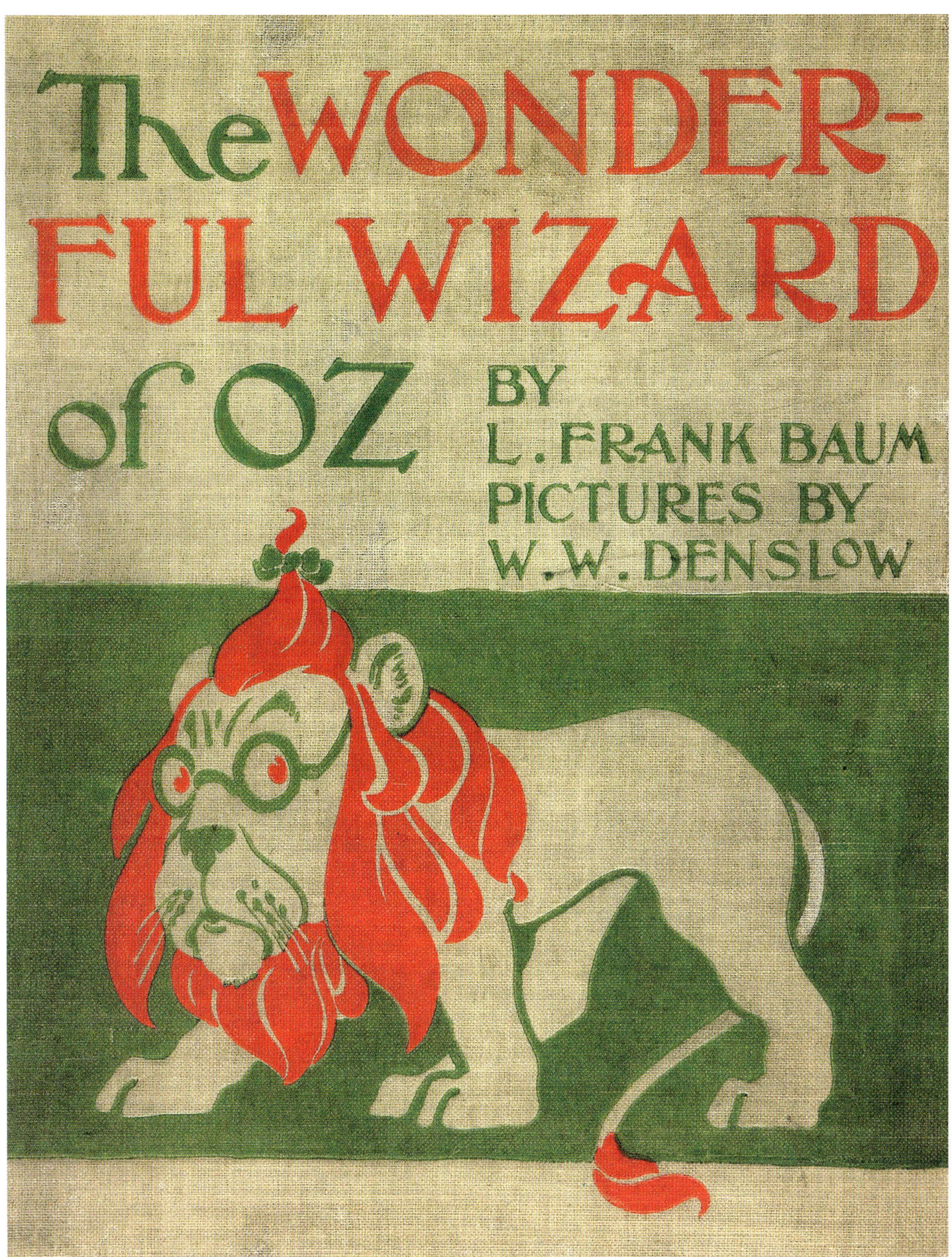

L Frank Baum and **William Denslow**
The Wonderful Wizard of Oz, 1900

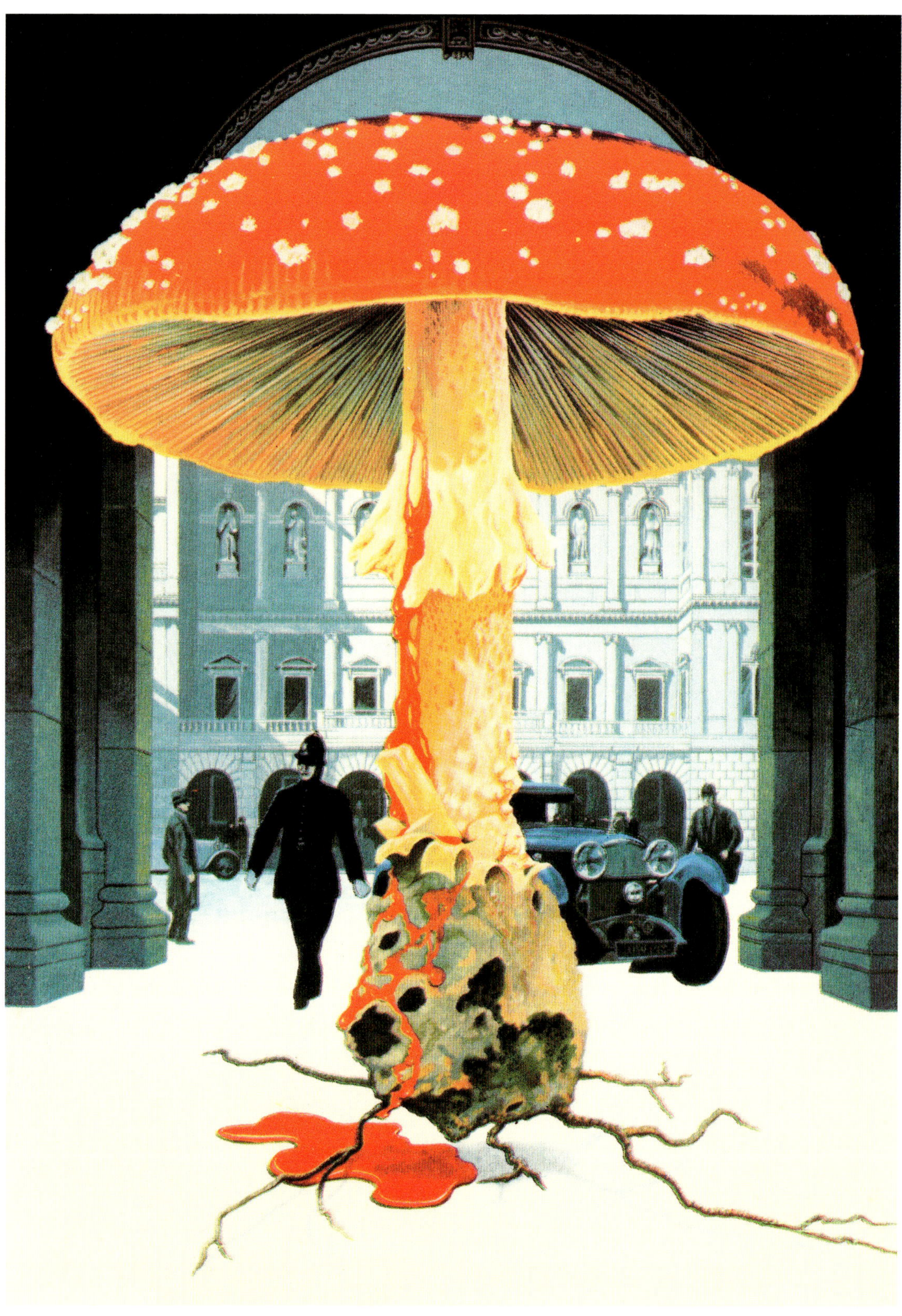

Dorothy L Sayers
The Documents in the Case, 1930 (1981 cover)

I wrote it as a story and sold it to a Hitchcock series. I sent them all a copy of it when it was published… as far as I know we have all been off mushrooms ever since." Considering Bradbury is a writer who anticipated the iPod, interactive television, electronic surveillance and live, televised police chases, his species of mushroom alien might not be as far-fetched as we hope.

When it comes to love, the mushroom has a chequered history. HG Wells sends his unhappily married protagonist in *The Purple Pileus* (1896) into the woods to contemplate taking his own life with a toxic mushroom. Instead, he has a mind-opening experience that changes the course of his life, and marriage, decisively for the better. But it's the opposite in Tolstoy's evergreen 1878 masterpiece *Anna Karenina,* in which mushrooms are the death knell of a marriage proposal: "It would have been better for Varenka to be silent. After a silence it would have been easier for them to say what they wanted to say than after talking about mushrooms," writes the Russian literary lion. As it turns out, the question "What is the difference between the birch mushroom and the white mushroom?" decisively destroys the mood. "Varenka's lips quivered with emotion as she answered: 'In the top part there is scarcely any difference; it's in the stalk.' And as soon as these words were uttered, both he and she felt that it was over…"

Mushrooms don't only murder love, they've proven handy murder weapons in crime fiction. In Dorothy L Sayers's *The Documents in the Case* (1930), an apparently accidental death leaves "a grotesquely grinning corpse" in a Devonshire cottage, discovered with a dish of mushrooms at its side. And deadly mushrooms crop up in no less than four Agatha Christie stories, including 1925's *The Secret of Chimneys* (poisoned sage and mushroom soup) and 1968's *By the Pricking of My Thumbs* (poisoned mushroom stew). In children's fiction, the King of the Elephants in *Babar* (1931) dies by accidentally eating a mushroom, leading the beloved titular elephant to be crowned. Unlike in Christie's murder mysteries, though, there's no suggestion of skulduggery.

Sylvia Plath credited the mushroom with a different kind of power — one that belies their mostly diminutive form. Her poem "Mushrooms" was completed in 1959 when she was 27 and pregnant with her first child. It was written at an artist's retreat in Saratoga Springs, where local woods brimmed with fungi. Plath anthropomorphises them as a quietly subversive, resilient and ever-multiplying force of nature: "Overnight, very / Whitely, discreetly, / Very quietly / Our toes, our noses / Take hold on the loam, / Acquire the air…" Often interpreted as an allegory for feminist liberation, Plath sees a thread of hope in the mushroom, or at least a drive as indomitable as the fetus growing in her womb: "Nudgers and shovers / In spite of ourselves. / Our kind multiplies: / We shall by morning / Inherit the earth. / Our foot's in the door."

Back in the 1950s, the ill-starred writer couldn't have known that the subjects of her poem might also have provided a lifeline through her deep depressions. As author and essayist Maria Popova writes of Plath: "It is both a hope and a heartache to consider that, today, mushroom species from the genus *Psilocybe* are being used in clinical trials to effectively allay treatment-resistant depression — a breakthrough she never lived to see that might have saved her life."

Fairy Rings & Satanic Milk Churns

Fungi in Folklore

Shakespeare's *A Midsummer Night's Dream,* Act II, opens with a conversation between resident trickster Puck and a fairy, who recounts her royal duties: "And I serve the Fairy Queen / To dew her orbs upon the green." This is a poetic reference to the natural occurrence known as fairy rings (aka elf rings or pixie rings). These circles of mushrooms spring up naturally in woodlands and grassy areas, with around 60 different mushroom species known to appear in such a pattern. Although modern science reveals fairy rings to be the product of fungal mycelium forming around necrotic zones of dead grass, Western European folklore has other ideas. According to legend, when the fair folk gather to perform their round dance, rings of mushrooms sprout up from each tiny footstep.

Richard Dadd is a famous practitioner of the 19th-century art genre called fairy painting, and his narrative, extravagant pictures often include mushrooms as convenient seats for sprites. In his *Titania Sleeping* from 1841, Dadd treats us to a dreamy scene where the titular Fairy Queen, from *A Midsummer Night's Dream,* is lulled into slumber by the drops of a magic flower administered to her eyelids by her royal counterpart, King Oberon. Titania is comfortably thronged by dancing fairy servants to her side; an impish orchestra perches upon an arch of blossoming flowers above her head; and many toadstools glisten in the grass below. Perhaps this compositional spiral — featuring fairy and fungi in circular harmony — is Dadd's romantic nod to the lore of fairy rings.

As enchanting as all this might sound, visiting these mushroom-dotted, hallowed sites is not recommended. To the Victorians, fairies were unpredictable tricksters at best. If a wayward traveller is lured into their merrymaking, folk wisdom warns they might never escape. Rendered invisible to other humans and unable to escape the ring, interlopers are damned to dance until the point of exhaustion, death or madness.

Leaning further into mischief — and perhaps evil — another sinister superstition, hailing from the Netherlands, attributes the curious circles to where the Devil, weary from a day of evil deeds, sets down his accursed milk churn. The Germans also blamed Satan and his devotees for the fungal phenomenon. Substitute sorcerers for fairies and you get the *Hexenringe* or "witches ring". In this tradition, the dancing affair is called Hexennacht (Witches' Night) and happens exclusively from dusk on 30th April to dawn on 1st May. Also known as Walpurgisnacht, this twilight festival makes use of a temporary window when the veil between worlds becomes thin, amplifying all magical endeavours. The sorcerers seeking to carouse with the Evil One would assemble on the Brocken, the highest peak on the Harz Mountains in Northern Germany. God-fearing local peasantry would burn fires on the surrounding hillsides in an attempt to ward off blasphemous influences threatening themselves and their livestock. The alleged aftermath of this night, besides charred bonfire remains and terrified German children, was the unholy circles of mushrooms borne from the witches' anticlockwise dance steps.

When it comes to fairy rings, science and legend agree on one fundamental aspect: a circle of growth, movement and life surrounding a territory of stillness, death or worse. Poetic to be sure, but for your next hike on the Brocken, a healthy dose of trepidation just might save you from a danceathon involving a satanic milk churn.

OPPOSITE
John Anster Fitzgerald, *The Intruder,* c.1860

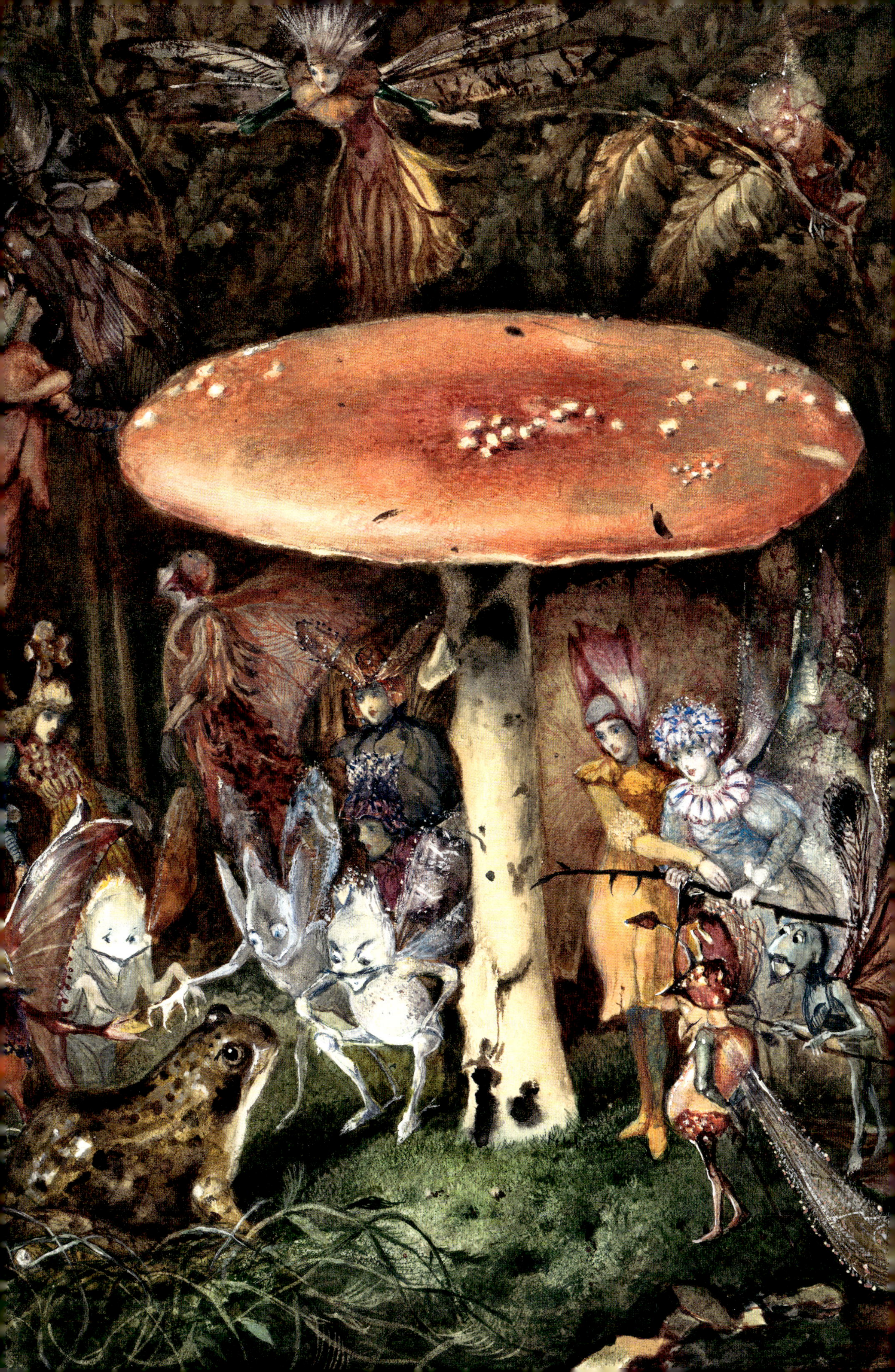

Lingzhi, the Enchanted Mushroom

For millennia, mushrooms have had such a venerated status in Chinese culture that some have achieved the level of myth. In particular, the lingzhi mushroom (more commonly known by its Japanese name reishi) has a longstanding place in traditional Chinese medicine and folklore. Today, it is used mainly as a supplement, prized for enhancing energy, vitality and mental clarity. The word *lingzhi* (灵芝) translates as "herb of spiritual potency", and appears in ancient documents and artwork dating back as far as 2,400 years. The mahogany fan-shaped fungus was likely used medicinally for thousands of years before that, and is most often consumed in teas, powders and tinctures.

Not content with having an impressive name and being one of China's earliest rulers (around 3,000 BCE), legend says Yan the Flame Emperor was also the founder of agricultural farming in China, and the patron of a seminal text on medicinal plants. In *Shennong Ben Cao Jing* (The Divine Farmer's Materia Medica), Yan extolled the lingzhi's virtues, claiming that "it may make the body light, prevent senility, and prolong life". Unsurprisingly, this supposed giver of eternal life was a favourite among rulers. Ceremonial sceptres called *ruyi*, meaning "fulfilment of wishes", took the shape of the lingzhi, and were wielded by generations of Chinese emperors as the ultimate symbol of imperial power.

But deathlessness is an idea that flourished beyond palace walls. Prevalent throughout ancient China, Taoism held that people could become immortal by deeply connecting with nature, whether via meditation, redirecting sexual energies — through practices described as testicle breathing and ovarian kung fu — or eating certain foods, including the lingzhi. The quest for eternal life via mushrooms is often woven into the Taoist myths of the Isles of the Blessed, said to be the home of immortals, free from death and suffering.

Once free-floating in the ocean, legends say these islands were stabilized by great turtles after sages residing there petitioned the highest gods to stop the islands from drifting. Quite possibly

OPPOSITE The Eight Immortals with the God of Longevity saluting the Queen Mother, Qing dynasty (1644–1911)

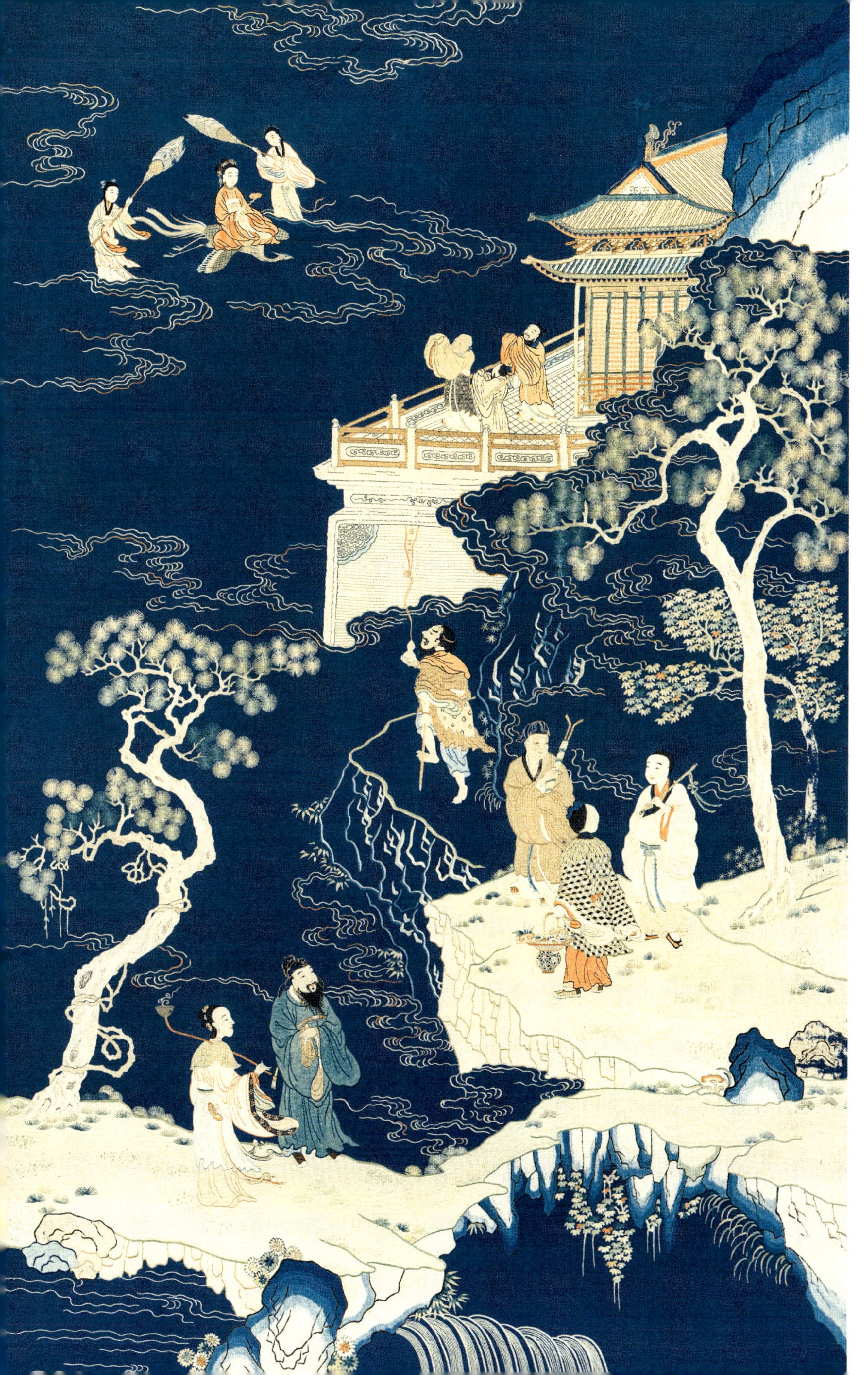

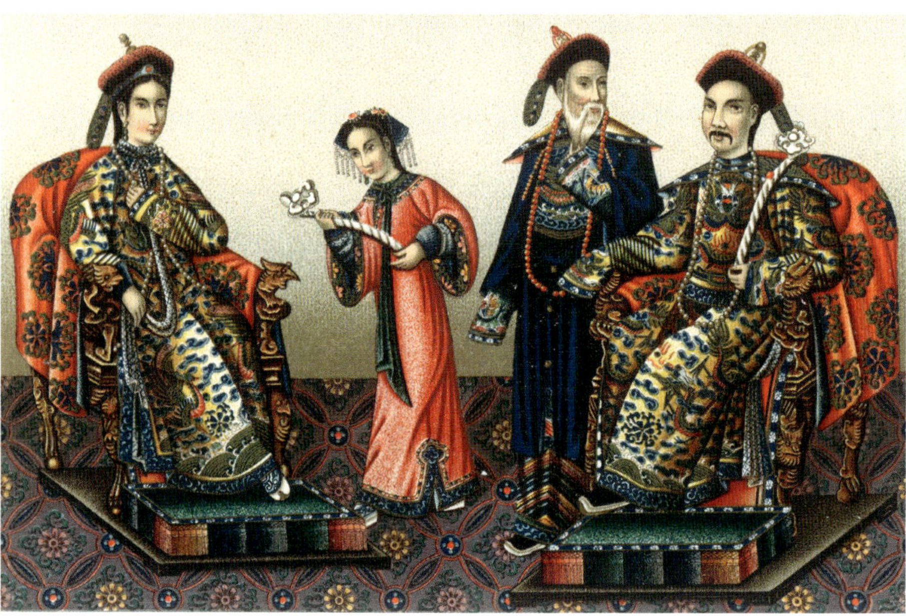

the first superhero group, these beings were known as the Eight Immortals (or The Blessed), who had achieved everlasting life after practising Taoism — and munching on mushrooms.

According to the myths, the islands' soil was so rich and potent that anyone who consumed its flora or fruit restored their youth and — in some legends — gained the ability to float from island to island. This primordial superfood was believed to sprout from the trunk of the mythical Chinese Tree of Life, a divine plant that grew only in the most holy and unspoiled areas of the islands' mountainous terrain. The mystical lingzhi was said to be an essential part of the Immortals' diet, allowing island denizen and Taoist wizard Anqi Sheng — on top of his invisibility superpowers — to grow to a ripe and wrinkly age of 1,000 years.

The Isles of the Blessed were not just allegory; they were believed to exist in the East China Sea, off the coast of Shandong Province. Emperors regularly dispatched expeditions to find them, including two in 219 and 210 BCE by Emperor Qin Shi Huang, ruler of the Qin Dynasty, who feared death more than anything else and became obsessed with discovering a cure. Qin Shi Huang dispatched loyal mariner Xu Fu to find the islands and retrieve lingzhi mushrooms — or whatever life-giving elixirs he could get from the Immortals. In some retellings, Xu Fu does indeed find the islands, only to be sent packing by wrathful deities.

In another version, his path is blocked by a sea monster. In still another, he is sent with 3,000 virgin boys and girls to appease any god that might stand in his way. All versions of the myth end the same way: Xu Fu never returns, and Emperor Qin Shi Huang dies — likely poisoned by mercury he mixed into a concoction that he hoped would grant him eternal life.

Another tale speaks of the Taoist sage Peng Zu, a nutrition expert, promoter and practitioner of sex therapies, libertine and all-around philanderer who lived over 800 years, had over 100 wives and fathered countless children well into his 450th year. Alongside Taoist practices, Peng is sometimes said to have attributed his longevity to lingzhi. He was also known to cook a stellar ginseng–chicken soup. Then there's the myth of

Racinet Albert Charles Auguste
Imperial Family of China, c.1888

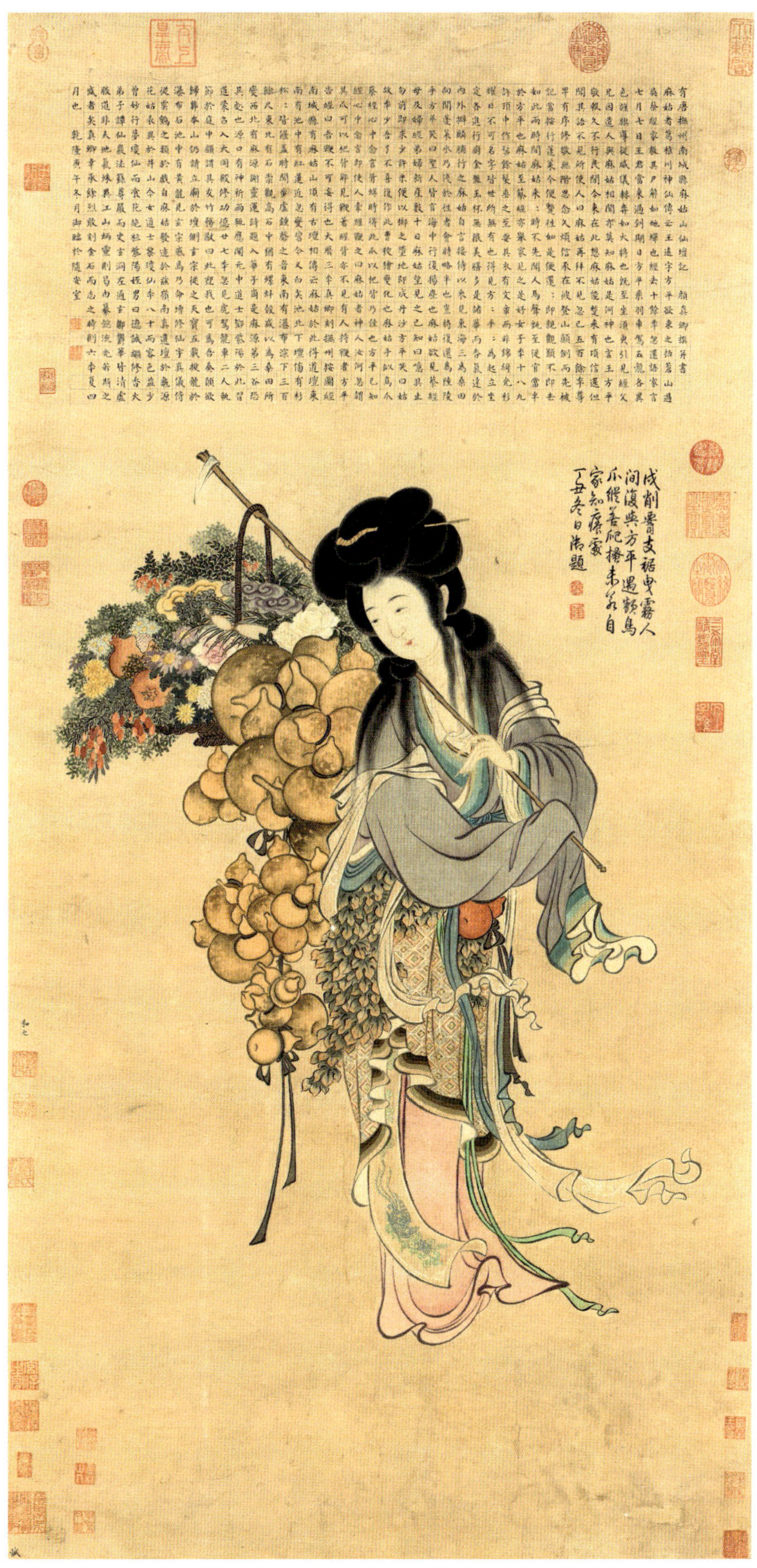

Ma Hezhi
Portrait of the Immortal Hemp Lady Magu, 12th–17th century

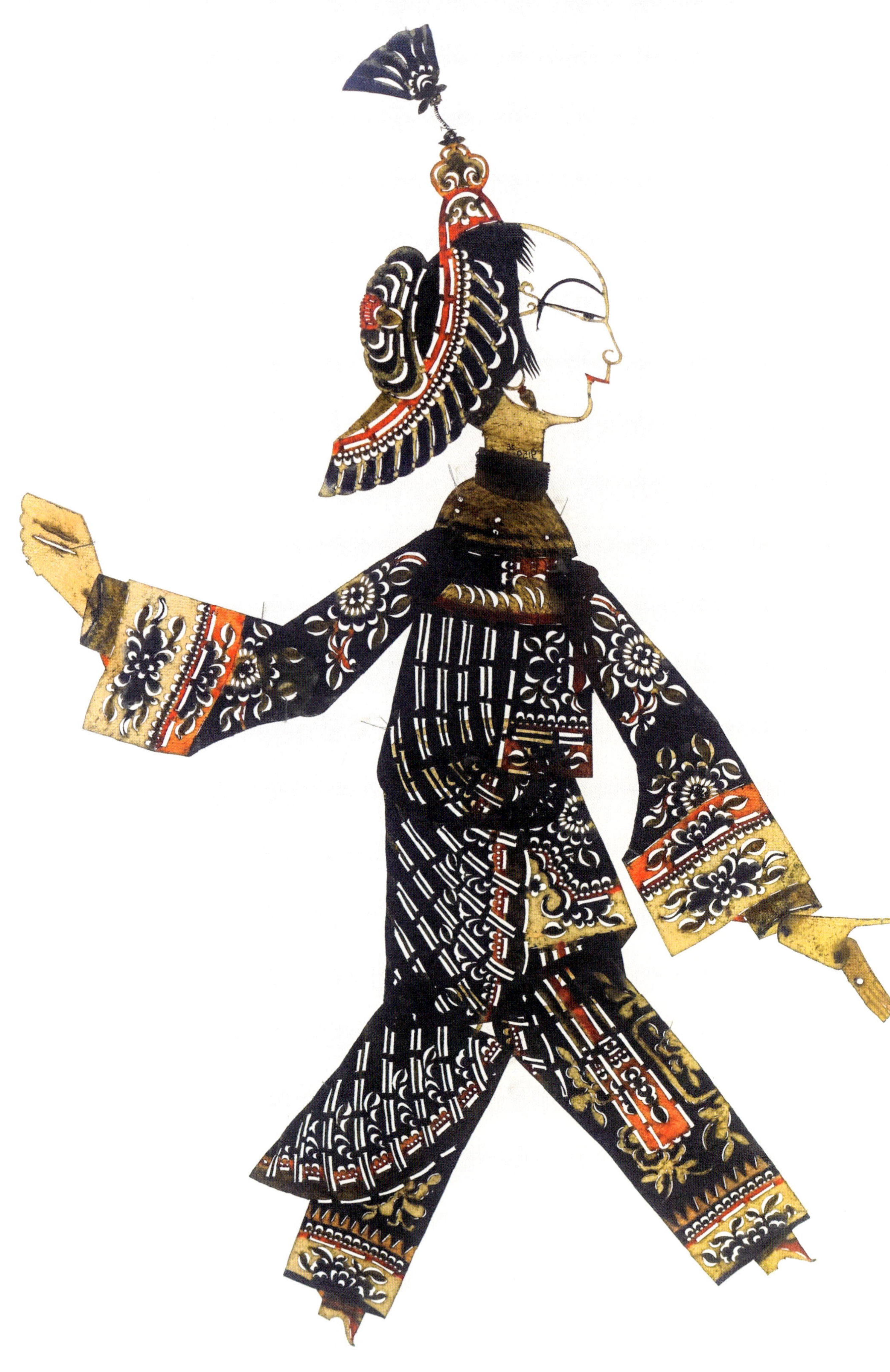

party animal Magu, who lived on one of the Isles of the Blessed and used water from 13 mountain springs to brew lingzhi wine for the queen's birthday. After letting it age for 13 years, Magu changed her mind and drank the wine herself, becoming immortal. To this day, Magu is associated with birthday celebrations and wishes of fortune and longevity. She is portrayed as having healing powers, and is believed to have gifted the world with both cannabis and lingzhi.

Arguably, the most famous lingzhi tale is the legend of the white snake. After a mystical serpent from Mount Emei transforms into a young woman named Bai Suzhen, she meets Xu Xian, a young man who offers up his umbrella one rainy day. In true meet-cute fashion, they instantly fall in love, tie the knot and open a medicine shop. Soon, however, a meddling local abbot warns Xu Xian of his new wife's true serpentine nature, one that can be revealed by drinking a wine made from realgar, a ruby red crystalline mineral also known as "arsenic blende".

Despite his initial disbelief, Xu Xian can't shake the idea that his wife might be a serpent in disguise, and eventually Bai Suzhen is tricked into drinking the wine, which indeed reveals her true form to be a white snake. Shocked by his wife's true nature, Xu Xian dies on the spot. The grieving Bai Suzhen, desperate to bring her beloved back to life, embarks on a perilous quest to the Kunlun Mountains to procure the magical lingzhi. Her unwavering resolve touches the heart of the Old Man of the South Pole — the divine guardian of the lingzhi — who grants access to the enchanted mushroom. With the magical fungus in hand, Bai Suzhen resurrects her beloved. Upon waking, Xu Xian realizes the depth of her genuine love and accepts her true nature, not caring that she is a snake or, apparently, that he is a zombie. This poignant and casually misogynistic tale of cross-species love has inspired countless literary works, theatrical performances, cinematic adaptations and artistic depictions throughout Chinese culture for centuries.

While its mythical properties are now viewed more symbolically, lingzhi retains its elevated status in China — to the tune of several thousand tonnes cultivated annually and a billion-dollar industry. Traditional Chinese medicine practitioners prescribe lingzhi to control blood glucose levels, improve the immune system, regulate liver function, calm the mind and relieve asthma, while Taoist teachings continue to revere it as a symbol of health, longevity, wisdom and spiritual enlightenment. In the end, whether resurrecting dead lovers, fuelling sex gurus or giving gods a good buzz, the lingzhi mushroom has secured its own immortal reputation.

OPPOSITE
A shadow puppet of Xu Xian, Qing dynasty (1644–1911)

A Trip to the Moon

Mushrooms at the Movies

Mushrooms were present during cinema's infancy, notably in magician-turned-film-mogul Georges Méliès 1902 silent short, *A Trip to the Moon,* widely considered the first-ever science fiction film. More than a century before *Avatar* (2009) put bioluminescent mushrooms on planet Pandora, Méliès took them galactic in his 12-minute Jules Verne-inspired spectacular, featuring a frenetic band of scientists who are shot into space in a tin-pot capsule which then crash lands into the moon's right eye.

The crew's subsequent investigation of an underground cavern turns up plentiful lunar mushrooms. Méliès was ahead of his time; these days, NASA is exploring the possibility of growing moon homes using a mixture of fungi and lunar dust. But Méliès' story was something of a warning against expansionist ambitions — his astronauts are beset by hostile insectoid extraterrestrials and forced to retreat to Earth.

Despite his status as a pioneer of film sci-fi, Méliès ended up selling toys in a Paris train station, and we're fortunate to be able to watch his sprouting moon mushrooms today. The film was nearly confiscated and melted down to make boot heels for soldiers during World War I — the fate of 400 other Méliès films. *A Trip to the Moon* survived, resurfacing in Spain in 1993 when it was donated by an anonymous collector to Filmoteca de Catalunya in Barcelona, its celluloid nitrate a little disintegrated but now restored to its Belle Époque glory.

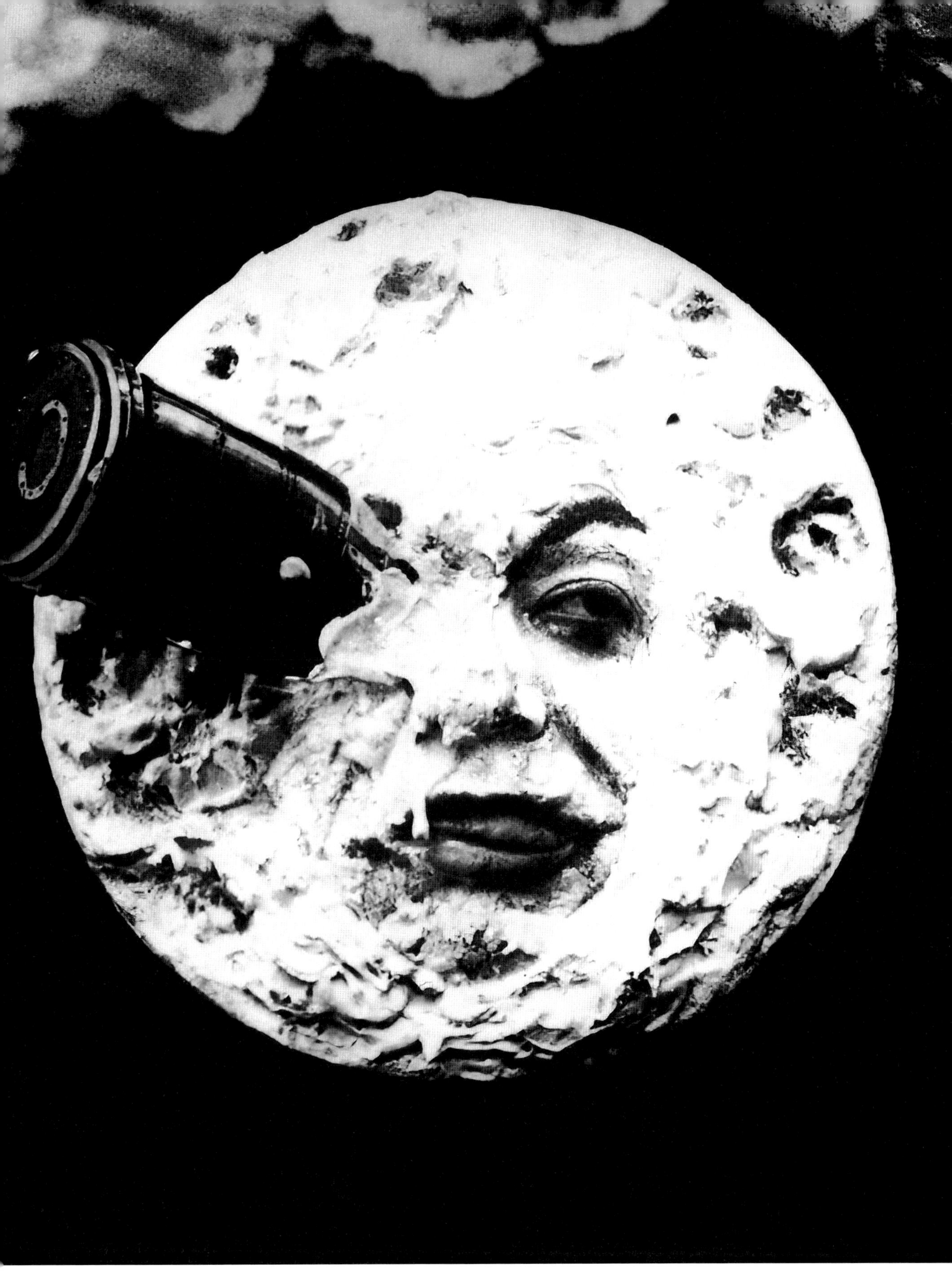

Georges Méliès
A Trip to the Moon, 1902 (still)

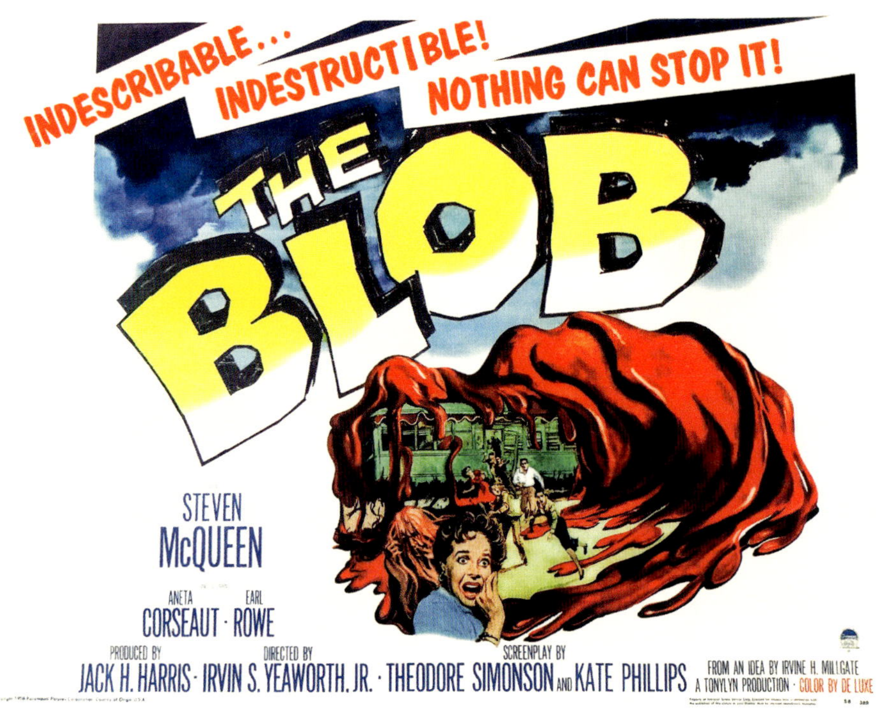

Perhaps because fungi are so adept at shape-shifting, more sci-fi films were to come. In 1958 schlocker *The Blob*, a blood-red organism, behaving like a slime mould, crashes to Earth in a meteorite and slithers around small-town Pennsylvania absorbing and digesting its human inhabitants until Steve McQueen, in his first starring role, figures out its vulnerability to cold temperatures. The Blob is eventually ditched in the Arctic, rendering it harmless (assuming the Arctic remains cold). Real slime moulds have differing traits to their celluloid counterpart but are every bit as remarkable: *Physarum polycephalum*, nicknamed "Le Blob" by French researcher Dr Audrey Dussutour, can heal itself, find the fastest way out of a maze, and has not one but 720 sexes — all without a central nervous system.

Like McQueen's film nemesis, some slime moulds, including Le Blob, are fairly invincible. In the 1970s, a Texan woman found a bright yellow slime mould known as dog vomit (*Fuligo septica*). "She used a garden hoe and smashed it, but the next day it had doubled in size," Dussutour said. "She tried to poison it with things she found in the garage, but it only changed colour and was still fine. She was scared, so she called the firemen, and they sprayed it with water, but it continued to grow. She then decided to call the police, and they shot it. The slime mould continued to grow, but then it simply disappeared because it went into sporulation."

Although many mycologists still study slime moulds, they are now considered to be protists, a catch-all term for any organism that is not quite animal, plant or fungus. Which is a good description for the monstrous creatures imagined by Japanese director Ishirō Honda, best known for *Godzilla* (1954) and much less known for atmospheric body horror *Matango* (1963), or *Fungus of Terror*. The plot centres on a wealthy group of holidaymakers whose yacht is shipwrecked on a tropical island. Tired of eating turtle eggs,

Irvin S Yeaworth Jr
The Blob, 1958 (poster)

they succumb to the mushrooms proliferating around them during the rainy season, despite dark warnings about their effects. At first, fungoid growths appear on their skin, and soon the castaways are mutating entirely into nightmarish mushroom-people.

Honda liked to smuggle serious social messages into his populist entertainments, and *Matango* has been interpreted as anti-drug, but it's also a devastating nuclear-age allegory: the ill-fated party's physical ailments resemble the radiation burns of victims of Hiroshima and Nagasaki so closely that the film was allegedly nearly banned. (*Matango* might have also inspired goofy 1960s US shipwreck sitcom *Gilligan's Island*, featuring a similarly motley crew of passengers but no parasitic mushrooms.)

Also dangerous to consume, but blowing the mind rather than the body, was the whipped-cream filling of colourful candy mushrooms in 1971's *Willy Wonka & the Chocolate Factory*. Some viewers have found it telling that shortly after these sweets are devoured, the Oompa-Loompa-paddled boat filled with sugar-guzzling children enters a tunnel in which some terrifyingly trippy visuals unfold — flying cockroaches, millipedes crawling over faces, a scorpion's mouth in close-up, a chicken being decapitated — as though they're experiencing a collective psychedelic freak-out. Director Mel Stuart was nonplussed by the charge in his book *Pure Imagination* (2001), explaining he simply intended to "heighten the drama".

"Here's their theory," he wrote of the rumours. "The mushroom filling eaten by the group before the boat enters the tunnel is peyote, a form of psychedelic mushroom. Their rationale for this theory is that Willy Wonka is a 'candy man', a street term for a drug dealer." (Conversely, Oliver Stone, the director of 1994's hallucinatory *Natural Born Killers*, has admitted to shooting pretty much the whole film under the influence of magic mushrooms.)

But the ultimate mushroom-trip-gone-sideways must surely have been endured by actor James Fox, in Nicolas Roeg and Donald Cammell's

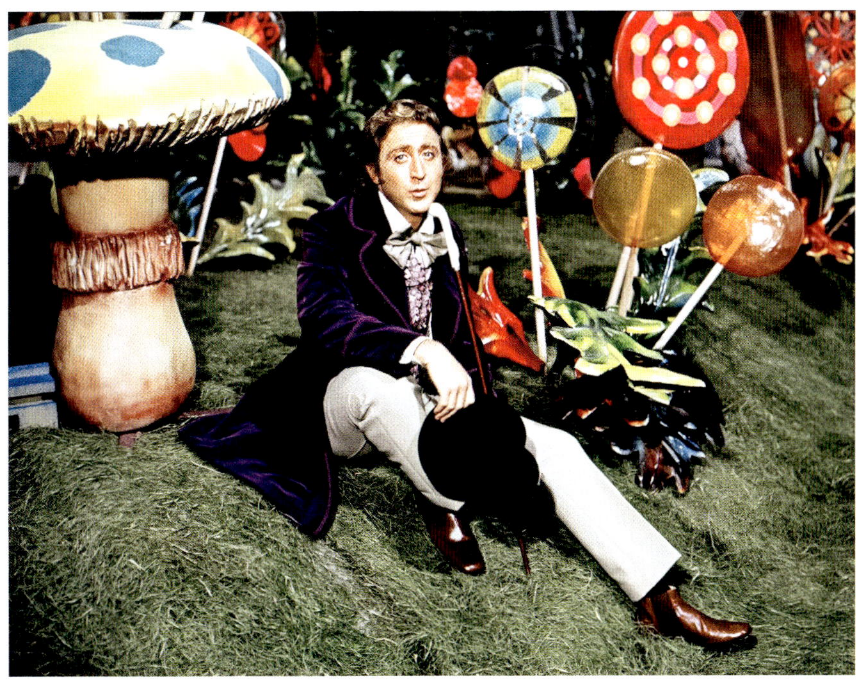

Mel Stuart
Willy Wonka & the Chocolate Factory, 1971 (still)

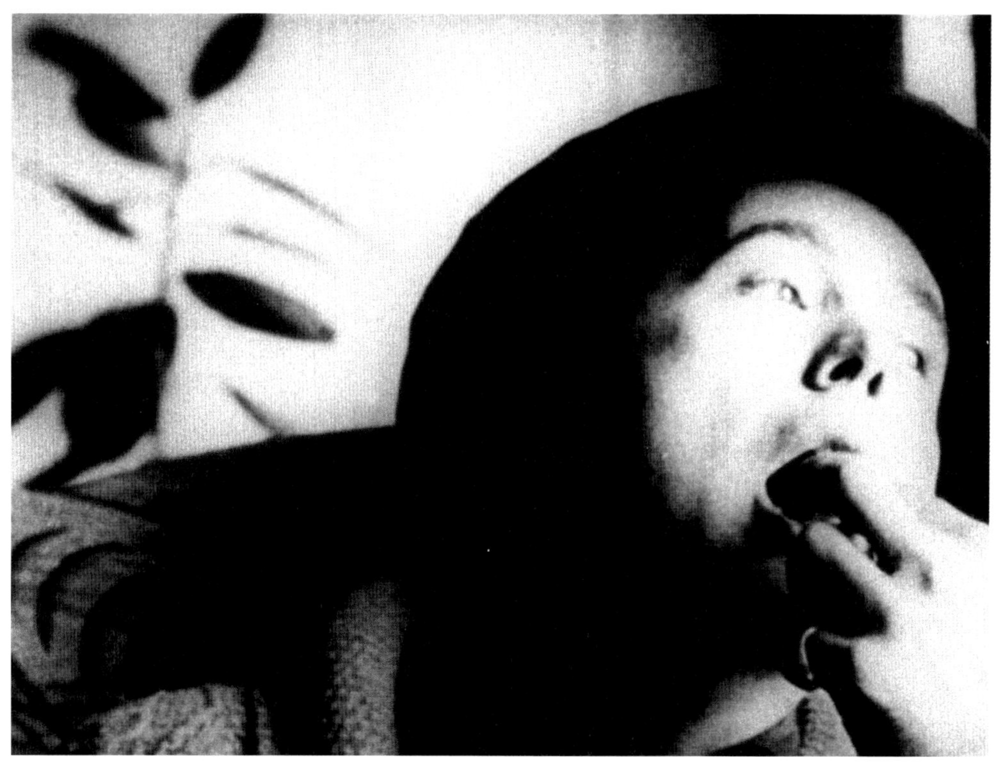

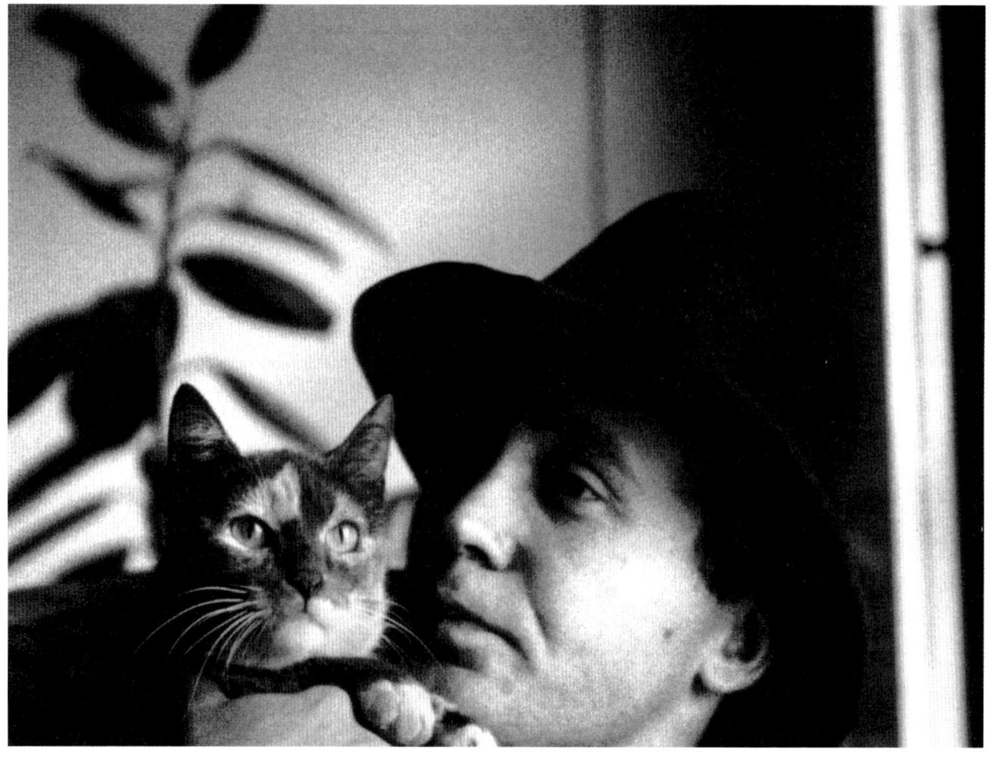

Andy Warhol
Eat, 1964 (stills)

Performance (1970), a phantasmagorical feature set in the seedy underside of libertine London. Starring Fox as a psychopathic East End gangster who's fed magic mushrooms by a reclusive rock star (Mick Jagger) and his sorceress of a partner (Anita Pallenberg) while hiding out in their crumbling Notting Hill lair, it's a tale of shattered identity that somewhat imitated the reality on set.

The role first possessed Fox and then propelled him into the wilderness, specifically the embrace of an evangelical Christian sect in northern England, for a decade. He eventually returned to acting in the early 1980s, but not to hallucinogens. Roeg meanwhile did revisit the mushroom much later with his supernatural horror *Puffball* (2007), named for *Calvatia gigantea,* a fungus so large it's often mistaken for an abandoned football in fields and hedgerows.

Some mushrooms are harder to spot. Truffles are mushrooms that have evolved to grow underground and thereby require the sensitive nose of a clever animal to seek them out, picking up on their earthy, aromatic smell. In *Pig* (2021), Nicolas Cage plays a former Michelin-starred chef turned intractable hermit, who returns to Portland's high-end dining scene when his precious truffle-hunting pig is stolen. The extreme lengths he's willing to go to retrieve his porcine companion aren't in the end about the eye-watering price a truffle can fetch — often a few thousand pounds per kilogram — but deeper motives buried, truffle-like, under the surface. The film's depiction of the multi-million-pound business isn't so far-fetched though — in reality, the high price of truffles has created a dangerous climate for animals, especially in Italy, where dogs have been surreptitiously dispatched with poisoned meatballs in truffle wars.

Poisonous mushrooms are employed as a twisted method of power and control in Paul Thomas Anderson's *Phantom Thread* (2017). Neatly chopped into a buttery omelette with chives, they're fed to Daniel Day-Lewis's impossibly fastidious haute couture dressmaker by his lover, sending him off to bed with a delirious fever and finally achieving her domination. The same year, Sofia Coppola's haunted collection of Southern belles in Civil War-era drama *The Beguiled* sauté poisonous wild mushrooms in butter and wine to dispose of a violent Yankee soldier. Adding the mushroom-murder-over-breakfast of an authoritarian father-in-law in *Lady Macbeth,* that year prompted multiple essays about the status of fungi as the undetectable feminist weapon of choice against male aggressors.

Despite their reputation, mushrooms have been eaten on film without adverse or apocalyptic effects. In 1964, Andy Warhol gave a single mushroom more than its 15 minutes when he shot artist Robert Indiana chewing one for a full 45 minutes, an experiment titled *Eat.* (Indiana was preoccupied with the word at the time, it being his mother's final one before she died.)

Indiana sits in a wooden rocking chair at his studio on Coenties Slip, a waterfront street at the tip of Manhattan, then home to a group of soon-to-be-famous artists who banded together for warmth and cheap warehouse space. He eats the mushroom, looks around the room, and is occasionally joined in the frame by his cat. The minimalist short was reportedly inspired by the lascivious, gluttonous tavern scene in Tony Richardson's adaptation of *Tom Jones* (1963). According to lore, Indiana deliberately starved himself the day before and brought a smorgasbord of fruits and vegetables to the shoot, but contrary Warhol chose just one mushroom and told him to make it last.

While Indiana's was an impressive feat of endurance, the last word in mushroom film magic goes to culinary French rat Remy, who rustles up an electrifying recipe in Pixar's *Ratatouille* (2007), with the help of a thunderstorm. The enthusiastic rodent combines a foraged chanterelle with tomme de chevre de pays, a fruity and nutty cheese, and is cooking it over a smoking chimney when it's accidentally struck by a bolt of lightning, causing his concoction to puff up like popcorn. A "burny, melty" dish it would be unwise to recreate at home.

FOLLOWING
Georges Méliès, *A Trip to the Moon*, 1902
(still from the colourised restoration, 2011)

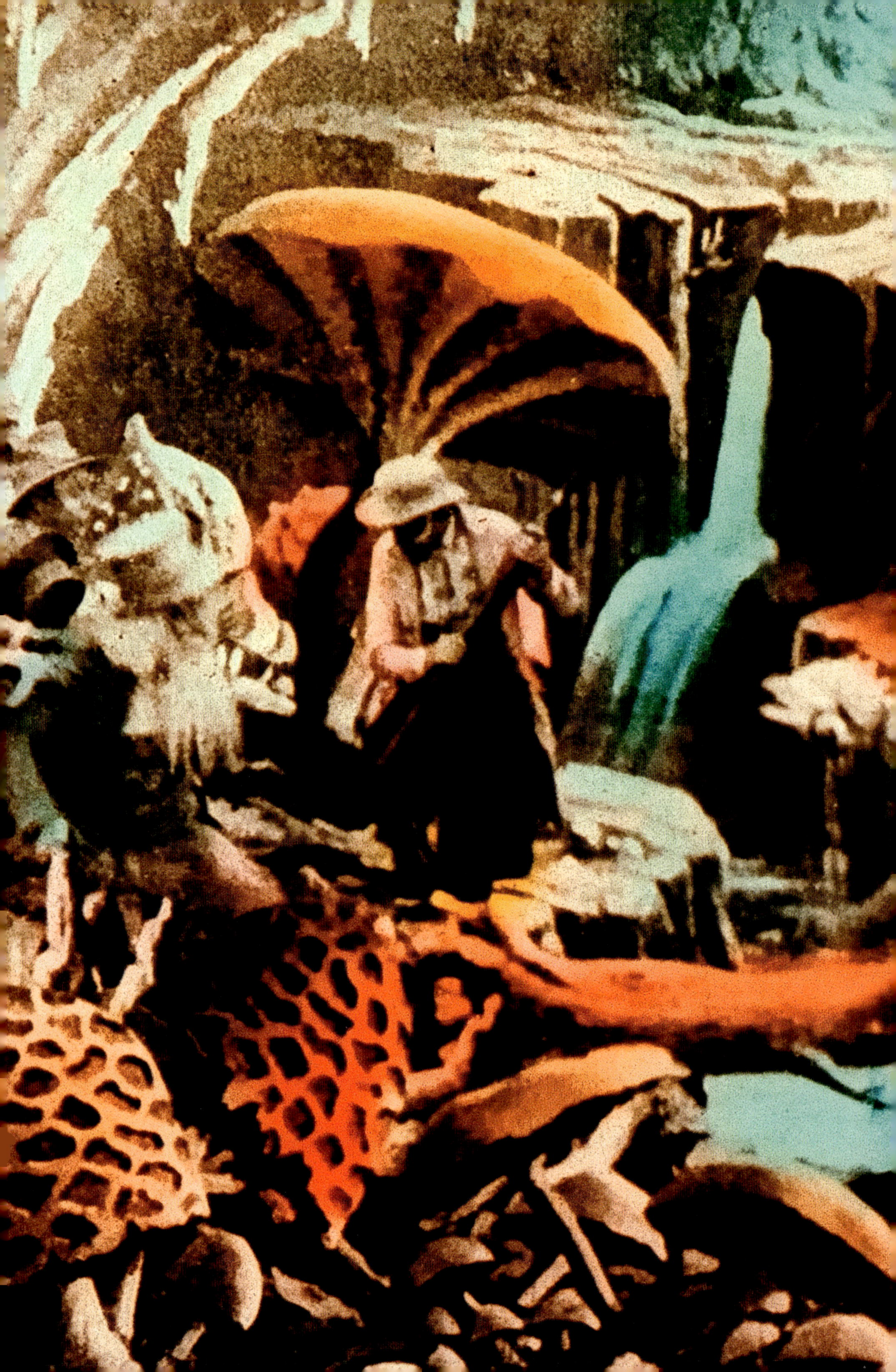

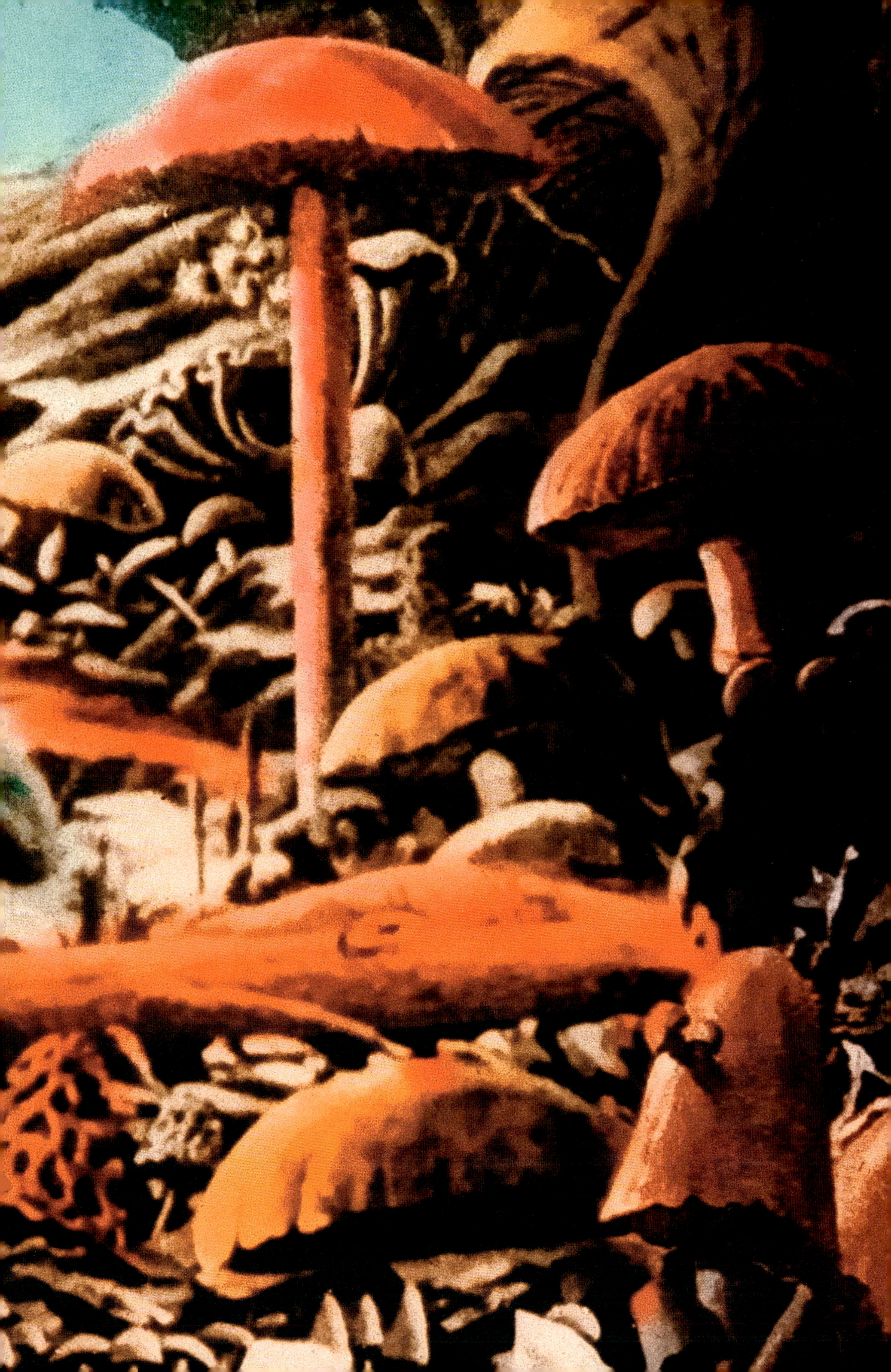

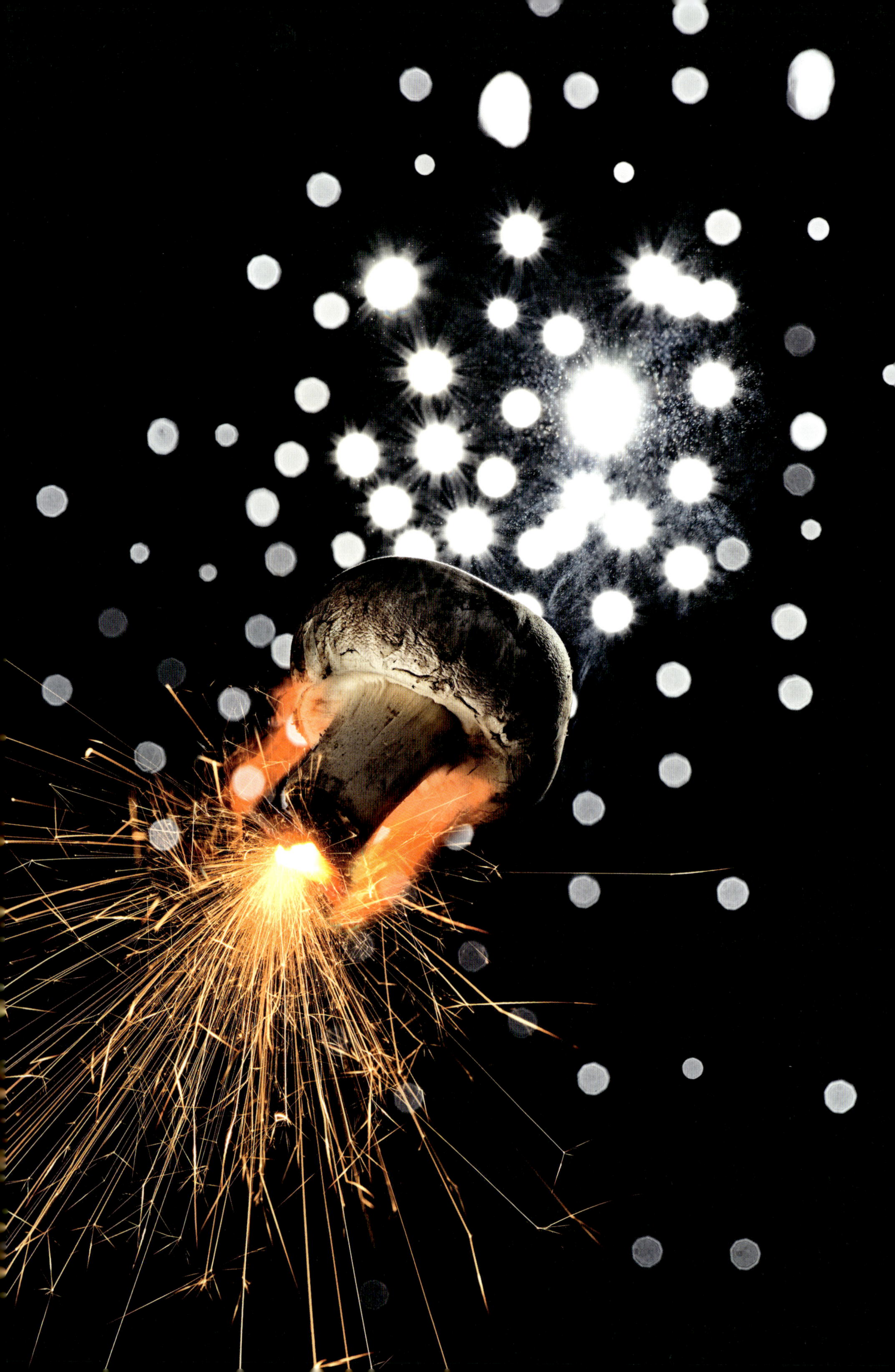

Mushrooms in Space

The nascent field of astromycology, the study of fungal biology throughout the universe, has an appropriately sci-fi origin story. Lauded American mycologist Paul Stamets was honoured by the writers of *Star Trek: Discovery*, who named a major character after him. The TV show, which ran for five seasons — from 2017 to 2024 — thus inspired Stamets to investigate the extraterrestrial applications of fungi.

Cementing his reputation as the closest thing mycology has to a bona fide rockstar, Stamets is partnering with NASA to explore how fungi might be used in a cosmic sense, and he projects that mushrooms will be indispensable to future space exploration. This collaboration has already identified the oyster mushroom's unparalleled ability to break down a synthetic version of Martian regolith, the layer of loose dust and small rocks that makes up the surface of planetary and other celestial bodies. Decomposing and restructuring regolithic hydrocarbons into carbohydrates — an essential nutrient for most life forms — is a critical step in producing rich soils to grow healthy food sources. Done on a massive scale to facilitate habitat regeneration, terraforming like this means your astronaut descendants won't be stuck slurping freeze-dried Tang for millennia.

In further tests, Stamets chose reishi mushrooms for their tough, woody and dense mycelium, growing it into large, solid mycelial blocks. To gauge their strength as a sustainable building material, the blocks were subjected to the crushing power of a stainless-steel hydraulic press — but it broke instead. Despite being able to withstand damage from enormous external pressure, these blocks are nonetheless easy to saw through.

Mushrooms, including reishi, also have excellent insulation properties. Made of carbon-rich, porous biological material that doubles as an excellent capacitor, mushroom mycelium can be processed into solar panels, essentially turning them into natural batteries. Some fungi exhibit remarkable resistance to radiation, suggesting they could be used to counter the harmful effects of cosmic radiation during space travel. What does this all amount to? Instead of launching tonnes of nails, AAA batteries and lead aprons across the solar system, we may only need a few spores to grow a sustainable, powered-gated community on Mars.

OPPOSITE
Bobby Doherty, *Untitled*, 2025

Mushrooms don't just have the right stuff to survive (and help humans thrive) in space, they might have originated there too. Stamets believes fungi were one of the first biological organisms on Earth, after the space debris that hosted them crash-landed here. This would make mushrooms a literal alien species, and one that might proliferate on other planets. Indeed, mushrooms seem to offer it all to the space traveller — food, housing, power, protection — but the next question is: how do we combat the feeling of crushing interplanetary loneliness that will surely impede the mental health of the first Martian colonies? With an abundance of research detailing how they help with PTSD, isolation and depression, psilocybin mushrooms could assist astronauts feel connected to both the universe and long guitar solos, while boosting creativity and emotional resilience to stay on mission.

But it's not all good news. Common fungi can form corrosive compounds which, coupled with their root-like hairs, called hyphae, allow them to deeply penetrate and damage materials like wood, stone and steel. This means spaceships are not immune to fungal infestations. In fact, hyphae were discovered on the Mir space station blossoming into mould that spread over windows and control panels, degrading critical components and parts of the interior hull.

Still, imagine this fungal future: you zip up your radiation-proof mushroom spacesuit, pull on your mushroom space boots, nibble on a magic mushroom to recalibrate your mental health, and wolf down your mushroom-enriched meal before rushing out of your insulated mushroom house to make it to your job at the mushroom-battery factory on time. Now, if only mushrooms could do your Mars taxes for you...

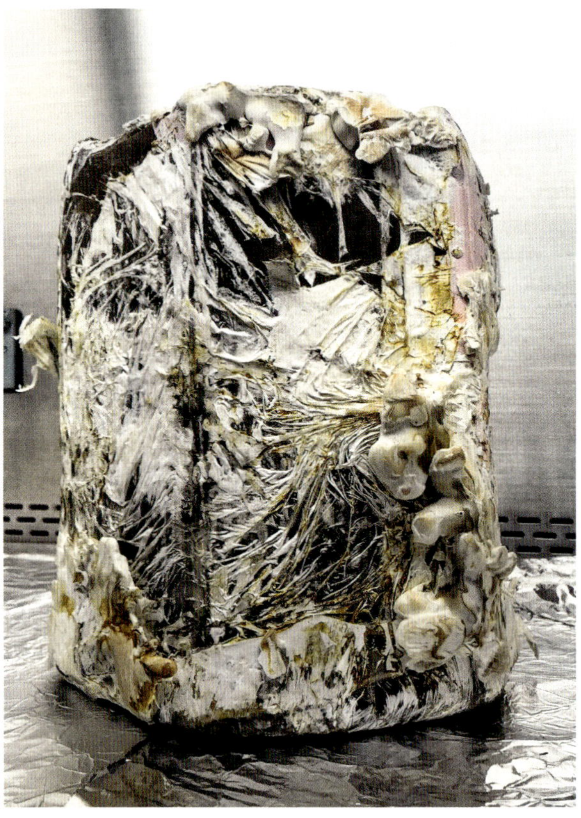

Stool by NASA constructed from mycelia after two weeks' growth, 2018

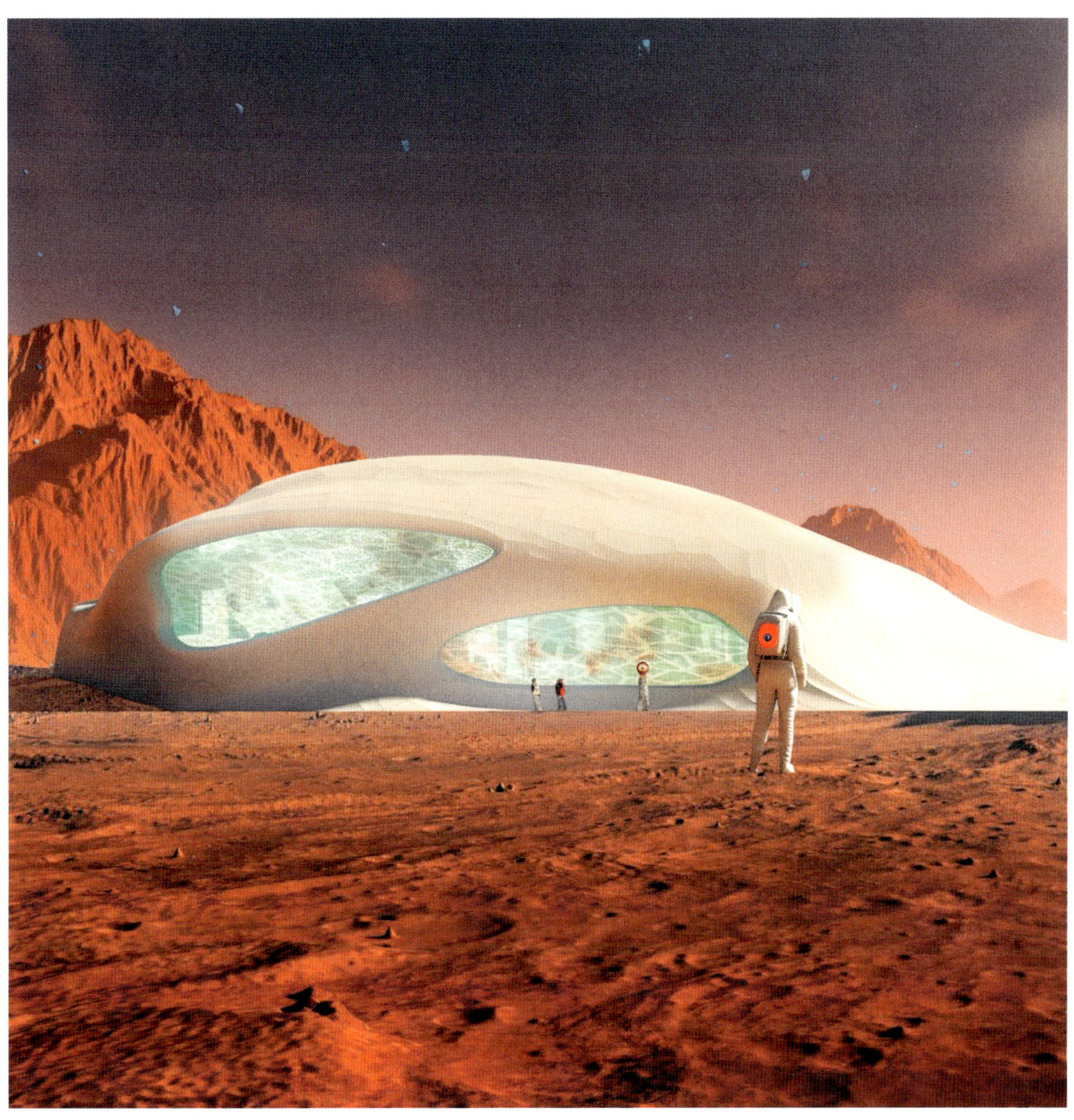

Redhouse Architects, mycelium architecture concept for Mars: MYCO for Mars, 2018
FOLLOWING **Takashi Homma**, *Fukushima*, 2011; **Takashi Homma**, *Fukushima, #14*, 2011

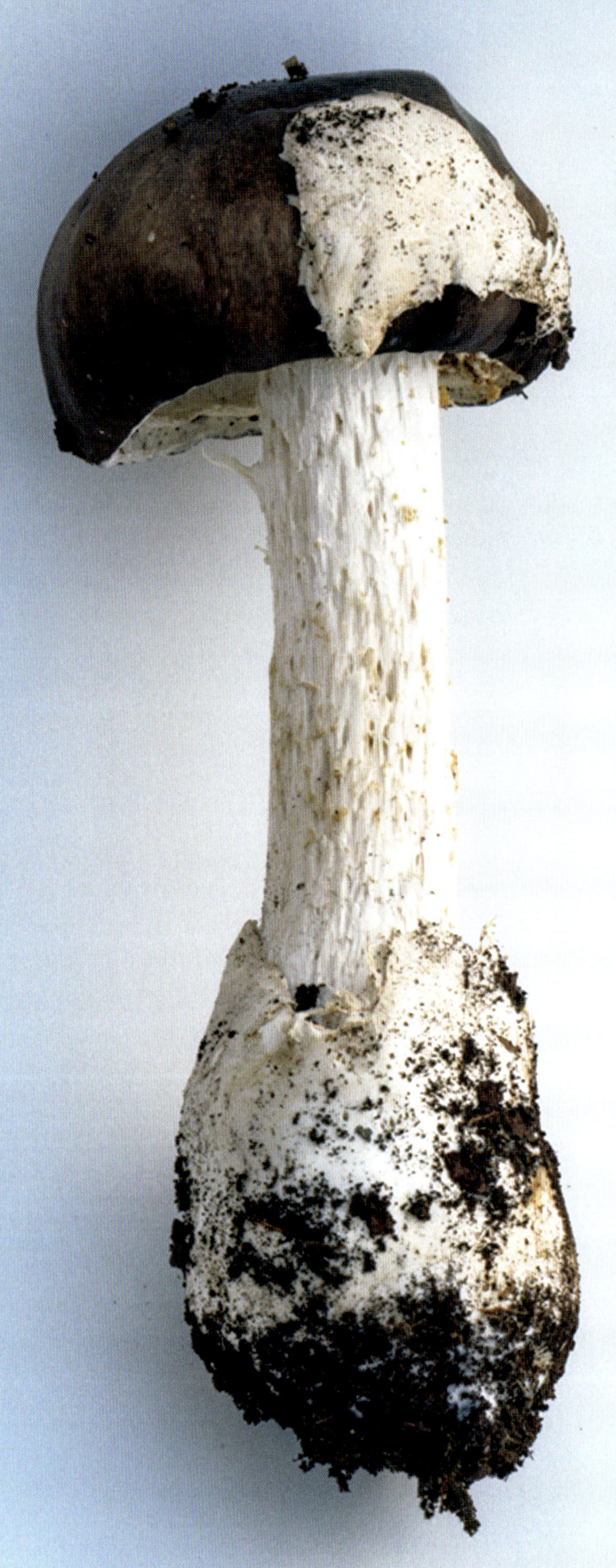

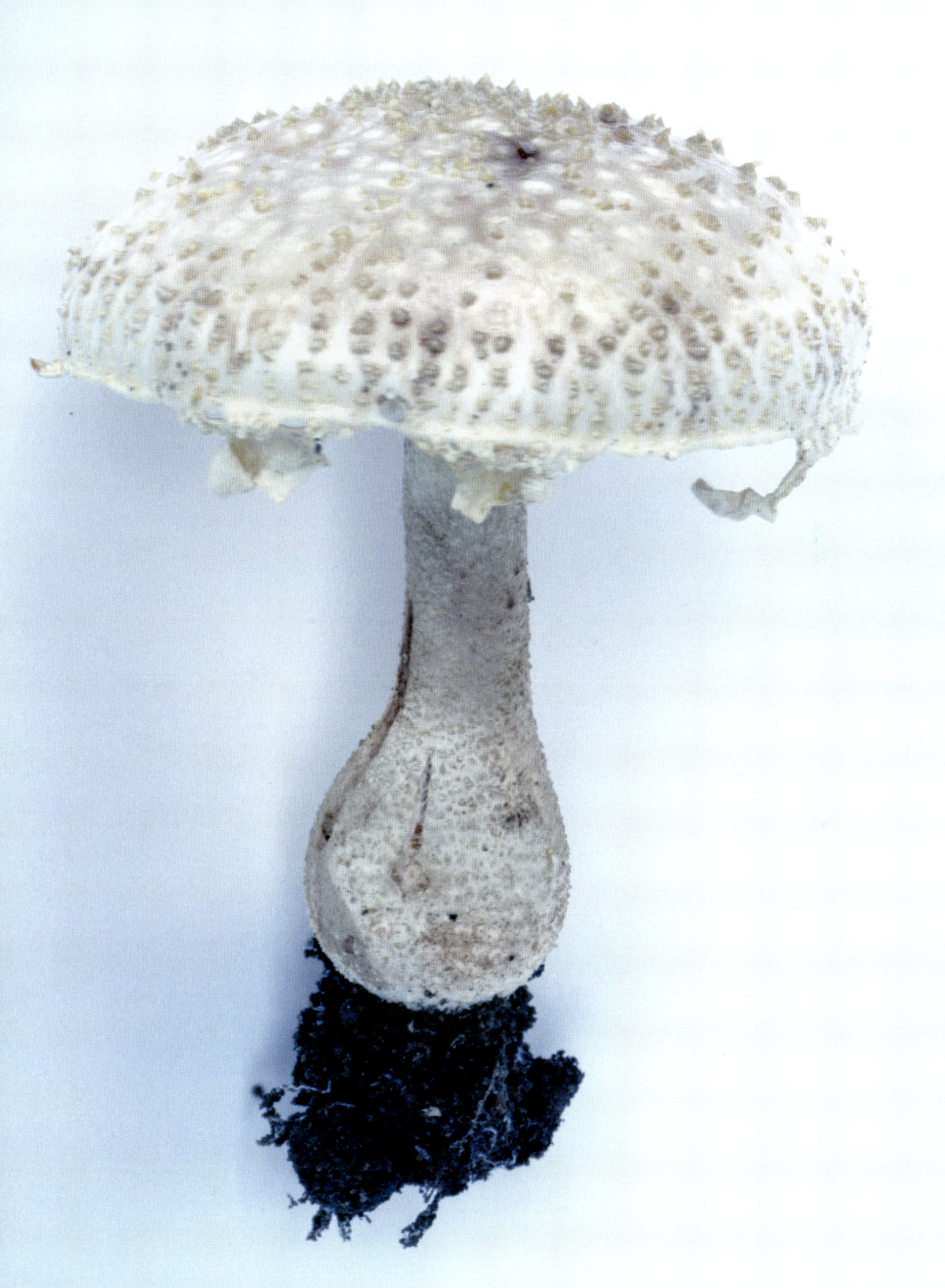

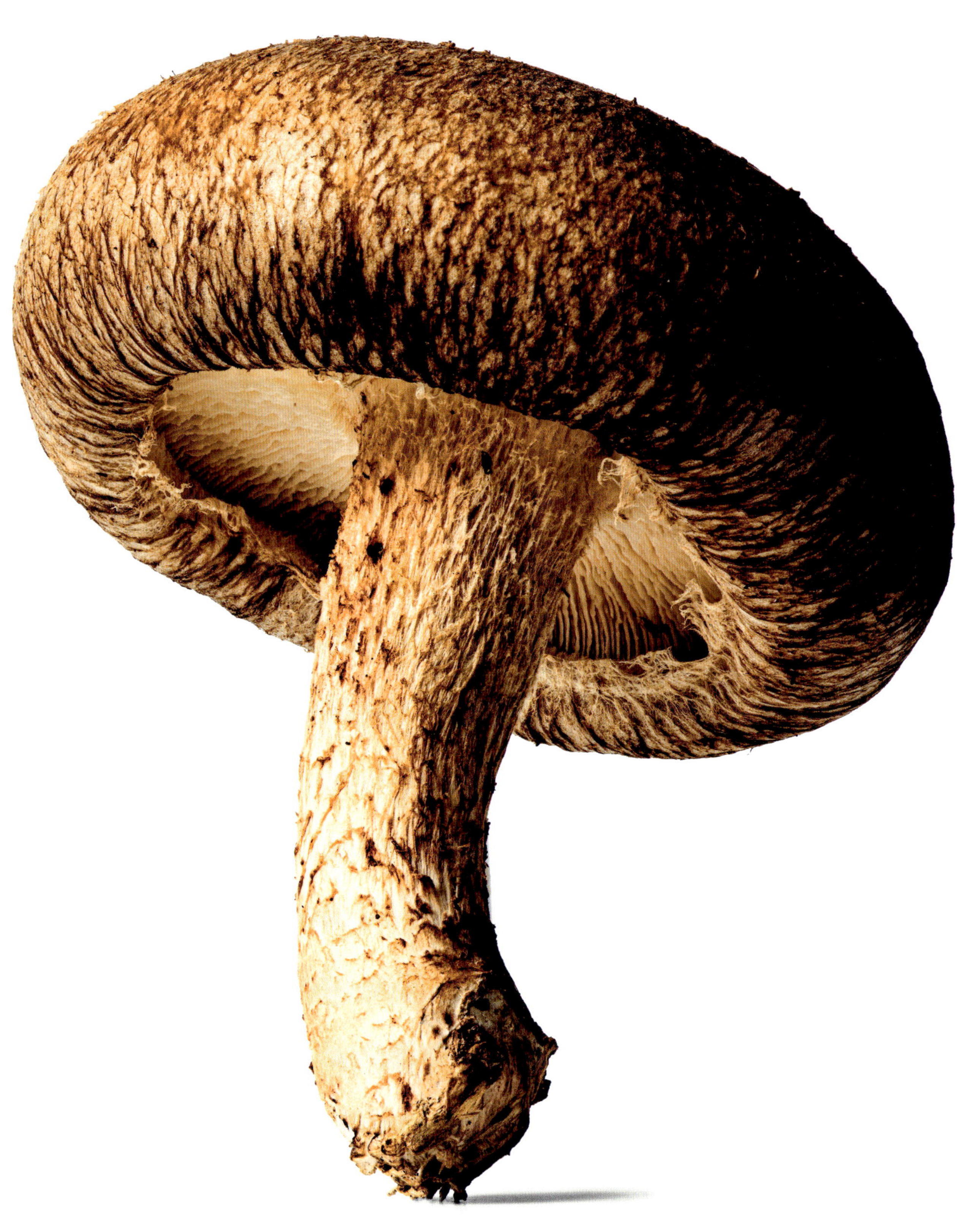

Recipes

RECIPE PHOTOGRAPHY **Bobby Doherty**
Food styling by **Jamie Kimm,** set design by **Noemi Bonazzi**
OPPOSITE **Bobby Doherty**, *Untitled,* 2025

Mushroom Tips

Cultivated mushrooms
Almost all fresh mushrooms found in shops are the same species (the common mushroom, *Agaricus bisporus*). Different names are used to indicate the maturity and colour of this cultivated mushroom:

Button mushrooms are the young, white variety with small, tightly closed caps. These have a mild flavour.

Closed-cup mushrooms are the white form that has started to mature; they are a bit larger and their caps are starting to open. These are still mild but have a firmer texture.

Chestnut mushrooms (also called cremini or baby bella) are also just maturing, but they are a brown variety. These are firmer than white mushrooms and have a deeper, earthier flavour.

Portobello or flat mushrooms are the fully mature brown type with a large, flat cap. These have a meaty texture and a rich, intense flavour — perfect for grilling or stuffing.

Wild mushrooms
In cooking, wild mushrooms such as porcini or morels are prized for their unique, earthy flavours. Some cooks use the name exclusively for foraged mushrooms; others include those fungi even when cultivated. But common shop-bought varieties like button mushrooms are always excluded. The term is best understood as a culinary category highlighting flavour and species rather than where or how mushrooms grow.

Sometimes, "field mushroom" is casually but incorrectly used for any edible mushroom that naturally grows in meadows, whether foraged or cultivated. This can be confusing, as a field mushroom is actually a species of wild mushroom (*Agaricus campestris*) with a delicate, aromatic flavour.

Eating raw porcini is special, but they must be perfect specimens: very fresh, firm to the touch, white on the inside, and no bruising, perforations or signs of wildlife.

Preparing
Fresh mushrooms are delicate and should be handled gently. To clean them, use a brush to remove dirt and debris, then wipe with a clean damp cloth if needed. Avoid washing fresh mushrooms — if left soaking or wet, they will absorb water and become slimy. Trim the stem ends to remove any dry or dark root area. Some mushrooms like shiitake have a stem with a woody, fibrous outer layer that is unpleasant to eat, so scrape this off with a knife.

To reconstitute dried mushrooms, gently shake or brush off any visible dust. The stems of some types of dried mushrooms can be a bit tough when reconstituted, so cut these off shiitakes and portobellos before rehydrating. Put the mushrooms into a bowl, cover with lukewarm water and leave to soak for at least 30 minutes (overnight if possible — the longer the better). Strain through a paper coffee filter or kitchen paper in a sieve over a bowl to catch the liquid — keep this and use it to make a soup or stock or add to a sauce (it can be frozen and used later). Lastly, rinse the mushrooms under cold water to remove any remaining debris, and drain.

Disclaimer
Mushroom foraging can be risky. Always be absolutely certain of a mushroom's identity before cooking or eating; if you're unsure, don't eat it. While care has been taken with these recipes, you use them at your own risk. The authors and publisher cannot guarantee your safety, and strongly recommend consulting an expert before eating any foraged mushrooms.

Recipe Conventions

Egg sizes used throughout the book are UK large. All spoon measurements are level unless stated otherwise.

All recipes in this book have been tested in the same oven at the temperatures given. All ovens vary — some run hot, some are cooler — so adjust temperatures and timings to compensate where required. An oven thermometer will tell the truth!

Sterilizing Jam Pots, Jars and Bottles

Preheat the oven to 160°C/140°C fan/gas mark 3.

Wash the jars, lids and any sealing rings in hot soapy water; rinse and drain.

Steep the lids in boiling water for a few minutes, then drain and arrange these with the pots/jars on a clean baking sheet, and place in the oven for ten minutes to dry. Remove and let them cool until warm — they are now ready to fill. Alternatively, run the pots and jars through a hot dishwasher cycle.

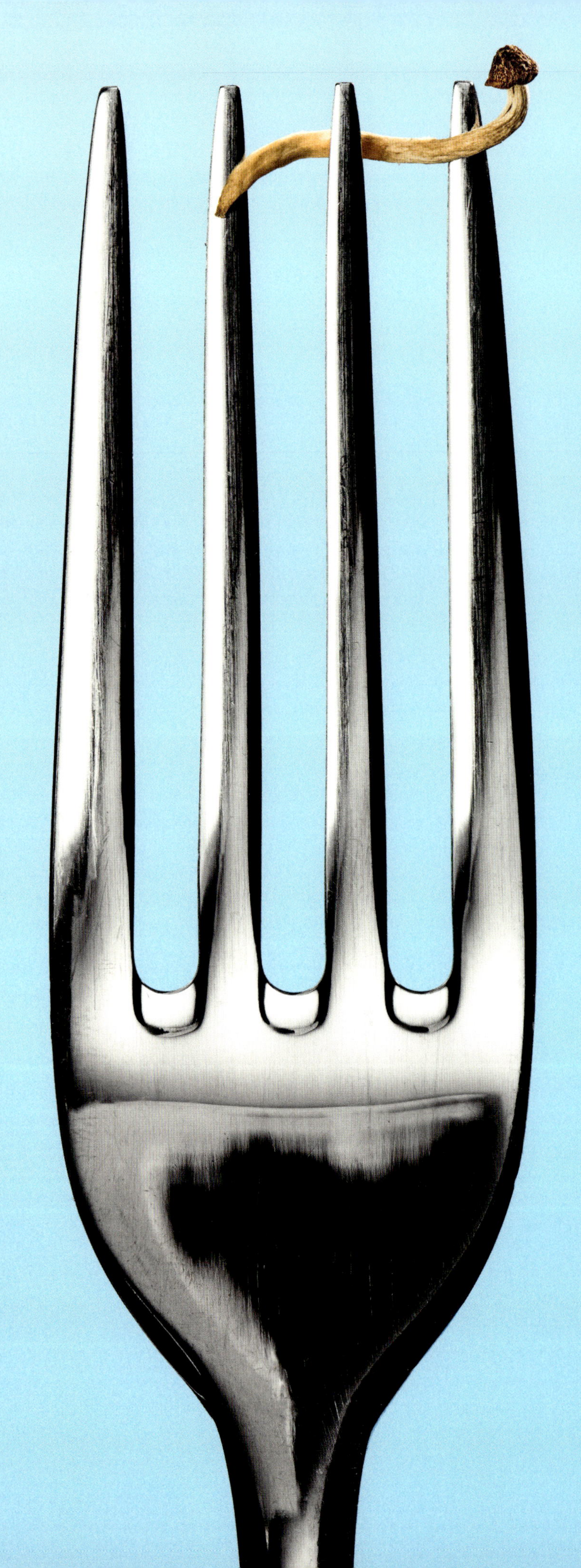

Appetising Mushrooms

Steamed Cantonese Stuffed Mushrooms

This delicately flavoured steamed dish is much enjoyed by the Cantonese and Fujianese. The egg white lightens the pork, and the bamboo shoots or water chestnuts add a delicate bite to the otherwise smooth texture; the sauce glistens on the stuffing, giving the dish an enticingly shiny, translucent glaze.

Serves: 6

INGREDIENTS
28 thick medium dried shiitake mushrooms with slightly curled edges, reconstituted
100 g minced pork (shoulder or leg)
2–4 thin slices of fresh ginger, finely minced
½ tsp salt
½ tsp sugar
2 tsp thin soy sauce
1 tsp shaoxing wine or medium dry sherry
½ tsp potato flour
1 tbs egg white
50 g drained canned bamboo shoots or 3–4 canned water chestnuts, finely chopped
5 spring onions, finely sliced
1 tsp toasted sesame oil
1 tbs light vegetable oil

Sauce:
1½ tsp potato flour, dissolved in 1 tbs water
1 tbs oyster sauce
1 tbs thick soy sauce
1½–2 tbs light vegetable oil

Garnish:
Spring onion "brushes" or curls

EQUIPMENT
Small bowl
Heatproof dish (to fit the steamer)
Steamer
Small saucepan

Drain and squeeze out the excess water from the mushrooms but leave damp, reserving 175 ml of the liquid.

Make the stuffing. Put the pork mince into a small bowl, then add the ginger, salt, sugar, soy sauce, wine, potato flour and 1 tbs of water. Stir vigorously with a spatula, always in the same direction, until well mixed. Add the egg white, and stir again until smooth and light. Leave to marinate for about 15 minutes. Then beat the bamboo shoots, spring onions, sesame oil and vegetable oil into the pork. Cover and set aside.

Hold a mushroom cap in one hand with the hollow side up. Using a small knife, fill the hollow generously with the stuffing, shaping into a slightly sloping mound. Repeat with all the mushrooms.

Arrange the mushrooms, stuffing side up, in one layer on a heatproof dish that will fit in your steamer. Steam, tightly covered, over a high heat for 10 minutes.

Just before the mushrooms are cooked, mix the potato flour, mushroom water, oyster sauce and thick soy sauce together in a small saucepan. Bring to the boil, stirring continuously with a wooden spoon as it thickens, then blend in the oil to give the sauce its sheen.

Lift the dish of steamed mushrooms from the wok. Arrange them on a warm serving dish, and pour over the sauce. Serve very hot.

* To make spring onion brushes: Trim the white ends of the spring onions into 6.5 cm lengths. Using a very sharp, small knife, make repeated cuts through both ends, leaving the central section intact. Place the onions in iced water, cover and refrigerate for at least an hour. This will make the ends curl up, forming the brushes. Remove them from the water and pat dry with paper towels.

To make spring onion curls: Trim then cut spring onions into long sections and slice them lengthwise very thinly — the finer you cut them, the more curly they will become. Place in iced water, making sure they are submerged, cover and refrigerate. After ten minutes, the spring onions will curl up. Remove them from the water and pat dry with paper towels.

Parmesan and Panko Breaded Mushrooms

Baking breaded mushrooms is a healthier and safer alternative to deep frying them, and they will be just as crisp and golden. However, this recipe would also work using a deep-fat fryer (remember to drain the cooked mushrooms on kitchen paper) or in an air-fryer.

Serves: 4

INGREDIENTS
75 g panko breadcrumbs or regular dried breadcrumbs
30 g freshly grated parmesan
1–2 tsp seafood seasoning mix (with celery salt and paprika)
2 tsp dried oregano
55 g chickpea (gram) flour
125 ml milk
20 bite-sized fresh white button mushrooms or small chestnut mushrooms

EQUIPMENT
Large baking sheet
Medium shallow bowl
Medium mixing bowl
Slotted spoon

Preheat the oven to 230°C/210°C fan/gas mark 7.

Select a baking sheet large enough to take the mushrooms in a single layer without touching each other, and line with baking parchment.

Put the breadcrumbs, seafood seasoning, parmesan cheese and oregano into a medium shallow bowl and gently mix together.

In a separate medium bowl, whisk the chickpea flour with the milk until smooth and having the appearance of pancake batter, then gently stir in the mushrooms to coat them evenly.

Using a slotted spoon, remove the mushrooms from the batter one by one, allowing excess batter to drip back into the bowl. Drop each into the breadcrumb mixture, and carefully roll around to coat evenly with the crumbs, then place on the lined baking sheet.

Bake the mushrooms for 10–15 minutes or until golden brown and crispy. Remove them from the oven and place on a warm serving plate with a dipping sauce of your choice. Serve immediately before they lose their crispiness.

Mushroom Pâté

Serves: 4

INGREDIENTS
50 g butter
175 g shallots, finely chopped
1 tbs anchovy paste*
450 g fresh chestnut mushrooms, chopped
1 tbs Madeira or medium sherry
100 g fresh parsley (or mix of parsley and dill), chopped
225 g full-fat cream cheese or fresh goat's cheese/curd
¼ tsp cayenne pepper or a dash of hot pepper sauce
Freshly ground black pepper

EQUIPMENT
Large frying pan
Food processor or stick blender
800 ml deep serving dish

Originating in the 12th century, pâté is traditionally a mixture of meat (typically game), herbs and spices, baked in a pastry casing. Today, we refer to this version as *pâté en croute*, while the name "pâté" is now used in short for *pâté en terrine*, where the meat is cooked in a terrine dish — without a pastry casing. Mushrooms are frequently used as a hearty meat substitute, and this pâté recipe calls for chestnut mushrooms, which are known for their firmness and nutty taste. Best served on toast.

Melt the butter in a large frying pan over a medium heat until foaming. Add the shallots, and cook gently for about 15 minutes until softened and golden. Add the anchovy paste, mushrooms and Madeira, and stir well. Cook, stirring occasionally, for about five minutes until the mushrooms are soft. Stir in the parsley.

Spoon the mushroom mixture into a food processor, then add the cheese and cayenne pepper, and season with black pepper — it shouldn't need extra salt as the anchovy paste is salty. Process in short bursts until it forms a thick, slightly rough paste (or process for longer if you prefer it smoother).

Spoon into a deep serving dish and let it cool. Then cover and chill for at least two hours until firm. Serve spread on toast, or in a sandwich with pickles and watercress.

This dish will keep in the fridge for up to one week.

* Vegan replacement for anchovy paste: 2 tsp of rinsed and chopped salted capers and a dash of dark soy sauce.

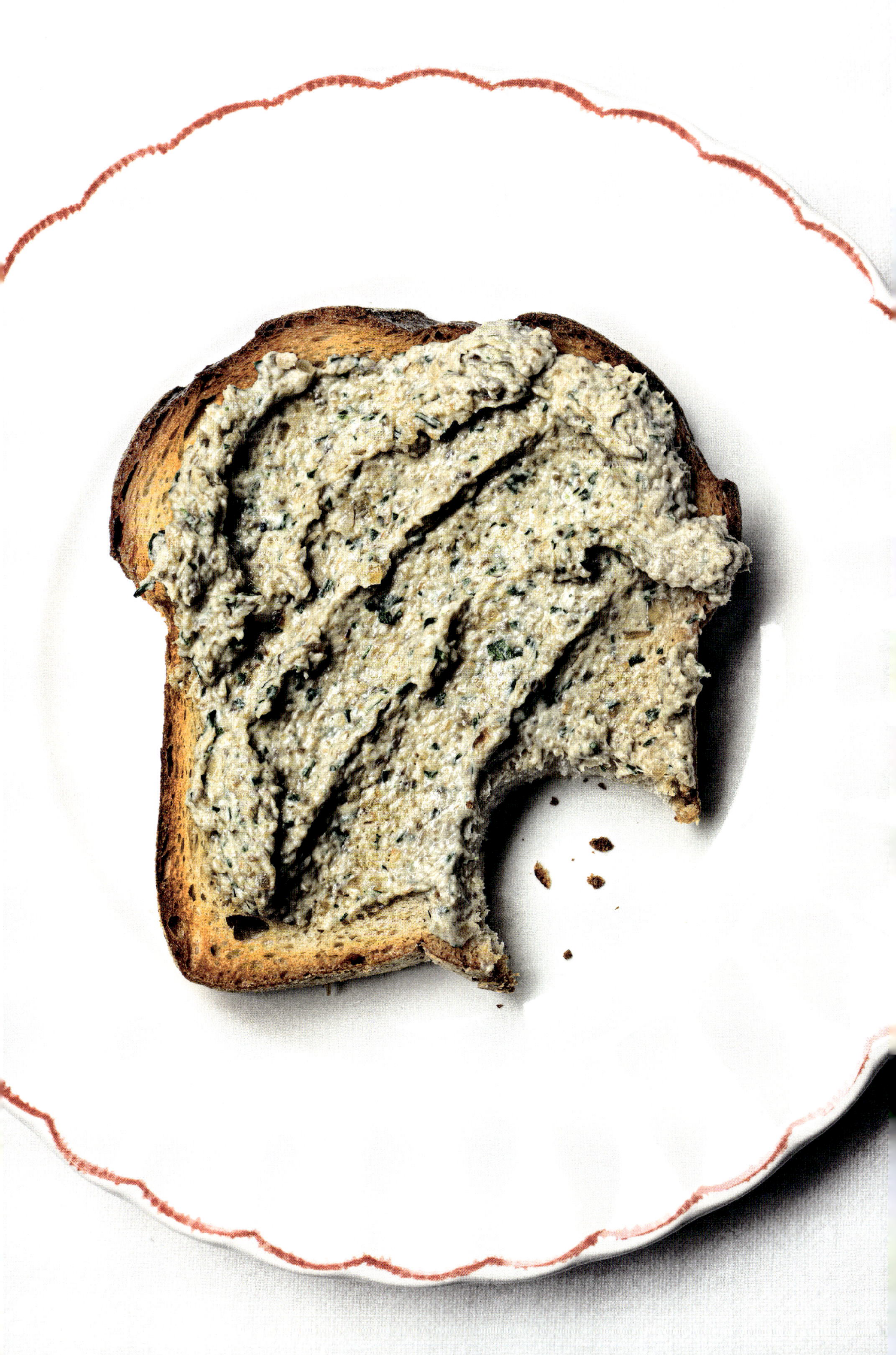

Chorizo, Feta and Olive Stuffed Mushrooms

Life isn't too short to stuff a mushroom — especially if you use a big and bold open-cup, black-gilled cultivated one that bursts with umami when cooked with the flavours of Spain. The sherry vinegar makes all the difference — don't leave it out.

Serves: 4

INGREDIENTS
4 large fresh flat mushrooms 6–7 cm in diameter (or 8 smaller open-cup portobello mushrooms)
Salt and freshly ground black pepper
75 g chorizo, diced
1 small red onion, finely chopped
1 tbs sherry vinegar
½ garlic clove, crushed
55 g fresh breadcrumbs (pita bread is good)
8–12 stoned dry black olives with herbs, chopped
1 tbs salted capers, rinsed and chopped
2 tbs fresh parsley, chopped
2 tbs feta cheese or salted ricotta, freshly crumbled

EQUIPMENT
Shallow ovenproof dish (to fit the mushrooms in a single layer)
Medium frying pan

Preheat the oven to 180°C/fan 160°C/gas mark 4.

Cut the stems off the mushrooms, then dice and set aside.

Arrange the mushroom caps in a single layer in a shallow ovenproof dish. Season with salt and pepper.

In a medium frying pan, sauté the diced chorizo in its own fat for one minute over a medium-high heat, then reduce the heat to medium and add the red onion and the sherry vinegar. Cook for a further four minutes, stirring frequently. Add the diced mushroom stems, and continue to cook until the chorizo is lightly browned and the onions are beginning to turn golden (about two minutes). Stir in the garlic, and cook for a further minute. Remove from the heat. Stir in the breadcrumbs, olives, capers, and parsley. Season to taste with salt and pepper.

Heap the stuffing mixture into the mushroom caps, pressing down lightly with the back of a spoon. Sprinkle with the feta cheese. Bake in the oven for 20–25 minutes, or until the mushrooms are tender when pierced with the tip of a sharp knife and the cheese is golden brown.

Chinese Salt and Pepper Mushrooms

In this classic Chinese dish, the distinctive and bold flavour of Sichuan peppercorns (which are technically not from a pepper at all, but the husks of a berry, harvested from prickly ash trees) is combined with spices, chilli, garlic and a splash of sesame oil. An elevated, moreish dish that gets attention when served.

Serves: 4

INGREDIENTS
900 g large fresh oyster mushrooms or other firm mushrooms
1 tsp salt
160 g cornflour (plus more if needed)

Spicy salt and pepper mix:
2 tsp salt flakes
1 tsp toasted Sichuan peppercorns
1 tsp white peppercorns
½ tsp Chinese five-spice powder
1 tsp soft brown sugar

Sauce and garnish:
1 tbs vegetable oil
4 garlic cloves, finely chopped
2 long red chillies, seeds removed, finely chopped
4 trimmed spring onion stalks, finely sliced on the diagonal (plus more for garnish)
Toasted sesame oil (to drizzle)

EQUIPMENT
Large tray
Clean kitchen towel
Large saucepan
Mortar and pestle, coffee grinder or spice mill
Colander
Large mixing bowl
Large saucepan or deep fat fryer
Slotted spoon
Kitchen paper
Large wok

Pull the clusters of mushrooms apart, then if still too large, trim and cut them lengthways into bite-sized pieces.

Bring a large saucepan of cold water to the boil while making the spicy salt and pepper mix. Put all the ingredients into a mortar and pestle, and grind to a fine powder. Alternatively, do this in a clean coffee grinder or spice mill. Set aside in a small bowl.

When the water is boiling, add 1 tsp of salt, and stir. Carefully drop handfuls of mushrooms into the water, and bring back to the boil, making sure all the mushrooms are submerged. Boil for about 2–3 minutes. This breaks down the structure of the mushrooms and enables water to be squeezed out of them easily.

When cooked, strain the mushrooms through a colander, and tip onto the kitchen towel-lined tray and allow to cool. When cool enough to handle, gently squeeze to remove excess water.

Next, put the cornflour into a large mixing bowl and add 2–3 tsp of the spicy salt and pepper mix. Mix well. Tip in the mushrooms, and using clean hands, toss the mushrooms with the seasoned flour to coat generously, massaging it into the gills. If the mushrooms stick together, add a little more cornflour.

Fill a large saucepan halfway with oil (or use an electric deep fat fryer), and heat to 180°C. Check if the oil is hot enough by dropping in a piece of mushroom — if it sizzles immediately, the oil is ready.

Carefully drop a few mushrooms at a time into the hot oil, making sure not to overfill, and fry until golden brown. Lift out of the oil with a slotted spoon and transfer to a tray lined with kitchen paper to absorb excess oil. Continue to fry in small batches to avoid the mushrooms sticking together, until they are all done.

To finish, heat a large wok with 1 tbs of vegetable oil and sauté the garlic, red chillies and spring onions over a high heat for 1–2 minutes. Add the mushrooms and another 2 tsp of the spicy salt and pepper mix, then toss a few times to mix. Drizzle with a splash of toasted sesame oil, and tip out onto a shallow serving dish. Garnish with the extra sliced spring onions and serve whilst still very hot.

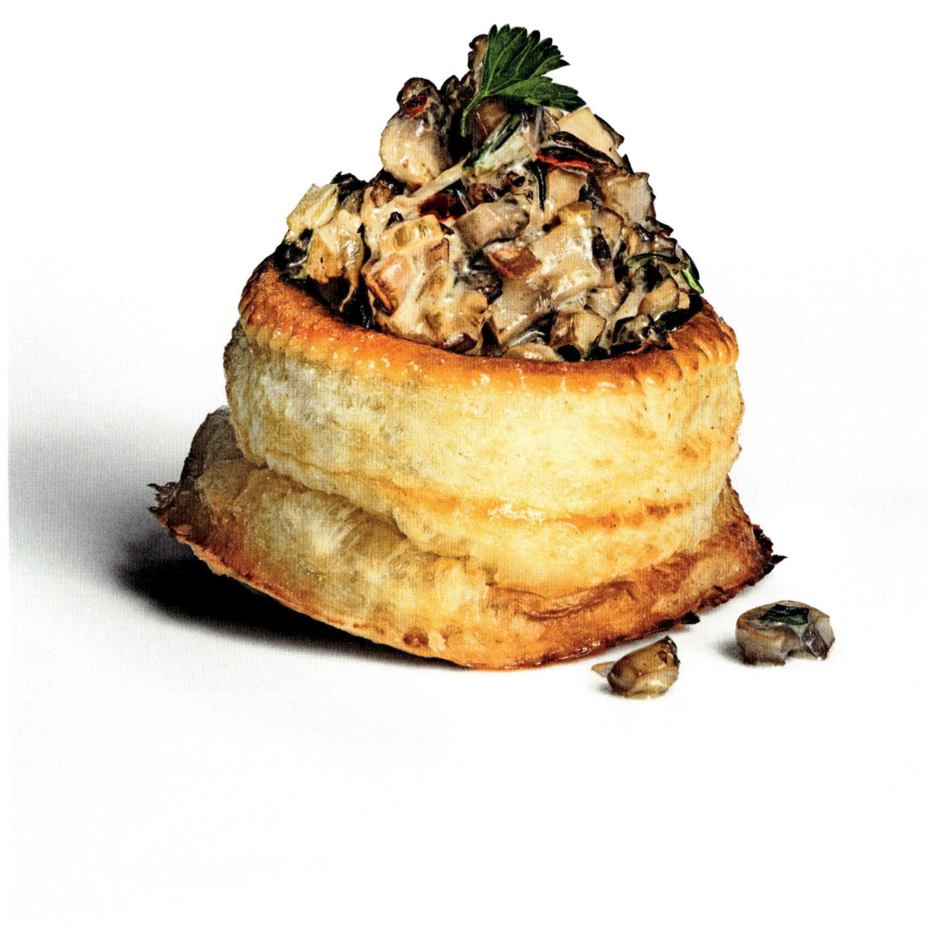

Creamy Mushroom Vol-Au-Vents

Makes: 12 (small)

INGREDIENTS
Plain flour (for dusting)
Two 500 g blocks of ready-made all-butter puff pastry
1–2 eggs, beaten with a little salt

Creamy mushroom filling:
55 g butter
500 g fresh mushrooms, finely chopped
2 garlic cloves, finely chopped
½ lemon, juiced (or to taste)
3 tbs crème fraîche
2 tbs fresh parsley, chopped
2 tsp fresh tarragon or chervil, chopped
Salt and freshly ground black pepper

Garnish:
A few sprigs of fresh flat leaf parsley, taragon or chervil

EQUIPMENT
2 large, heavy baking sheets
Baking parchment
Rolling pin
7 cm plain round biscuit cutter
6 cm plain round biscuit cutter
Pastry brush
Large frying pan

Popular in 18th-century France and revived in buffet-enthused 1970s Britain, vol-au-vents have truly stood the test of time. Made from a ring of puff pastry, creating a crisp and light shell, the name translates from French as "windblown". Whilst there is debate around who first created these delights, it's widely agreed that they will forever be a party favourite.

Preheat the oven to 220°C/200°C fan/gas mark 7.

Line a large heavy baking sheet with baking parchment.

On a lightly floured work surface, roll out the pastry until it is 4–5 mm thick. Using the 7 cm cutter, stamp out 24 rounds. Then stamp the centres out of 12 of them using the 6 cm cutter so you are left with six rounds and six rings. (As a cook's perk, brush the leftover cut-outs with beaten egg, dip in some freshly grated parmesan, arrange on a baking sheet and cook separately to make 12 little nibbles.)

Arrange the larger 7 cm rounds on the prepared baking sheets, leaving plenty of space between each one. Using a pastry brush, lightly brush the pastry rounds with beaten egg.

Top each round with a pastry ring so the edges match up neatly, press down lightly to seal the join, then brush the tops of the rings with beaten egg.

Prick the exposed bases with a fork to prevent them from rising too much during baking. Bake for about 12–15 minutes, or until risen, deep golden brown and cooked through. If not quite cooked through, lower the heat to 150°C/130°C fan/gas mark 3 and leave to dry out for ten minutes or so.

In a large frying pan, heat the butter until foaming, then add the mushrooms and garlic, and cook over a medium-high heat for about 5–6 minutes until the mushroom edges start to turn golden. Take off the heat, squeeze in the lemon juice, then stir in the crème fraîche and chopped herbs. Taste and season well. If the mushrooms are too dry, add a splash of milk or water to loosen the sauce.

Using a dessert spoon or teaspoon, fill the pastry cases with the creamy mushrooms, garnish with the herbs, and serve immediately while hot and the pastry is crisp.

Mushroom Tempura

Serves: 4

INGREDIENTS
60 g cornflour
Vegetable oil (for frying)

Tempura batter:
100 g fine white rice flour
80 ml chilled sparkling water (more may be needed)
¼ tsp salt
Pinch of baking soda
½ tsp red Kampot pepper or szechuan pepper, freshly ground (optional)
½ tsp garlic granules (optional)

Filling:
300 g fresh mushrooms (any, or a mixture)

Dipping sauce:
6 tbs soy sauce
1 tbs freshly squeezed lemon juice
1 tsp rice vinegar
2 tsp honey
1 small red chilli, seeds removed and finely chopped

EQUIPMENT
Small bowl
Large bowl
Deep saucepan, wok or electric deep fat fryer
Heatproof tray
Paper towels
Small bowl
Wire scoop or slotted spoon

Japanese tempura is a light, crisp batter that's perfect for all kinds of vegetables but particularly mushrooms. During Lent, when Catholics refrain from eating meat, a dish of green beans coated in flour and fried was popular with Portuguese sailors based in 16th-century Japan. The word "tempura" originates from the Portuguese word *têmpora*, Latin for "times" or "seasons", and relates directly to the Ember Days — periods of fasting. This recipe is a modern, plant-based tempura batter that is egg, dairy and gluten free.

To get ahead, prepare everything beforehand, so that you are ready to fry and have no last-minute panics.

The batter must be kept very cold, so place the water in the freezer to chill for ten minutes before you start. Also, sit the bowl of batter in a larger bowl of iced water while you are frying.

Make the dipping sauce. Whisk the soy sauce, 1 tbs of water, the lemon juice, vinegar, honey and chopped chilli together in a small bowl. Taste and adjust as desired. Set aside.

If the mushrooms are large, trim and cut into long slices. Small button mushrooms can be cooked whole. Medium-sized closed-cup mushrooms can be quartered. Oyster mushrooms can be torn into segments. Then toss the prepared mushrooms in the cornflour to lightly coat them, so that the batter will stick to them.

Heat the oil in the deep saucepan to 175°C. If you don't have a thermometer, use a drop of the batter — if it sizzles immediately, the oil is at the right temperature.

While the oil is heating up, make the batter. In a small mixing bowl, whisk together the rice flour, chilled sparkling water, salt and baking soda, and the pepper and garlic if using. More water may be needed to make a thin batter, depending on the humidity of the flour. The batter should not be thick — more like pouring cream.

Dip the mushrooms into the batter one at a time, gently shaking off the excess, then drop into the hot oil for 3–4 minutes or until crisp and bubbly. Fry 3–4 pieces at one time to give them room to crisp — overloading can make the mushrooms stick together, and can lower the temperature of the oil so the mushrooms stew instead of crisp. Once cooked, the tempura should be a pale cream colour (not brown), semi-transparent, bubbly and crisp. Lift out of the oil with a wire scoop and transfer to the lined tray to drain.

Repeat with the remaining mushrooms, pile up on a warm serving dish and serve immediately with the dipping sauce.

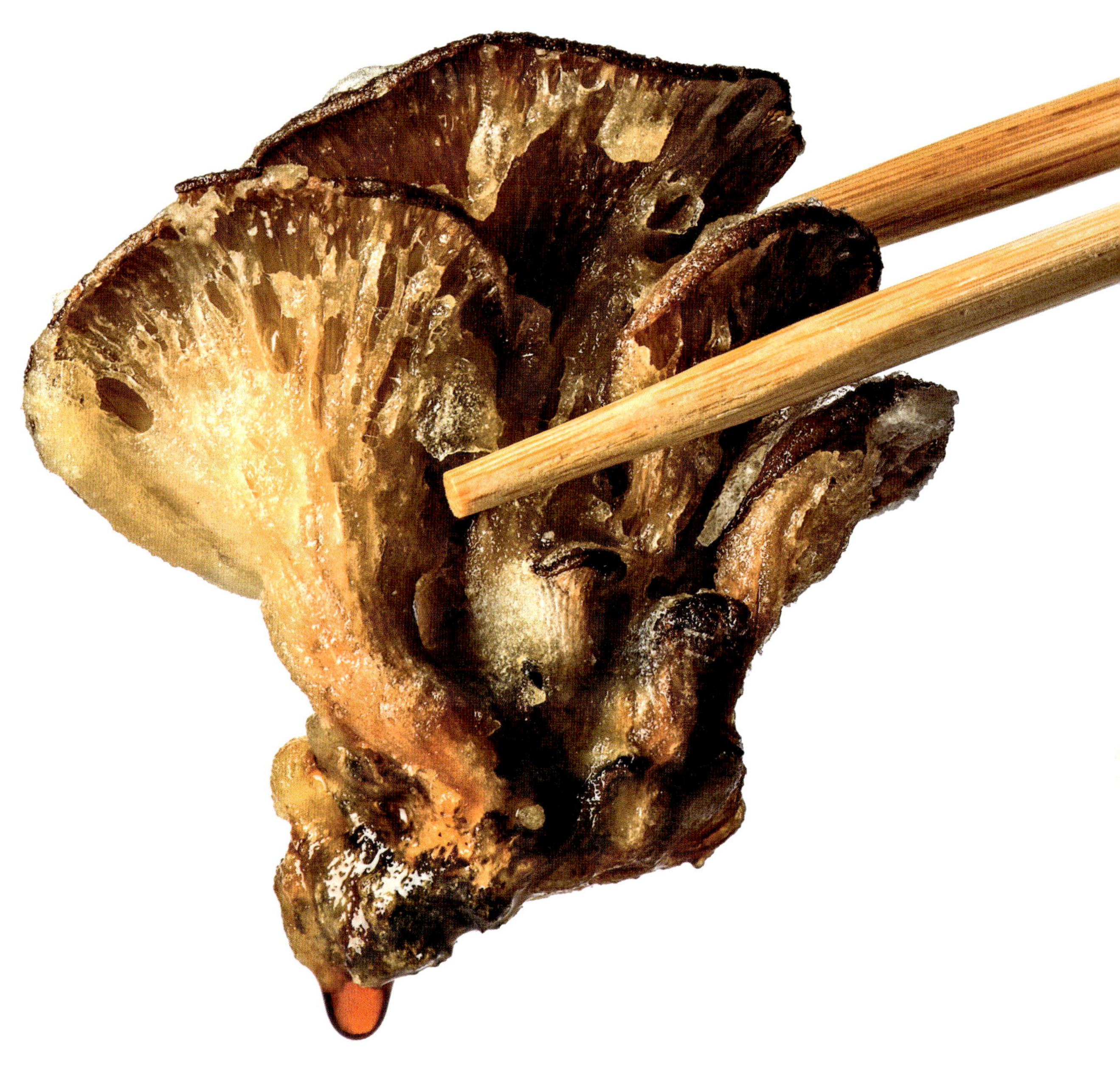

Mushroom and Tofu Gyoza

Makes: 30

INGREDIENTS
1 packet (about 30 sheets) gyoza wrappers
1–2 tbs vegetable oil
1 spring onion, green part only, finely sliced on the diagonal

Mushroom filling:
40 g dried shiitake mushrooms, reconstituted
175 g mixed fresh mushrooms
2 spring onions, trimmed and roughly chopped
100 g firm tofu (drained for 20 minutes on kitchen paper)
1 tsp ginger, finely grated
2 garlic cloves, finely grated
1 tbs soy sauce
1 tbs oyster sauce
1 tsp toasted sesame oil
Salt

Dipping sauce:
6 tbs soy sauce
6 tbs rice vinegar
1 tsp chilli oil
1 tsp toasted sesame oil
Salt and freshly ground black pepper (to taste)

EQUIPMENT
Food processor
Medium bowl
Small bowl
Large tray
Baking parchment
Clean kitchen towel
Large non-stick frying pan with lid

Gyoza are the Japanese version of the Chinese dumpling—jiaozi (considered to be ancient). Both are crescent-shaped dumplings encasing meat and vegetable fillings that can be steamed or pan fried. However, gyoza are made with thinner wrappers, the ingredients are more finely chopped and they feature more garlic than jiaozi.

To make the filling, strain the soaked shiitake mushrooms (reserving the soaking water for later), then squeeze out excess water, roughly chop and put into a food processor with the fresh mushrooms, spring onions and tofu. Pulse in short bursts until very finely chopped but not pureed. Scrape out into a medium bowl, and add the ginger, garlic, soy sauce, oyster sauce and sesame oil. Stir well to mix, adding salt and pepper to taste. Cover and set aside.

Make the dipping sauce by mixing all the ingredients, except the spring onions, together in a small bowl. Cover and set aside.

Line a large tray with baking parchment. Take six gyoza wrappers at a time (keep the rest in the packet or plastic bag, to prevent them drying out). Place a wrapper on one hand and put 1 tsp of filling in the centre of the wrapper. Wet your index finger, and run it around the inner edge of the gyoza wrapper to dampen it. Bring the two edges up on either side of the filling but do not seal yet—the trick is to pleat only one side of the dumpling, leaving the other side untouched. So, starting on one edge, make three pleats moving towards the centre on the left, then do the same working from the right, or vice versa. Now press and seal the top, making sure no air is trapped inside. Place the dumpling on the baking parchment, and cover with a damp clean kitchen towel to prevent it from drying out. Fill the remaining dumpling wrappers the same way.

To cook the gyoza, preheat a large non-stick frying pan over a medium heat. Add the vegetable oil and swirl to coat the pan, then arrange the dumplings so that they don't touch. This may have to be done in batches, depending on the size of the pan. Turn up the heat to medium-high, and fry the dumplings fairly briskly to sear and colour their bottoms—about one minute. Now add about 200 ml of the reserved mushroom soaking water. This should be roughly a quarter of the way up the dumplings' sides.

Cover the pan with its lid, and cook the dumplings over a medium-high heat for 7–9 minutes until you hear a sizzling sound, telling you that the water has evaporated and the dumplings are starting to fry, not steam. Uncover, and cook for another 1–2 minutes to crisp up the bottoms, shaking the pan once or twice to make sure they don't stick. Pile the gyoza onto a warm serving dish and serve immediately with the dipping sauce, topped with the sliced spring onion.

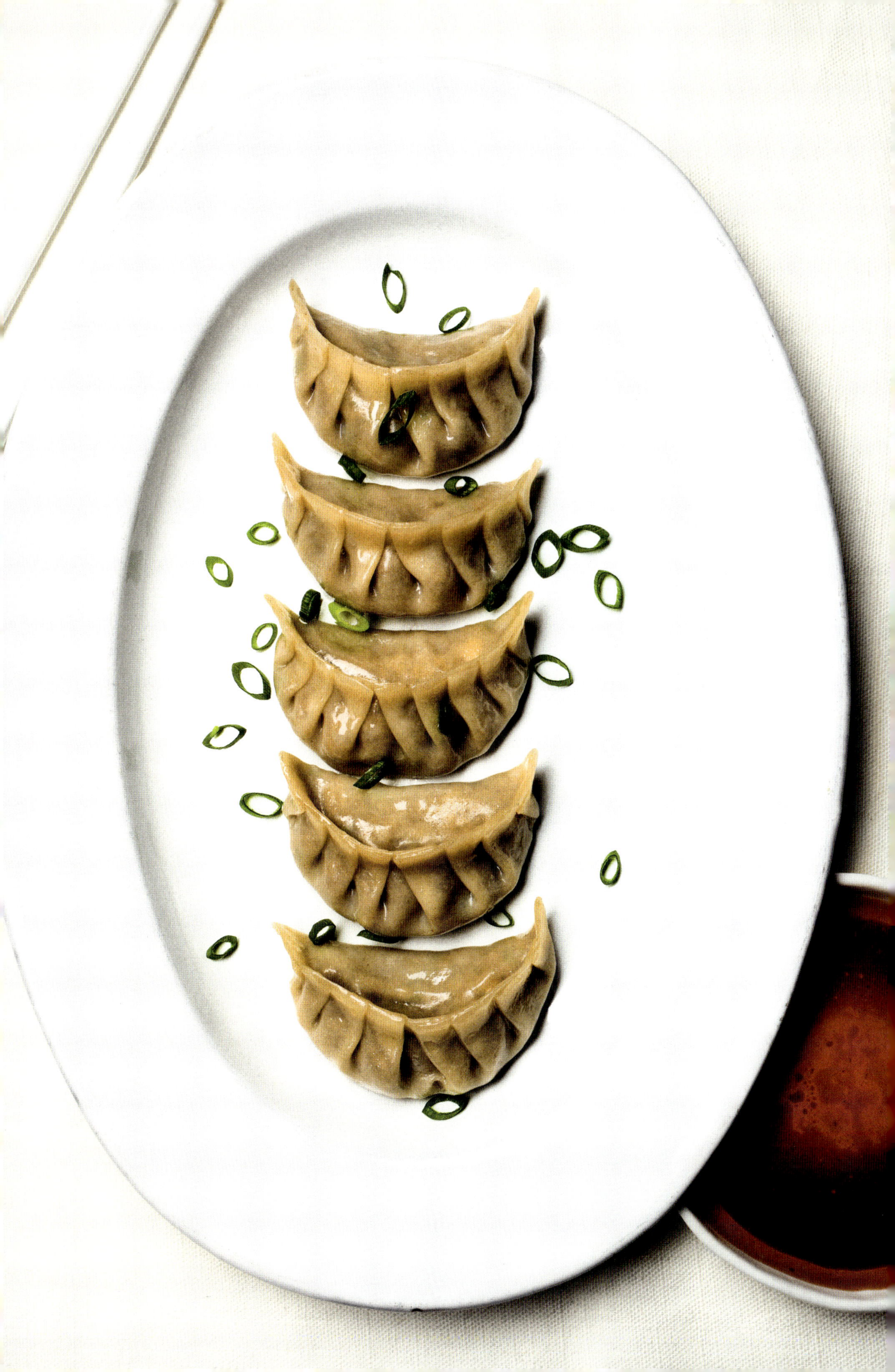

Mushroom Pierogi with Breadcrumbs

Makes: 30

INGREDIENTS
50 g butter, melted, seasoned with salt and freshly ground black pepper

Dough:
450 g plain flour (plus extra for dusting)
30 g butter, melted
120 ml milk, warmed

Mushroom filling:
550 g assorted fresh mushrooms
1 tbs olive oil
30 g butter
2 large shallots, finely chopped
1–2 tbs fresh lemon juice (to taste)
Salt and freshly ground black pepper
3 tbs crème fraiche
1 tsp fresh thyme leaves, chopped
1 tbs flat-leaf parsley, chopped

Crispy toasted breadcrumbs:
3 slices of stale bread
2 tbs extra-virgin olive oil
2 garlic cloves, finely chopped
Handful of fresh parsley leaves, finely chopped
20 g parmesan, freshly grated

This popular take on the dumpling originates in Poland. Pierogi have a shell made from unleavened dough and are typically filled with potato, cheese, meat or mushrooms (sometimes with sauerkraut). They are boiled and served warm (sometimes fried), with a topping of sour cream and/or onions fried in butter. It's a Polish custom to enjoy pierogi filled with the autumnal harvest of preserved forest-foraged mushrooms on Christmas Eve.

To make the dough, put the flour into a stand mixer, add the melted butter and warm milk, and start mixing on low speed. Add about 180 ml of warm water — a little at a time — until it is all used, and continue to mix for about five minutes. The dough should be smooth, elastic and no longer sticky. If the dough seems too firm, add more water, as some flours need more moisture. Cover the bowl with a damp clean kitchen towel and leave to rest for 30 minutes before attempting to roll out. The dough will be much more elastic after resting.

To make the filling, place the mushrooms in a food processor, and pulse in short bursts until finely chopped. Set aside.

In a medium, deep frying pan, heat the olive oil over a medium-low heat, then add the butter, and when foaming, add the shallots. Add 1 tbs of water, cover and cook for about three minutes until softened. Add the chopped mushrooms and lemon juice to taste, season with salt and pepper, and mix well. Raise the heat to medium, and cook, stirring occasionally, for 8–10 minutes until soft and reduced. Stir in the cream and chopped herbs, and cook for about one minute. Transfer to a medium bowl to cool.

Now make the crispy breadcrumbs. Pulse the stale bread in the food processor until it becomes breadcrumbs.

Heat the olive oil in a medium saucepan over a low heat, add the garlic, and when sizzling stir in the breadcrumbs, chopped parsley, parmesan and a pinch of salt. Continue to stir and toss around for 3–5 minutes until the breadcrumbs become golden brown. Transfer the mixture to a small serving bowl and set aside.

Line a large tray with a clean kitchen towel, and dust generously with flour to prevent the finished pierogi sticking.

Now fill and make the pierogi. Divide the dough into four, and put three pieces into a plastic bag. Roll out the first piece of dough on a lightly floured surface until it's thin but not see-through — a thickness of about 3 mm. Using a 7.5 cm round cutter, cut out as many rounds as you can. Cover with a damp clean kitchen towel

EQUIPMENT
Electric stand mixer
Clean kitchen towel
Food processor
(with a large mixing bowl)
Medium, deep frying
pan with lid
Medium bowl
Medium saucepan
Large tray
Clean kitchen towel
Plastic bag
Rolling pin
7.5 cm round cutter
or drinking glass
Large saucepan
Colander

to prevent them from drying out. Repeat with the remaining dough – you should have about 30 rounds in all.

Bring a large saucepan of water to boil and salt it generously.

To fill a pierogi, place a heaped teaspoon of the filling towards the front of a circle of pierogi dough. Moisten the edges of the dough with water, and fold in half around the filling, to form a crescent, firmly pinching the edges closed (or use the tines of a fork). Continue to fill and form the pierogi, transferring them to the lined tray until all the dough has been used.

Working in batches, drop the pierogi into the boiling water. Like gnocchi, they will sink to the bottom and then rise to the top. Once they have floated to the top, cook for about two minutes until cooked through.

Drain the pierogi in a colander and return them to the hot frying pan. Add the seasoned, melted butter, and gently toss to coat. Tip the pierogi onto a warmed platter and spread them out. Scatter the crispy golden breadcrumbs over the top and serve immediately.

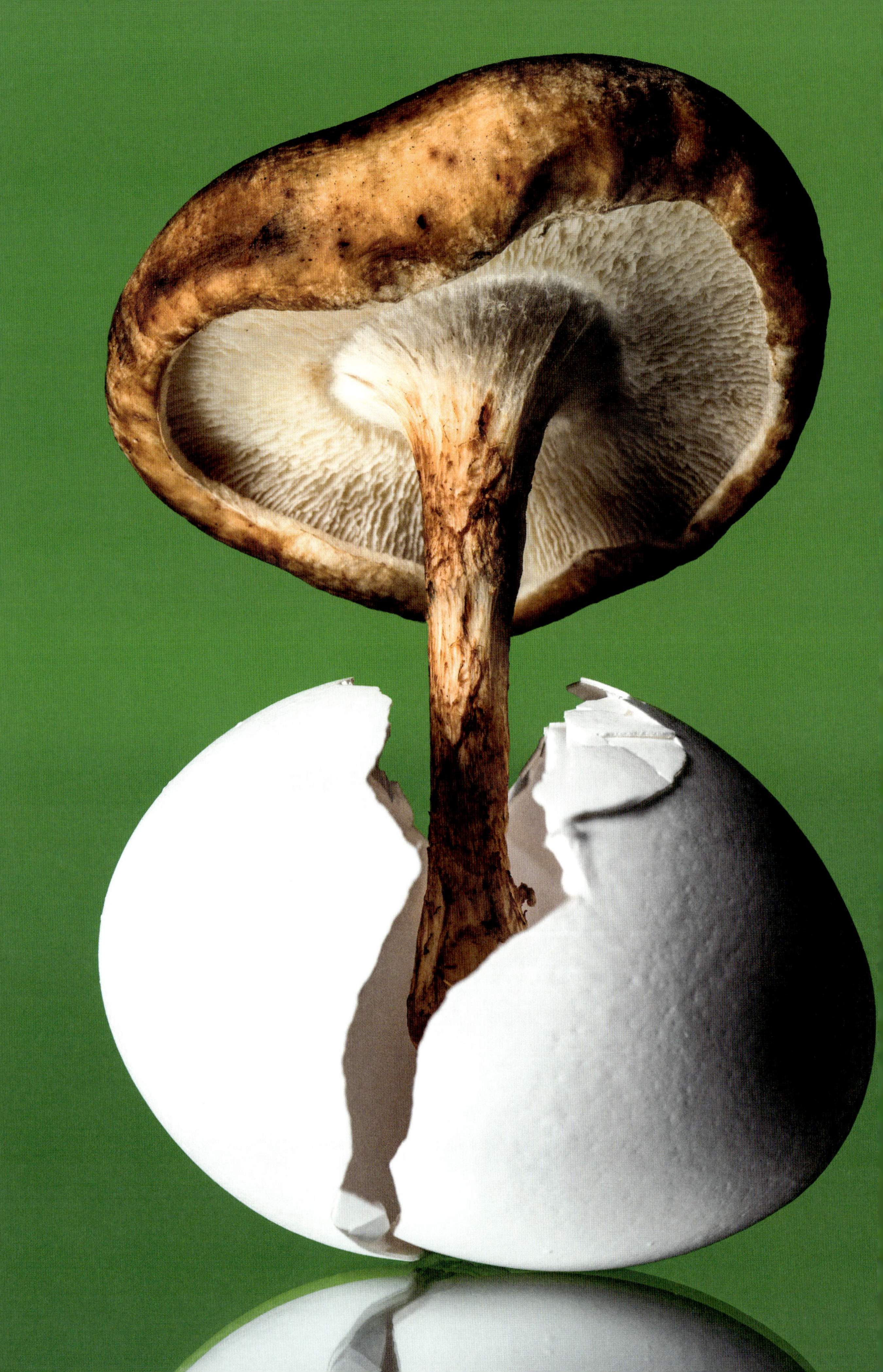

Mushrooms to Start

Mushroom Omelette

Serves: 1

This recipe uses a tiny amount of sherry vinegar or honeygar, a delicious blend of honey and apple cider vinegar, which brings a rich depth of flavour and sweetness to the mushrooms. The honeygar "mother" offers numerous health benefits, but the mixture has a powerful flavour, so use sparingly.

INGREDIENTS

Mushroom filling:
20 g butter
150 g fresh mushrooms (cultivated or wild), sliced or torn
1 garlic clove, finely chopped or grated
1 spring onion, trimmed and thinly sliced
3 fresh sage leaves, finely shredded
½ tsp thyme leaves, bruised
Salt and freshly ground black pepper
½ tsp sherry vinegar or honeygar
40 g grated pecorino or crumbled feta

Omelette:
3 medium eggs
1 tbs cold water
1 tsp grated pecorino (optional)
Salt and freshly ground black pepper
15 g butter

EQUIPMENT
Medium non-stick frying pan
Small bowl
15 cm non-stick heavy frying or omelette pan

First, make the filling. Heat a medium non-stick frying pan over a medium-high heat and add the butter. Once foaming, add the mushrooms, garlic, spring onion, sage, thyme and a generous seasoning of salt and pepper. Stir well, and turn with a spatula so that the mushrooms are coated in the buttery juices.

Cook for 3–4 minutes, stirring and turning occasionally, until the mushrooms soften and brown and any liquid has almost evaporated. Add the vinegar and stir fry for another minute. Cover and set aside to keep warm.

To make the omelette, break the eggs into a small bowl, add 1 tbs of cold water, the grated pecorino if using, and salt and pepper, and beat with a fork until just mixed with no streaks of egg white. Melt the butter in a 15 cm heavy non-stick frying pan, and swirl it around so that the bottom and sides are coated. When foaming, pour in the egg mixture.

Hold the frying pan handle with one hand, and move the pan gently back and forth over the heat. At the same time, with a spatula or wooden spoon, move the mixture slowly, scraping up large creamy flakes of egg mixture. As you do this, some of the liquid egg from the middle of the omelette will run to the sides of the pan, so tilt the pan to help this.

Leave the pan over the heat until the bottom of the omelette has set and browned lightly and the top is still creamy. Scatter half of the cheese all over the top of the omelette, then remove the pan from the heat and spoon the filling into the omelette centre.

With a spatula or palette knife, fold the nearside edge of the omelette towards its centre, and then flick the whole omelette over onto a warmed plate with the folded edges on the underside. Alternatively, fold the omelette in two and slide it on to a warm plate. Scatter the remaining cheese on top.

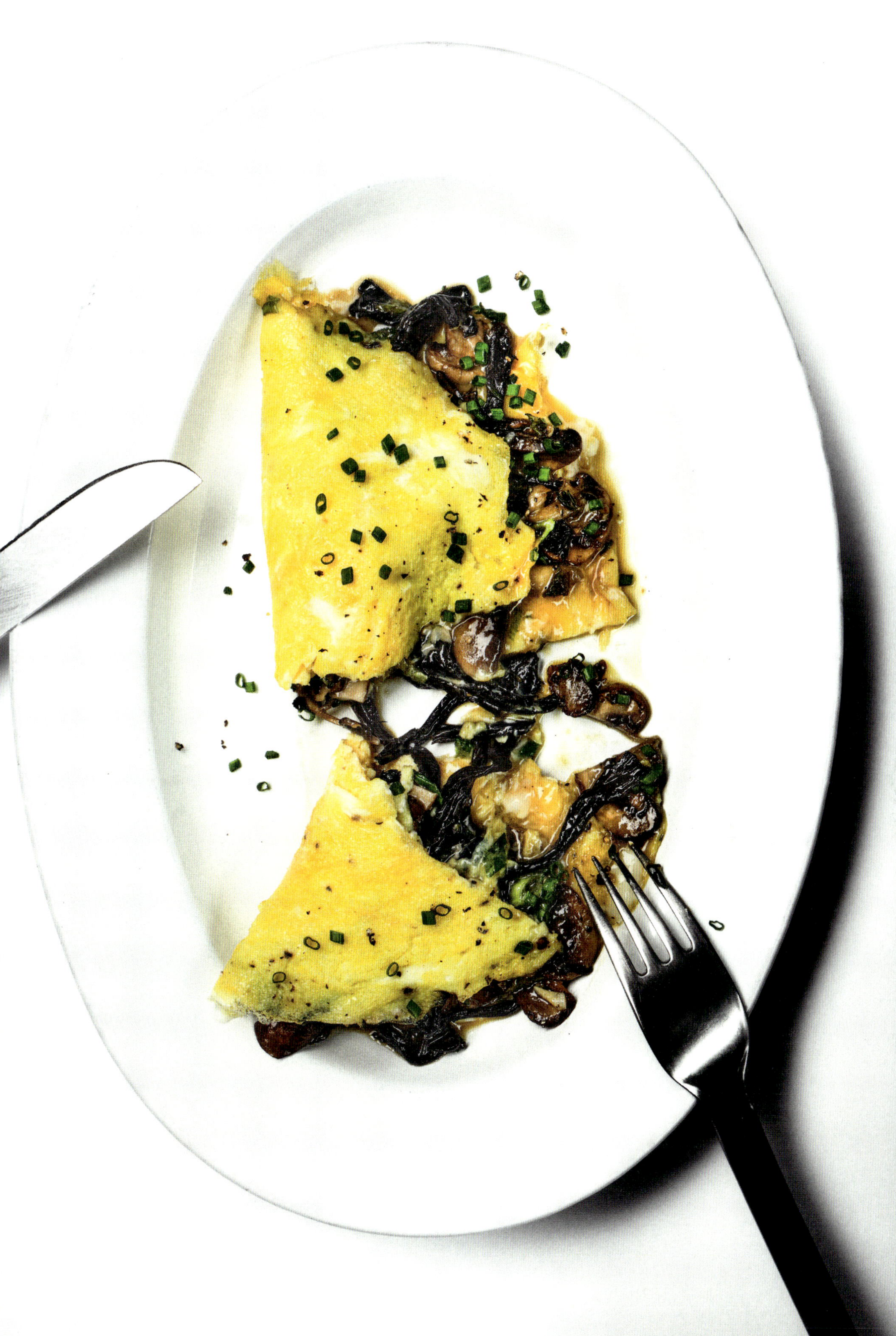

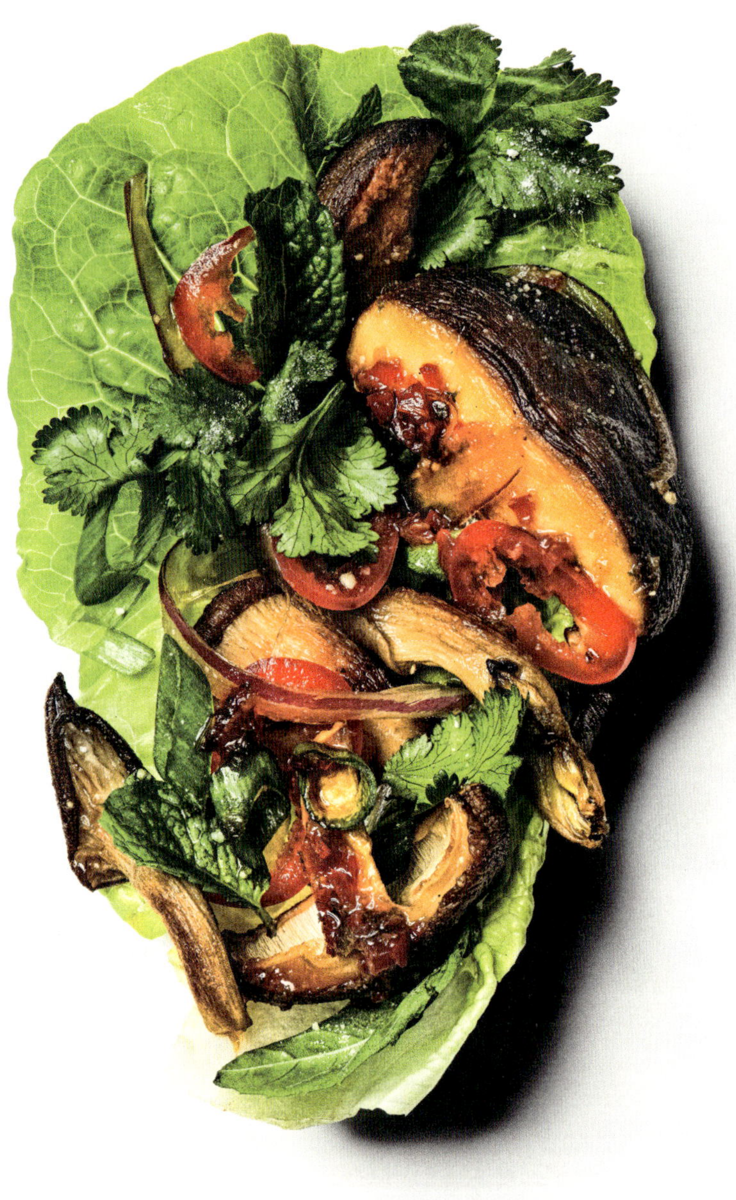

Mushroom Larb

Serves: 4

INGREDIENTS
900 g mixed fresh mushrooms (button, oyster or shiitake)
3 tbs vegetable oil
½ tsp salt
2 tbs uncooked glutinous or arborio rice

Dressing:
1 lime, finely zested, then juiced
1 tbs soft brown sugar
2 tbs soy sauce
1–2 tbs fish sauce (optional)
1 garlic clove, grated
2 red bird's eye chillies, sliced, or ½ tsp red chilli flakes
1 small red onion, thinly sliced
2 spring onions, trimmed and finely sliced on the diagonal
25 g fresh coriander leaves and stems, roughly chopped
15 g fresh mint leaves, torn
15 g fresh Thai or sweet basil leaves, torn

EQUIPMENT
Large mixing bowl
Large baking sheet
Small frying pan
Mortar and pestle or a spice grinder
Medium bowl

A dish that's popular in the northern and northeastern regions of Thailand, larb is a punchy, zingy combination of cooked minced meat, fresh herbs and a lime dressing. In this version, crisply roasted mushrooms replace the meat. A subtle, nutty crunch from toasted ground rice is an essential element of larb, so don't leave it out. Best served with a crisp, lightly pickled cucumber salad.

Preheat the oven to 220°C/200°C fan/gas mark 7.

Trim and quarter the mushrooms or tear into large pieces. Place these in a large mixing bowl, and add 3 tbs of oil and ½ tsp of salt. Using clean hands, toss well to coat with the oil. Spread the mushrooms in an even layer on a large baking sheet, and put into the oven to roast for about 25 minutes, stirring the mushrooms twice and spreading them out until golden brown and crisp around the edges.

Meanwhile, toast the rice in a small frying pan over a medium heat for about four minutes, stirring often to toast evenly, until it begins to smell nutty and turn golden. Remove from the heat, tip onto a plate and allow to cool. Transfer to a mortar and pestle, and pound to a medium-coarse powder. Set aside.

When ready to serve, put the lime zest and juice into a medium bowl. Add the sugar, soy sauce and optional fish sauce, stir to dissolve, then stir in the garlic and chillies. Add the roasted mushrooms to the bowl, and toss to coat. Gently stir in the onion, spring onions, coriander, mint and basil. Stir to combine, then sprinkle on the toasted rice powder.

Serve the mushroom larb on a platter, with a pile of crisp lettuce leaves, a bowl of steamed rice and plenty of lime wedges to squeeze.

Cream of Mushroom Soup

Serves: 4

INGREDIENTS
55 g butter
340 g fresh flat black cultivated mushrooms, chopped
3 tbs (heaped) fresh parsley, chopped
1 large garlic clove, crushed
2 large slices stale bread (preferably sourdough), crusts removed
1 litre good chicken or vegetable stock
Pinch of ground nutmeg or mace
Salt and freshly ground black pepper
150 ml double cream

EQUIPMENT
Large heavy-based saucepan
Electric liquidizer, stick blender or food processor

Cultivated flat black open-cup mushrooms are ideal for this well-loved soup, although the flavour can be deepened by adding some rehydrated dried wild mushrooms such as porcini, a good teaspoon of dried mushroom powder (see page 236) or a tablespoon of ultra-savoury homemade mushroom ketchup (see page 240). For a luxury version, use fresh porcini. The parsley is essential.

Melt the butter in a large heavy-based saucepan over a medium heat, and when foaming, add the mushrooms along with two-thirds of the parsley. Lower the heat, and cook gently, stirring, until the mushrooms are very soft and mushy — don't let the mushrooms dry out and brown. Now add the garlic and the bread, torn into pieces. Stir until the bread and mushrooms are well mixed, then add the stock, the nutmeg, and salt and lots of black pepper to taste. Raise the heat and bring to a simmer, then cook slowly for ten minutes.

Liquidize the soup. For a silky smooth soup, use an electric liquidizer or stick blender. For a hint of texture, pulse in a food processor.

Return the soup to the rinsed pan, add the remaining chopped parsley, and the cream, taste and check the seasoning, then reheat. Serve in warm bowls with grilled sourdough rubbed with garlic (or for pure extravagance, drape with thin slices of Italian lardo whilst the bread is still hot so that it softens).

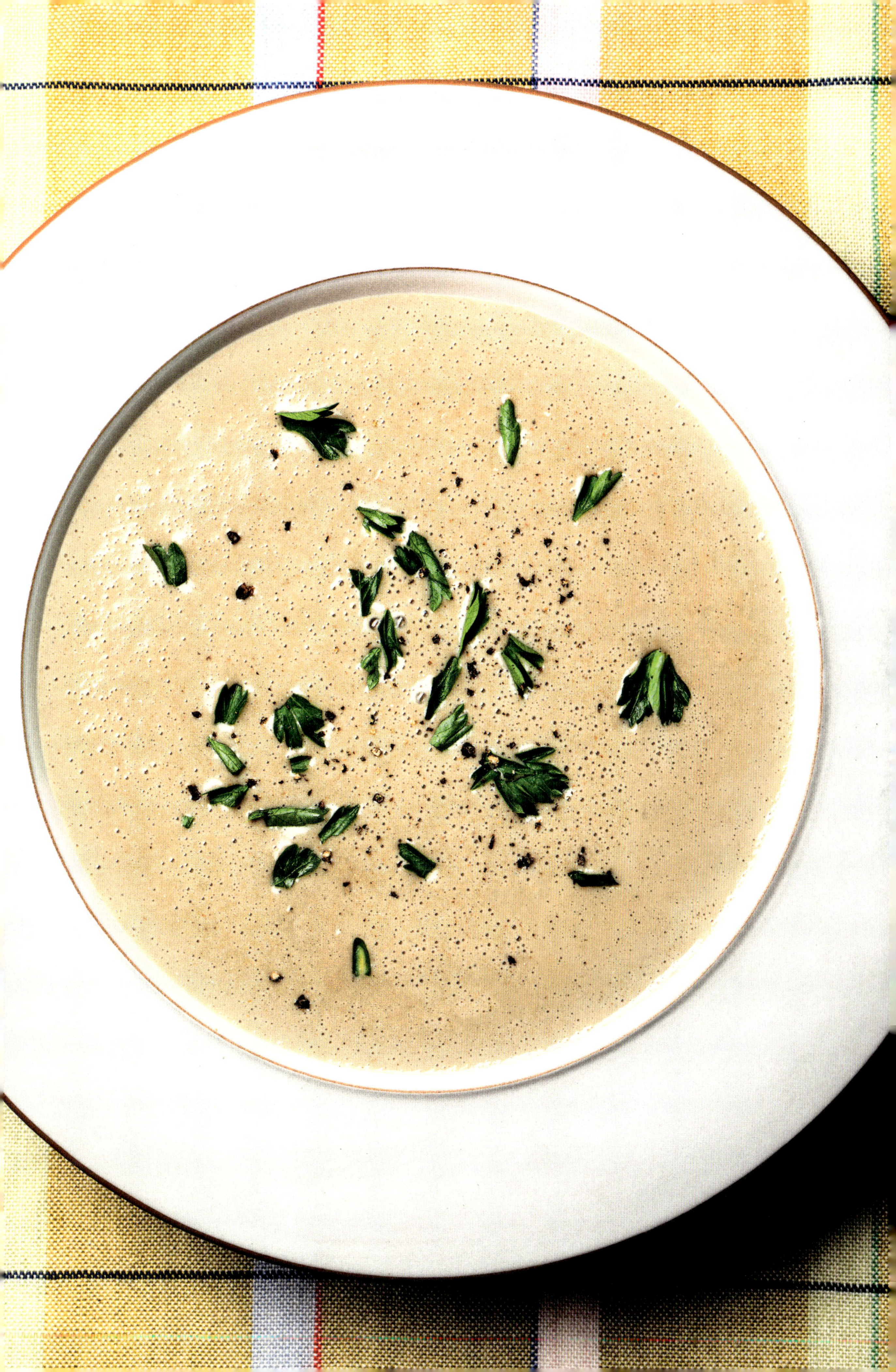

Christmas Barszcz with Uszka

Barszcz is a classic Polish soup traditionally served on Christmas Eve. It's made from beetroot, often flavoured with mushrooms, and has a clean, almost clear appearance. It's ladled into mugs or bowls to enjoy alongside miniature dumplings known as uszka ("little ears"), which are filled with dried and fresh mushrooms.

Serves: 10

INGREDIENTS

Dough:
450 g plain flour
30 g butter, melted
120 ml milk, warmed

Mushroom filling:
25 g dried porcini mushrooms, reconstituted
2 tbs unsalted butter
1 medium onion, chopped
450 g fresh cultivated mushrooms, chopped
Salt and freshly ground black pepper

Barszcz:
4 medium carrots, cut into chunks
1 medium parsnip, cut into chunks
350 g celeriac, cut into chunks
1 leek, thickly sliced
4 parsley sprigs
40 g dried porcini mushrooms
1 tbs salt
2 bay leaves
4 allspice berries
6 medium raw beetroot, peeled and thickly sliced
3 garlic cloves
1 eating apple, quartered with the skin on
2 tsp sugar
¼ tsp dried marjoram or oregano
2 tbs white wine vinegar
1 tbs freshly squeezed lemon juice
Salt and freshly ground

Filter and retain the water used for soaking the dried mushrooms (see page 155).

To make the dough, put the flour into a stand mixer, add the melted butter and warm milk, and start mixing on low speed. Add about 180 ml of warm water — a little at a time — until all used, and continue to mix for about five minutes. The dough should be smooth, elastic and no longer sticky. If the dough is too firm, add more water, as some flours need more moisture than others. Cover the bowl with a damp clean kitchen towel, and leave to rest for 30 minutes before attempting to roll out. The dough will be much more elastic after resting.

To make the mushroom filling, put the porcini mushrooms into a small saucepan and cover with cold water. Bring to the boil over a high heat, then lower the heat and simmer for about an hour until tender. Meanwhile, melt the butter in a medium frying pan over a medium heat, and when foaming, add the chopped onions. Cook for 15 minutes, stirring occasionally, until translucent. Add the chopped fresh mushrooms to the onions, season with salt and pepper, and cook for about 15 minutes until soft and fully cooked. Put the mushroom and onion mixture into a food processor with the cooked dried mushrooms, season with salt and pepper, then pulse a few times until finely chopped, but not a paste. Tip into a bowl and set aside.

Line a large tray with a clean kitchen towel, and dust generously with flour to prevent the finished uszka sticking.

To make the uszka, divide the rested dough into four, and put three pieces into a plastic bag. Roll out the first piece of dough on a lightly floured surface until it's thin but not see-through — a thickness of about 3 mm. Using a 3.5 cm diameter round cutter or upturned glass (e.g. a shot glass), cut out the rounds from the dough.

To fill and shape the uszka, working with one round at a time, place ½ tsp of the filling in the centre. Wet the edge of one-half of the round, and fold over to meet the other side. Seal the edges together to make a half moon. Take the two points at opposite sides from the straight edge, and press them together to create an ear-shaped dumpling a little like a tortellini, and set it on the lined tray.

black pepper

EQUIPMENT

Electric stand mixer
2 clean kitchen towels
Small saucepan
Medium frying pan
Food processor
Medium bowl
Large tray
Plastic bag
Rolling pin
3.5 cm round cutter or a shot glass
Large saucepan
Slotted spoon
Large baking sheet
Small bowl
Very large saucepan
Colander

Continue making uszka with the rest of the dough and filling. Bring a large saucepan of water to the boil, salt it generously and add no more than ten uszka at a time. Like gnocchi, they will sink to the bottom and then rise to the top. Once they have floated to the top, boil for about two minutes until cooked through. Once cooked, lift them out of the water with a slotted spoon onto a baking sheet, making sure they are all separate, cover with a damp clean kitchen towel and set aside. If serving immediately, place the uszki in warm serving bowls and cover with the barszcz.

To make the barszcz, put the carrots, parsnips, celeriac, leek, parsley sprigs and dried porcini mushrooms, along with the strained water used for soaking the mushrooms used for the uszka, in a very large saucepan, cover with 2.5 litres water, add 1 tbs of salt, the bay leaves and allspice, bring to the boil then lower the heat and simmer uncovered for about 30 minutes.

Add the beetroot, garlic, apple, sugar and marjoram to the vegetable broth with 1 tbs each of wine vinegar and lemon juice, to preserve the beautiful colour of the beetroot. Bring back to a simmer and cook uncovered for 30 minutes. Then add the remaining vinegar, taste and adjust the seasoning with more vinegar, sugar, salt and pepper, as needed. The soup should taste bright and sharp but have a good depth of flavour.

Strain the barszcz through a colander placed over a large pan or bowl. Discard all the vegetables, and ladle the liquid into either mugs to drink or bowls to be served with the mushroom uszka. Barszcz is best served on the day it is made as it can lose its wonderful colour if reheated to boiling.

Wild Chanterelles on Toast
(Svamptoast)

Swedes who pick their own chanterelles make this dish, known as svamptoast. The delicate chanterelles are cooked in nothing but butter and cream (though a splash of brandy can be added). The mushrooms are almost slow cooked to concentrate their delicate woodland flavour, and served neatly on toast.

Serves: 1

INGREDIENTS
35 g butter
125 g fresh chanterelle mushrooms
Dash of brandy (optional)
60 ml double cream
Salt and freshly ground white pepper
Thick slice of white bread, toasted (e.g. sourdough or crunchy French loaf)

EQUIPMENT
Medium frying pan

In a medium frying pan, melt the butter until foaming, add the chanterelle mushrooms, and gently fry in the butter for about five minutes until they release their juices and this liquid has all but evaporated. Add a dash of brandy now, if using.

Turn the heat to low and add the cream. Simmer the mixture, stirring occasionally, for about ten minutes to further stew and soften the mushrooms and thicken the cream. Season to taste, and pile high on top of your favourite toasted crusty bread. For a treat, instead of toasting the bread, butter each side and fry on both sides until golden.

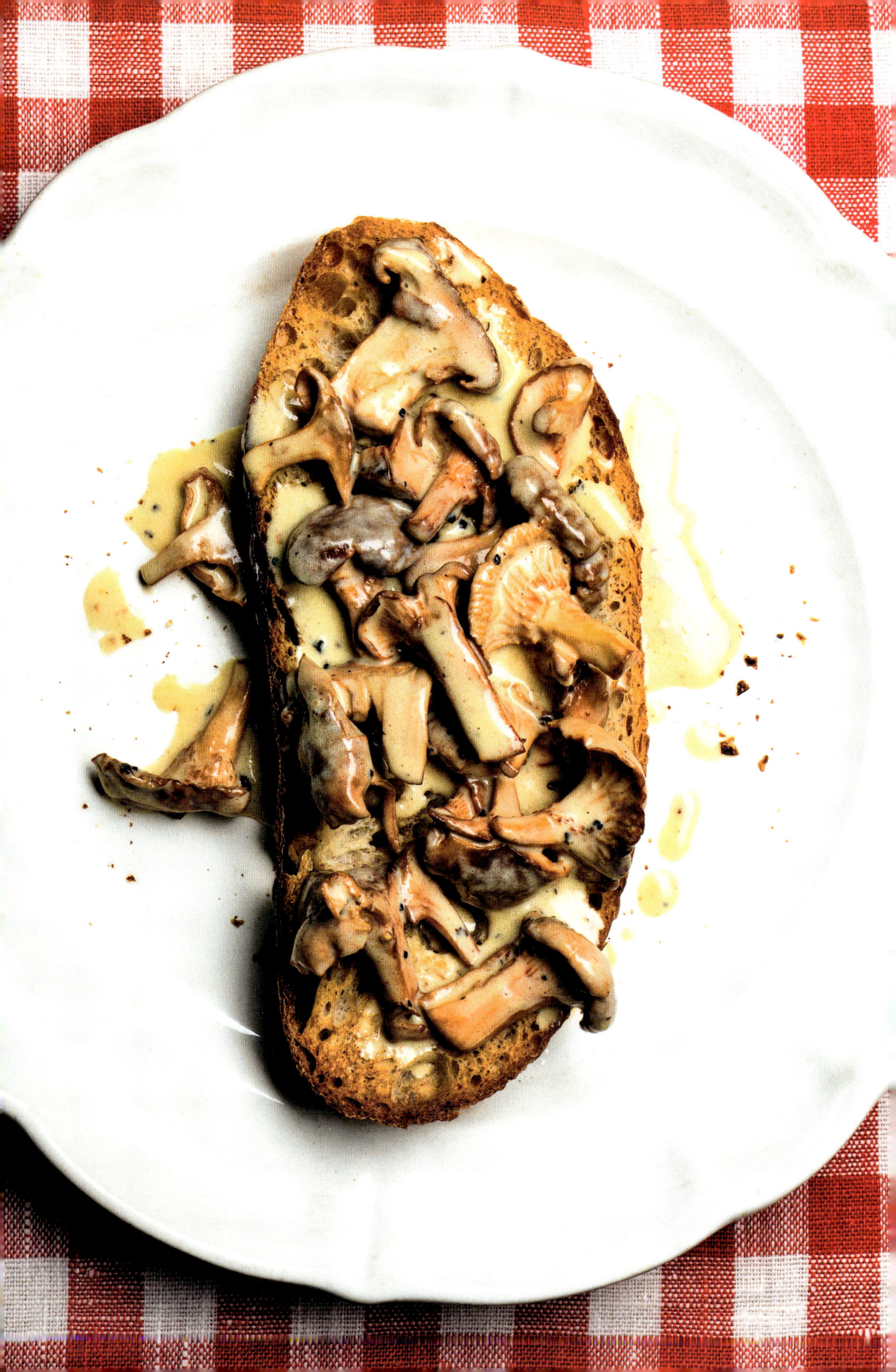

Mushroom Okonomiyaki

Makes: 2 as a light lunch or 6 as a starter

INGREDIENTS
2–3 tbs butter
300 g fresh firm mushrooms, thickly sliced
2 eggs
60 g plain flour
1 tbs potato starch
80 ml dashi or water
150 g hispi or white cabbage, finely shredded
2 spring onions, finely sliced
Salt and freshly ground black pepper
Japanese mayonnaise (Kewpie) (to garnish)

Okonomiyaki sauce:
3 tbs tomato ketchup
1 tbs Worcestershire sauce
1 tsp soy sauce

EQUIPMENT
Large non-stick frying pan
Baking sheet
Medium bowl
20 cm non-stick frying pan with lid
Kitchen foil

This is a versatile Japanese pancake/omelette that can be used as a vehicle for all sorts of ingredients – and it's particularly delicious when made fresh with mushrooms. Originally, matsutake were the sought-after mushrooms for okonomiyaki because of their prized spicy, aromatic flavour, but they're costly now, so rare to find used in this dish.

Heat a large non-stick frying pan over a medium-high heat, add half the butter, and when foaming, stir in half of the mushrooms and season with salt. Turn up the heat, and sauté briskly for about five minutes or until the mushrooms have exuded their water and begun to caramelise on their edges. Tip them onto a baking sheet to cool. Repeat with the remaining mushrooms and butter, then add them to the cooked mushrooms and leave for ten minutes.

Make the okonomiyaki sauce by mixing together the tomato ketchup, Worcestershire sauce and soy sauce in a small bowl. Set aside.

To make the pancake batter, put the eggs, flour, potato starch and dashi into a medium bowl, season well and whisk to mix to a thickish batter, then fold in the shredded cabbage, half of the cooked mushrooms and the spring onions.

For two large okonomiyaki, ladle half of the mixture into a 20 cm non-stick frying pan at a medium heat, and spread to evenly cover the base. It should be about 2.5 cm thick. Turn down the heat to medium low, cover with the lid and cook this first side – shaking the pan occasionally to ensure the mixture doesn't stick – about five minutes or until just set. Uncover, and using the lid or a plate, flip the pancake onto this, then slide the okonomiyaki back into the pan and cook for one more minute. Remove the okonomiyaki and wrap it in kitchen foil, and keep it warm while the second is made in the same way.

Cook smaller pancakes in muffin/chef's rings in a large frying pan or in shallow patty tins and bake in the oven.

To serve, spread the pancakes/omelettes with the okonomiyaki sauce and then drizzle the mayonnaise over in a zig-zag fashion. Pile the remaining mushrooms on top. Katsuobushi (bonito flakes), beni shoga (red pickled ginger) and aonori (kelp powder) are all optional but delicious serving additions.

Sizzling Garlic Mushrooms

Serves: 4

INGREDIENTS
450 g small/medium fresh brown mushrooms (chestnut or portobello)
3 large garlic cloves, crushed
1 black garlic clove, grated (optional)
175 g butter (at room temperature)
1–2 tbs chopped fresh parsley
1 tbs lemon juice
Salt and freshly ground black pepper

EQUIPMENT
Large, shallow heatproof gratin dish (to fit under the grill/broiler)
4 small heatproof gratin dishes (optional)
Baking sheet (to fit all 4 small gratin dishes) (optional)

These sizzling mushrooms are a vegetarian take on French snails in garlic butter (or make it vegan by using plant-based butter). They can be pan fried, but grilling is easier, and the mushrooms look better for taking straight to the table. Serve with a pile of crusty bread to mop up the garlicky, buttery juices.

Preheat the grill (broiler) to medium high.

Pull the stalks off the mushrooms and chop finely.

In a small bowl, beat the garlic with the softened butter, then beat in the chopped stalks, parsley and lemon juice. Season well with salt and pepper.

Arrange the mushroom caps, insides facing up, in a large, shallow gratin dish (or in four individual dishes). Place a teaspoon of the garlic butter mixture into each cap and dot the remainder around them.

Place the dish (or individual dishes set on a baking sheet) under the grill, but not too close. Cook for 10–15 minutes or until the butter is sizzling and the mushrooms lightly browned. Serve immediately.

Mushroom Galettes

Makes: 4

INGREDIENTS
55 g parmesan, finely grated
Small bunch of chives, chopped (to serve)

Buckwheat batter:
85 g buckwheat flour
85 g plain flour
½ tsp salt
1 egg, beaten
175 ml milk
50 g butter, clarified and melted (or light olive or sunflower oil)

Mushroom and leek filling:
3 tbs olive oil
400 g fresh chestnut mushrooms quartered
1 large leek, thinly sliced
2 garlic cloves, finely chopped
2 sprigs of fresh tarragon, roughly chopped
3 tbs crème fraîche (plus extra to serve)
1 tsp dijon mustard or mushroom ketchup (see page 240)
1–2 tbs freshly squeezed lemon juice (or to taste)
Salt and freshly ground black pepper

EQUIPMENT
Food processor or stick blender
Medium jug
Large, deep pan or wok
Medium bowl
20 cm heavy crêpe pan or non-stick frying pan
Large baking sheet (to fit under the grill/broiler)

Galettes can be dated back to ancient Rome, and have become a cherished part of French culture. Related to crêpes, galettes are savoury and served as a main dish. They are traditionally made from buckwheat flour, bringing a nutty flavour.

To make the batter, put the flour, salt, milk, 100 ml water, half of the melted butter, and the egg into a food processor, and blend until smooth. Pour into a jug, cover and leave to rest in a cool place for at least an hour—this will make the batter lighter. After resting, add a little more water if necessary, to give the consistency of thick pouring cream. The addition of the melted butter adds to the flavour and texture of the galettes and helps them to not stick to the pan. Use the remaining clarified butter for greasing the pan.

Meanwhile, make the mushroom filling. Heat 1 tbs of olive oil in a large, deep pan over a medium-high heat. Add the mushrooms, and cook, stirring occasionally for about ten minutes until the juices have evaporated and the mushrooms have caramelised. Tip the mushrooms into a medium bowl.

Add the remaining oil to the hot pan, add the leeks and stir fry for 3–4 minutes or until softened, then add the garlic and tarragon and stir fry for a further minute. Stir in the crème fraîche and mustard, tip in the set-aside mushrooms, and simmer for a minute or so. Turn off the heat and stir in lemon juice to taste and season with salt and pepper. Cover and keep warm while you cook the galettes.

Wipe a heavy crêpe pan with the clarified butter, and heat it until a drop of batter sizzles as soon as it hits the pan. Pour in a ladleful (about 100 ml) into the hot pan, and swirl so it covers the base. Cook for a minute or two, until the edges have set and the underside is lightly golden, then flip over with a spatula and cook for about ten seconds more, then transfer to a large plate as you make them. Repeat with the remaining batter to make four galettes. They should be soft and pliable, and not too browned or crisp, to make them easier to shape.

Heat the grill (broiler) to medium. Butter a large baking sheet, and lay the four galettes on it, pale side up. Spoon a quarter of the filling into the centre of each galette, mounding it up in the centre, then fold over the edges of each galette towards the centre, to make a square border with some of the filling exposed. Scatter the parmesan over the galettes. Grill (broil) the galettes for 3–4 minutes until the cheese is melted and golden. Then lift them onto warm plates and serve with a dollop of extra crème fraîche and chives on top.

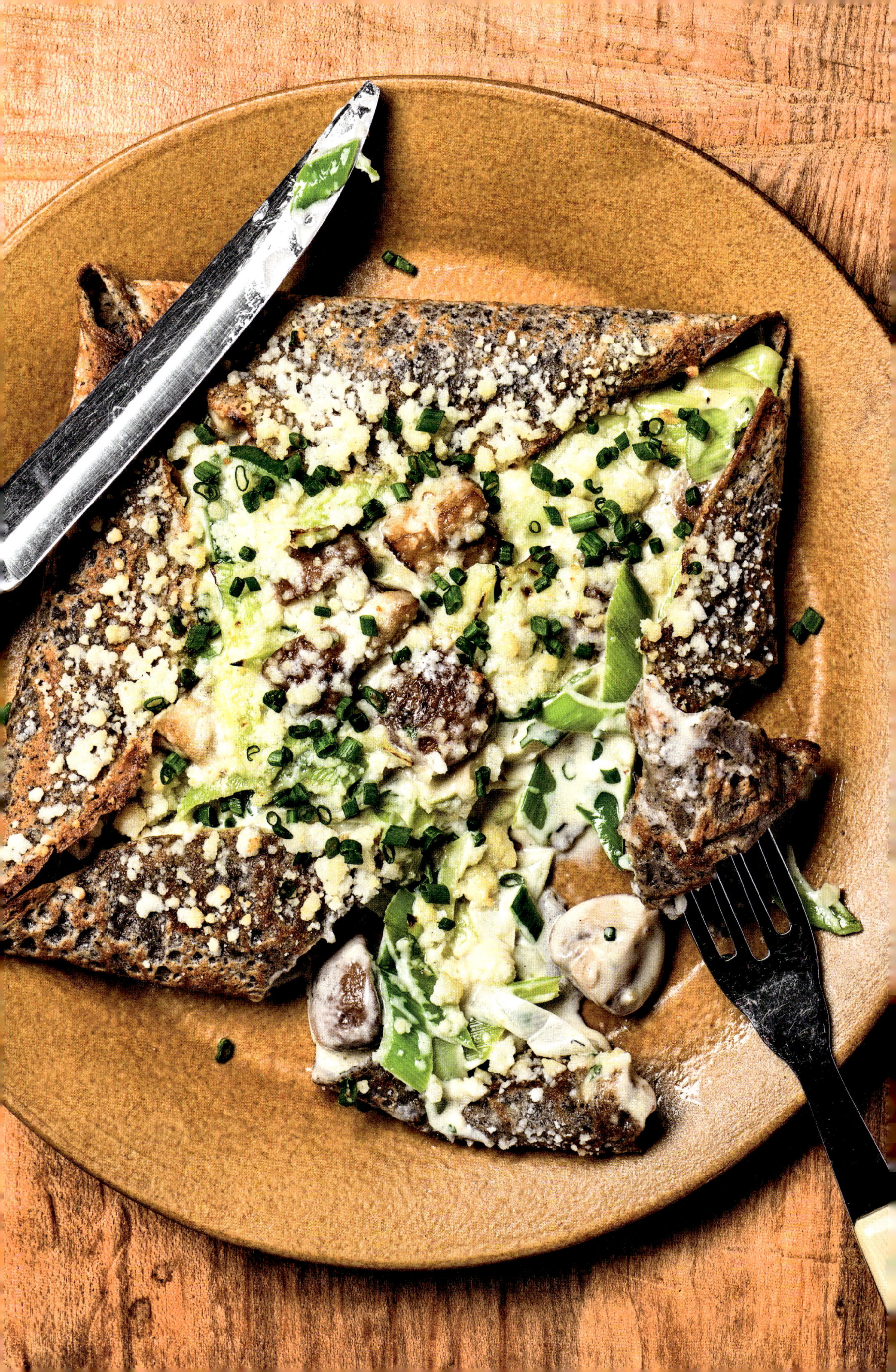

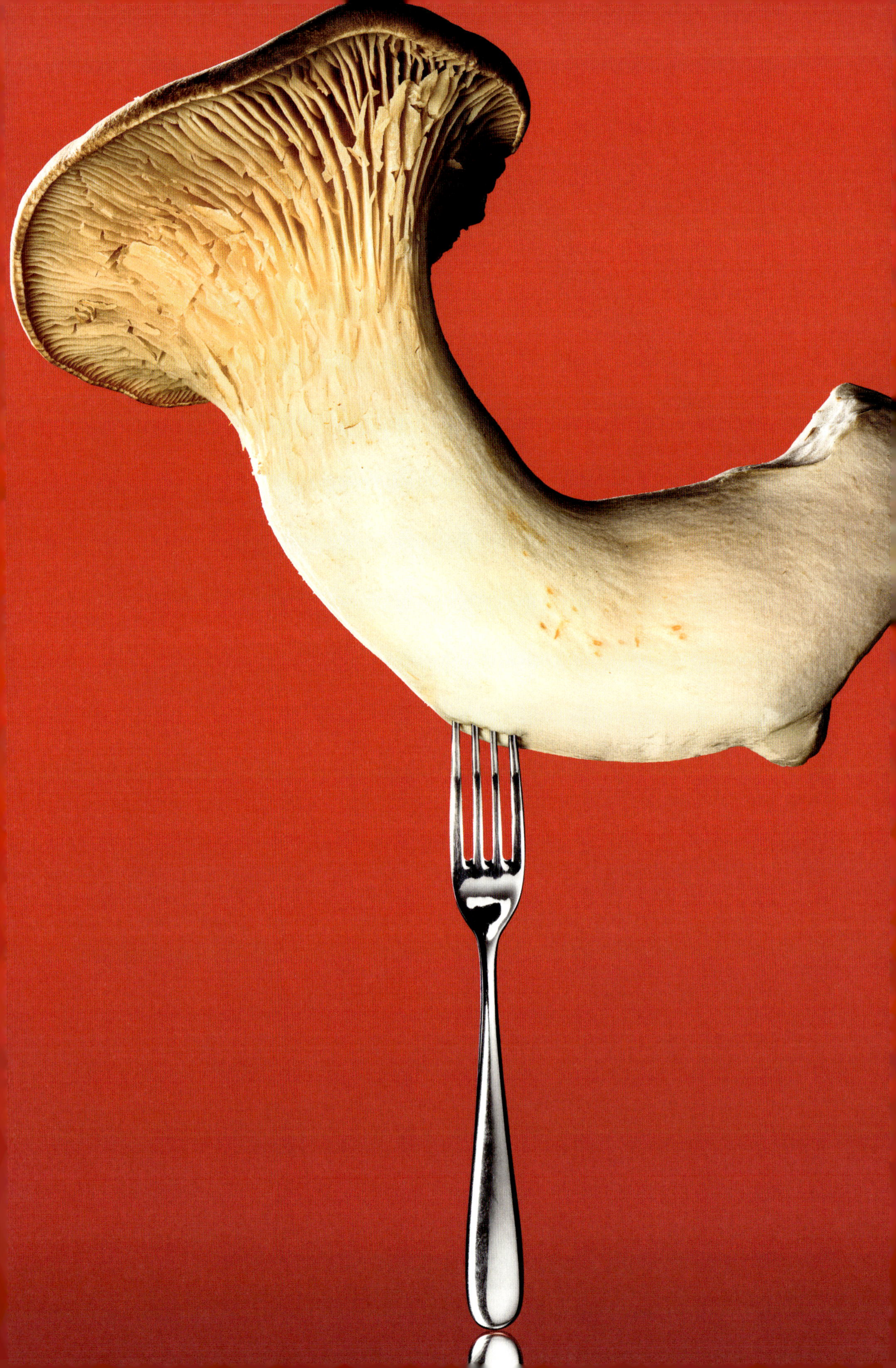

Main Mushrooms

Wild Mushroom Risotto

Serves: 6

INGREDIENTS
1.5 litres chicken or vegetable stock
125 g unsalted butter
1 large onion, finely chopped
2 garlic cloves, finely chopped
250 g mixed fresh wild mushrooms, coarsely chopped*
150 ml dry white wine or vermouth
500 g risotto rice
1 tbs freshly chopped thyme
1 tbs freshly chopped marjoram or nepitella
75 g freshly grated parmesan (plus extra to serve)
Salt and freshly ground black pepper

EQUIPMENT
Large frying pan with lid
Large, heavy saucepan
Large ladle

Any type of fresh, wild mushroom will make this taste wonderful — black trompettes de mort or deep golden musky girolles, for example. But a combination of cultivated mushrooms and reconstituted dried Italian porcini or French cèpes is a great alternative. In Italy, a wild herb called nepitella, a wild catmint, is often used when cooking wild mushrooms. Use Carnaroli risotto rice for best results.

Put the stock in a large saucepan and keep at a gentle simmer.

Melt half the butter in a separate large, heavy saucepan and add the onion and garlic. Cook gently for ten minutes, until soft, golden and translucent but not browned. Stir in the mushrooms and cook over a medium heat for about three minutes to heat through. Pour in the wine and boil hard until it has reduced and almost disappeared. This will remove the taste of raw alcohol and concentrate the flavour. Stir in the rice, and fry gently over a medium heat with the onion and mushrooms until dry and the rice is slightly opaque, having absorbed the butter.

Begin adding the stock, a large ladleful at a time, stirring — traditionally with a wooden spoon — until each ladleful has been absorbed by the rice. It is said that the stock should "sigh" as it hits the pan, showing that all is at the right temperature. Continue ladling and stirring until the rice is tender and creamy, but the grains are still firm. This should take 15–20 minutes, depending on the type of risotto rice used — check the packet instructions. Taste and season well with salt and pepper, and add the herbs.

Remove the pan from the heat and beat in the remaining butter and parmesan. Cover, and let it rest for a couple of minutes to become even creamier. Serve immediately with extra grated parmesan.

* Or a mixture of wild and ordinary mushrooms, or 200 g of cultivated mushrooms plus 25 g of dried porcini soaked in warm water for 20 minutes, drained and chopped.

Tagliatelle with Porcini Sauce

Serves: 4

INGREDIENTS
125 g butter
1 small onion, finely chopped
10 g dried porcini mushrooms, reconstituted and finely chopped
500 g fresh mushrooms (chestnut, portobello or porcini), finely chopped
Salt and freshly ground black pepper
3 tbs finely chopped parsley
500 g dried tagliatelle
50 g freshly grated parmesan cheese (plus extra to serve)

EQUIPMENT
Sieve
Paper coffee filter
Soft pastry brush
Medium non-stick frying pan with a lid
Very large saucepan
Colander

Made with fresh porcini, this dish is sublime — and the dried mushrooms aren't essential. If you don't have a supply of wild fungi, this simple recipe will make cultivated mushrooms taste almost as good.

Filter and retain the water used for soaking the dried mushrooms (see page 155).

Heat a medium non-stick frying pan over a medium heat and add half of the butter. When foaming, add the onion, and cook for 5–7 minutes, stirring occasionally until soft and golden but not brown. Add the soaked and chopped dried mushrooms and their filtered water, and cook over a medium-high heat until all the liquid has evaporated, watching that it doesn't catch and burn. Stir in the chopped fresh mushrooms, season with salt and pepper, and cover the pan. Turn down the heat, cover and gently simmer for 25–30 minutes. This long cooking will help the wild mushroom flavour to permeate into the ordinary mushrooms. After the cooking time, reduce any residual liquid remaining in the pan by boiling fast. Turn off the heat and set aside.

Cook the pasta in a very large saucepan of boiling salted water according to the manufacturer's instructions. When it is cooked al dente, drain through a colander, keeping aside a ladleful of the cooking water to add to the sauce.

Toss the pasta immediately with the reserved mushroom sauce, the reserved cooking water, the remaining butter, the parsley and the parmesan, and warm through gently. Serve with a bowl of extra freshly grated parmesan.

Wild Mushroom and Herb Ravioli

Serves: 4

INGREDIENTS
100 g butter
Freshly grated parmesan (to serve)

Fresh herb pasta:
200 g* plain white flour or Italian "00" flour
Pinch of salt
3 medium eggs, beaten
3 tbs mixed chopped fresh rocket, marjoram and parsley (plus extra to serve)
1 tbs olive oil

Filling:
250 g fresh mixed wild mushrooms, finely chopped
50 g butter or 2 tbs olive oil
2 shallots, finely chopped
25 g black semi-dried (black crinkly) olives, stoned and finely chopped
4 sun-dried tomato halves in oil, drained and finely chopped
2 tbs dry vermouth or white wine
Salt and freshly ground black pepper
Freshly grated nutmeg

EQUIPMENT
Soft pastry brush
Food processor (optional)
Large frying pan
Small plastic bag
Rolling pin
2 clean kitchen towels
Large saucepan with lid
Serrated pasta wheel or pastry wheel (or sharp knife)

This is a pretty, green, herb-speckled ravioli filled with a mixture of wild mushrooms with a hint of olive and sundried tomato to give an intense smoky flavour. The dish needs nothing more than some melted butter, extra herbs and fresh parmesan to complete it.

First, make the pasta. Do not make the dough too far in advance or it can discolour. Sift the flour and salt onto a clean work surface, and make a large well in the centre with your hand. Beat two eggs with the herbs and oil, and pour this into the well. Gradually mix the eggs into the flour with the fingers of one hand and bring it together into a stiff dough. Knead the pasta for about five minutes until smooth. Wrap and allow it to rest for at least 30 minutes at room temperature, before attempting to roll out—the pasta will be much more elastic and ready to roll out after resting.

Melt the butter or olive oil in a large frying pan. Add the shallots and cook for about five minutes until soft and golden but not browned. Stir in the mushrooms, olives and tomatoes, and cook, stirring over a high heat for about two minutes (no longer or the mushrooms will become too dry). Sprinkle with the wine, and cook for one minute longer. Season well with salt, pepper and the grated nutmeg. Transfer to a bowl, and allow to cool.

Unwrap the pasta and cut the dough in two. Put one-half in a plastic bag. Using a rolling pin on a very lightly floured surface, roll one-half of the pasta as thinly as possible, to a rectangle about 30 × 30 cm.† Cover with a slightly damp clean kitchen towel, and repeat with the remaining pasta.

Place 16 tsp (heaped) of filling in four even rows of four on the pasta rectangle, keeping them well spaced to allow for sealing of the ravioli edges later. Brush the dough spaces between the mounds with beaten egg with a pastry brush.

Using the rolling pin, lift the remaining sheet of pasta over the dough with the mounds of filling. Press the pasta gently down between these mounds, pushing out any trapped air, then press down firmly to seal properly. Cut the filled pasta into 16 neat squares with a serrated pasta wheel. Transfer to a floured kitchen towel.

Bring a very large saucepan of salted water to the boil, and carefully add the ravioli. Bring back to the boil, turn off the heat and cover with a tight-fitting lid. Leave for five minutes, then uncover, drain well (keeping back 4 tbs of the cooking water) and return the ravioli and the reserved water to the hot pan. Toss with the melted butter and extra herbs, and place four ravioli on each of four warm plates, spooning over the herby butter sauce remaining in the pan.

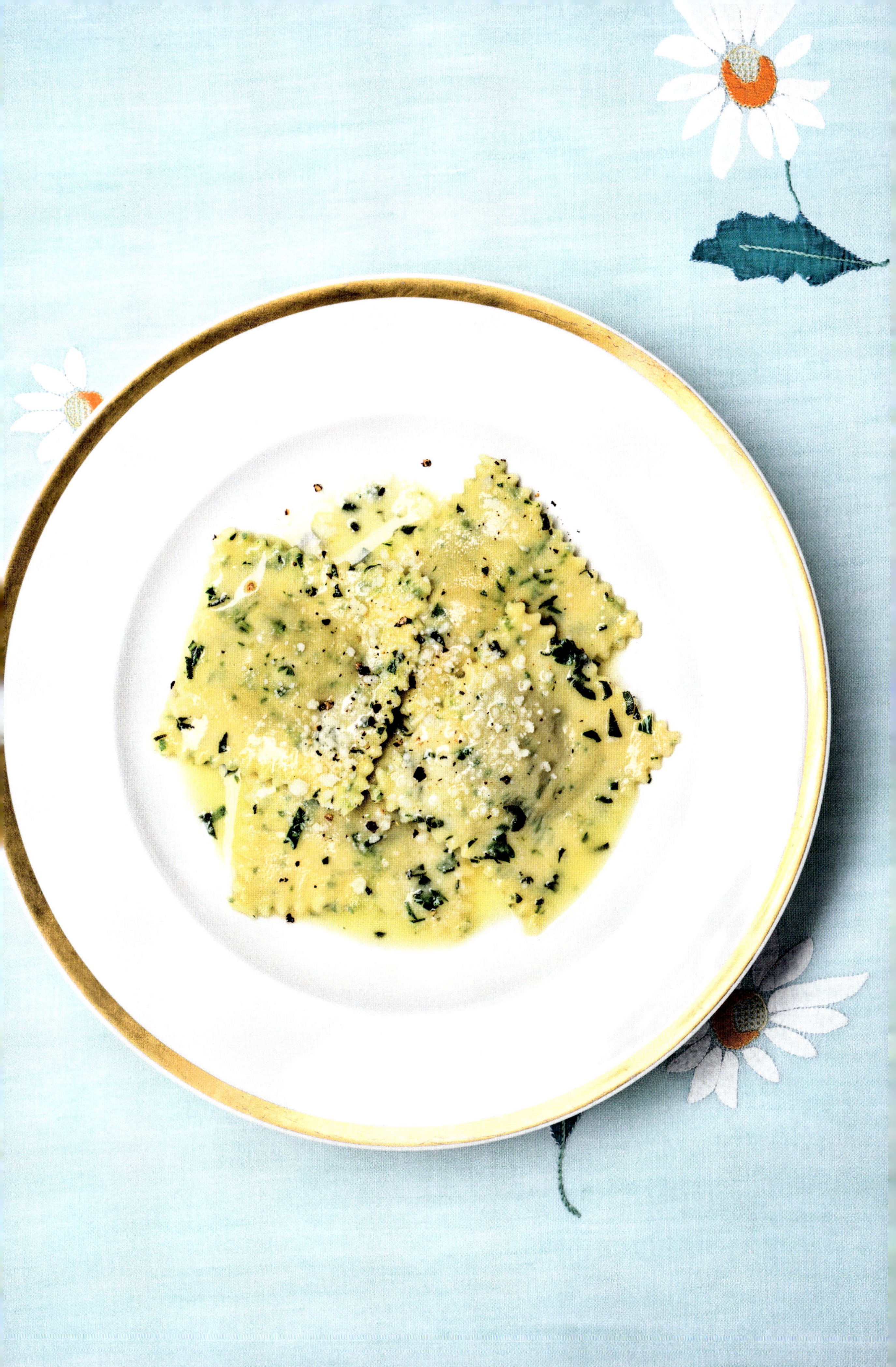

Serve with freshly grated parmesan.

* This quantity is only a guide — depending on humidity, type of flour, etc., you may have to add more or less flour. The dough must not be too soft — it should be quite hard to knead but will soften somewhat after resting. Adding too much extra flour will make the pasta tough, taste floury and difficult to roll. Replacing a proportion of the flour with semola (Italian fine semolina flour made from grano duro) will give the pasta more texture and bite.

† If you have one, use a pasta machine to roll out the pasta dough thinly into long strips, and use these to make the ravioli as above but in one row, flipping over the long side of the pasta sheet.to cover the filling so that you have one rounded, folded side and three open edges. Brush the inside edges with beaten egg, press out the air with your finger while sealing them together, then cut and trim these three edges with the serrated pasta wheel.

Hungarian Mushroom Pie
(Gombas Lepény)

Serves: 4

INGREDIENTS
350 g ready-rolled all-butter shortcrust pastry, thawed if frozen
50 g butter
1 red onion, finely chopped
3 garlic cloves, finely chopped
Salt and freshly ground black pepper
500 g mixed fresh mushrooms, sliced
3 eggs
75 g quark
150 ml crème fraîche or double cream
3 tbs fresh sourdough breadcrumbs
100 g freshly grated Gruyère cheese
2 tbs fresh mixed dill and parsley, chopped
3 tbs freshly grated parmesan or pecorino
2 tbs olive oil
2 red peppers
2 red onions, quartered
1 tsp caraway seeds

EQUIPMENT
23 cm pie dish
Medium non-stick frying pan
Kitchen foil
Baking beans
Baking sheet
Medium mixing bowl
Wooden spoon or balloon whisk

This is a dish from the little-known cuisine of the Magyars, who settled near the Matra mountains and Bakony forest in Hungary. The area would have been teeming with highly prized wild mushrooms. This is a refined version, with a nod to its rustic roots. The country version is not baked in pastry but has added breadcrumbs to make it more substantial — a puffy golden bread and mushroom pudding. It is delicious served warm, and makes good picnic food when cold.

Use the ready-rolled shortcrust pastry to line the pie dish (roll out thinner if wished). Trim the edges with a sharp knife, then prick the base all over with a fork, and chill or freeze for 15 minutes to set the pastry.

Preheat the oven to 190°C/170°C fan/gas mark 5.

Meanwhile, heat a medium non-stick frying pan and add the butter. When the butter stops foaming, add the onions and garlic, season well with salt and pepper, then add the mushrooms, and scoop and stir over a high heat until the mushrooms are browning around the edges and their juices have reduced to almost nothing. Cool in the pan for five minutes.

Once chilled or frozen, line the pastry case with kitchen foil, and pour in enough baking beans to come two-thirds the way up the sides. Flick the edges of the foil inwards over the baking beans so that it doesn't catch on the pastry. Set on a baking sheet, and bake blind in the centre of the oven for 15–20 minutes. Remove the foil and beans, and return the empty pastry case to the oven for a further 7–10 minutes to cook and dry out completely. Leave to cool. Lower the oven to 180°C/160°C fan/gas mark 4.

In a medium mixing bowl, beat the eggs and mix with the quark, crème fraîche, breadcrumbs, Gruyère cheese and fresh herbs, and season well with salt and pepper. Spread the mushroom mixture evenly over the base of the cooled pastry case, and spoon over the egg and cream mix, spreading to the edges. Sprinkle with the parmesan, place on a baking sheet and bake for 30–40 minutes until golden brown and risen. If it is cooking too quickly, cover the top with kitchen foil to protect it.

Meanwhile, toss the red peppers, onions and caraway seeds with the olive oil and roast for 30 minutes until soft and lightly charred.

Remove the pie from the oven, cool in the dish for five minutes, then cut into wedges to serve with the roasted red peppers, onions and caraway seeds.

Simple Mushroom Tarts

A dish so simple because it uses shop-bought puff pastry, and fresh, frozen or dried mushrooms, these creamy mushroom tarts punch above their weight. A perfect lunch served alongside a rocket or a bitter leaf salad with a parmesan dressing.

Serves: 4

INGREDIENTS
Flour (for dusting)
450 g fresh/frozen or 110 g dried reconstituted porcini mushrooms, thinly sliced
225 g fresh flat mushrooms (the dark, open kind), thinly sliced
500 g all-butter puff pastry
125 g butter
Salt and freshly ground black pepper
3 tbs crème fraîche
1 lemon, zested
4 garlic cloves, thinly sliced
2–3 tbs fresh parsley, chopped
50 g dry breadcrumbs
1 egg, beaten
2 tbs freshly grated parmesan

EQUIPMENT
Paper coffee filter (if using dried mushrooms)
Sieve
Rolling pin
15 cm saucer
Large baking sheet
Large frying pan
Medium bowl
Pastry brush
Large 32 × 38 cm baking sheet

Filter and retain the water used for soaking the dried mushrooms (see page 155).

On a floured work surface, roll out the pastry to a thickness of 3 mm. Cut out four 15 cm circles of pastry using a saucer as a guide. Arrange on a large, floured baking sheet and chill.

Preheat the oven to 200°C/180°C fan/gas mark 6.

Heat the butter in a large frying pan until it stops foaming. Add the mushrooms, and season with plenty of salt and pepper. Cook briskly over a high heat, scooping and turning until the mushrooms are browning around the edges and golden brown all over, driving off all the moisture as it is released. Add the crème fraîche, lemon zest, garlic, parsley and breadcrumbs, and mix well. Tip into a medium bowl and leave to cool.

Remove the pastry from the fridge, and brush the flat rim of each round with a 1 cm band of beaten egg. Pile the mushrooms into the centre of each round and spread them out to just touch the internal edge of this band of beaten egg. Sprinkle evenly with the grated parmesan, and carefully slide onto a large greased baking sheet.

Bake in the oven for 15–20 minutes or until the pastry has risen up around the edges, encasing the filling, the edges are beautifully golden, and the bases are cooked and crisp underneath. Serve immediately with a rocket or bitter leaf salad with a parmesan dressing.

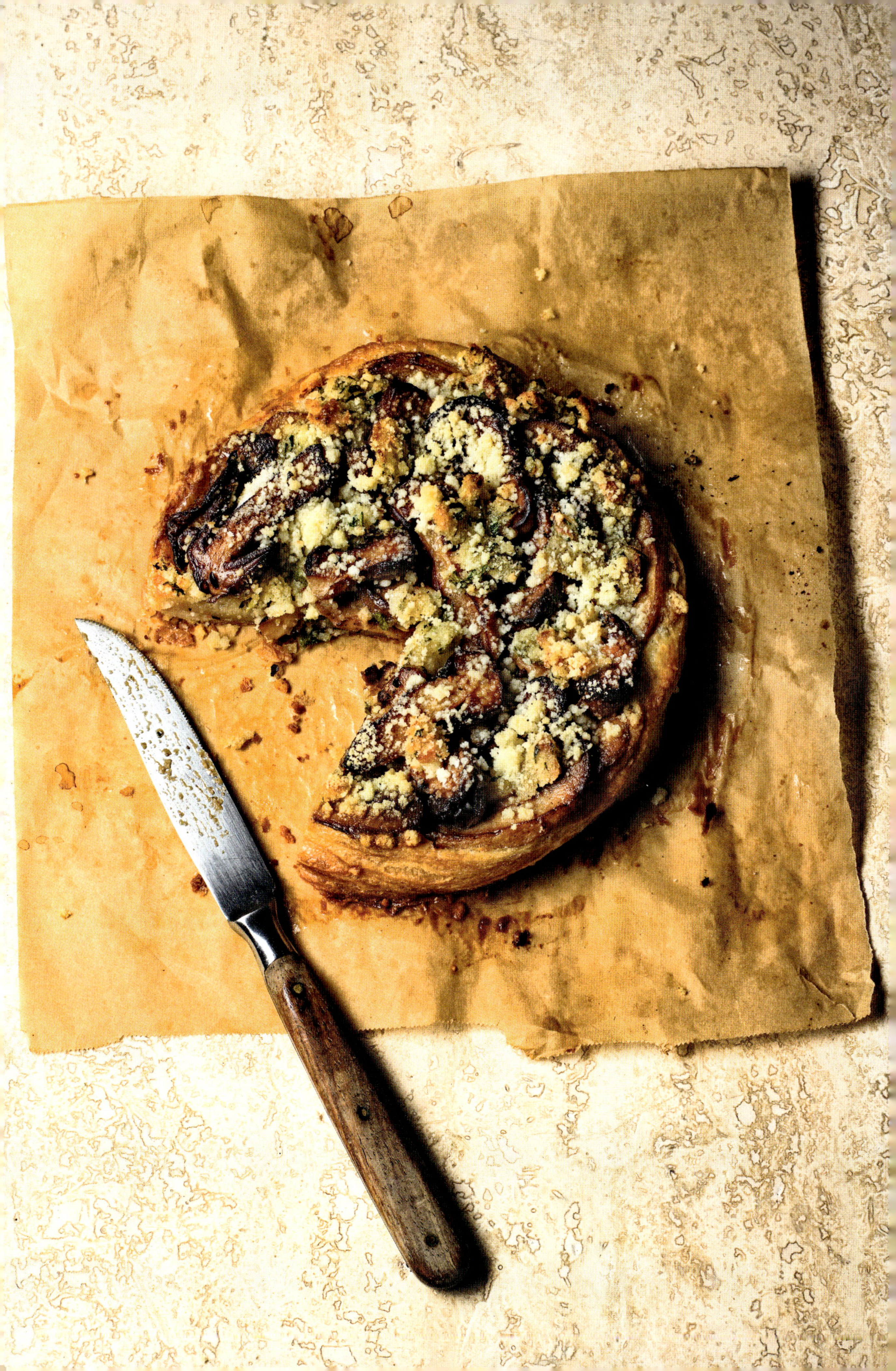

Mushroom Stroganoff

Serves: 4

INGREDIENTS
3 tbs olive oil
50 g butter
3 large shallots or 1 onion, finely chopped
3 garlic cloves, crushed
900 g fresh chestnut mushrooms, sliced
1 tbs dijon mustard
2 tsp smoked paprika (pimentón)
1 tbs plain flour
1 tbs mushroom ketchup (see page 240) or Worcestershire sauce
450 ml mushroom (or vegetable or chicken) stock
250 g long grain rice
300 ml soured cream
½ lemon, juiced
Salt and freshly ground black pepper
3 tbs parsley, roughly chopped (to serve)
2 lemon wedges (to serve)

EQUIPMENT
Large frying pan
Large saucepan

Popular post-war in the 1950s and 60s (using what were then expensive ingredients), beef Stroganoff exploded around the world into restaurants – often cooked tableside for the added thrill of brandy flaming. There is no traditional recipe for this, but it has Russian origins and was adopted into French haute cuisine (hence the mustard) and must include onions and soured cream; the rest is up to the cook. Noodles or pasta were the precursors to the ubiquitous rice accompaniment. This version makes the mushroom the star of the dish, supported by enticing non-Russian starlets like Spanish pimentón and dijon mustard.

Heat a large frying pan over a medium heat and add the oil, then the butter. Once the oil and butter start to foam, add the onion, garlic and a pinch of salt, turn down the heat and cook gently for 5–7 minutes or until soft but not coloured, stirring occasionally. Stir in the mushrooms, raise the heat to medium and continue to cook gently for 5–6 minutes, or until the mushrooms are tender and beginning to turn golden brown. Add the mustard, paprika and flour, and mix well to coat.

Mix the mushroom ketchup with the stock, and pour over the mushrooms, stirring as you pour. Simmer gently for five more minutes whilst you start cooking the rice in a large, heavy saucepan. Cook the rice according to the packet instructions in a separate saucepan until tender.

Whilst the rice is cooking, remove the mushrooms from the heat, stir in the soured cream and fresh lemon juice, and gently but thoroughly mix it all together. Taste, and add salt and pepper as needed and reheat. Scatter generously with chopped parsley and serve with the rice, and lemon wedges on the side.

Mushroom Bourguignon

Serves: 4

INGREDIENTS
2 tbs olive oil
40 g butter
85 g bacon lardons or cubed pancetta (optional)
600 g fresh mushrooms (e.g. medium chestnuts)
1 large carrot, thickly sliced
125 g shallots, halved and peeled
1 medium leek, thickly sliced
2 garlic cloves, crushed
1 tsp plain flour
125 ml burgundy-style fruity red wine
2 sprigs of thyme
1 bay leaf
200 ml mushroom or vegetable stock (more if needed)
Salt and freshly ground black pepper
Extra thyme leaves chopped with fresh parsley (to serve)

EQUIPMENT
Medium-sized heavy-based pan or casserole (not too deep)
Slotted spoon
Medium bowl
Kitchen paper

The word "bourguignon" refers to a recipe that is prepared in the style of the French region of Bourgogne (Burgundy), one of France's major wine-making regions. A recipe prepared à la bourguignon will usually feature meat or poultry, or in this instance mushrooms, braised in a hearty Beaujolais or young Burgundy, with baby (pearl) onions, button mushrooms and bacon lardons.

Heat 1 tbs of the olive oil with butter in a medium-sized heavy-based pan or casserole. Add the lardons (if using) and fry over a medium heat until they become crisp and golden brown. Remove with a slotted spoon and drain on kitchen paper. If not using lardons, skip this step and begin with the mushrooms.

Add the remaining olive oil to the remaining fat in the pan. Add the mushrooms and cook over a high heat, scooping and tossing them as they cook for a few minutes until they start to look golden and begin to brown at the edges. Using a slotted spoon, transfer them to a medium bowl, leaving the cooking fat behind.

Put the pan back on the heat and add the carrots and cook for five minutes, then add the shallots and leeks (cut sides down) and cook for five minutes more until all the vegetables are lightly caramelized. Stir in the garlic, sprinkle in the flour and cook, gently stirring for one minute.

Pour in the wine, add the reserved lardons (if using), and the thyme and bay leaves, and mix gently. Bring up to a steady simmer and cook for about five minutes, to reduce the wine by half. Now add the stock and reserved mushrooms with their juices, and simmer for a further ten minutes until everything is tender and the sauce lightly syrupy. Taste and season. Remove the bay leaf, and serve scattered with chopped parsley and extra thyme leaves. It is extra-delicious with crushed new potatoes or a buttery creamy mash.

Mushroom Ragù with Soft Polenta

In Italy, there is an ancient communal feasting tradition of eating polenta and ragù directly off the table, called *polenta alla spianatora*. Everyone has a spoon, and they dig in. Great fun and no washing up!

Serves: 4–6

INGREDIENTS

Mushroom ragù:
30 g dried wild mushrooms
600 g mixed fresh mushrooms
1 medium onion
2 medium carrots
2 celery stalks
4 garlic cloves
45 ml olive oil
150 ml red wine
1 tbs mushroom ketchup (see page 240), Worcestershire sauce or tamari
1 mushroom or vegetable stock cube
Two 400 g cans plum tomatoes
300 g passata
1–2 tsp (to taste) dried chilli flakes
2 tsp dried oregano
2–3 sprigs fresh thyme
2 bay leaves

Soft polenta:
250 g polenta (traditional bramata or "instant")
200 g grated parmesan, grated (plus extra to serve)
100 g butter, diced
Salt and freshly ground black pepper

EQUIPMENT
Paper coffee filter
Sieve
Food processor
Medium bowl
Medium heatproof casserole with a lid
Large, heavy saucepan
Balloon whisk

Filter and retain the water used for soaking the dried mushrooms (see page 155).

A food processor will make chopping the soaked and fresh mushrooms much easier than doing it by hand. Process the mushrooms in four batches, pulsing them in short bursts until "minced" but not purèed. Do the same with the onion, carrots and celery, and the garlic, tipping them into a medium bowl as you go.

Preheat the oven to 140°C/120°C fan/gas mark 1.

Heat the oil in the casserole, over a medium heat, then tip in the chopped onion, carrot, celery and garlic, and stir well to coat. Cook, stirring occasionally, for about ten minutes until the vegetables have softened and the onions are translucent. Now stir in the chopped mushrooms and allow to cook for about five minutes until the mushrooms release their juices.

Add the wine, the mushroom ketchup, the reserved mushroom water, the crumbled stock cube and 250 ml of water, stir well and boil fast for five minutes to reduce the liquid and boil off the alcohol. Stir in the chopped tomatoes and passata with the chilli flakes, oregano, thyme sprigs and bay leaves, and bring up to a simmer.

Cover and transfer to the oven, and cook for at least one hour, but preferably 2–3 hours to really concentrate the flavours. When cooked, keep warm or reheat when you have made the polenta.

The cooking method is the same for both traditional and "instant" polenta— the cooking times are just very different. Instant takes about 5 minutes, and traditional polenta bramata can take as long as 40–50 minutes. Bring 1.5 litres of water to the boil in a large, heavy saucepan. Slowly shower in the polenta, stirring constantly with a balloon whisk. When it starts to boil again, reduce the heat to low and cook, stirring constantly with a wooden spoon or spatula (the whisk may not be strong enough at this stage). The polenta is ready when it leaves the sides of the pan but is still runny like a very sloppy mashed potato. When cooked, beat in the parmesan and butter, taste, and season well with salt and pepper.

Spread the polenta over a long, narrow, shallow dish, and top with the ragù, or serve individually in shallow bowls with plenty of extra parmesan. Or serve family style — directly on the table.

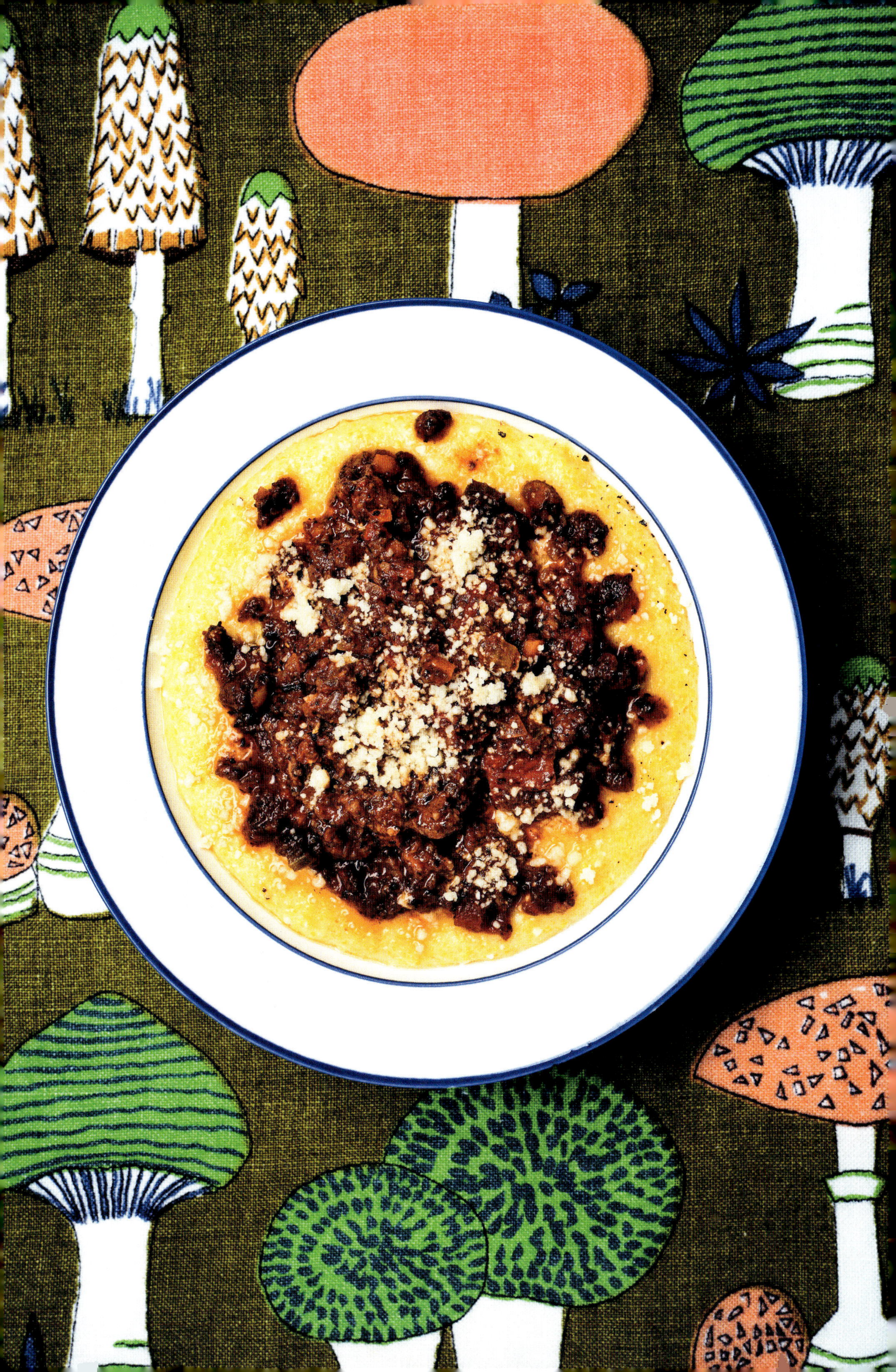

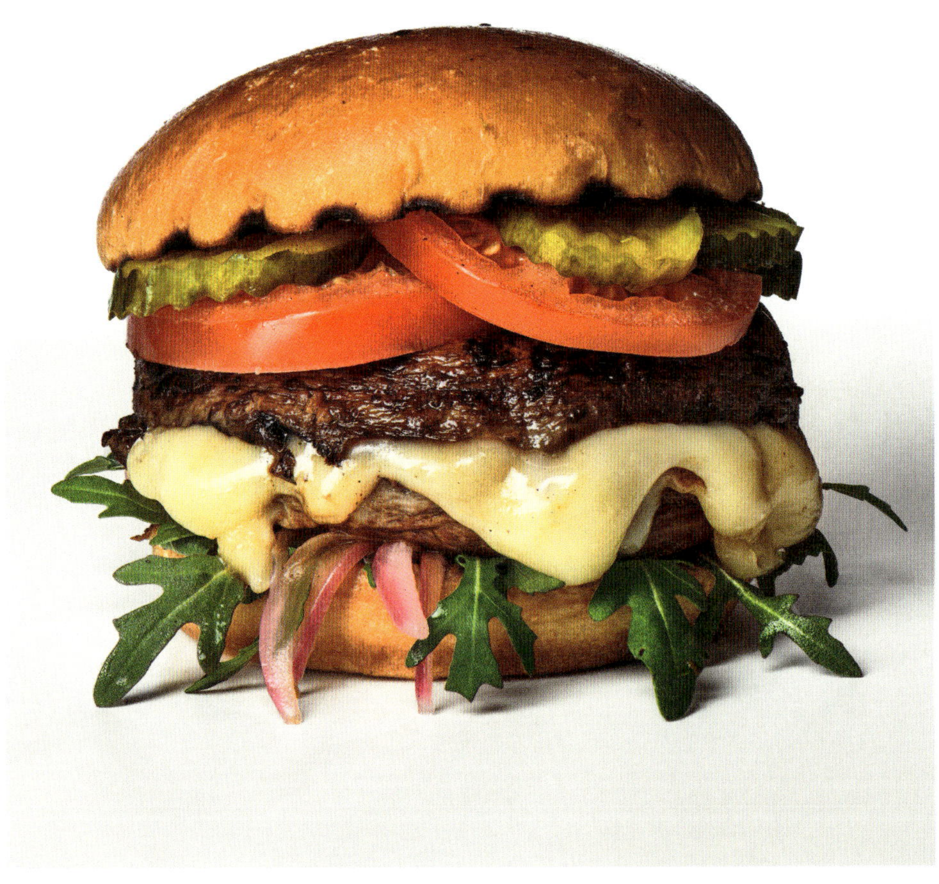

Mushroom and Taleggio Burgers

Serves: 4

INGREDIENTS
4 thick slices of Taleggio cheese
4 hamburger buns
Selection of salad leaves, watercress or rocket, sliced tomato, sliced or pickled red onion, favourite pickles, mayonnaise, mustard, chilli sauce/relish, etc.

Burger:
8 large fresh portobello mushrooms (chosen to fit the bun)

Basting sauce:
8 tbs extra-virgin olive oil
1 tbs balsamic vinegar
2 tbs tamari
½ tsp dijon mustard with tarragon
2 large garlic cloves, finely grated (black garlic is better)
Salt and freshly ground black pepper

EQUIPMENT
Soft pastry brush
Large baking sheet
Large, ridged grill pan

If big wild porcini caps are available, they are ideal for this recipe. Alternatively, a large portobello mushroom will work perfectly well. This recipe uses Taleggio; a ripe and semi-soft cheese with a strong aroma and an almost fruity flavour that melts perfectly on top of the mushroom.

Halve the buns, and toast their cut sides.

Choose the mushroom size to fit the buns. Remove the stems (keep for a stock or discard).

Place the mushrooms top side up on a large baking sheet. Whisk the basting sauce ingredients together with salt and pepper to taste in a small bowl, and pour over the mushrooms, then turn them in the sauce to coat.

Heat a large, ridged grill pan on the hob, or barbecue until hot.

Arrange the mushrooms top side down on the grill pan, and brush the insides with the remaining sauce.

Turn the mushrooms over after 2–3 minutes, and cook for a further 1–2 minutes until the mushrooms are sizzling and cooked through. Turn two mushrooms over to their gill side, and top with slices of Taleggio — halved if necessary and stacked together to stay within the mushroom edges — and let them begin to melt.

Working quickly, place a cheesy mushroom on the base of each burger bun, then a handful of greens on the cheese and enclose each with a plain mushroom cap (top side up) and add the extras of your choice. Spread some mayonnaise or burger sauce on the bun lids, and press one lightly on top of each burger. Eat immediately.

Soba Noodles in Mushroom Broth with Mushroom Dipping Sauce

Serves: 2–4

INGREDIENTS
Noodle dipping sauce:
200 ml dark or light soy sauce (depending on desired intensity)
200 ml mirin
100 ml sake
1 piece of kombu (dried kelp)
4 tbs bonito flakes (katsuobushi)
3 fresh shiitake mushrooms, sliced

Noodle broth:
200 g dried soba noodles
400 g assorted fresh mushrooms, sliced
4 spring onions, finely sliced on the diagonal (to serve)
2 tbs toasted sesame seeds (to serve)
Coarsely ground shichimi togarashi (Japanese seven-spice seasoning) (to serve)

EQUIPMENT
Large saucepan
Paper coffee filter
500 ml screw-top jar
Large slotted metal spoon or a spider
2 noodle bowls

It's truly comforting to eat a hot bowl of noodles in cold weather. Both nutritious and warming, noodles are instantly satisfying and warm you up from inside. Japanese mushrooms such as shimeji and enoki have become increasingly easy to buy in the West, but if unavailable, try using fresh shiitakes mixed with portobello or chestnut mushrooms.

First, make the dipping sauce. Put all the ingredients into a large saucepan and stir. Bring to the boil over a high heat, then lower the heat to a simmer and cook gently for 5–7 minutes. The sauce should reduce and thicken very slightly. Remove from the heat, and strain through a paper coffee filter into a warmed screw-top jar to remove the kombu, bonito flakes and mushrooms, and allow to cool completely before using. Tightly screw on the lid, and store in the fridge for up to a week.

Now cook the noodles. Bring a large saucepan of water to the boil over a high heat. Add the soba noodles, and give a quick stir to ensure the noodles are separated. Return the water to the boil, and when boiling once more, add a glass of cold water and bring it to the boil again — this is to ensure both the outer and central parts of the noodle strands are cooked at the same speed. When the water returns to the boil for the third time, they should now be properly cooked. Drain the noodles, and rinse them under cold running water. Drain well, and set aside (but not for too long).

Alternatively, follow the manufacturer's cooking instructions on the packet.

In the same large saucepan, heat the noodle dipping sauce with 750 ml of water to make a broth. Bring to the boil over a medium-high heat. Taste, and add more water if too strong or more dipping sauce if too bland. When the broth reaches the boil, add the noodles and cook for one minute to reheat them. Lift out the noodles using a large slotted spoon, and divide the warm noodles between two warmed bowls.

Add the mushrooms to the broth, and cook for 2–3 minutes. Ladle the broth over the noodles, and finish with the chopped spring onions and sesame seeds. Provide the ground shichimi togarashi separately in a spice grinder or a small bowl.

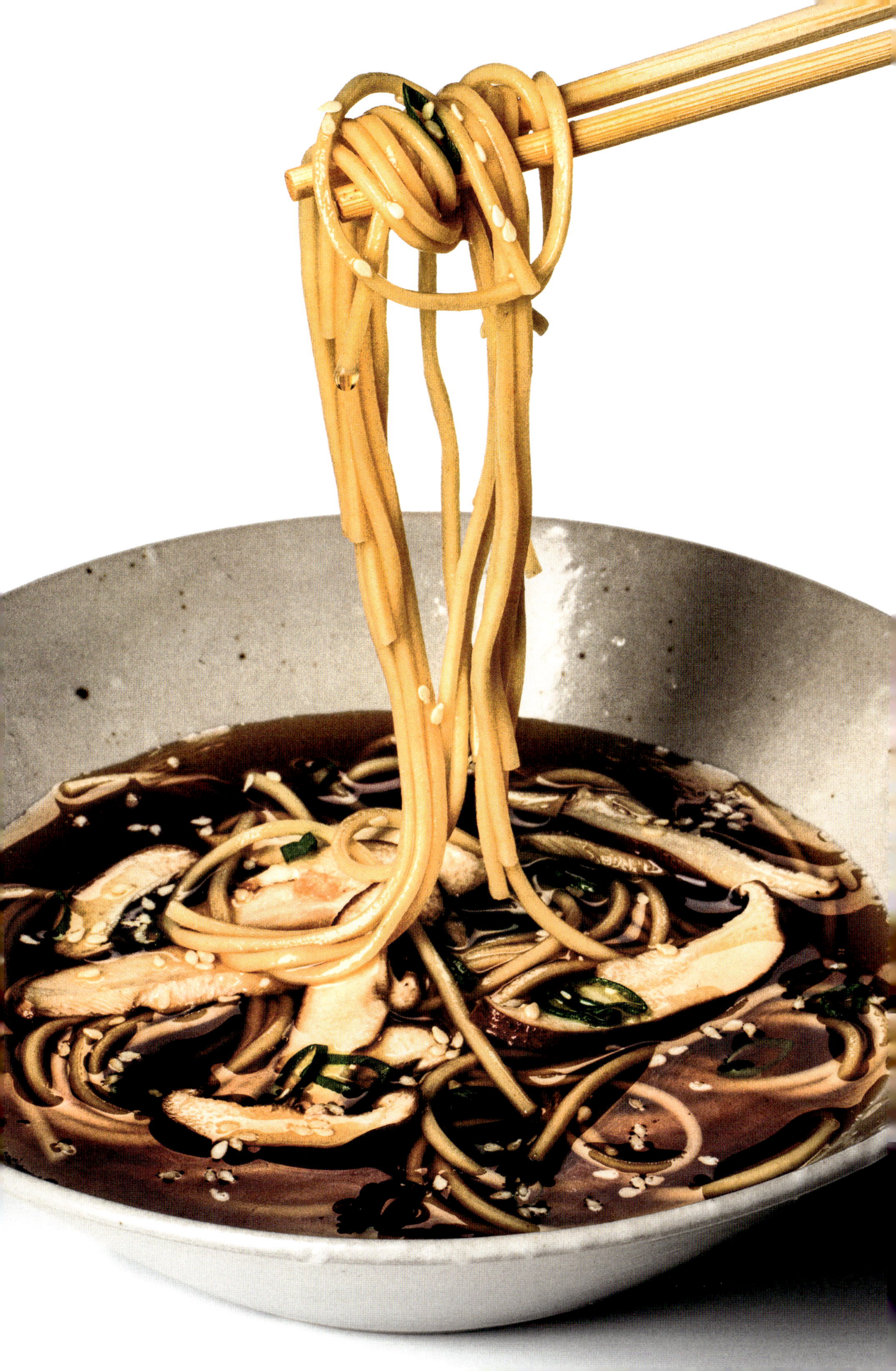

Mushroom, Ricotta and Pesto Lasagne

Serves: 6

INGREDIENTS

Pasta:

4-egg quantity of fresh egg pasta dough, 12 fresh shop-bought lasagne sheets (about 15 × 20 cm) or 400 g dried pasta sheets (cook according to manufacturer's instructions)

Mushroom sauce:

25 g dried wild porcini mushrooms, reconstituted and roughly chopped
4 tbs olive oil
125 g butter, plus a bit extra
900 g fresh mushrooms (porcini, field or open cup), thinly sliced
1 medium onion, finely chopped
4 garlic cloves, chopped
3 tbs dry vermouth
2 or 3 sprigs fresh thyme, leaves chopped
300 ml mushroom, vegetable, chicken or meat stock
4 tbs fresh parsley, chopped

Pesto:

3 garlic cloves, peeled
75 g pine nuts
75 g fresh basil leaves including young stems (or wild garlic leaves in season)
100 ml olive oil
75 g butter, softened
Salt and freshly ground black pepper
4 tbs freshly grated parmesan or pecorino

A rich and robust dish inspired by the area around Tuscany, Umbria and Le Marche where wild mushrooms abound, and fresh egg pasta is made regularly. Cultivated mushrooms are also good here, but use flavoursome, dark, open-cap ones or field mushrooms (do not use shiitakes — they are completely the wrong flavour). The dish takes time to make, but it's worth it. A proper lasagne has more pasta layers than filling and won't collapse all over the place when lifted out of the dish.

Make the fresh pasta, if using,* and wrap it and leave aside to rest; do not refrigerate. Filter and retain the water used for soaking the dried mushrooms (see page 155).

Heat half of the oil in a large non-stick sauté pan and add the butter. When foaming, add half of the fresh and dried mushrooms, half of the chopped onion and all of the chopped garlic, and sauté over a high heat for 4–5 minutes until tender, reduced and beginning to soften.

Tip into a medium bowl, and repeat with the remaining half, then combine the two batches back in the pan, stir in the vermouth and thyme, and cook for a further two minutes, then pour in the stock and the reserved dried mushroom liquid, bring to the boil, and boil rapidly for 4–5 minutes until the sauce reduces and turns syrupy. Stir in the parsley. Set aside to cool.

To make the pesto, put the garlic in a mortar and pestle with a little salt and the pine nuts. Pound until broken up. Add the basil leaves, a few at a time, pounding and mixing to a paste. Add the mixture to a small bowl, and gradually beat in the olive oil, little by little, until the mixture is creamy and thick. Beat in the butter, and season with pepper, then beat in the cheese. Alternatively, put everything in a blender and process until smooth. Store in a jar in the refrigerator — with a layer of olive oil on top to exclude the air — until needed.

Now make the ricotta mix. Place the ricotta, eggs and grated cheese in a medium bowl, and season to taste. Mix thoroughly with a spatula until the mixture is smooth, and set aside.

Fresh home-made pasta can be used without pre-cooking, as it absorbs the mushroom sauce. If using shop-bought fresh pasta sheets, remove them from the packaging — gently separating if necessary — and place in a medium roasting pan. Cover with water, and leave to stand for two minutes, then drain before using — they will be easier to handle this way.

INGREDIENTS (CONT.)

Ricotta mix:
500 g whole milk ricotta
2 large eggs
4 tbs freshly grated parmesan or pecorino (plus to finish)
Salt and freshly ground black pepper

EQUIPMENT
Soft pastry brush
Paper coffee filter
Large non-stick sauté pan
2 medium bowls
Mortar and pestle, mini food processor or hand-held stick blender
Small bowl
Medium roasting pan
23 × 33 × 5 cm deep ovenproof dish
Kitchen foil
Oven tray

Butter a 23 × 33 × 5 cm deep ovenproof dish and spread 3 tbs of ricotta sauce evenly over the base. Cover this with a layer of pasta, cutting the sheets to fit the dish — butting them together, not overlapping them, as they swell as they cook, absorbing the mushroom sauce. Cover with a thin layer of ricotta sauce, another layer of pasta, then a thin layer of mushroom sauce, and a layer of pasta, and repeat these layers until everything is used up, finishing with a final layer of pasta.

Dredge this with extra grated parmesan and dot with any remaining butter. This will give a delicious, crunchy, golden topping.

Cover with oiled kitchen foil, set on an oven tray and bake at 180°C/160°C fan/gas mark 4 for 20 minutes. Uncover, turn the heat up to 200°C/180°C fan/gas mark 6, then bake for a further 15 minutes until bubbly with a wavy golden top. Allow to stand for ten minutes before serving, cut into squares.

*Fresh egg pasta
400 g plain white flour or Italian "00" flour
Pinch of salt
4 medium eggs
1 tbs olive oil

These quantities are only guidelines — depending on the humidity, type of flour, etc., you may have to add more or less flour. The dough must not be too soft — it should be quite hard to knead but soften somewhat after resting. Adding too much flour will make the pasta tough, taste floury and difficult to roll. Replacing a proportion of the flour with semola (Italian fine semolina flour made from grano duro) will give the pasta more texture and bite.

As a rough guide, allow one medium egg to 100 g of flour per portion of pasta for one generous plateful.

Sift the flour and salt onto a clean work surface, and make a large well in the centre with your hand. Beat the eggs and oil together, and pour the mixture into the well. Gradually mix the eggs into the flour with the fingers of one hand, and bring it together into a stiff dough.

Knead the pasta for about five minutes until smooth. Wrap and allow it to rest for at least 30 minutes at room temperature before rolling it out — the pasta will be much more elastic after resting.

To make lasagne sheets, roll out the pasta thinly by hand or machine, cut it into 6–8 strips slightly smaller than the size of your dish, laying them on a clean, flour-dusted cloth as you go. This will allow the pasta to dry a little and prevent it sticking together when cooking. There is no need to cook this fresh pasta — it is much more delicate than bought pasta, and also doesn't require soaking.

Chicken and Mushroom Pie

Serves: 4–6

INGREDIENTS
*Shortcrust pastry:**
200 g plain white flour
40 g lard, chilled and diced
55 g unsalted butter, chilled and diced
1–2 tbs ice-cold water
1 medium egg

Filling:
4 skinless, boneless chicken thighs
2 large skinless, boneless chicken breasts
100 g bacon or pancetta lardons (or 3 thick slices of dry cure bacon, sliced into short strips)
1 onion, thinly sliced
250 g fresh chestnut mushrooms, quartered
3 tbs chopped fresh parsley
Salt and freshly ground black pepper
2 tbs plain flour
100 ml chicken, mushroom or vegetable stock
2 tsp mushroom ketchup (see page 240), Worcestershire sauce or soy sauce
4 tbs crème fraîche

EQUIPMENT
Large bowl
Food processor (optional)
Plastic bag
900 ml deep pie dish
Pie funnel
Rolling pin
Pastry brush
Baking sheet

Simple to make and one of the very best everyday pies, this dish is made even more delicious by the addition of mushroom ketchup – a deeply flavoured seasoning sauce dating back to Elizabethan England. It isn't thick or tomato-based like classic ketchup, and is used to enrich meat, poultry and game dishes. Alternatively, you can use Worcestershire or even soy sauce – all these sauces add a deep savouriness to the dish.

First, make the pastry. There are two ways.†

The classic way: Sift the flour and salt together into a large mixing bowl. Add the lard and butter, and rub in until the mixture resembles breadcrumbs. Add enough of the ice-cold water to bring the pastry together, and stir in. Tip onto a lightly floured surface and knead lightly to bring the dough together. Shape into a flattened ball, pop into a plastic bag and chill for at least 30 minutes before rolling out and using in the recipe.

The food processor method: Sift the flour and salt together into the bowl of the machine. Add the lard and butter, and process for about 30 seconds until the mixture resembles fine breadcrumbs. Pour in some of the ice-cold water and pulse for ten seconds. The dough should start to come together in large, raggy lumps. If not, add another tablespoon of water and pulse again. As soon as the dough forms one big lump (don't overprocess or the pastry will be tough), tip out onto a lightly floured surface and knead lightly. Shape into a flattened ball, pop into a plastic bag and chill for at least 30 minutes before rolling out and using in the recipe.

While the pastry is chilling, preheat the oven to 190°C/170°C fan/gas mark 5 and place the pie funnel in the centre of the pie dish.

Cut the chicken into chunky bite-sized pieces and place these in a large bowl, and add the bacon lardons, sliced onion, mushrooms and parsley, and season well with salt and pepper. With clean hands, mix well. Pile the mixture around the pie funnel in the pie dish. With a small whisk, mix the flour with the chicken stock, mushroom ketchup and crème fraîche until smooth. Pour over the filling (this is enough liquid – the mushrooms will release their liquid as they cook). Remove the pastry from the fridge and let it stand at room temperature for five minutes.

On a lightly floured surface, roll the pastry out to an oval shape that is about 2 cm larger than the top of the dish. Cut off an extra-long strip of pastry that will fit around the lip of the pie dish (joining bits together if necessary). Lightly brush the lip of the pie dish with beaten egg, and press the pastry strip all around the lip.

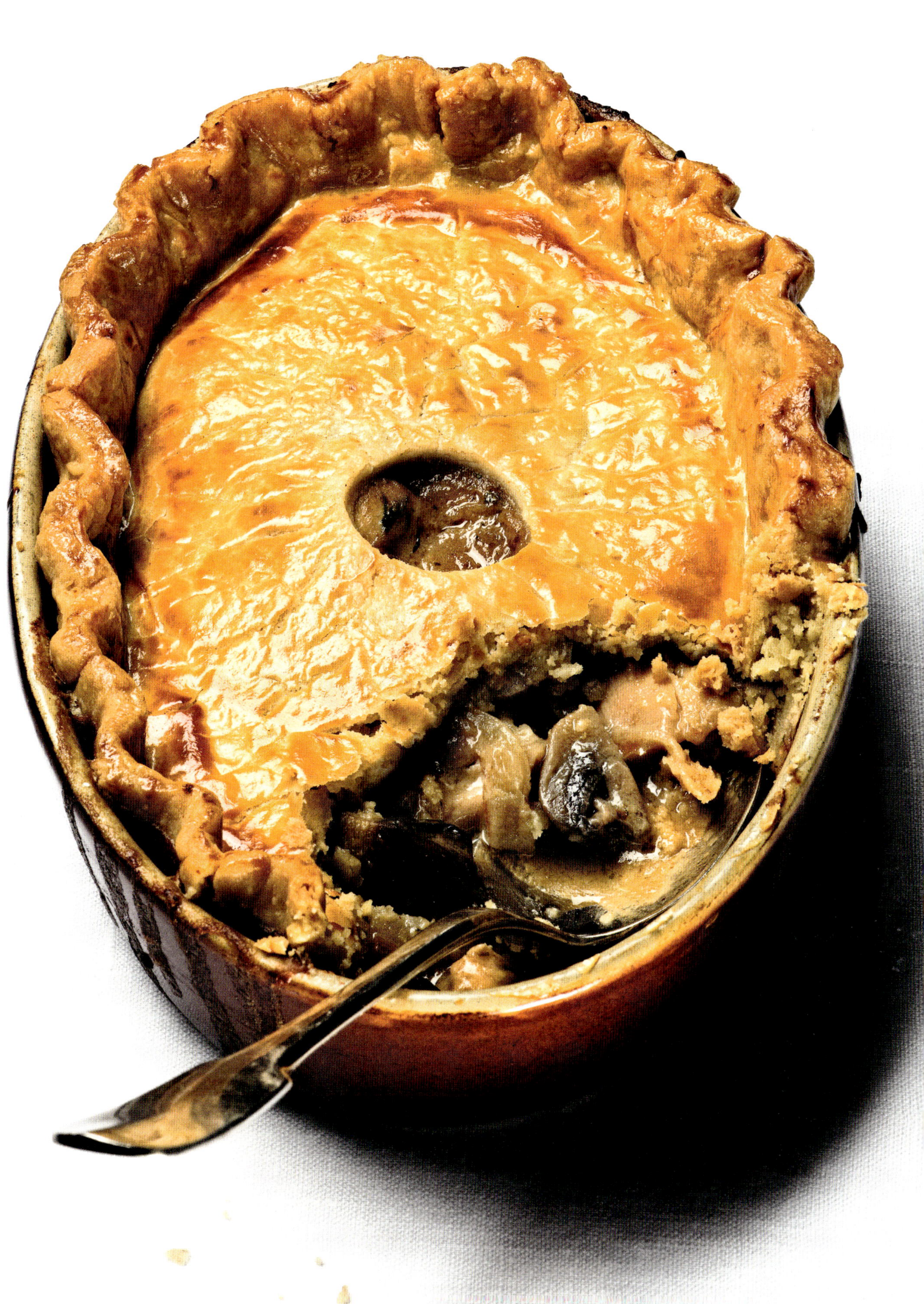

Brush this with beaten egg, and using the rolling pin, lift and lay the pastry oval over the dish, letting it fall on top of the pie funnel in the centre. Quickly cut a cross in the pastry that sits on top of the pie funnel, and gently push it down over the funnel. Press the pastry onto the lip of the dish to seal and trim off the excess pastry. Crimp, scallop or fork the edges firmly to seal. Alternatively, for a more rustic look, just drape the pastry over the pie and let it hang over the edges. Brush with beaten egg mixed with a pinch of salt, set on a baking sheet and bake for 25 minutes in the preheated oven to set the pastry, then reduce to 150°C/130°C fan/gas mark 3 and bake for a further 25–30 minutes until the pastry is golden and the filling cooked. Serve with creamy mashed potatoes and green vegetables.

* Or buy 350 g of ready-rolled shortcrust pastry instead of the ingredients for making fresh pastry.

† The classic method for making short and crumbly shortcrust pastry is given here — it is made with half butter and half lard: the butter for colour and flavour, and the lard for shortness. If you have cool hands, the hand method is best, as it will incorporate more air than in a food processor. If you have hot hands, the food processor is a blessing! The quantities of water added vary according to the humidity of the flour. Always add less than it says — you can always add more if it is dry, but it's disastrous once it becomes a sticky mess!

Mushroom Dum Pukht Biryani

Serves: 4

INGREDIENTS
500 g basmati rice
1 tbs salt
1 tbs vegetable oil
1 small stick of cinnamon
1 tsp whole peppercorns
6 green cardamom pods, lightly bruised

Crispy onions:
5 medium red onions, thinly sliced
150–200 ml vegetable oil
125 g raw cashew nuts

Mushrooms:
30 g unsalted butter
400 g fresh mushrooms, quartered
¼ tsp salt
½ tsp ground turmeric
½ tsp garam masala

Biryani sauce:
1 tbs vegetable oil
1 medium red onion, sliced
6 large garlic cloves
2.5 cm fresh ginger
5 green chillies
2 medium ripe tomatoes, chopped
Small handful of fresh mint leaves
Small handful of fresh coriander leaves
1 tbs garam masala
Salt
200 ml plain yoghurt
2–3 tbs fresh lemon juice
Large pinch of saffron threads, soaked in 4 tbs hot water

A spectacular dish to make as the centrepiece of a special meal. This method of cooking is of Mughal origin – *dum pukht* means "cooking on a slow fire". Layers of under-cooked rice traditionally encase a bed of marinated meat. The dish is then sealed using a bread dough, and finished in an oven so that it cooks in its own steam, infusing it with aromatic spices and herbs. Birista (crispy fried onions) is added here as a nod to the Hyderabadi style of cooking.

Wash the basmati rice in lots of cold water to remove the starch. Tip into a medium bowl and cover with cold water. Leave to soak for 20 minutes. Drain well through a sieve and set aside.

Fill a very large saucepan (important – prevents the rice from sticking together) with lots of water, and bring it to a rolling boil. Add the salt, oil, cinnamon, peppercorns and cardamom pods.

Tip in the drained rice, stir and bring back to the boil, then boil rapidly for about seven minutes or until three-quarters cooked.* Drain through a large sieve sitting in a colander until the rice is as dry as possible. Spread it out on a large tray lined with a clean kitchen towel, and allow it to cool completely.

To make the crispy onions, add the sliced onions to a wide, deep frying pan, then add enough oil to just cover the onions. Cook the oil and onions from cold – this will produce a crisper result, as the onions release their water over the cooking time and then will start to fry. Place the pan over a high heat, and using a slotted spoon, stir the onions every five minutes to make sure they are cooking evenly. After about 20 minutes the onions will start to look slightly brown at the edges. Reduce the temperature to medium, and stir constantly to ensure even cooking. When the onions turn a light golden brown, reduce the heat to low, and slowly start lifting out the onions and spreading them over a large tray lined with kitchen paper. Allow the onions to cool completely. Reserve and bottle the flavoured oil to use in other cooking.

Now fry the cashews. Put 75 ml of the reserved onion oil into the pan, add the cashews and stir fry over a medium-high heat for a couple of minutes until golden. Scoop them out of the oil with the slotted spoon, and drain well on kitchen paper. Set aside. Wipe out the pan.

To make the mushroom mix, add 2 tbs of the onion oil and the butter to the pan, and set on medium-high heat. When the butter has stopped foaming, add the quartered mushrooms and ¼ tsp of salt, and stir fry for five minutes until they begin to release their juices.

INGREDIENTS (CONT.)
2 tbs chopped fresh coriander leaves
2 tbs chopped fresh mint leaves
2 pinches of garam masala

EQUIPMENT
Medium bowl
Large sieve
Very large saucepan
Large sieve
Colander
Large tray
Clean kitchen towel
Wide, deep frying pan with a lid or a wok
Slotted metal spoon or a spider
Kitchen paper
Food processor or electric or stick blender
Medium, heavy ovenproof casserole with lid
Kitchen foil

Stir in the turmeric and the garam masala, and continue to stir over a high heat for 2–3 minutes until the juices have evaporated and the mushrooms have nicely browned. Tip the mushrooms onto a plate, and set aside to cool. Wipe out the pan.

To make the sauce, add 1 tbs of oil to the pan, and place over a medium heat. When hot, add the sliced onion, and stir fry gently for 5–8 minutes until the onions soften but do not colour.

Meanwhile, using a food processor, blitz the garlic, ginger, chillies, tomatoes, mint and coriander with 100 ml of water until smooth. Pour this into the softened onions, then add the garam masala and a good pinch of salt. Bring up to a simmer, and simmer for 5 minutes. Whisk the yoghurt with 4 tbs of water, and stir into the sauce. Cover and cook for 3–4 minutes on a medium heat. Add the crispy onions (keeping a handful back for the garnish), mix well, re-cover the pan and simmer for another 4–5 minutes until the sauce reduces and thickens. It should not be watery. Remove from the heat and stir in the lemon juice. Taste and add more salt if necessary.

Preheat the oven to 200°C/180°C fan/gas mark 6.

Take a heavy ovenproof casserole, and ladle in half of the sauce, spreading it evenly over the bottom. Place half of the rice in spoonfuls over the sauce, and spread it out to cover. Cover this layer with half of the mushrooms, and spread out evenly. Sprinkle evenly with half of the saffron water and half of the chopped coriander and mint, and then sprinkle with half of the cashews and a pinch of garam masala. Repeat these layers once more, finishing with a layer of cashews and garam masala. Cover tightly with kitchen foil and a lid.

When ready to cook, place the casserole in the oven and bake for 15 minutes. Remove from the oven, and let it rest for another ten minutes before you open it at the table to serve. Garnish with the reserved crispy onions.

* To make a biryani, the pre-cooked rice should still have some bite to it after cooking — it should be cooked on the outside, but the centre should be a little hard — so don't overcook it at the first stage. It will cook properly and fluff up in the last stage. Season the rice well with salt at this stage, to bring out the full flavour of the rice in the biryani.

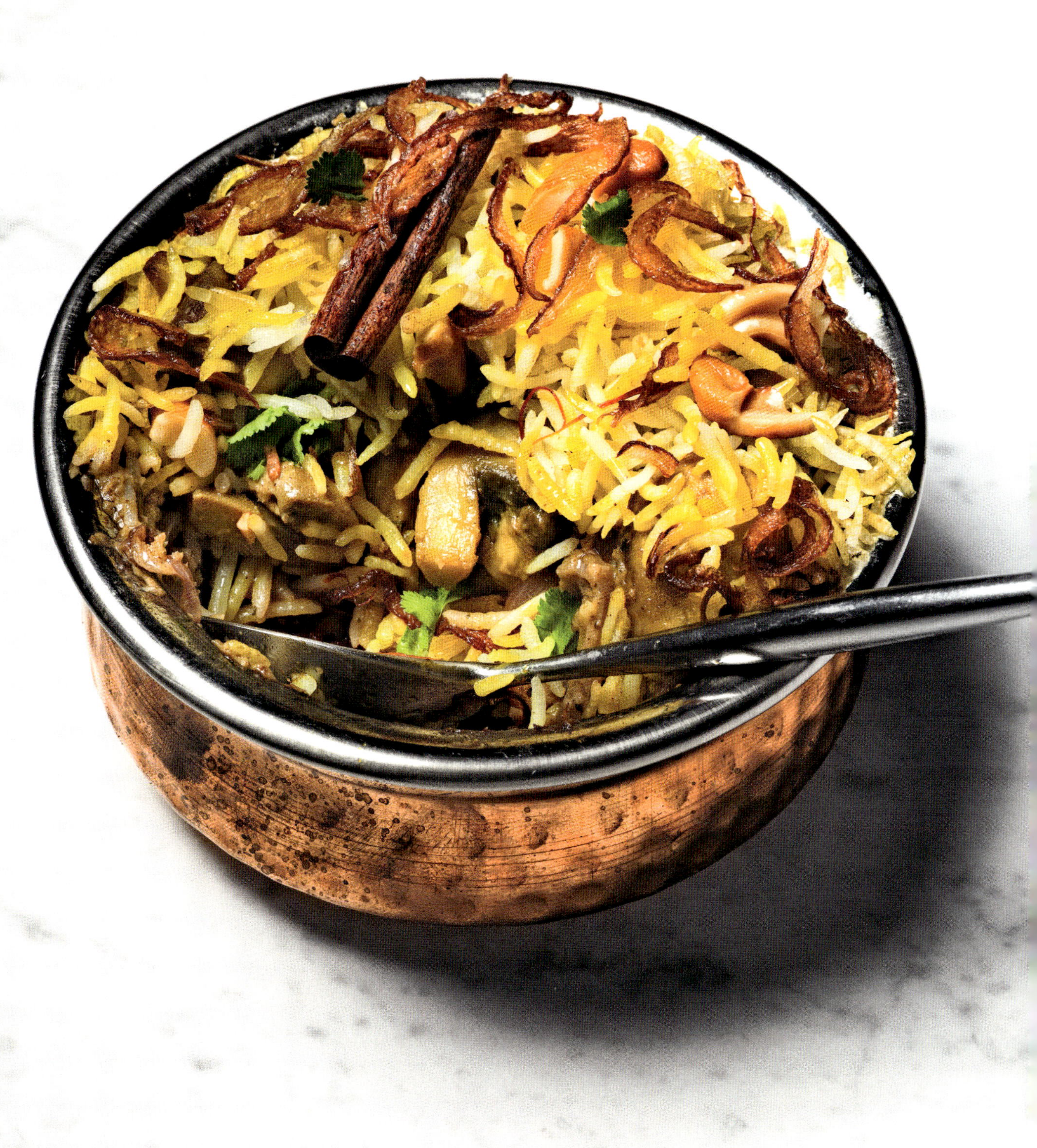

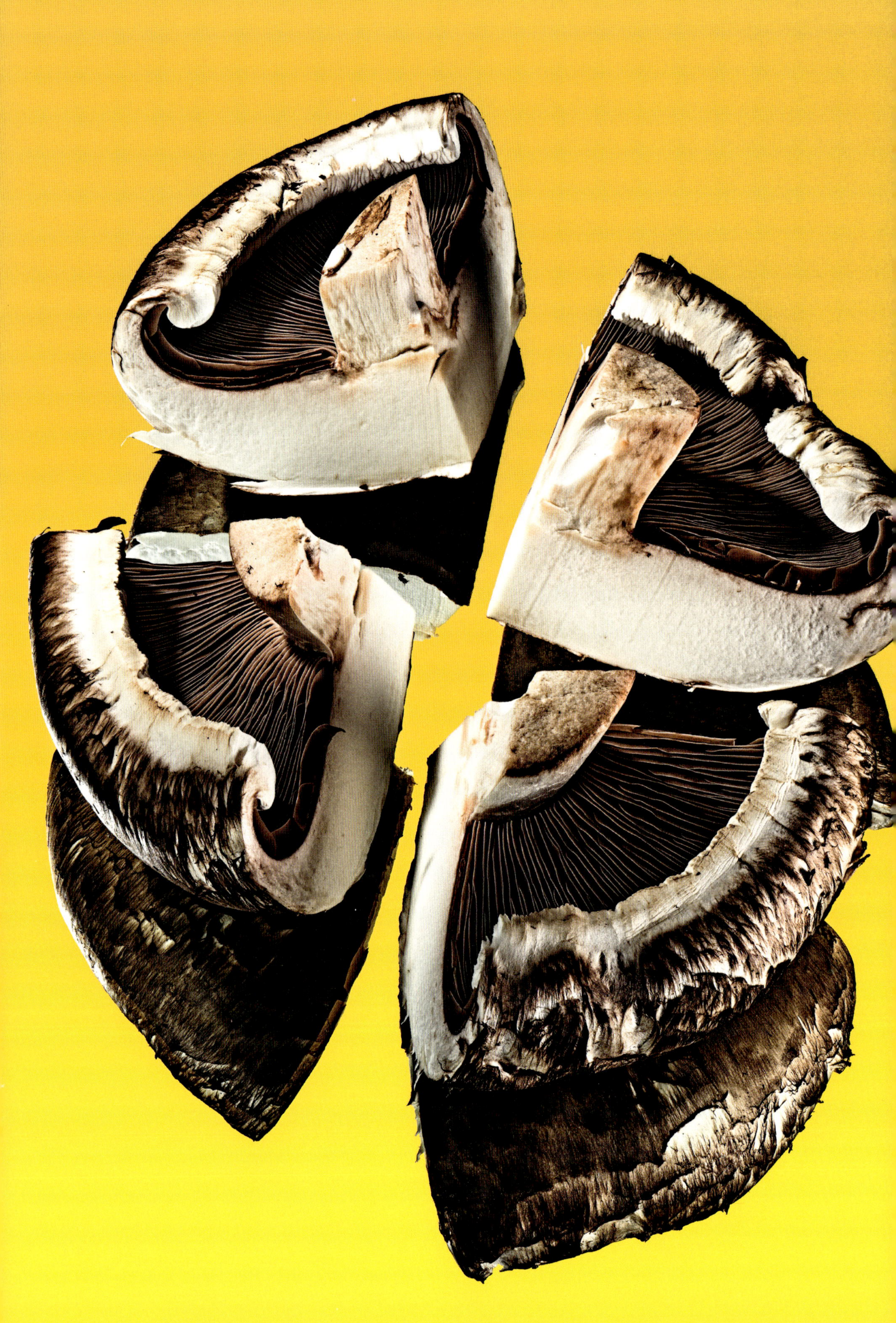

Mushrooms to Share

Cèpes à la Bordelaise

Serves: 4 as a side

INGREDIENTS
500 g fresh porcini mushrooms
4 tbs extra-virgin olive oil
2 large banana shallots, finely chopped
4 garlic cloves, finely chopped
3 tbs (or more) flat-leaved parsley, chopped
Salt and freshly ground black pepper
Freshly squeezed lemon juice
2–3 tbs stale white breadcrumbs, fried until crisp in a little oil (optional)

EQUIPMENT
Large non-stick sauté pan or frying pan with lid

Nearly every region in France has its own way of cooking the revered wild cèpe, known elsewhere as porcini (among other names). This recipe is Bordeaux's contribution to the repertoire, a simple method for cèpes a l'etuvée — mushrooms cooked in olive oil. Only the best and freshest porcini will do, so look for firm caps and stalks (a sign that there are no unwelcome visitors). Parsley is a key ingredient — don't hold back.

Separate the mushroom caps from the stems. Thickly slice the caps cross-wise and the stalks into thick rounds.

Heat a large non-stick sauté pan over a medium-high heat. Add the olive oil, and when almost smoking, throw in the mushrooms together with the shallots, garlic and parsley, stir well, then immediately turn the heat to low (a heat mat helps here). Cover tightly and simmer very gently for ten minutes. Uncover, taste and season well with salt and pepper and a hint of lemon juice, then serve immediately, sprinkled with the breadcrumbs if using.

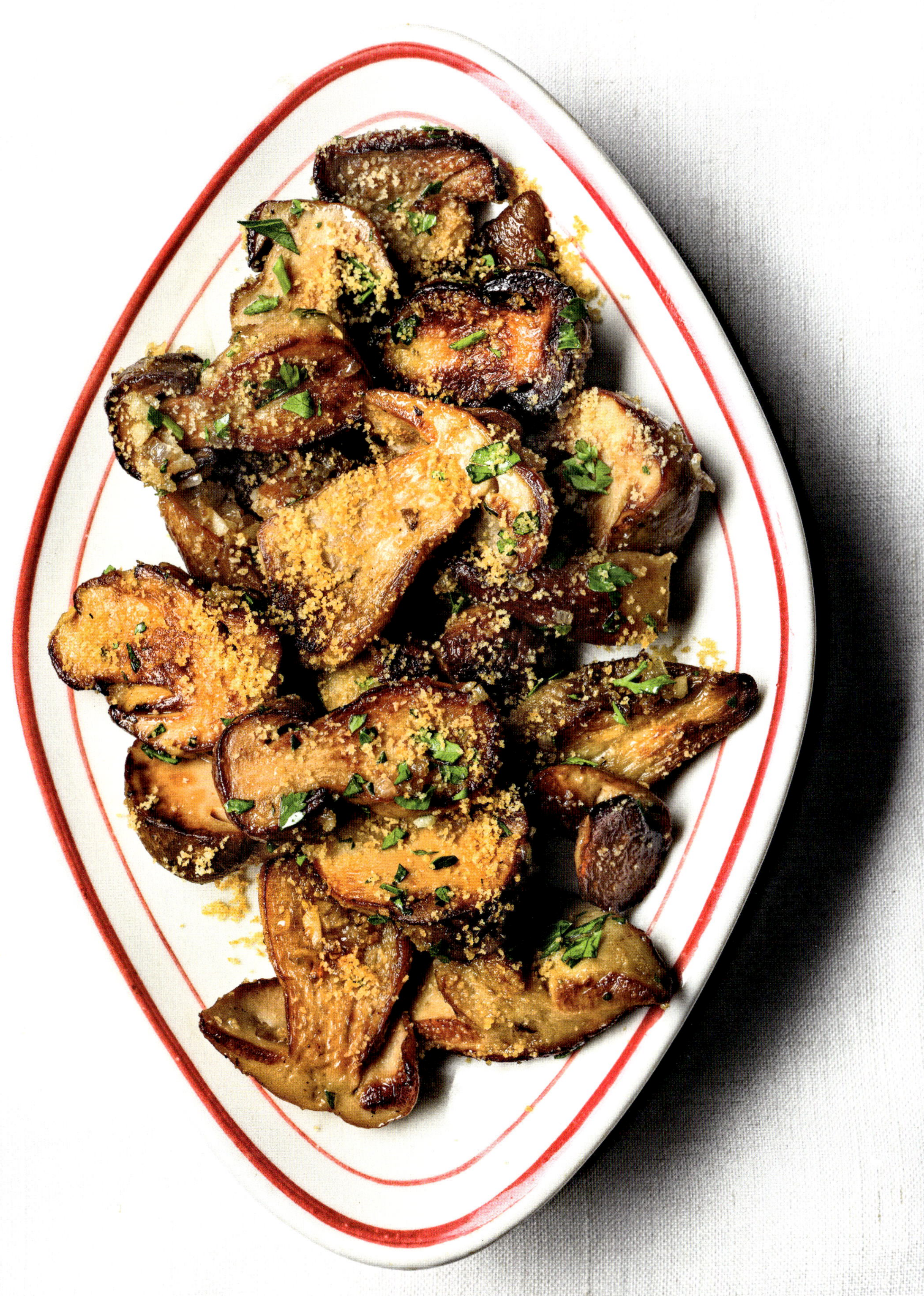

Finnish Mushroom Salad with Soured Cream and Mead (Sienisalaatti)

A Finnish Christmas spread wouldn't be complete without sienisalaatti, a salad made from mushrooms picked in the summer and then salted to preserve them over the winter months. Every family has its own version, but traditionally the mushrooms are reconstituted, finely chopped, then mixed with chopped onion and thick or soured cream. This recipe uses fresh mushrooms that are blanched in heavily salted water to give them a slightly firmer texture and a subtle saltiness.

Serves: 4

INGREDIENTS
900 g fresh closed-cap mushrooms, quartered
125 ml single cream
125 ml soured cream
1–2 tbs cider vinegar or fresh lemon juice
2–3 tsp mead, brown ale or medium sherry
4 tbs fresh chives (or wild garlic in season), chopped
Salt and freshly ground black pepper

EQUIPMENT
Large saucepan with lid
Colander
Tray
Kitchen paper
Medium bowl
Small bowl

To blanch the mushrooms, fill a large saucepan half full of cold water and add 3 tsp of salt. Bring to the boil, then add the mushrooms, stir once and bring back to the boil. Reduce the heat to a simmer, cover with a lid and simmer further for one minute. Have a colander ready in the sink, and immediately after the one-minute simmering, tip the mushrooms into the colander to drain – do not rinse. Then tip them onto a tray lined with kitchen paper and spread them out to cool and drain thoroughly. Next, tip them into a medium bowl, and cover and chill for 30 minutes.

In a small bowl, whisk both of the creams with 1 tbs of vinegar, the mead and half of the chives. Taste and season with salt and pepper, adding more vinegar if necessary.

Uncover the mushrooms, spoon over the dressing and mix well to coat. Re-cover and chill them for at least one hour before serving. Serve in a shallow bowl scattered with the chopped chives.

Porcini Gratin

Serves: 4 as a side or starter

INGREDIENTS
600 g fresh porcini mushrooms
45 g unsalted butter (plus extra if needed)
Salt and white pepper
100 ml double cream
50 g aged Gruyère or parmesan, finely grated
½ small garlic clove, grated
Nutmeg, freshly grated

EQUIPMENT
Very sharp knife
Large non-stick frying pan
Baking sheet
Baking parchment
Shallow ovenproof dish
gratin dish

Gratiner is a French culinary technique in which an ingredient is topped with a browned crust, using grated cheese, breadcrumbs, butter, eggs or cream. Hence, gratin. A gratin is usually prepared in a shallow heatproof dish and baked in a hot oven or cooked under a hot grill and served in the same dish. This recipe is so simple, and allows the taste and texture of the mushrooms to shine through the rich cream and cheese crust. It will work with any firm, fresh mushroom, but porcini are ideal.

Preheat the oven to 250°C/230°C fan/gas mark 9 – or as high as the oven will go.

Using a very sharp knife, cut the mushrooms lengthways into 5 mm slices so that the stem and cap remain together.

Place a large non-stick frying pan over a medium heat, and when hot, add the butter. When the butter stops foaming, add enough mushroom slices to cover the base (work in batches), and fry until golden on one side, then turn them over and fry the second side. Turn the heat down to medium low, and fry until all the moisture from the mushrooms disappears and the mushroom flesh still holds its shape. Lift the slices out with a spatula and lay them on a parchment-lined baking sheet to cool while you cook the rest (don't overlap them).

Once all the mushroom slices are all cooked, season them with salt and pepper, and arrange them in layers in a shallow ovenproof dish gratin dish – the layers should not be too thick, no more than 1 cm.

Mix the double cream, grated cheese, garlic and grated nutmeg (to taste) in a small bowl. Pour the cream mixture over the mushrooms as evenly as possible, set the dish on a baking sheet, and place in the oven and bake for about 8–12 minutes (depending on the oven) until deep golden brown on top. Watch closely, as the hotter the oven, the quicker the gratin will brown. Remove from the oven and leave to settle for 3–4 minutes before serving.

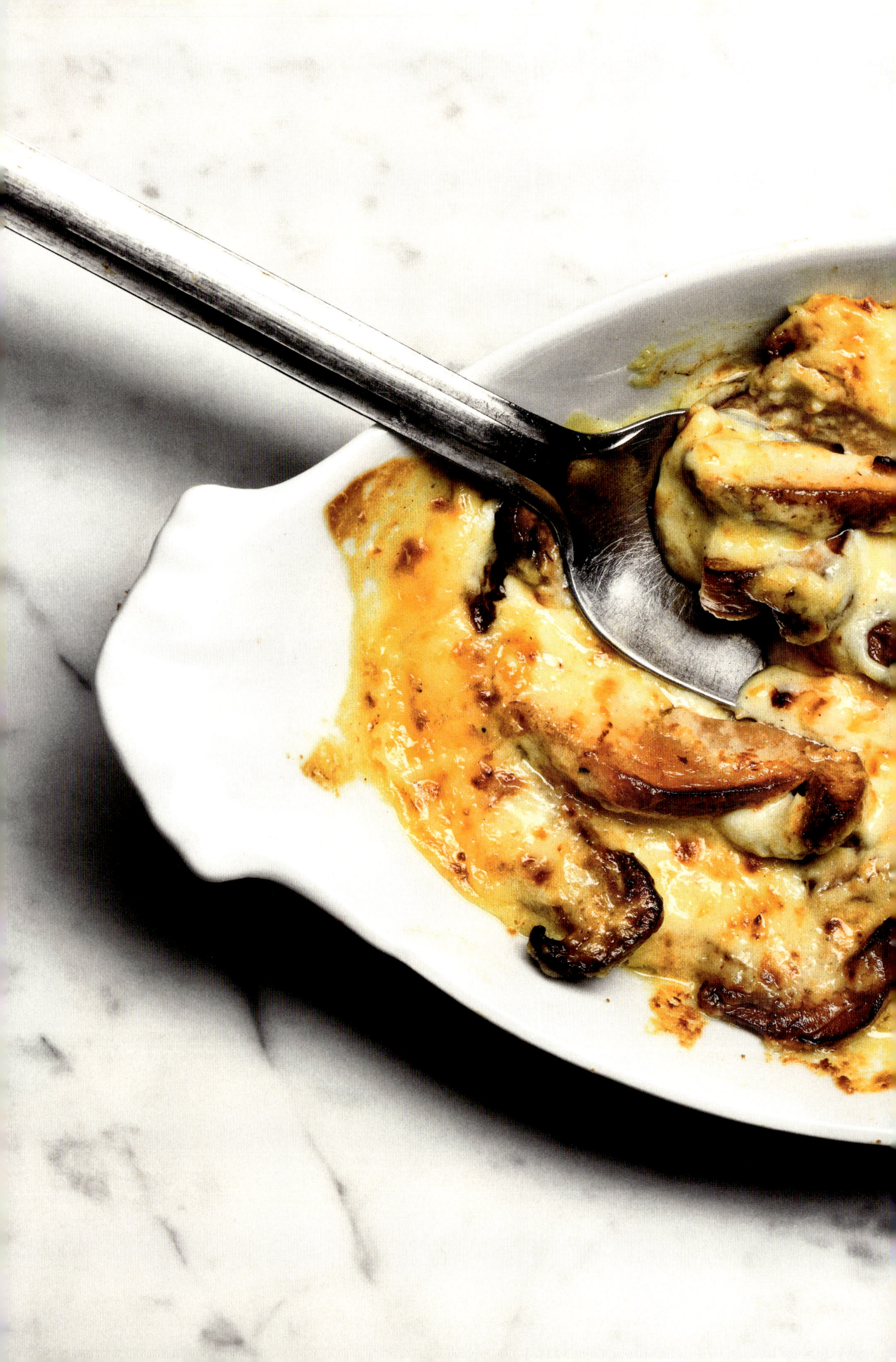

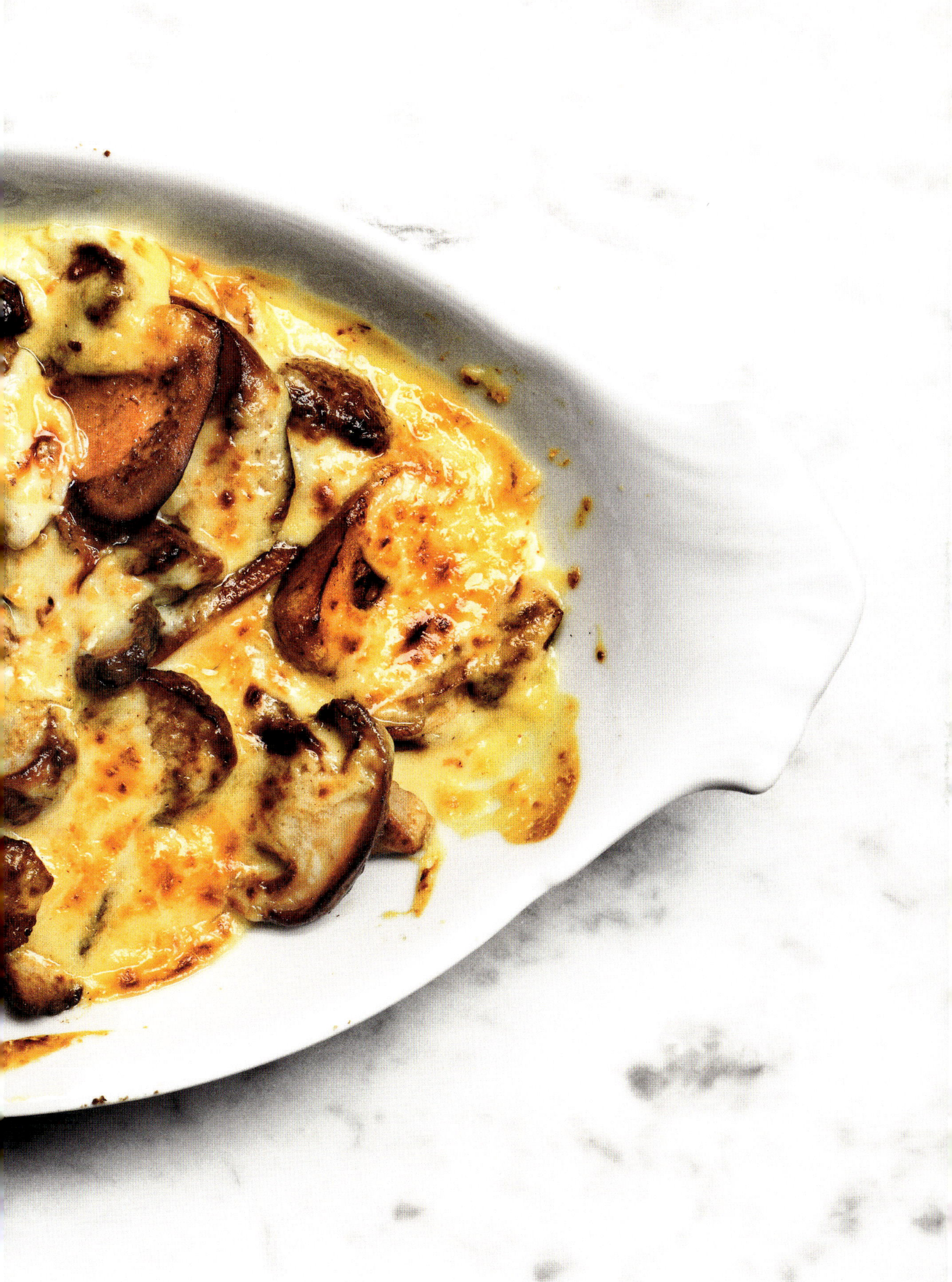

Mushroom Fried Rice

Serves: 4–6

INGREDIENTS
400 ml jasmine or basmati rice
100 g fresh oyster mushrooms
120 g fresh shiitake mushrooms
140 g fresh button mushrooms
2 large eggs
1½ tbs shaoxing wine or dry sherry
A few drops of toasted sesame oil
3 tbs vegetable oil (preferably groundnut)
1 small onion or banana shallot, chopped
Salt and freshly ground white pepper*
3 spring onions, white and green parts finely sliced diagonally (to garnish)

EQUIPMENT
Large bowl
Medium heavy pot with tight-fitting lid
Tray
Clean kitchen towel
Large bowl
Small bowl
Wok
Wok scoop

In China, traditional fried rice is usually served at the end of a meal to cleanse the palate. It is made with freshly cooked rice, does not include soy sauce and should not be sticky. The version here is cooked the Chinese way — long before serving; it requires no weighing of ingredients and brings the right texture and flavour. A wok is crucial for this dish. The rice and mushrooms need to be on the move the whole time to ensure everything cooks quickly and evenly.

Pour the rice into a large bowl, and fill with cold water. Swish it around, then tip the water out. Do this until the water is clear — this removes any loose starch, which would make the rice sticky. Drain the rice, put it into a medium heavy pot with 900 ml water, and bring to the boil. Boil rapidly for about 15–20 minutes until most of the surface liquid has evaporated and the surface is covered with small "pock marks" or little craters. At this point, cover the pot with a tight-fitting lid (a clean kitchen towel underneath the lid makes a good seal). Reduce the heat to the lowest setting and let the rice steam undisturbed for 15–20 minutes — sometimes a heat mat will help regulate it here. Uncover, and the rice will be fluffy and dry and ready to eat — or can be cooled for later. For this dish, tip the rice onto a tray lined with a clean kitchen towel, and gently spread it out. This way, the rice cools quickly and becomes dry enough on the outside to stir fry. When cold, gather it up in the towel and transfer it to a large bowl. Set aside.

While the rice is cooling, prepare the mushrooms. Tear or pull the oyster mushrooms into pieces. Trim the tough stems off the shiitake mushrooms, and thinly slice the caps. Slice or quarter the button mushrooms. Keep in separate piles.

Whisk the eggs, ½ tbs of shaoxing wine, the sesame oil and a large pinch of salt together in a small bowl. Set aside.

Put a wok over a medium-high heat, and heat until a drop of water instantly sizzles when it hits the side. Splash 1 tbs of oil around the edge of the wok and add the onion or shallot. Stir-fry for about one minute, until the onions are beginning to turn translucent. Quickly add the sliced shiitake mushrooms and stir-fry them for about 30 seconds.

Splash another tablespoon of oil around the edge of the wok, then add the sliced button and oyster mushrooms. Add the remaining 1 tbs of shaoxing wine, and stir fry for 1–2 minutes, or until the mushrooms are lightly browned and caramelized.

Add the remaining 1 tbs of oil, then the rice. Use the wok scoop to alternate between stir frying the rice and flattening it against the surface of the wok, to break up any clumps and heat it through until steaming hot. This should take 3–5 minutes with freshly cooked rice. Now add the beaten egg mixture, and stir fry for two minutes until the egg sets. Taste and add white pepper, and extra salt if needed. Turn into a warmed serving dish and garnish with the spring onions. Serve immediately.

* Ground white pepper is the norm in most Chinese food, but deliciously fragrant red Kampot pepper would be very good in this dish. The beaten egg is always added at the end of cooking and not scrambled beforehand — this way it doesn't dry out.

Raw Porcini with Salad Greens and Parmesan

So simple, so good. This dish relies on the best and freshest of ingredients. Serve with a chilled, dry white wine or sparkling water with a splash of lemon juice (avoid sweet drinks — these will clash with the savoury, earthy porcini).

Serves: 2

INGREDIENTS
110 g fresh perfect porcini mushrooms*
Extra-virgin olive oil (not too pungent) (to taste)
Salt and freshly ground black pepper
½ lemon, juiced
125 g fresh young greens (rocket, watercress, wood sorrel, Japanese mustard greens, mustard and cress or any micro-greens)
Lump of fresh parmesan
Lemon wedges (to serve)

EQUIPMENT
Very sharp knife
Small salad bowl

Trim the bases of the mushrooms. Slice the mushrooms in half to inspect for slug damage to the caps, and worm tunnelling — especially in the stems. Discard any damaged mushrooms — or these can be dried (see page 236) for use at another time. Slice the perfect mushrooms lengthways in 5 mm slices, keeping the cap and stem intact as much as possible.

When ready to serve the salad, divide the mushroom slices between four small salad plates, drizzle with a little olive oil, and season with salt and pepper to taste.

Just before serving, in a salad bowl, whisk 4 tbs of olive oil with 1 tbs of lemon juice with salt and pepper to taste. Drop in the chosen leaves/greenery, and carefully turn to coat in the dressing, adding a few parmesan shavings.

Lift out the salad a handful at a time, leaving any unused dressing behind, and add a mound to the centre of each plate on top of the mushrooms. Shave some more parmesan over the top, and serve with lemon wedges on the side.

* Part of what makes eating raw porcini special is that they must be perfect specimens. Whether bought or foraged, inspect the mushrooms for quality and wildlife. They should not be bruised and must be firm to the touch and white on the inside — no perforations. Older porcini are best dried or slow cooked in sauces or soups to really bring out their flavour.

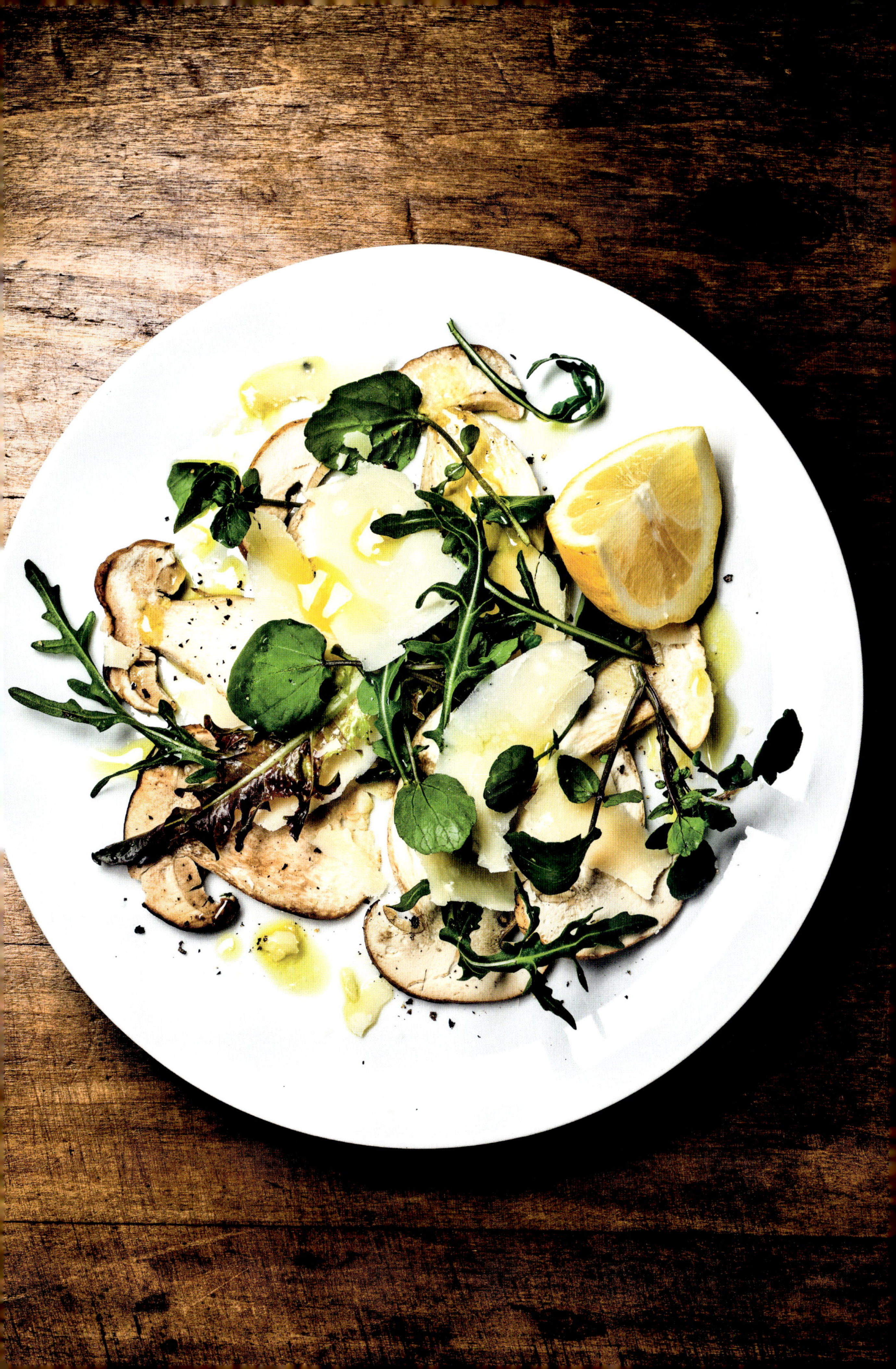

Sautéed Japanese Mushrooms with Soy Butter Sauce

Serves: 4 as a side

INGREDIENTS
150 g fresh shiitake mushrooms
150 g fresh shimeji mushrooms
150 g bunch of fresh enoki mushrooms
2 tbs groundnut oil
1 garlic clove, grated
45 g soft unsalted butter
1 tbs Japanese soy sauce
Salt and freshly ground white pepper
2 spring onions, finely sliced (to garnish)

EQUIPMENT
Medium wok
Wok scoop

A quick and moreish recipe that is so easy to make. The perfect side dish for any Japanese-style feast.

Cut the stems off the shiitake mushrooms, and slice the caps in half. Slice the bottom off the shimeji mushrooms, and separate or pull into small bite-size pieces by hand. Slice the bottom 2.5 cm from the bunch of enoki mushrooms and pull apart into small bunches.

Place a medium wok over a high heat until a drop of water will sizzle in it. Swirl in the oil, and add the mushrooms and garlic, and stir fry for a couple of minutes until just softened. Add the butter and soy sauce, stir once, then taste and season with salt and pepper. Stir for a few more seconds, then tip out onto a warmed serving dish. Sprinkle with the chopped spring onions. Serve immediately.

Enokitake Mushrooms Steamed in a Foil Package
(Enokitake Mushi-yaki)

Serves: 4 as a side

INGREDIENTS
2 bunches of fresh enokitake mushrooms
30–40 g butter (plus extra for greasing the foil)
3 thin lemon slices or a few drops of yuzu juice
Kinome* leaf sprigs or bruised yuzu leaves (plus extra to garnish)
Yuzu leaves, bruised

EQUIPMENT
35 cm square of heavy-duty kitchen foil or a double piece of lighter foil
Baking sheet

The rather cute Japanese mushrooms called enokitake have a unique texture and a subtle, earthy flavour, and they easily absorb flavours, especially when steamed. The combination of ingredients in this recipe makes a delicious, citrusy side dish. Place the foil package on a warm serving dish, and open before passing around.

Preheat the oven to 250°C/230°C fan/gas mark 9 (or as high as you can go).

Prepare the cleaned enokitake mushrooms by discarding any spongy base.

Butter the centre of a 30 cm square of heavy-duty kitchen foil, and place the mushrooms in the centre, but do not divide them. Dot the mushrooms with butter, the lemon slices and a few sprigs of kinome for a bright citrusy aroma and season with salt.

Carefully fold the foil up and over the enokitake, making a loose envelope, and twist the edges to seal to keep in all the steam, flavours and juices. Set on a baking sheet, and bake in the oven for five minutes. Remove from the oven and set on a warm serving dish.

* Also called sansho or Japanese pepper.

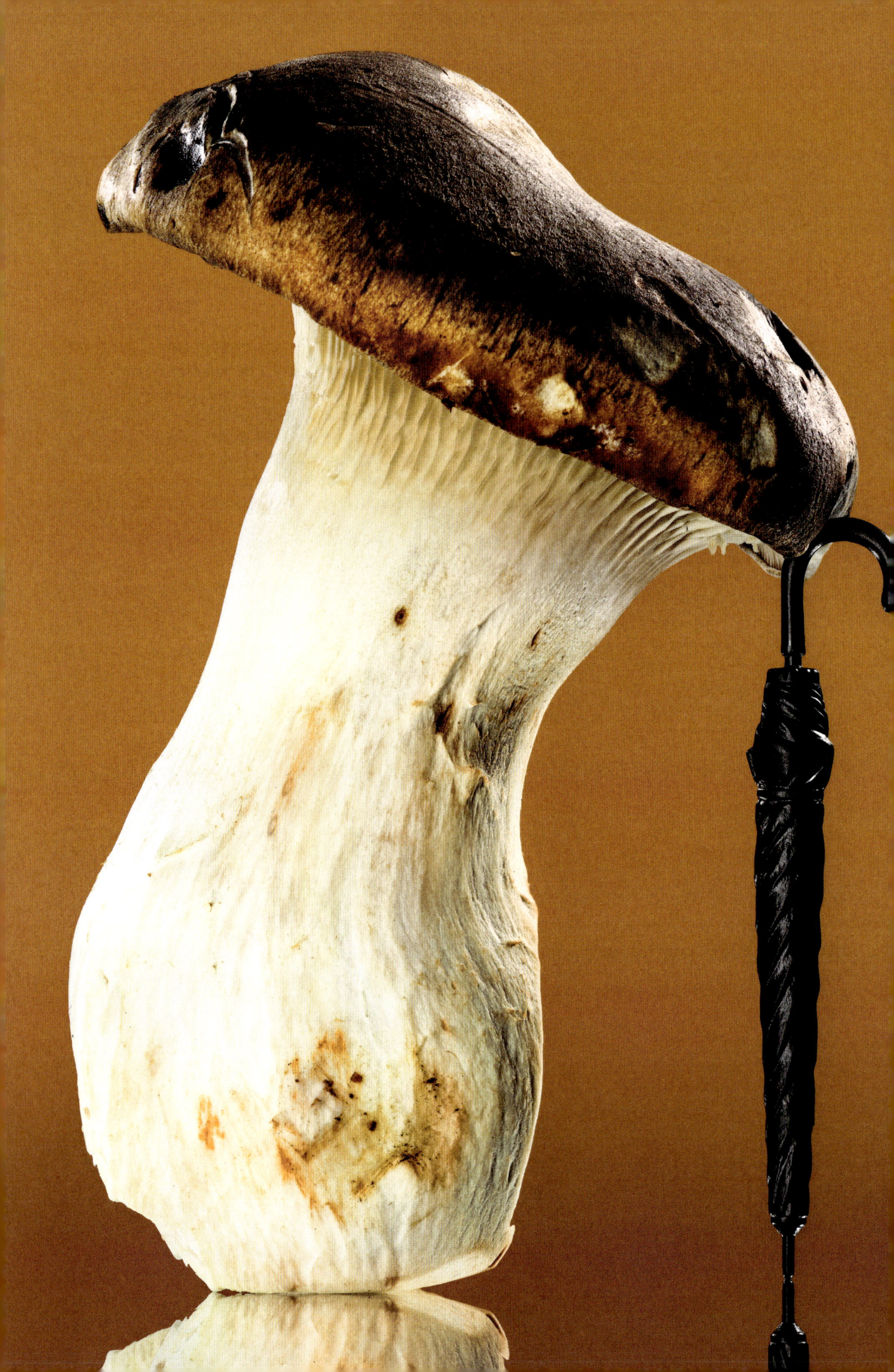

Accompanying Mushrooms

Pickled Mushrooms

Makes: four 300 ml jars

INGREDIENTS
1 kg perfect fresh button mushrooms
250 ml good white wine vinegar
500 ml distilled white vinegar
3 small bird's eye chillies
2 generous sprigs of rosemary
A few sprigs of thyme
3 fresh bay leaves
2 tbs salt
Few peppercorns
2 tbs of salted capers or caper berries (optional)
3 whole garlic cloves, lightly bruised (optional)
Few dried chillies (optional)
Olive oil

EQUIPMENT
Large, deep saucepan
Slotted spoon
Four 300 ml preserving jars with lids, sterilized (see p. 155)

Button mushrooms are best for this recipe as they have little flavour and will absorb the flavourings you add to the pickling mix. There are no rules – this recipe has fresh herbs, but it is equally delicious with, say, Middle Eastern dried spice mixes. Remember, a pickle is only as good as its ingredients – use the best vinegars, and they must have a minimum acidity of 5% to preserve the mushrooms. Mix the pickle into a potato salad with lots of spring onions, use as a pizza topping, or simply eat with a rustic pâté or lump of cheese and good bread and butter.

Clean the mushrooms but do not wash or peel them. Pull out and discard the stalks (freeze for later to make a stock).

Put the mushroom caps into a large, deep saucepan with the vinegars, 300 ml of water, the chillies, rosemary, thyme, bay leaves, 2 tbs of salt and a few peppercorns. Bring up to the boil, then reduce the heat and simmer for about five minutes, then turn off the heat and leave to stand and settle for five minutes.

Lift the mushrooms out with a slotted spoon and pack into clean, warm preserving jars, sprinkling in the capers (if using), leaving about 2.5 cm headspace above the mushrooms. Bring the vinegar back to the boil, and strain over the mushrooms, making sure they are well covered. Tuck in extra herb sprigs, garlic cloves and dried chillies down the sides of the jars if desired.

Seal tightly and store somewhere cool and dark for at least two weeks to cure before using. The pickle will keep for up to six months. When ready to use, spoon the mushrooms out of the vinegar brine, drain them well and mix them with some good olive oil.

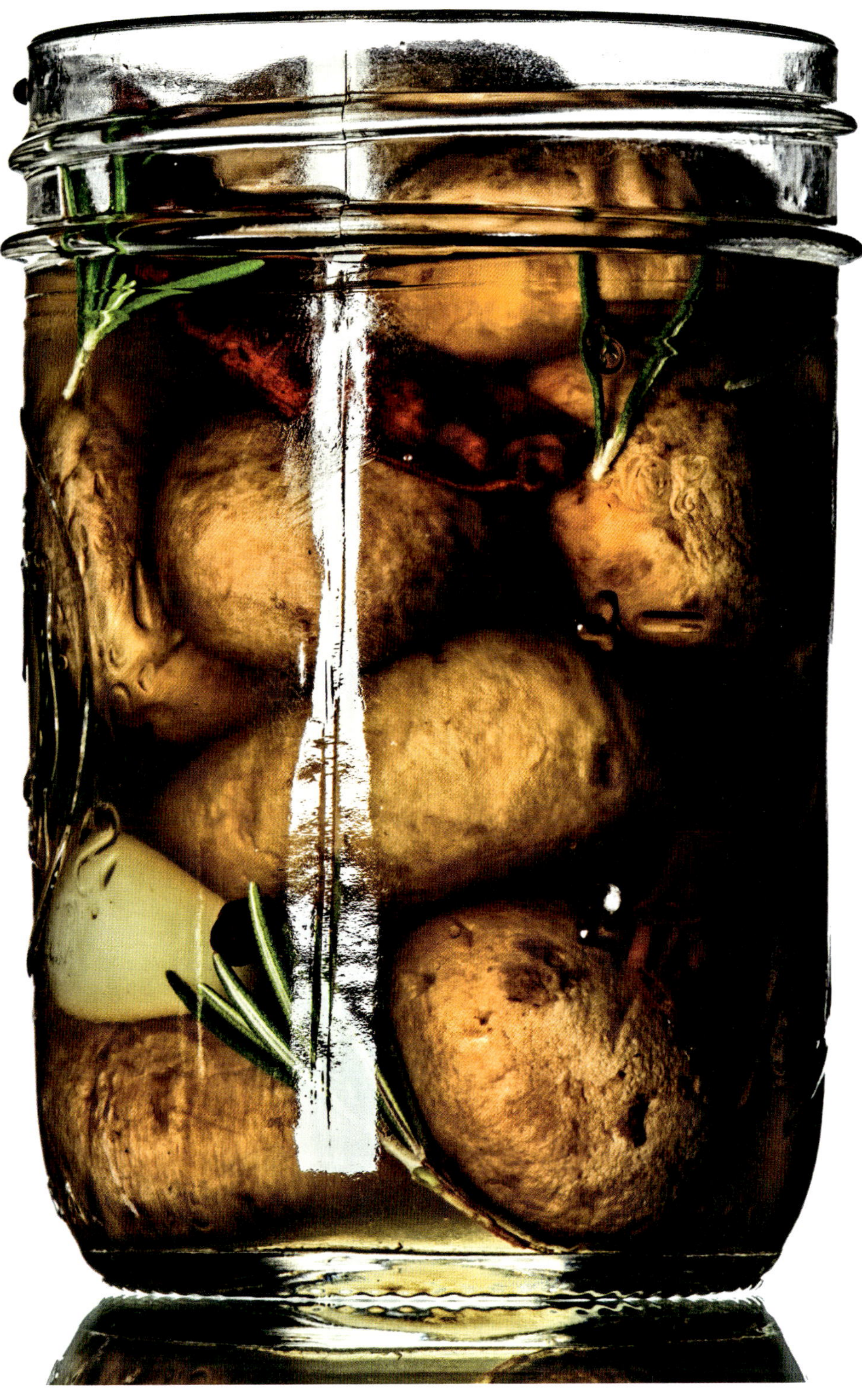

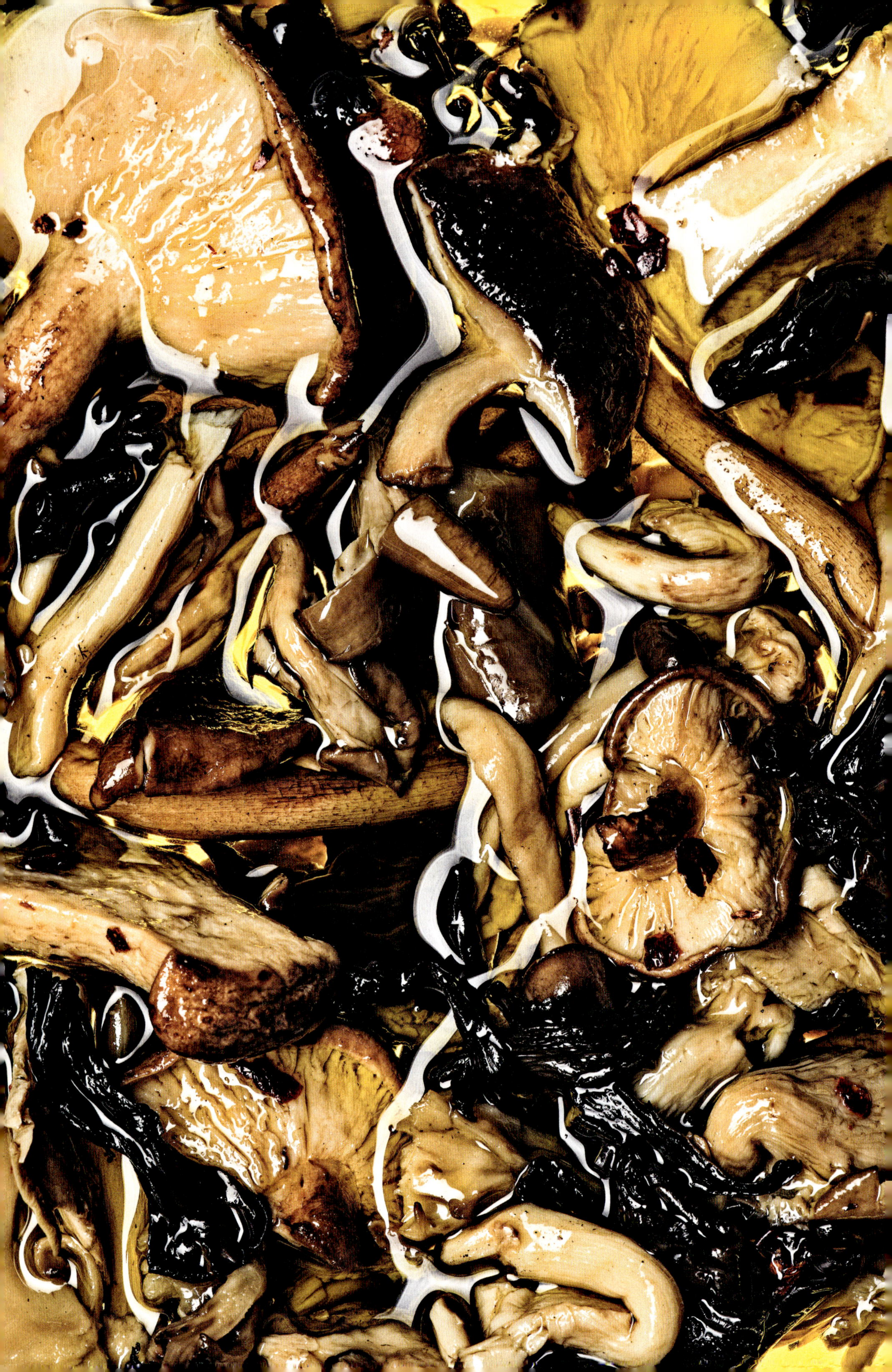

Funghi Sott'olio (Mushrooms Preserved in Oil)

Makes: two 300 ml jars

INGREDIENTS
1 kg mixed fresh mushrooms (any size, wild or cultivated)
2 tbs salt
500 ml good white wine vinegar
4 bay leaves
½ tsp chilli pepper flakes
16 whole black peppercorns
200 ml extra-virgin olive oil (plus extra if needed)

EQUIPMENT
Large bowl
Medium saucepan
Medium bowl
Two 300 ml preserving jars with lids, sterilized (see p. 155)

Mushrooms have been preserved in oil for centuries all over the world, allowing them to be enjoyed long past the harvest season. *Sott'olio,* meaning "in oil", is a very simple Italian method that can be adapted to your taste using different herbs, or chilli, and with any mushrooms you choose.

Prepare the mushrooms. Some prefer to scrape off the gills or sponge from inside the mushroom caps — but this isn't necessary. Slice the larger mushrooms thickly and halve the smaller ones. The mushrooms should be of a similar size.

Place the mushrooms in a large bowl and lightly toss with 2 tbs of salt. Place a plate on top of the mushrooms and weigh it down with a heavy object, such as a can of beans. Let the mushrooms sit for about one hour to disgorge their water, then drain and spread them out on a clean kitchen towel, and pat dry.

Bring the vinegar and half of the flavourings to a boil in a medium saucepan, add the mushrooms, return to the boil, and simmer for about 5–10 minutes (depending on the size of the pieces) or until the mushrooms have softened but still retain their texture.

Drain the mushrooms from the brine and spread them out on a tray lined with a clean kitchen towel, and pat dry. Leave them to cool, and dry further for 2–3 hours, then tip them into a medium bowl. Heat the olive oil over a medium-low heat with the remaining half of the flavourings for about five minutes, stirring occasionally — do not let the oil get too hot. Pour this over the mushrooms, and mix gently with a wooden spoon. Cover and leave to marinate overnight.

The next day, pack the mushrooms into the two jars in layers, pouring some of the residual oil and spices from the bottom of the bowl between each layer. When the jars are packed, pour in the remaining oil so that the mushrooms are completely covered — you may have to top up with extra oil. Screw the lids on tightly, and check after 24 hours to see if the oil needs to be topped up again.

Store in the fridge for at least a week before eating. Top the jar up with extra-virgin olive oil as the mushrooms are eaten, to keep them submerged.

Unopened, these preserved mushrooms will keep in the fridge or a very cool pantry for up to three months.

Classic Duxelles

Makes: 350–500 ml (depending on the mushroom)

INGREDIENTS
125 g butter
125 g shallots, chopped
500 g fresh open-cap (or field) mushrooms, roughly chopped
Salt and freshly ground black pepper
Nutmeg, freshly grated
30 g fresh parsley, chopped

EQUIPMENT
Deep non-stick frying pan
Food processor

Classically, all the ingredients in French duxelles, a mince of mushrooms, onions and herbs, are chopped very finely — but this method using a food processor is much quicker. Fresh field mushrooms are the perfect candidate for this recipe — the ones with fully opened flat caps with brown gills are the best choice here. Duxelles will enrich a sauce, make a soup or a stuffing for pasta or fish, fill an omelette or replace meat in a lasagne. Spread it on toast or crostini. Always keep some in the freezer.

First, heat the butter in a deep non-stick frying pan until melted, then, when it stops foaming, stir in the chopped shallots and cook over a medium-low heat for five minutes to begin softening.

Stir in the mushrooms, add 1–2 tsp of salt, lots of freshly ground black pepper and a little grated nutmeg to taste. Continue to cook gently at a medium-low heat, stirring occasionally for about 30 minutes (uncovered), until really soft and all the liquid evaporates, intensifying the flavour. Tip into a food processor with the parsley and process in short bursts until finely chopped but not a complete purée. Taste and adjust the seasoning.

Use immediately or transfer to a sealed container and store in the fridge for up to three days. Freeze in ice cube trays, then store in freezer bags for up to two months, for the ultimate convenience food — toss one or two cubes into a béchamel or pasta sauce.

Mushroom Stock

Makes: 1.5 litres

INGREDIENTS
2 tbs olive oil
1 large onion, sliced
1 garlic clove, thinly sliced
500 g fresh mushrooms, sliced (including stalks)
Bouquet garni of fresh herbs (optional)
Salt
Fresh lemon juice (to taste)

EQUIPMENT
Large saucepan or deep stock pot with a lid
Fine sieve
Paper coffee filter (optional)

This simple stock using fresh mushrooms relies on the initial gentle softening and browning of the onion, followed by long simmering to intensify its flavour. Almost any kind of mushroom can be used for a mushroom stock — whether fresh, dried, or half and half. Adding dried mushrooms to fresh will give a more intense flavour. This recipe is for a basic stock using fresh mushrooms.

Heat the oil in a large saucepan over a medium heat until a piece of onion sizzles instantly when it hits the oil. When hot enough, add the onions* and stir well, then turn the heat to low and cook the onions very slowly, stirring occasionally until they turn a rich russet brown. This will take at least 25 minutes — cook them any faster and they are sure to burn.

Now add 2 litres of water, the garlic, mushrooms, herbs (if using) and 1 tsp of salt. Stir well and bring to a boil, then turn down the heat and simmer gently, half-covered, for at least three hours. Now taste the stock and add 1 tbs of lemon juice — or more — to lift and brighten the flavour.

Strain the broth through a fine sieve and discard the mushrooms, which will have given up most of their flavour to the stock (or keep to pad out a soup).

To make the stock clear (not necessary), pour the stock through a paper coffee filter whilst warm.

The stock can be served as a broth on its own with a little extra seasoning, used as the base of a mushroom risotto, or in any mushroom recipe that requires a stock or broth for added mushroom flavour.

As with all stocks, it can be boiled fast to reduce, and frozen in ice cube trays, then turned out into a freezer-proof container or strong plastic bag, to be kept in the freezer for up to six months.

* You can add extra ingredients to the basic stock — cook these with the onion — but too many will mask the flavour of the mushrooms. Suggestions are previously saved mushroom stems, onion skins for extra colour, parsley stems, rosemary, thyme, bay leaves, celery and carrot (not too much). For an Asian flavour, use fresh or dried shiitake mushrooms, dried kombu, dried shrimp paste or fish sauce, bonito flakes and soy sauce.

Dried Mushrooms and Dried Mushroom Powder

Makes: 15 thin pancakes (depending on pan size)

INGREDIENTS
175 g plain flour
1 large pinch salt
1 tbs caster sugar
½ lemon, zested (finely grated)
2 large eggs plus 1 egg yolk
400 ml milk (for crisp, delicate pancakes use 50/50 milk/water)
2 tbs melted butter, plus more for greasing
1 bowl caster sugar and lots of lemon wedges (to serve)

EQUIPMENT
Balloon whisk, food processor or electric blender
Sieve
Medium bowl
Jug
15–18 cm frying pan
Thin spatula

Dried mushrooms
Not all mushrooms are suitable for drying. Some have a tough fibrous texture after drying, and some lose their flavour. The most accessible mushrooms to dry are fully open, brown-gilled cultivated or field mushrooms. Slice them thinly, then spread them out in one layer on baking trays and dry at a temperature not exceeding 50°C/30°C fan, until quite leathery — if your oven doesn't go that low, set it to its lowest setting and keep the door ajar. Once fully dry and crispy, leave until they are cold before storing. The time taken will differ from mushroom to mushroom, depending on type and water content. Pack loosely in airtight jars and keep in a dry place. See page 155 for how to reconstitute dried mushrooms.

A condensed guide to the best wild mushrooms for drying:
Porcini — the best for flavour and texture
Horn of plenty — ideal for drying, as it has a low water content
Bay bolete
Slippery jack
St George's mushroom
Fairy ring mushroom
Field mushroom
Hedgehog fungus

Sadly, the lovely chanterelle does not dry well.

Dried mushroom powder
This is more of a method than a recipe, but every mushroom lover will want to make this — mushroom powder is a pantry stalwart. You can use your own dried mushrooms, but ready-dried mushrooms are ideal, as the process is so simple.

To grind mushrooms to a fine powder, they must be fully dried to a crisp — they should snap when bent. If even the slightest bit humid or soft, the mushroom will not turn into "mushroom dust". So, pop the dried mushrooms in a paper bag, keeping it open at the top, and sit it on a radiator for 10–15 minutes to make sure they are fully dry, and allow to cool. They should be nicely crisp after this. Alternatively, spread the dried mushrooms out on a tray and put them in a low oven not exceeding 50°C/30°C fan with the door ajar.

Once dried and cooled, grind the mushrooms to a fine powder in a clean coffee grinder, food mill or similar. Sift out any bits that will not break down after grinding, and then store the powder in an airtight container to keep it dry and flavourful. Use to add extra mushroom flavour to sauces and stews, season scrambled eggs or boost the flavour of a mushroom omelette.

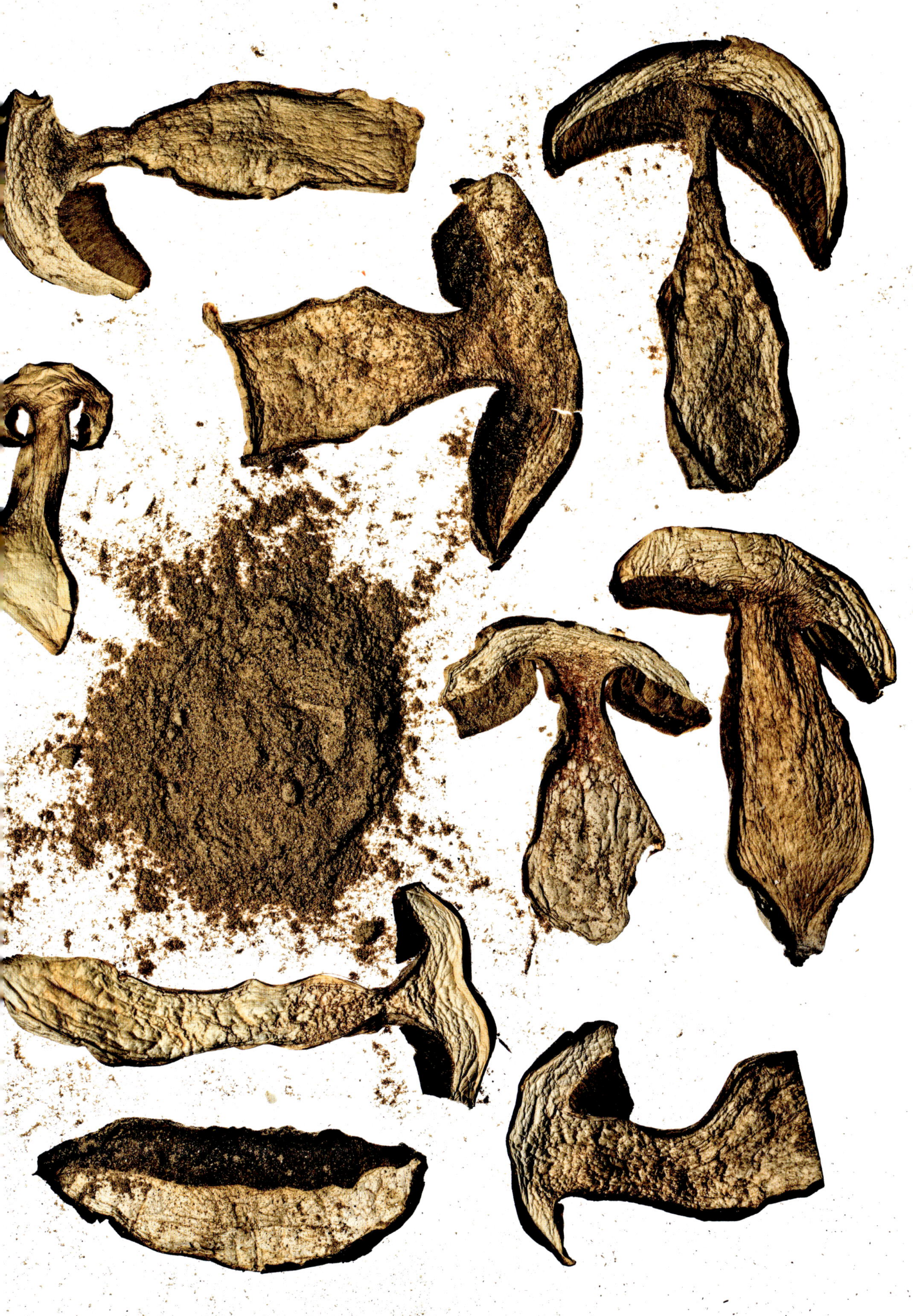

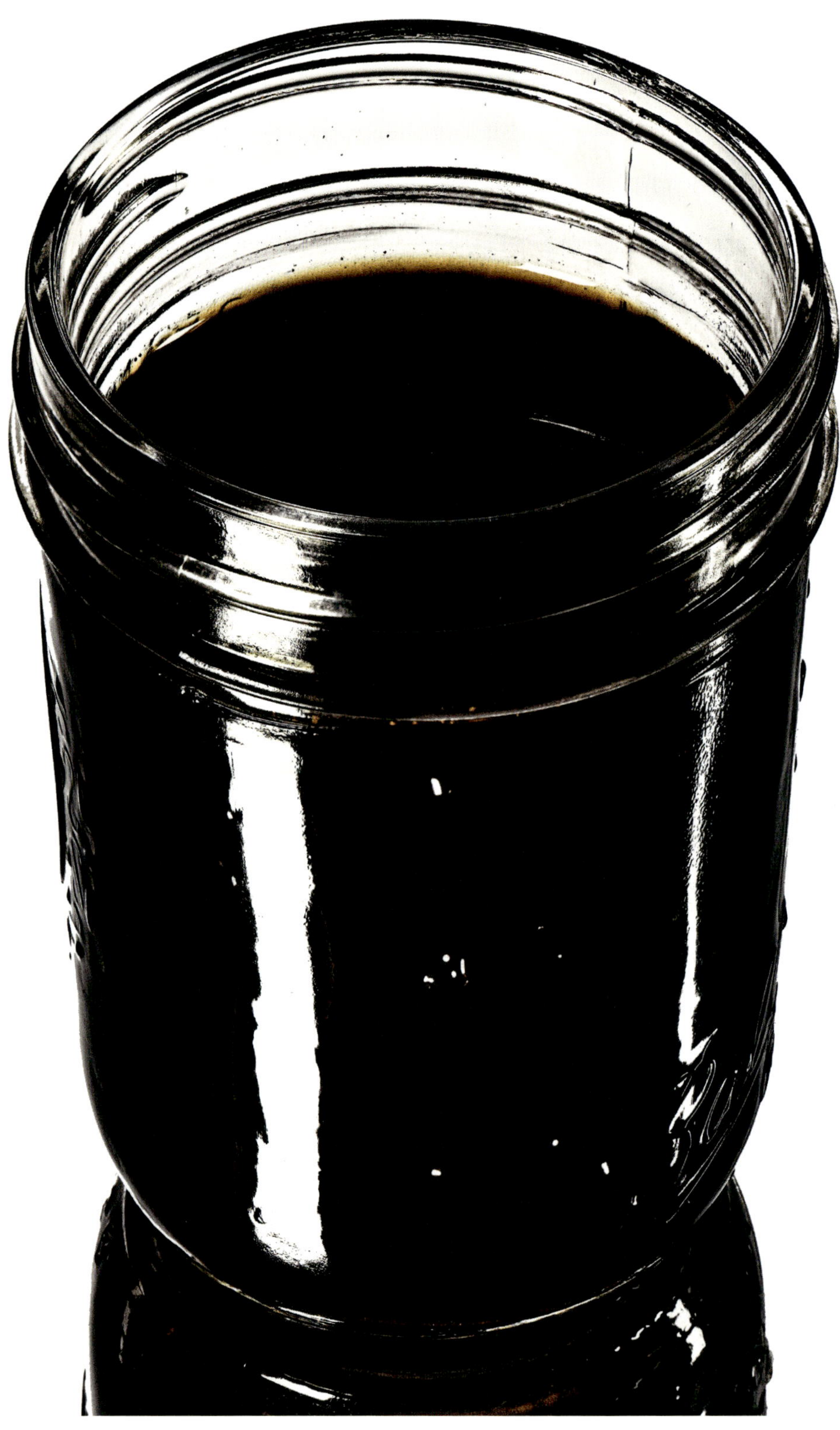

Japanese Mushroom Relish/Glaze

A concentrated relish full of umami, this mixture can be used as a glaze when grilling fish or vegetables or even a steak. Brush it on barbecued food for a mouth-watering finish, or add it to a rice bowl to liven it up.

Makes: 150 ml

INGREDIENTS
15 cm piece of kombu (kelp)
2 dried shiitake mushrooms
50 ml sake
50 ml soy sauce
100 ml mirin
15 g bonito flakes

EQUIPMENT
Large bowl
Medium saucepan
Fine sieve
200 ml glass jar with lid, sterilized (see p. 155)

Put the kombu and mushrooms into a large bowl, add 600 ml of water, cover and leave to soak overnight in the fridge. The next day, transfer the contents to a medium saucepan, add the remaining ingredients and bring to the boil over a high heat. Once boiling, reduce the heat to a simmer, and continue simmering for about 20 minutes or until reduced by half. At this stage, remove the kombu and mushrooms (keep to add to a rice dish).

Keep simmering until the sauce becomes shiny and syrupy. Strain through a fine sieve into a sterilized glass jar, screw on the lid and leave to cool. Store for up to 2–3 weeks in the fridge.

Old-Fashioned Mushroom Ketchup

Makes: about 750 ml

INGREDIENTS
1.5 kg large fresh open-cup (or field) mushrooms, roughly chopped
75 g salt
15 g fresh root ginger, chopped
1 tsp (heaped) black peppercorns
1 tsp (heaped) allspice berries
½ tsp ground mace or 2 large blades of mace
4 whole cloves
½ small cinnamon stick
2 fresh bay leaves
600 ml cider vinegar
½ tsp brown sugar

EQUIPMENT
Medium/large, deep ovenproof casserole with a lid
Potato masher
15 × 15 cm square of muslin or a reusable drawstring tea/coffee filter bag
Medium saucepan
Large, deep saucepan
Fine sieve
Large bowl
Paper coffee filter (optional)
750 ml swing-top bottle with rubber seals

There are two types of ketchup that can be made with mushrooms. One is the old English ketchup — an intensely spicy mushroom-flavoured sauce used to add extra umami to soups, sauces, stews and even cocktails. This condiment is not a table sauce. Its thicker, sweeter cousin is based on the American tomato catsup (ketchup) with a mushroom addition — and it is a table sauce. In days of yore, when field mushrooms were plentiful in meadows, the former was made with the remainder of a glut of them and was a pantry staple. It's particularly good added to meat pies or savoury puddings, and adds depth to a soup or stock.

Arrange the mushrooms in layers, sprinkled with salt, in a medium/large casserole, cover and leave in a cool place for 2–3 days, stirring and pressing them — use a potato masher every now and then to encourage their juices to leach. The mushrooms will collapse — this is normal.

After 2–3 days, preheat the oven to 140°C/120°C fan/gas mark 1. Cover the casserole and place it in the oven to gently cook for 2–3 hours to extract all the mushroom flavour.

While the mushrooms are cooking, make the spiced vinegar. The amounts of spices used here are just for guidance — adapt them for a stronger or milder flavour. Put all the spices onto a square of muslin, and tie up to form a little bag. Place the spice bag in a medium saucepan, pour in the vinegar and add the sugar. Bring to the boil, then turn down the heat to a simmer and cook gently for ten minutes. Remove from the heat, and allow the vinegar and spices to cool and infuse. Remove the spice bag when cold.

After around three hours, remove the casserole from the oven, and mash the mushrooms to break them up, or pulse in a food processor until roughly chopped. Tip the mushrooms and juices into a large, deep saucepan, add the cooled spiced vinegar and bring up to the boil. Reduce the heat and simmer gently for 30 minutes.

Strain the whole lot through a fine sieve set over a large bowl until all the liquid has strained out — this quantity will make about 750 ml. If it makes more, pour the liquid back into the saucepan and boil hard until reduced to 750 ml. Discard the spent mushrooms. At this stage, you can pass the ketchup through a paper coffee filter to remove any tiny particles of mushroom — this is purely cosmetic and isn't essential. Pour the ketchup into the warmed swing-top bottle to within 2.5 cm of its top, and seal.

To prolong the life of the ketchup, you can process the bottles in a water bath. Put a clean folded kitchen towel on the bottom of a very large, deep pan that will take all your bottles without them falling over. Wrap each sealed bottle in a clean kitchen towel to prevent them touching each other during processing. Half fill the pan with warm water, then stand the bottles in the pan next to each other. Top up with warm water, to about 2.5 cm below the stopper. Bring to the boil slowly, turn down the heat a little to a gentle boil and keep it there for 20 minutes. Turn off the heat and leave to cool in the water for ten minutes. Carefully lift out of the water using oven gloves or a clean kitchen towel, and leave to cool. Label and store for up to a year. Allow to mature for about two weeks before using.

This is a strong flavouring and a little goes a long way. Store in the fridge once opened.

Mushroom Sauce for Steaks

Serves: 4

INGREDIENTS
60 g butter
1 shallot, finely chopped
120 g fresh field mushrooms, sliced
1 tbs dry white wine or vermouth
300 ml good beef gravy or reduced stock
Pat of black garlic butter or dash of cream (optional)
Salt and freshly ground black pepper
1 tsp fresh chervil, tarragon or parsley, chopped

EQUIPMENT
Heavy-based frying pan (unwashed from cooking the steaks)
Wooden spatula

Make this sauce in a flash while the steaks you've cooked are resting, using the still-warm pan with all the good bits from frying the steaks clinging to its bottom. A good, strong beef stock is essential for a flavourful sauce with body. A pinch of mushroom powder (see page 236) and a dash of mushroom ketchup (see page 240) will up the umami. Any type of mushroom works for this recipe — field, cultivated or wild.

Using the unwashed frying pan that the steaks were cooked in with all the sticky bits and any fat that has collected, reset the pan over a medium heat and add half of the butter. Swirl around, add the shallot, and cook over a medium heat until the colour is just turning.

Add the remaining butter, then the mushrooms, to the pan, and begin to fry, scraping the bottom of the pan to loosen the sticky sediment from the fried steaks. Fry for about two minutes to lightly brown the mushrooms and evaporate their water, then stir in the wine or vermouth, the beef gravy and any juices surrounding the resting steaks.

Turn up the heat and boil rapidly to reduce and thicken the sauce to a syrupy consistency. Whisk in a pat of black garlic butter after reducing the sauce, for an extra special touch — or a dash of cream. Taste and adjust the seasoning, then stir in the freshly chopped herbs, and spoon over the steaks. Serve immediately.

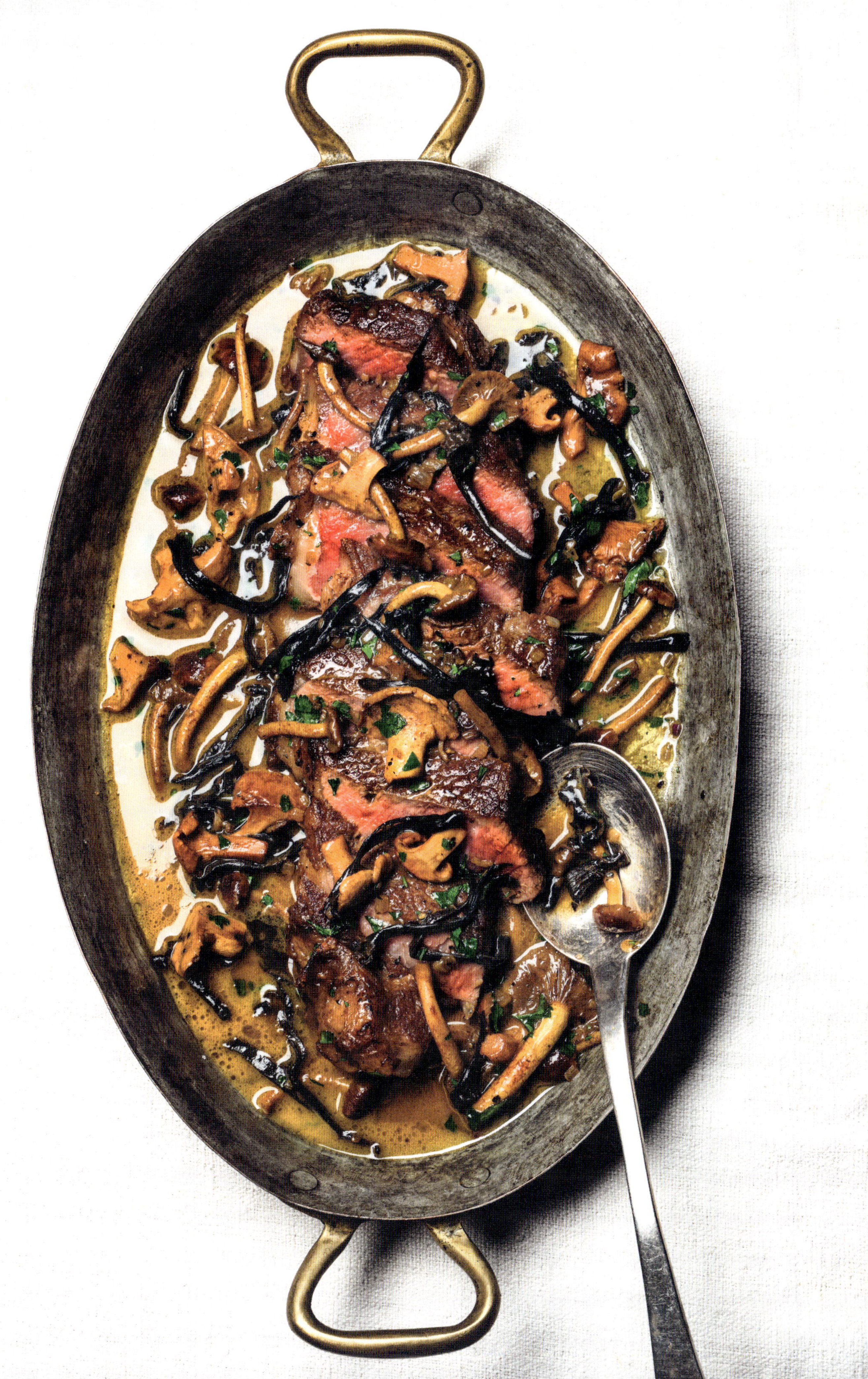

Mushroom and Chinese Leaf Kimchi

Makes: two 600 ml jars

INGREDIENTS
350 g fresh mushrooms, finely sliced
120 g coarse salt
750 g head of whole Chinese leaf

Kimchi paste:
75 g gochugaru (Korean chilli powder)
150 g leek or spring onions, finely chopped
1–2 tbs garlic, finely grated
1 tbs ginger, finely grated
1–2 tbs fish sauce
1 tbs coarse salt
2 tbs sugar

EQUIPMENT
Large saucepan
2 medium non-reactive bowls
Sieve
Colander
Latex gloves
Small/medium bowl
Two 600 ml wide-necked preserving jars with lids, sterilized (see p. 155)

Any type of meaty flavourful mushroom will work here – puffball, porcini, cultivated portobello, chestnut, shiitake, even field mushrooms – anything that can be cut into decent slices. Making kimchi takes a couple of weeks, but the preparation is quick, and the kimchi is left to do its own thing at each stage. The longer the finished kimchi is left to mature, the better the flavour. Use the kimchi straight from the jar in a salad, on a sandwich or with rice.

Salting stage
Put the sliced mushrooms in a large saucepan, add 20 g of salt, and pour in enough water to just cover them. Bring to the boil, stirring to dissolve the salt, and boil for 30 seconds. Turn off the heat and pour the mushrooms into a medium non-reactive bowl, and place a plate with a weight on top of the mushrooms, to keep them submerged. Leave to stand for 24 hours at cool room temperature.

Next, cut the Chinese leaf in half lengthwise, and place the halves, cut-side up, in another medium non-reactive bowl. Crush the remaining salt* and rub it all over the cut sides so that it will penetrate better once the water is poured over. Pour enough cold water over the cabbage to completely cover the halves, and place a plate with a weight on top to keep them submerged. Leave to stand for 24 hours at cool room temperature.

After 24 hours' salting, drain the mushrooms through a sieve, rinse and set aside. Drain the Chinese leaf (which will have become quite floppy) through a colander, and rinse several times in cold running water, making sure the insides of the leaves are rinsed as well – separate the leaves with your hands to open them up. Turn cut-side down, and leave to drain for five minutes.

Flavouring stage
Put on some latex gloves. In a small/medium bowl, mix together all the kimchi paste ingredients. Use a third of the paste, and mix with the mushrooms, making sure the paste coats them all.

Mix the Chinese leaf with the remaining kimchi paste, lifting the leaves and pushing the paste inside. Now, slice each half into four chunks, keeping the layers together.

Pack a layer of Chinese leaf into the bottom of each wide-necked preserving jar. Next, pack about a third of the mushrooms on top, then another layer of leaves, and continue until everything is inside the jar, packing down between layers.

Leave to stand at room temperature for 24 hours – do not open.

Fermentation stage

Transfer the jars to the fridge for ten days to mature — don't be tempted to open for the duration of the maturing process, as this will inhibit the fermentation. After ten days it should be ready, and will last for at least two months.

* A good kimchi contains the right amount of salt, but to get it right it's important to taste the vegetable after salting. If it's very salty after the salting stage — taste a bit of leaf from the centre of the head — rinse multiple times until it tastes just slightly too salty. On the other hand, if the salt level tastes just right it's probably under-salted. It's tricky to get the correct balance.

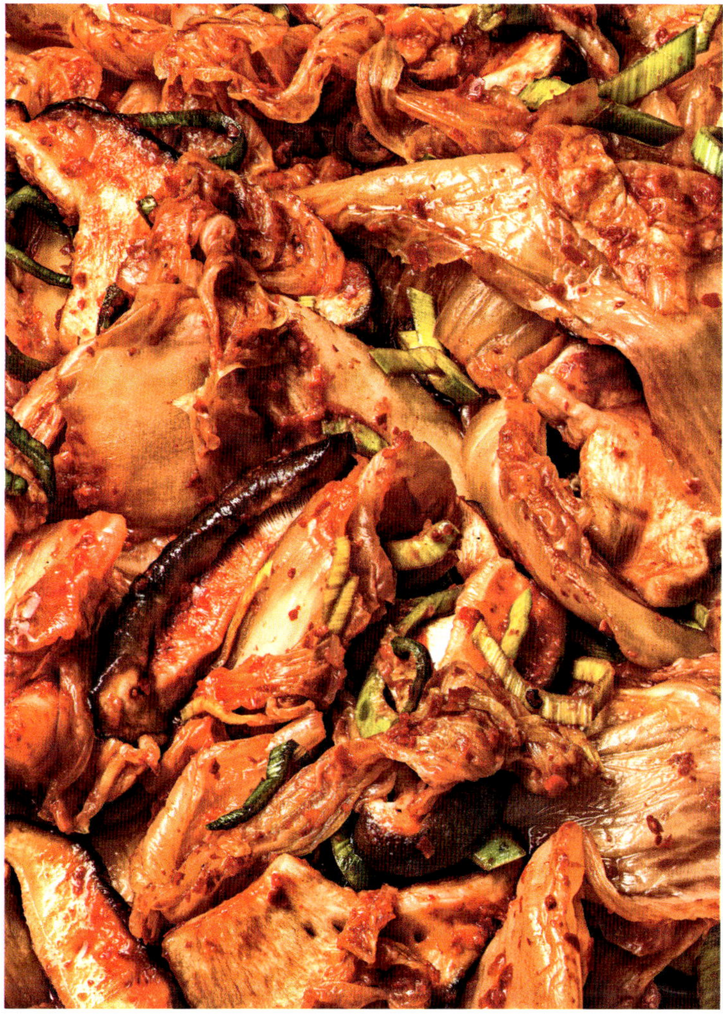

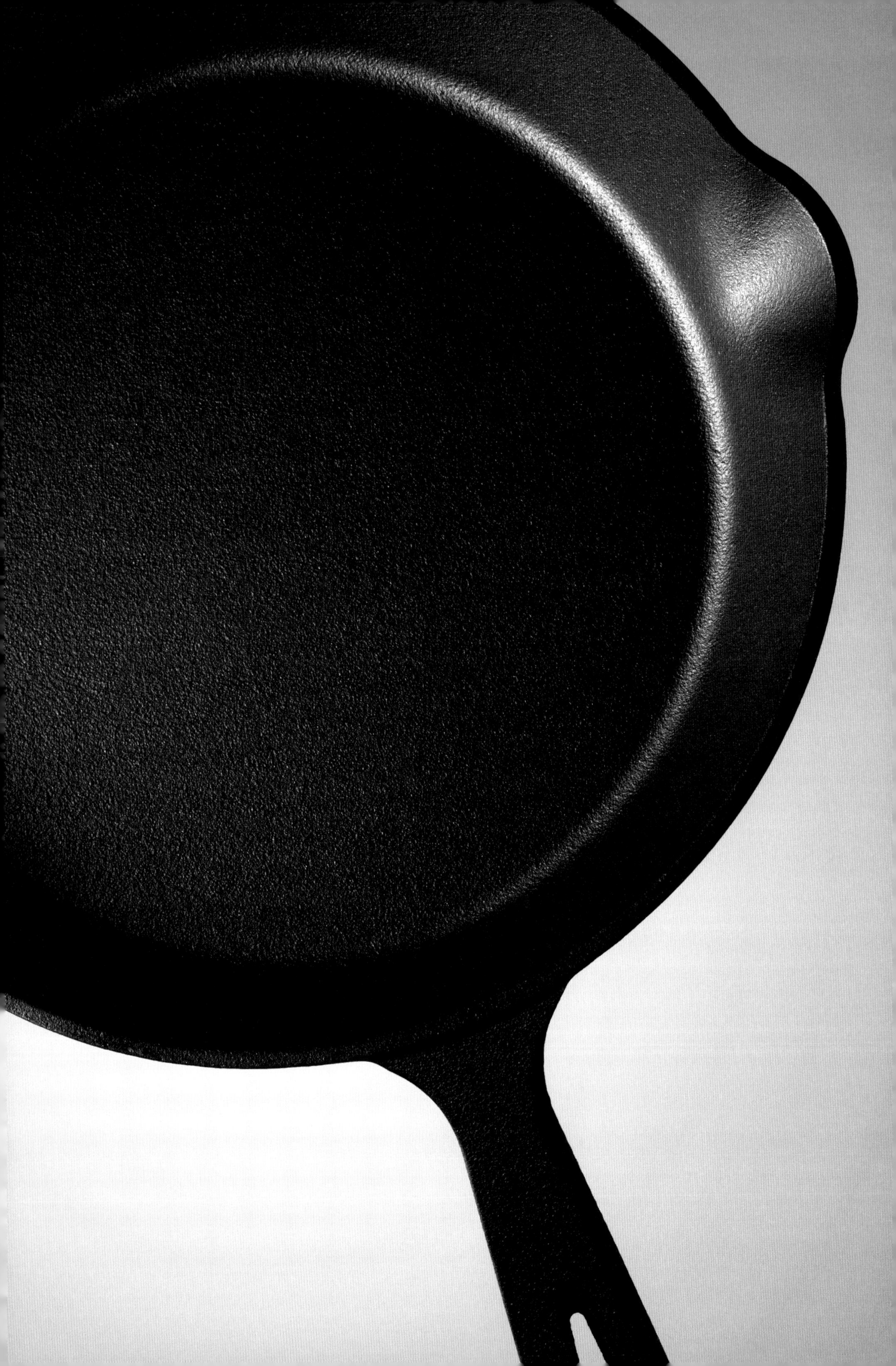

Mushroom Accessories

PHOTOGRAPHY
Robin Broadbent, 2025

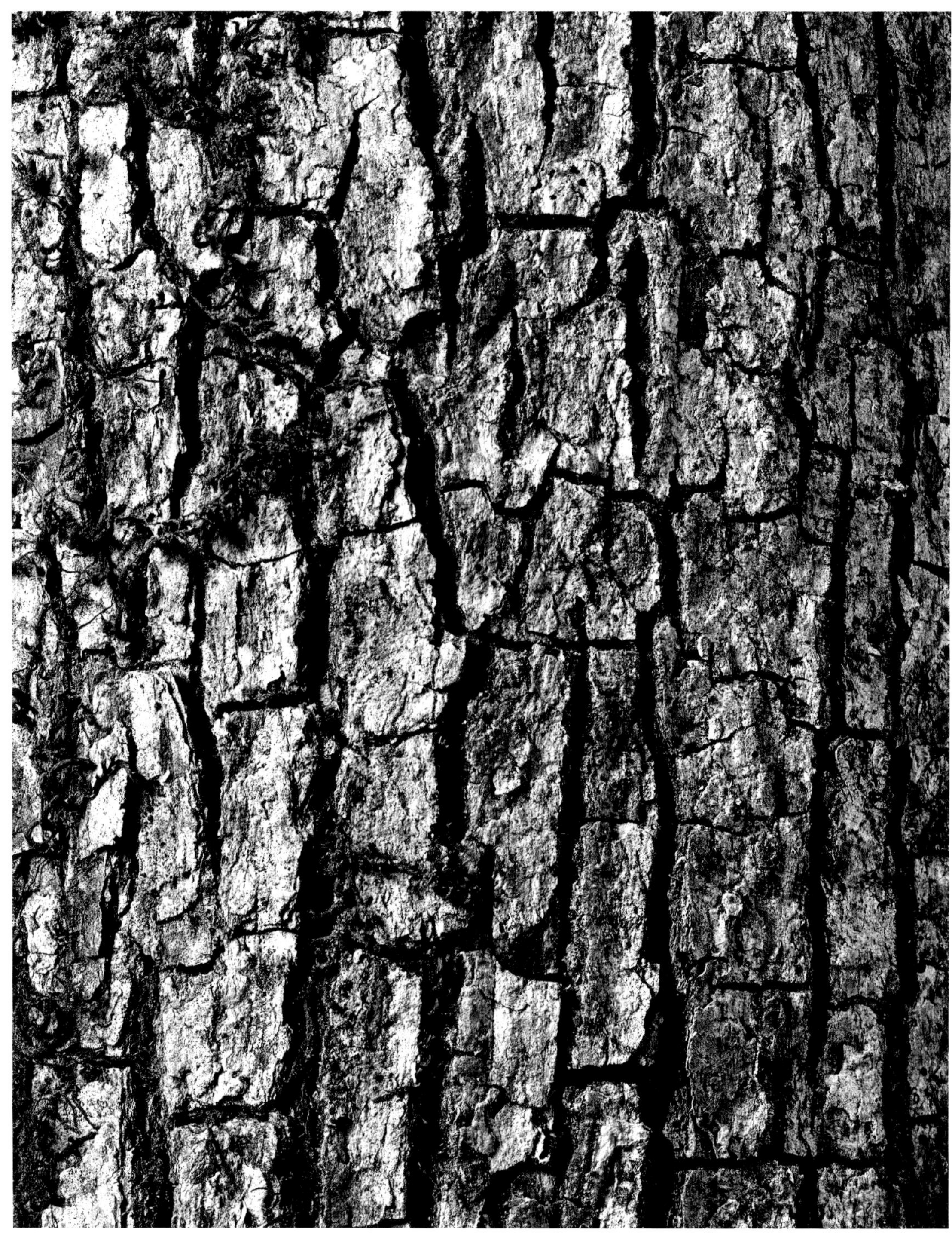

Tree Bark

Myriad mushrooms lurk as spores within tree bark, taken there on the breeze. Turkey tail, pheasant back and chicken of the woods, to name a few. When freed from their shady environs, these are sliced and served with their namesakes and a glass of pinot.

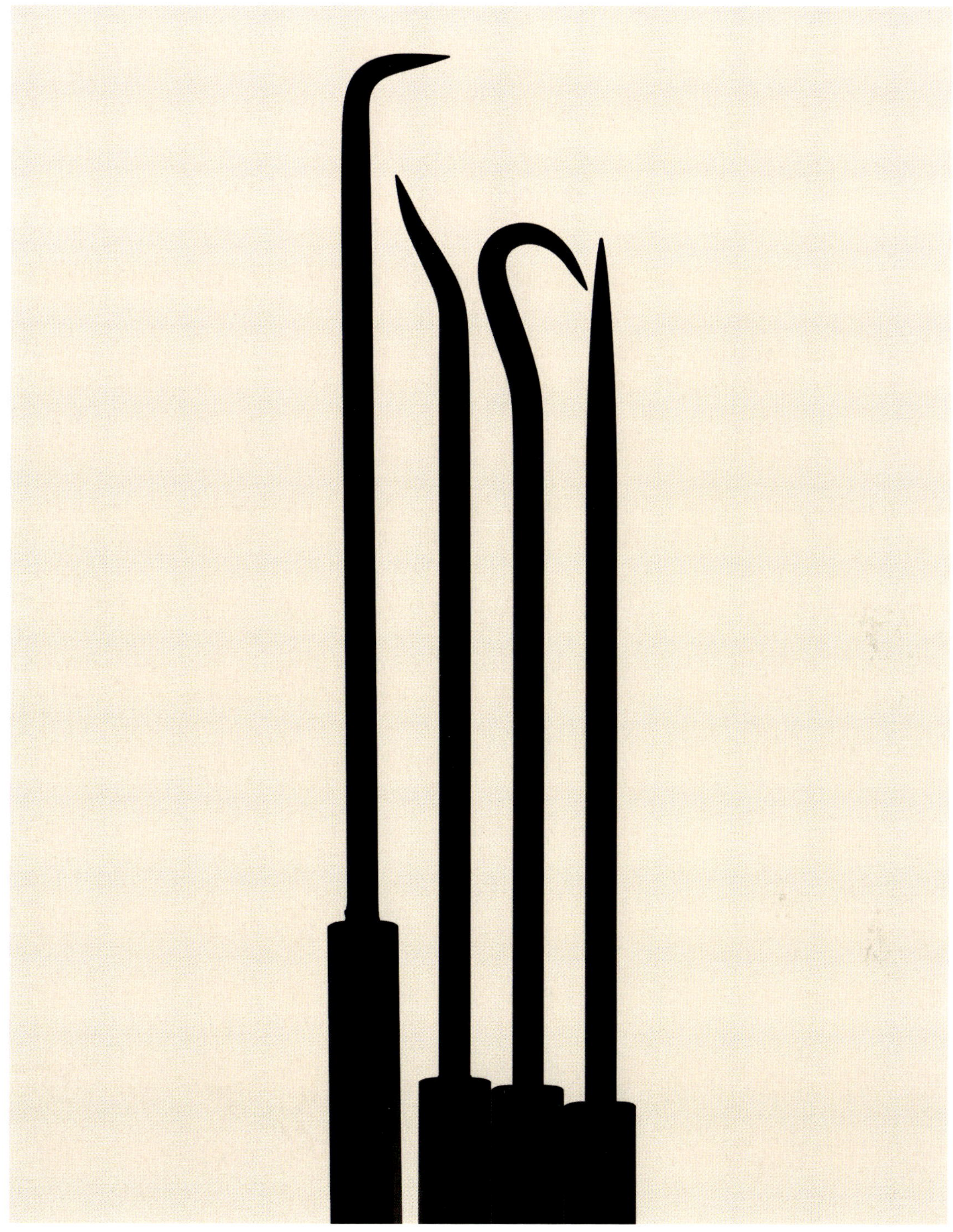

Tiny Picks

Few things take the fun out of an evening of fungal appreciation quite like stubborn grit lodged in the gills of a field mushroom or similarly creviced variety. Coming to the rescue, these mini-picks are the perfect way to delve for and discard unwanted detritus.

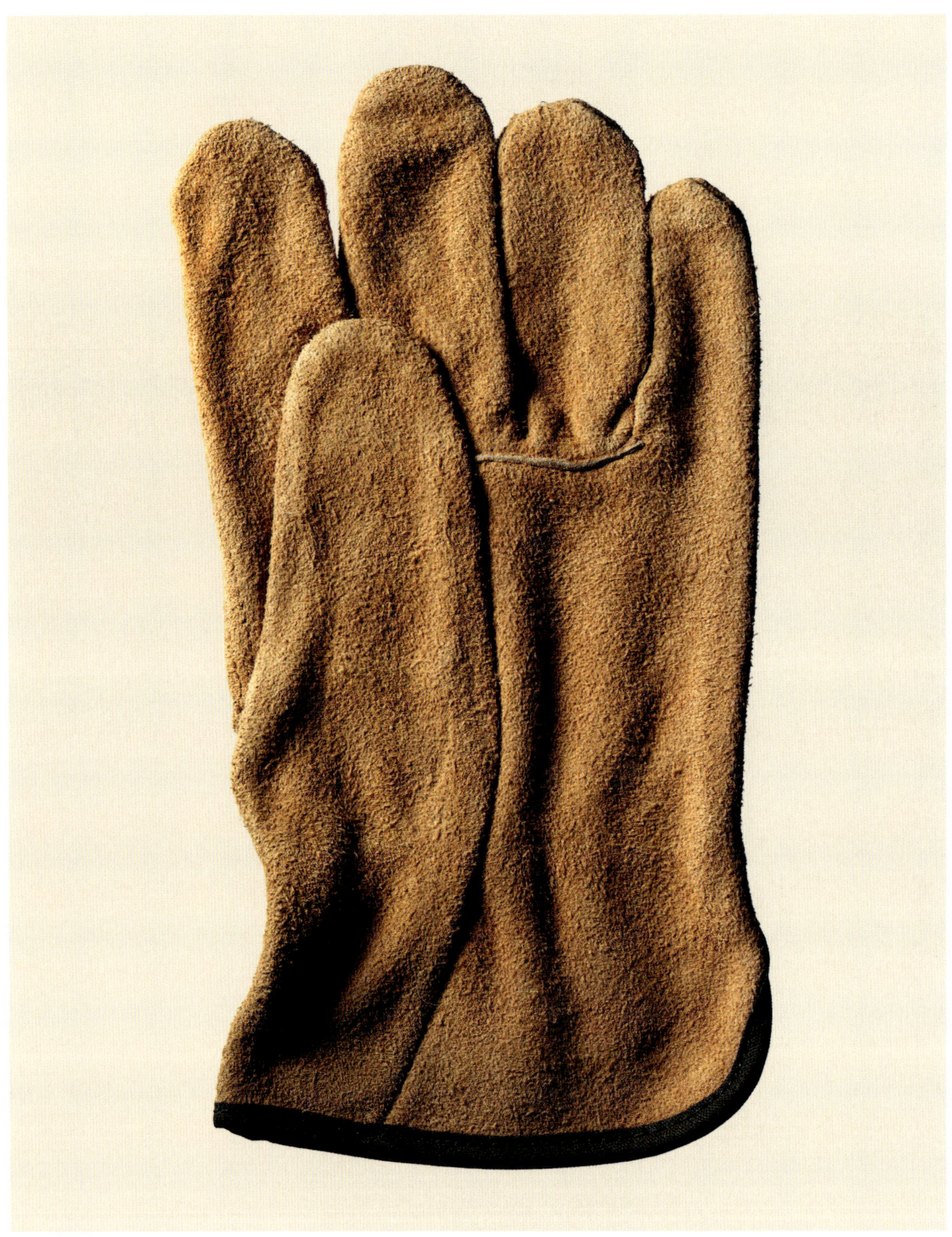

Gloves

The perfect marriage of softness and durability, a pair of cowhide gloves is a must for forest floor snack-seekers. With protection against thorns lurking in the leaf litter, yet able to yield enough for careful picking and handling, they keep both fungus and forager safe from harm.

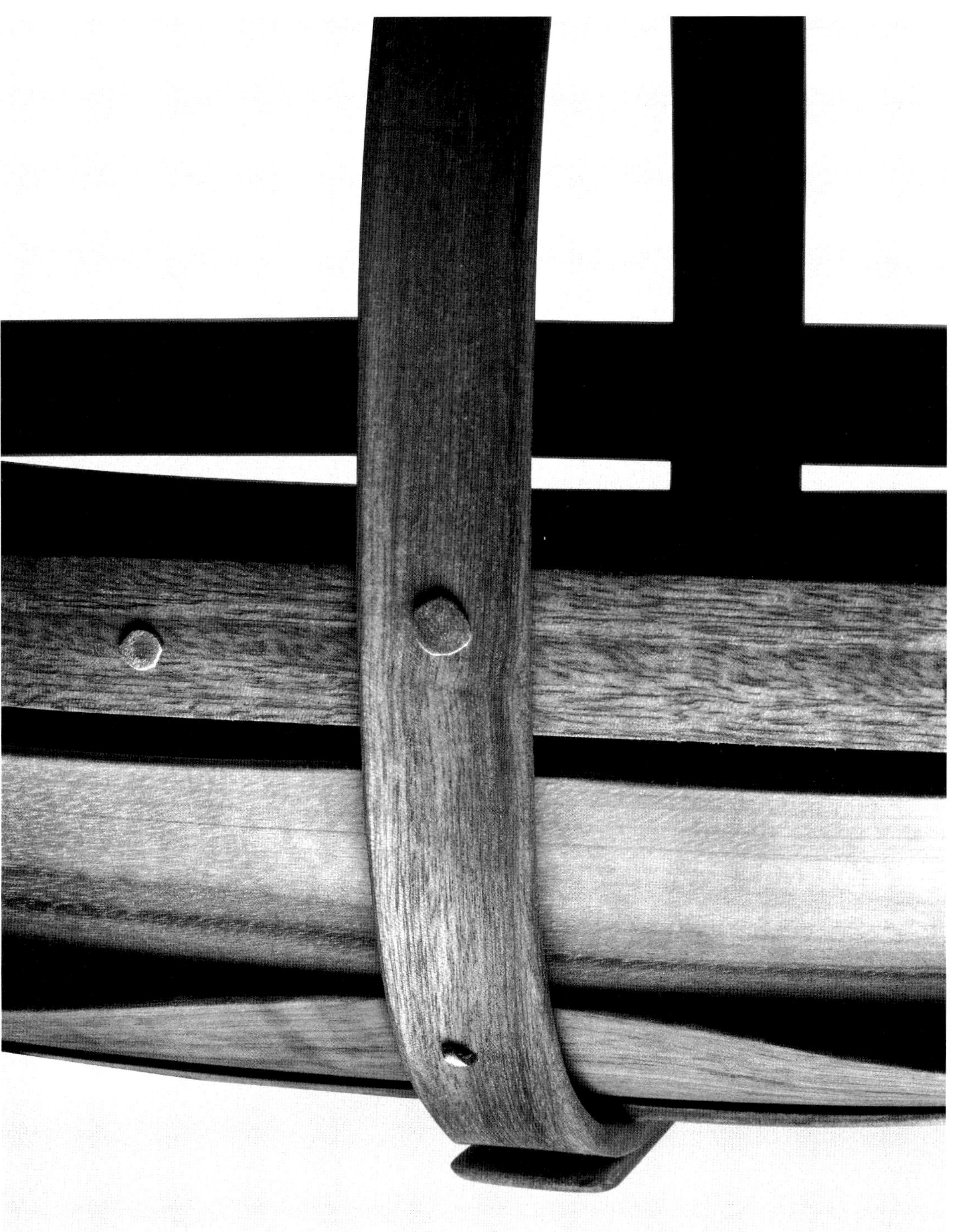

Sussex Trug

Shallow trug baskets — notably those crafted in the English county of Sussex since the early 1800s — replaced solid wooden carriers, thus lightening the load of fruit pickers and farmhands. Crafted in various sizes and slatted to keep air circulating, trugs allow fresh-picked mushrooms to stay free of dampness.

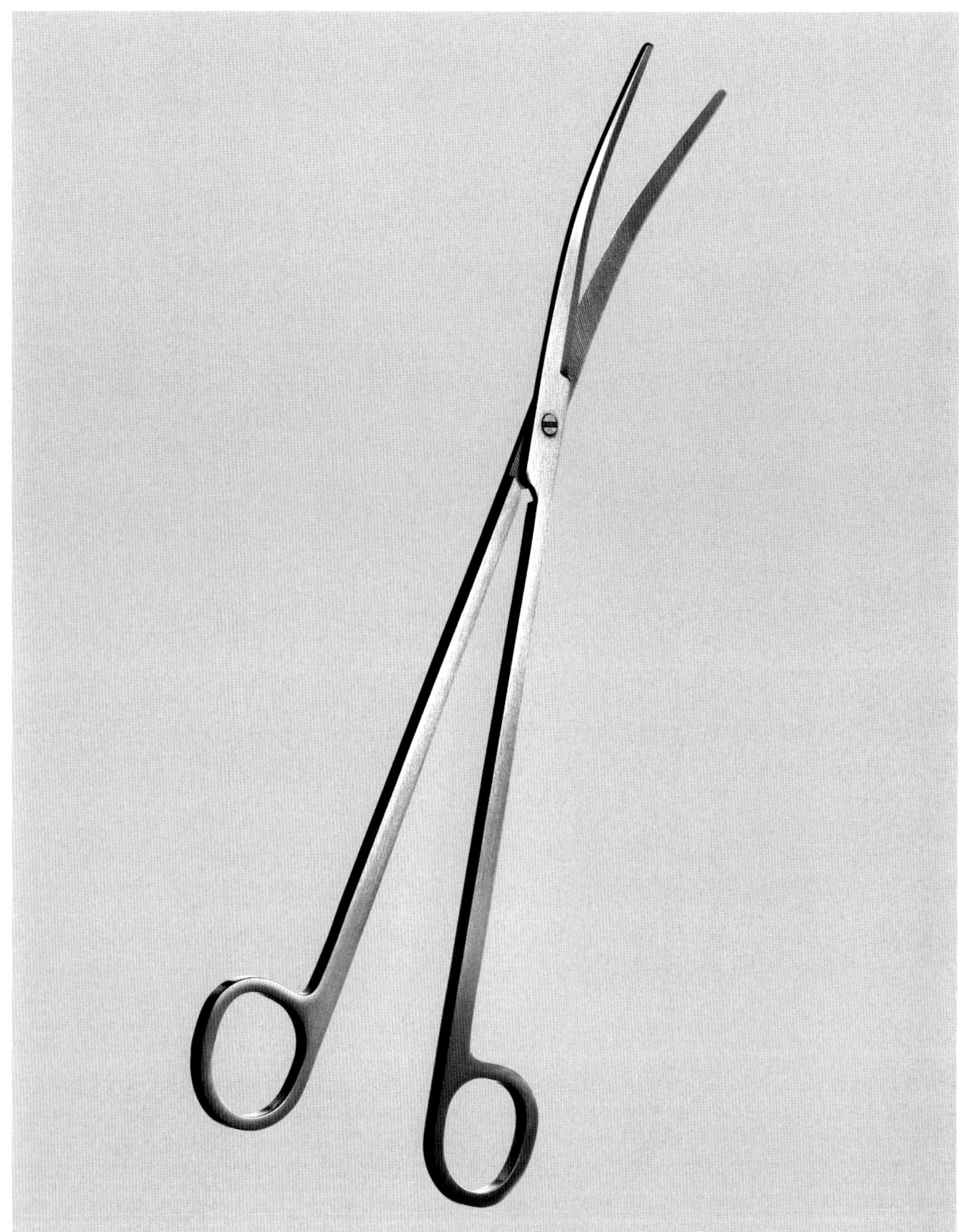

Metzenbaums

Invented by a surgeon with small hands and a need to reach inflamed tonsils, the structure of Myron Metzenbaum's eponymous scissors make them ideal implements to reach down towards the stem of a delicate mushroom to be duly snipped and served.

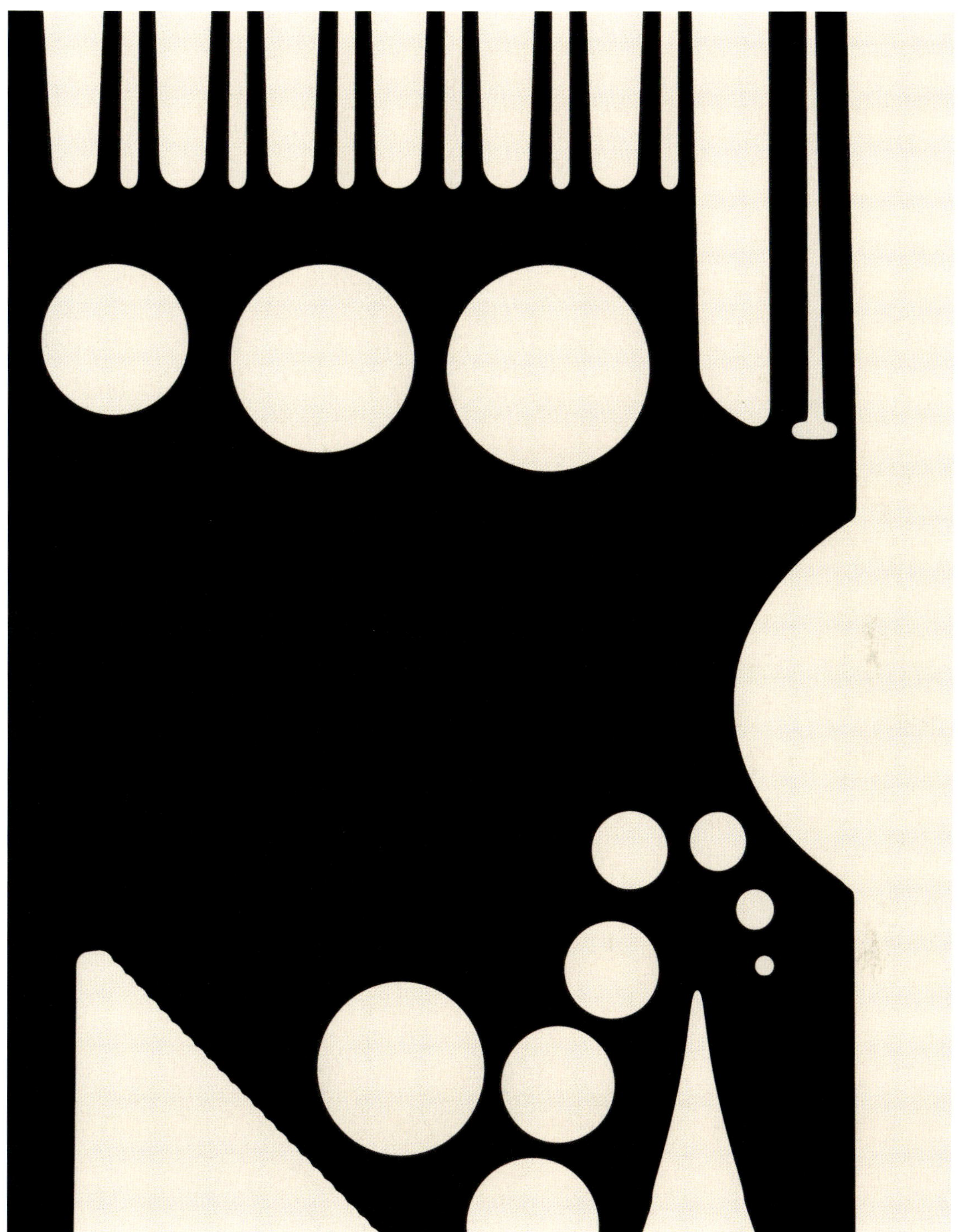

Forager Card

This credit-card-sized steel multi-tool is the perfect accessory for an impromptu spot of foraging. Of particular interest to mushroom hunters are its sharp edge for clean cuts, a ruler to size up the finds, and a stripper to ensure accompanying herbs are free of woody stalks.

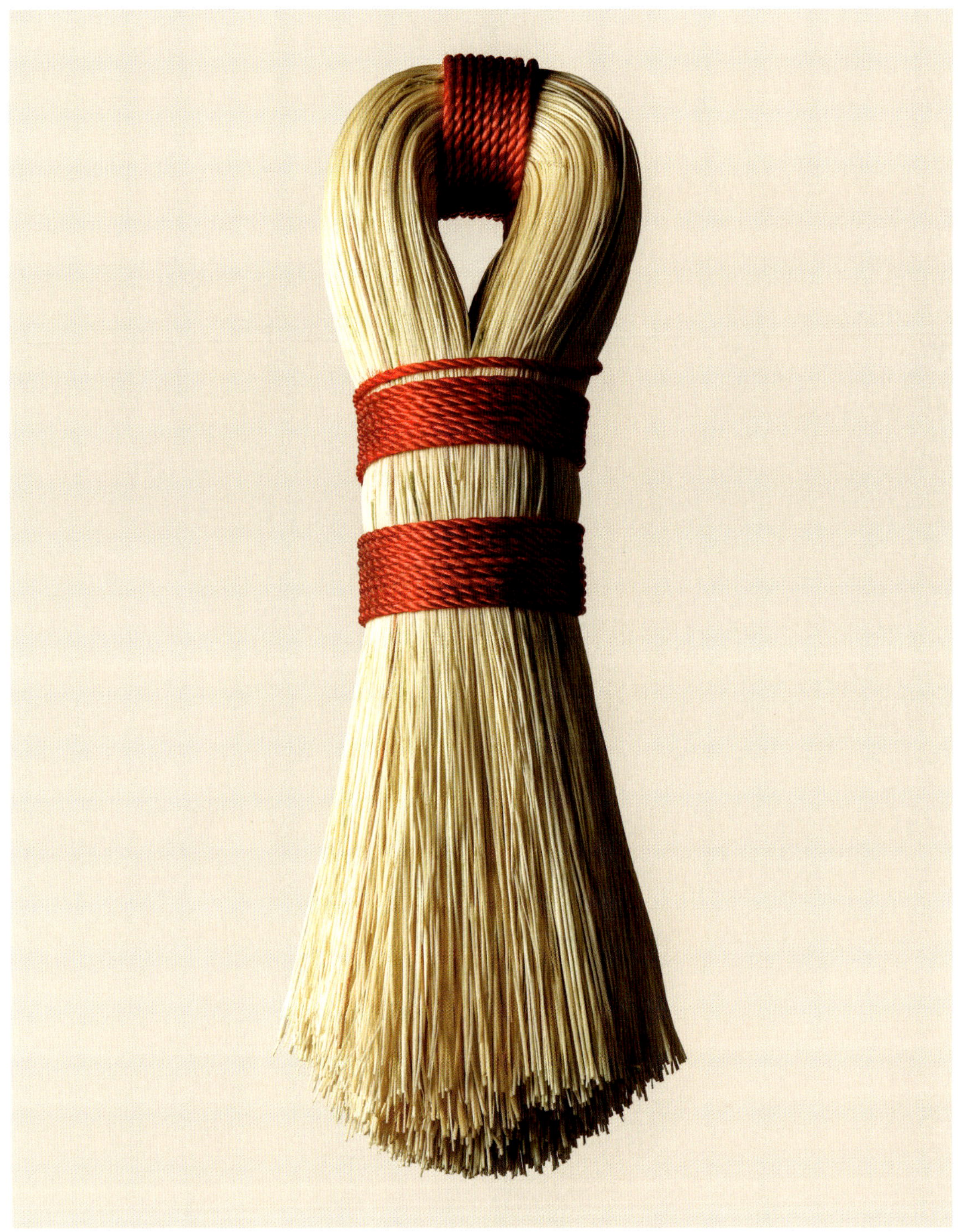

Tampico Brush

The bristles of the Tampico brush are sourced from the *Agave lechuguill*a plant, native to Mexico. A delicate, rough-textured composition retains just enough abrasive qualities to make these brushes perfect for loosening earth, muck and dirt from the cap and stem of a mushroom before preparation.

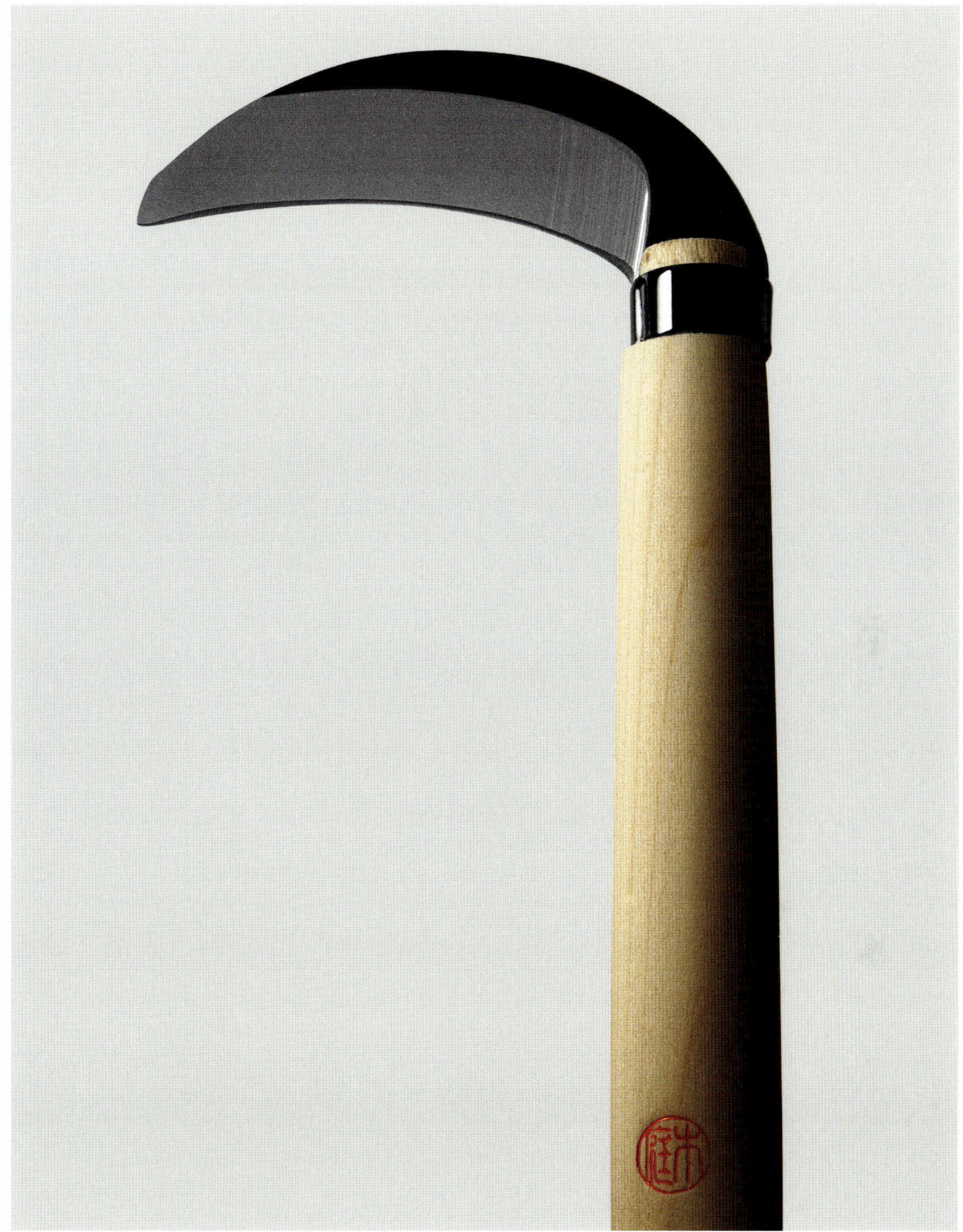

Mini Scythe

Set atop a circular handle, the bevelled carbon steel blade of the mini scythe makes it a perfect tool for the precise, single, sweeping cut favoured by harvesters of enoki mushrooms, whose tight clusters of tall, willowy stalks require the most unfaltering method of excision.

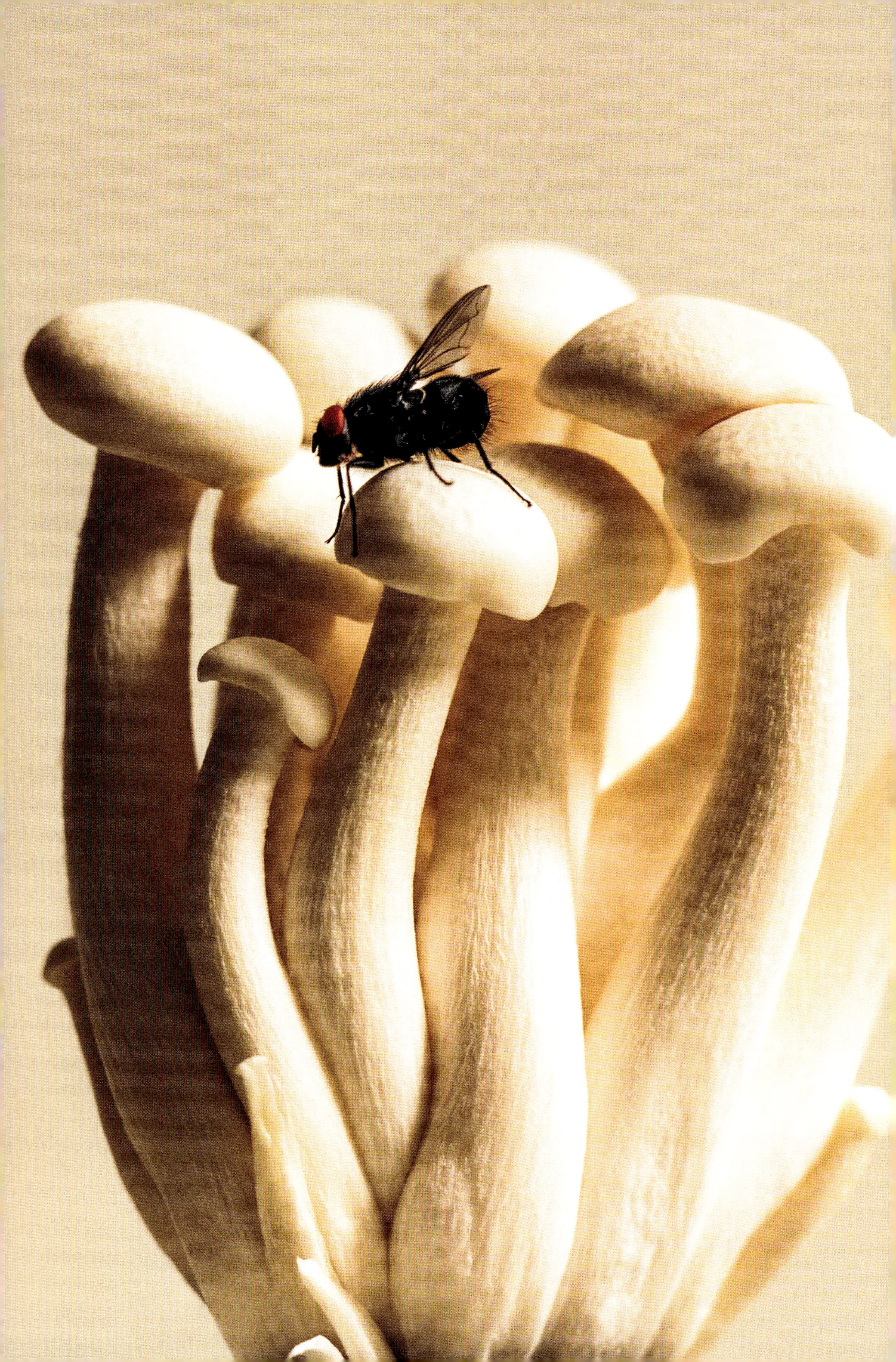

Index

OPPOSITE
Ben Toms, *Untitled*, 2021

A

B

C

H

I

J

K

L

M

N

O

P

U

V

W

X

Y

Z

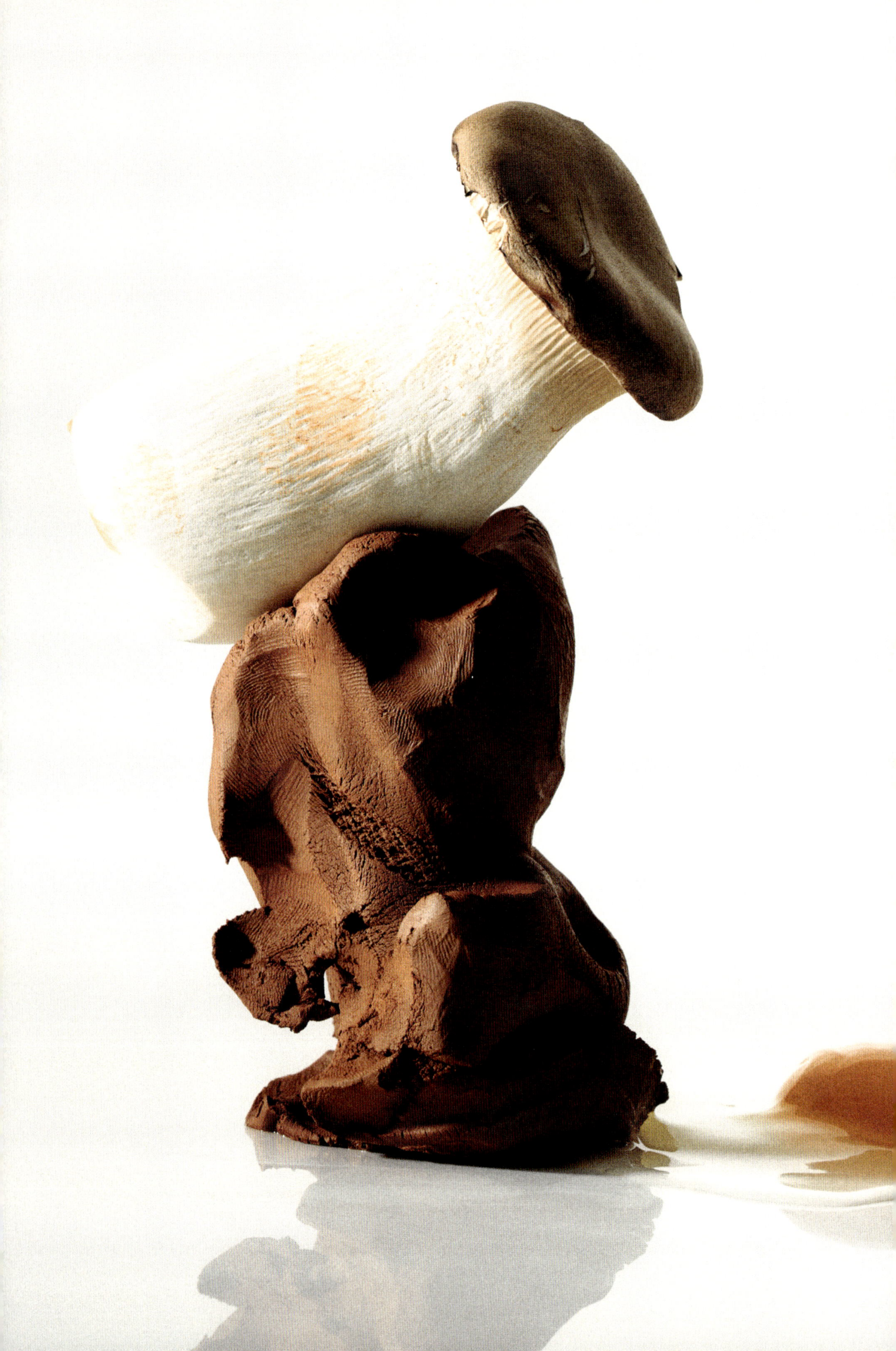

It's been such a pleasure to explore the mysterious and magical world of mushrooms by way of creating this book, and we could not have done it without our wonderful editorial team.

Firstly, we wish to thank our publisher, Marlene Taschen, and the rest of the team at TASCHEN; Alexi Alario, Kathrin Murr, Frank Goerhardt, Frauke Peters, Charlotte Broomfield. We also wish to thank our literary agent, Luke Ingram, at The Wylie Agency, our very talented team at The Gourmand; Editor Ananda Pellerin, Managing Editor Chloe Dixon-Goulden, Picture Editor Kate Suiter, Sub Editor and Proof-reader Rich Cutler, Designer Jordan Weaver, Copy Editor Myles Smith, Recipe Developer Maxine Clark, and Didi Ronan — who helped get the project off the ground in the first place.

We would also like to thank our contributing writers; Patrick Baglee, Jonathan Griffin, David Guimond, and Hannah Lack, Jennifer Higgie, who wrote our introduction, and Jeremy Lee MBE who penned our foreword.

Finally, we would like to thank our contributing photographers and stylists; Bobby Doherty, Robin Broadbent, Jamie Kimm, Anna Edqwist, Noemi Bonazzi, Grace Gem, Jesscia Do, the team at Minititle, and our typeface designer Gunnar Vilhjálmsson.

OPPOSITE **Charlotte Kreiger**, *Mushroom, Egg and Clay*, 2022
FOLLOWING **Optical Arts**, *Mushrooms in Times Square*, 2025

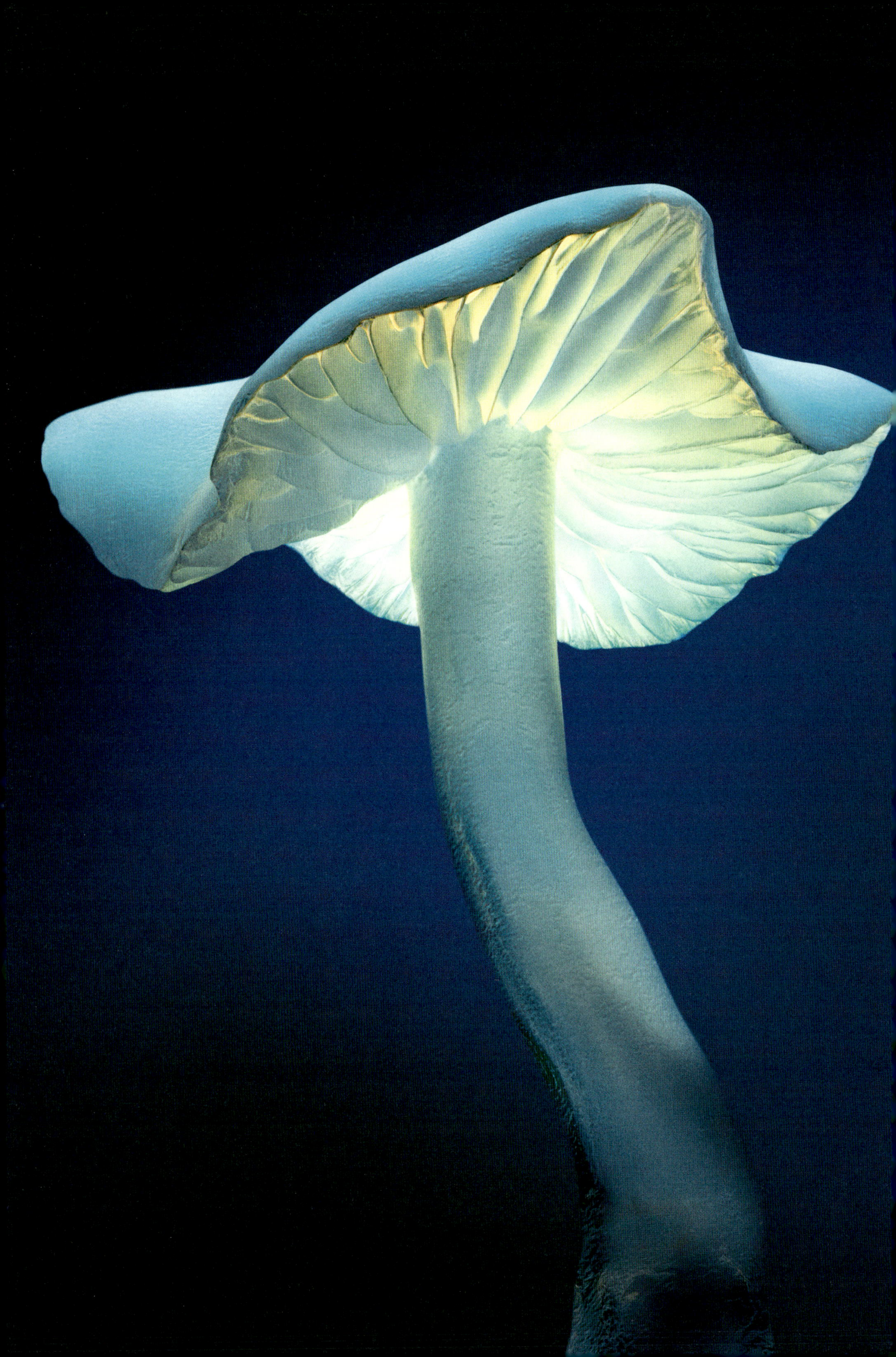

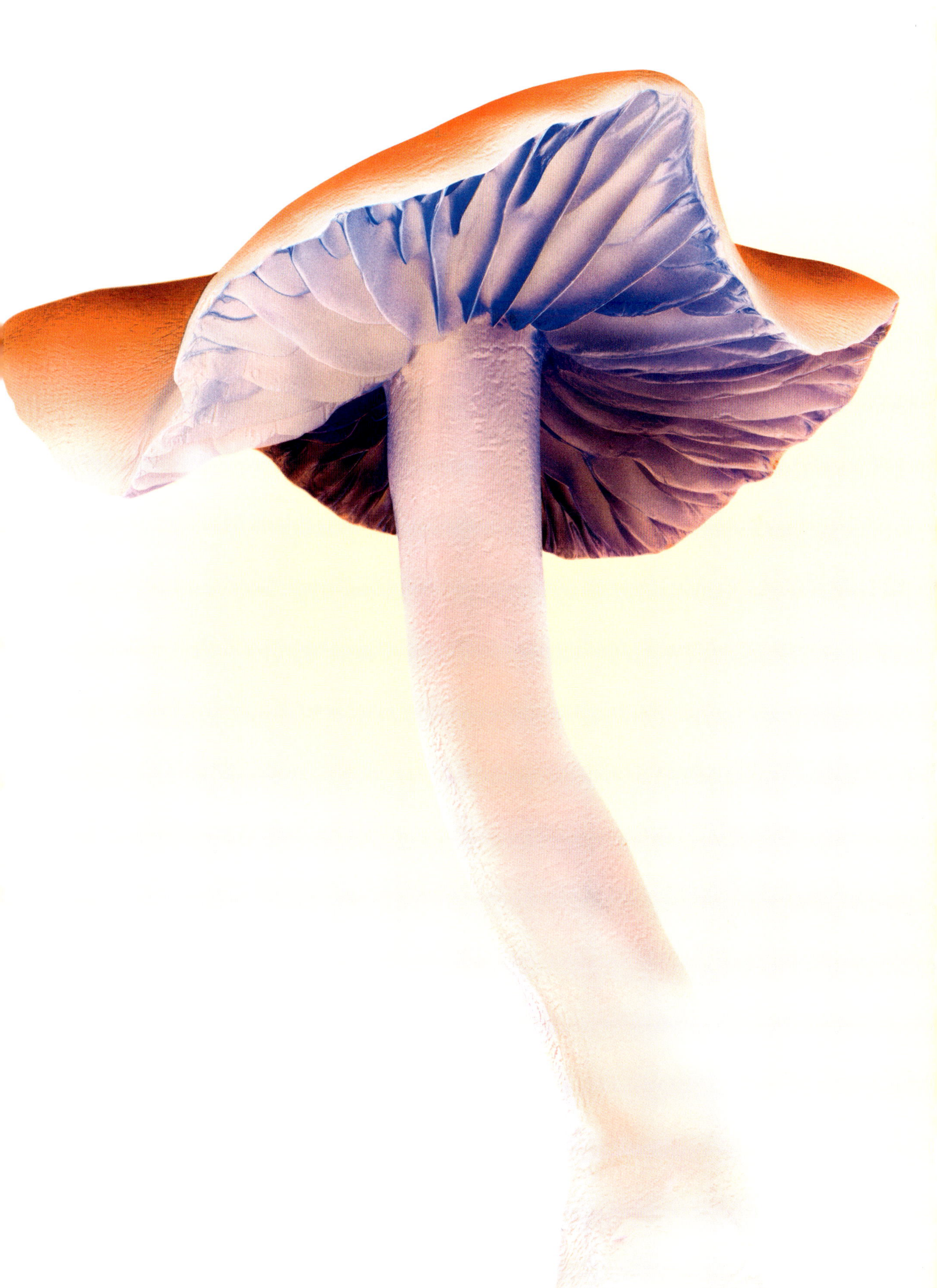

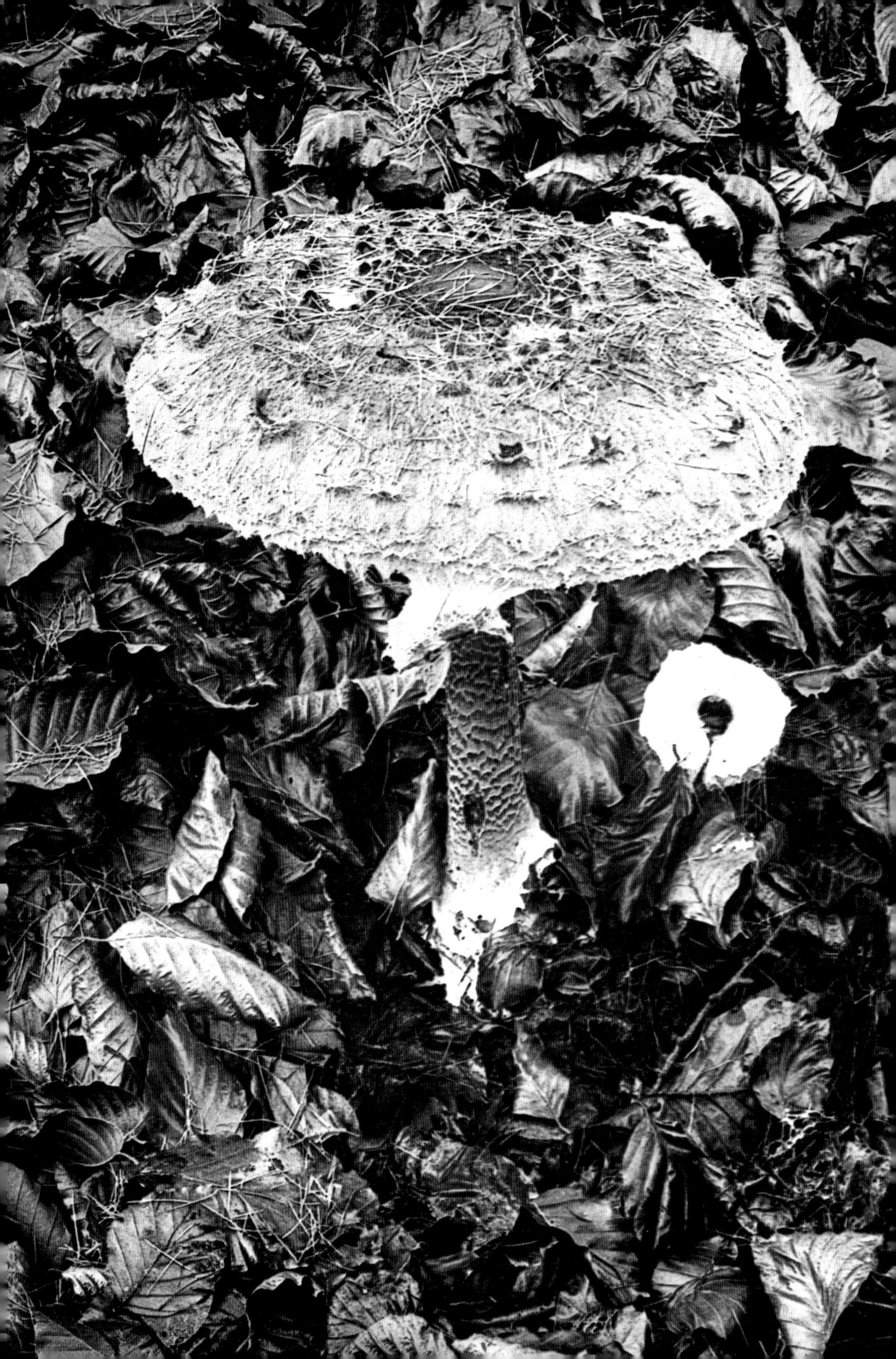

Reuters 2; © Photographic Archive Museo Nacional del Prado 3; British Museum 5; Alamy Stock Photo/CalimaX 6; Armitt Museum Gallery Library 11; Alamy Stock Photo/ Fine Art Images/Heritage Images 14; British Library Archive 15; Museum of Fine Arts, Boston/licensed 2026 by DACS, London and VG Bild-Kunst, Bonn 16; Statens Museum for Kunst 18; Courtesy of the Connor Family Trust, Thomas Dane Gallery and Michael Kohn Gallery, Los Angeles 20; © 2025 The Andy Warhol Foundation for the Visual Arts, Inc./licensed 2026 by DACS, London and VG Bild-Kunst, Bonn 21; Fibreglass, metallic car paint, 260 × 250 cm/© Sylvie Fleury, courtesy of the artist and Almine Rech/photo by Isabelle Arthuis 22; Grano-lithograph, collotype, photochrome from three offset reproductions. Printed in nineteen colours. Three elements hand-collaged and three passages drawn with crayon by the artist after printing. 29.9 x 22 in © Cy Twombly Foundation 23; Photo by Hiro Ihara, courtesy of Cai Studio 24; Gunpowder, ink, and dried lingzhi mushroom on paper, 20-page folding album. Album: Approximately 28 x 481.5 x 2.5 cm; Lingzhi mushroom: Approximately 16 x 10 x 9 cm irregular dimensions. Photo by Hiro Ihara, courtesy Cai Studio 25; Acrylic on canvas, 400 × 400 mm, © 2000 Takashi Murakami/Kaikai Kiki Co., Ltd, all rights reserved, courtesy of Perrotin 26; Acrylic on canvas mounted on board, 1800 × 1800 mm, © 2001 Takashi Murakami/Kaikai Kiki Co., Ltd, all rights reserved, 27; Symbionts: Contemporary Artists and the biosphere, MIT List Visual Arts Center, Cambridge 2022. Photo Dario Lasagni. Courtesy MIT List Visual Arts Centre 28; www.dalemreidphotography.com, info@dalemreidphotography.com 30; Courtesy of the Estate of the late Richard Giblett 38; The Metropolitan Museum of Art/Art Resource/Scala, Florence 40; Photo by James Klosty, courtesy of the John Cage Trust 45; New York State Museum 47; © 1971–72, permission John Cage Trust 51; © Lingholm Estate, Penguin Ventures 64; Penguin Ventures 65; Armitt Museum Gallery 66–68; Penguin Ventures 69; Getty 86; © Hergé-Tintinimaginatio 2025 89; © Disney 92–93; Acrylic on canvas mounted on wood panel, 1800 × 1800 mm, © 2003 Takashi Murakami/Kaikai Kiki Co., Ltd, all rights reserved 97; Oil paint, acrylic paint, synthetic resin, glass fibre and iron, 1524 × 3470 × 3470 mm/ installation view of Takashi Murakami Mononoke Kyoto, 2024, Kyoto City Kyocera Museum/photo by Joshua White, © Takashi Murakami/Kaikai Kiki Co., Ltd, all rights reserved 98; Acrylic on canvas mounted on board, 405 × 405 mm, © 1998 Takashi Murakami/Kaikai Kiki Co., Ltd, all rights reserved 99; Acrylic on canvas mounted on board, 1800 × 1800 mm, © 1999 Takashi Murakami/Kaikai Kiki Co., Ltd, all rights reserved 100; Acrylic on canvas mounted on board, 1800 × 1800 mm, © 1999 Takashi Murakami/Kaikai Kiki Co., Ltd, all rights reserved 101; www.tarquinbilgen.com 105; Christian Schallert/Jordi Garcia, Barcelona 106; Arxiu Mas, Fundació Institut Amatller D'Art Hispanic, Barcelona 107; Alamy Stock Photo/Gina Kelly 109; Photo by Gio Staiano 112; © Yayoi Kusama 115; © Yayoi Kusama 116; © Yayoi Kusama 118; © The Estate of Philip Guston, courtesy Hauser & Wirth/promised gift of Musa Guston Mayer to The Metropolitan Museum of Art/photo by Genevieve Hanson 121–22; © Peter Blake 202/DACS 125; Chazen Museum of Art 131; © NPL - DeA Picture Library/Bridgeman Images 134; Alamy Stock Photo/RTRO 138; Alamy Stock Photo/RTRO 139; Alamy Stock Photo/All Star Picture Library 141; © The Andy Warhol Museum, Pittsburgh, PA, a museum of Carnegie Institute/film still courtesy of The Andy Warhol Museum 142; FPA Classics 145; 2018 Stanford-Brown-RISD iGEM Team via NASA 148; NIAC 149; Estate of the artist/courtesy of Kicken Berlin 268

OPPOSITE
Ernst Fuhrmann, Basidiomycetes, *Lepiota procera*, parasol mushroom, c.1930

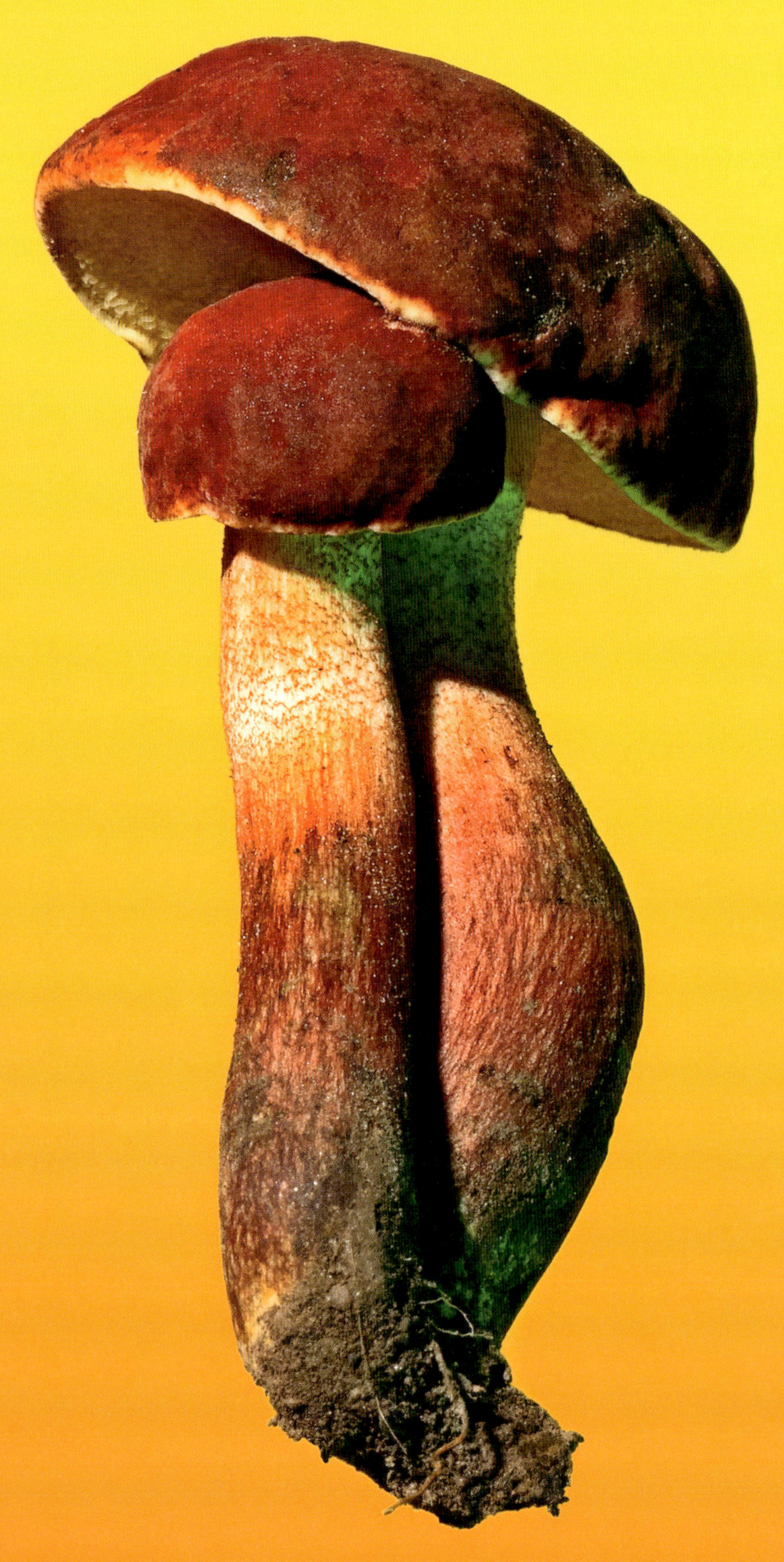

Editorial and Creative Direction
David Lane and **Marina Tweed**

Editor
Ananda Pellerin

Design & Art Direction
David Lane and **Jordan Weaver**
at **Lane & Associates**

Picture Editor
Kate Suiter

Managing Editor
Chloé Dixon-Goulden

Sub Editor and Proofreader
Rich Cutler

Copy Editor
Miles Smith

Contributing Editor
Didi Ronan

Contributing Writers

Patrick Baglee
Form Follows Fungi: The Mushroom in Design and Architecture

David Guimond
Rhizomatic Roots: A Deeper Understanding of Mushrooms and Mortals/The Death Cap: Mushroom Toxicity and Poisoning/Project Bluebird: Magic Mushrooms and Mind Control/Mushrooms in Space/Lingzhi: The Enchanted Mushroom

Jonathan Griffin
Earthly Etchings: Mycological Illustration from 15th-Century to John Cage/The Snuffler: Otto Marseus van Schrieck/The Cute Aggression of Takeshi Murakami/Yayoi Kusama's Obsession/Philip Guston's Mushroom Nail

Hannah Lack
Beatrix Potter: A Life of Flora and Fauna/Shady Stories: Mushrooms in Fiction/A Trip to the Moon: Mushrooms at the Movies/Melodic Mushrooms: Music for, About and by Fungi/Masters of the Mushroom: A Brief History of Notable Mycologists/The Characterful World of the Cartoon Mushroom/Mushrooms à la Mode: Fashion's Enduring Relationship with Fungi

Myles Smith
A Spotted History of Fly Agaric/Fungi, Fairies and Folklore

Recipe development
Maxine Clark

Recipe and cover photography
Bobby Doherty

Food Stylist
Jamie Kimm assisted by **Anna Edqwist**

Recipe set design
Noemi Bonazzi

Contributing photographers
Robin Broadbent and **Bobby Doherty**

Hohenzollernring 53, D-50672 Köln
www.taschen.com

Printed in Slovakia
ISBN 978-3-8365-8661-0

OPPOSITE
Phyllis Ma, *Hortiboletus rubellus*, 2021

“All mushrooms are edible;
but some only once.”

TERRY PRATCHETT

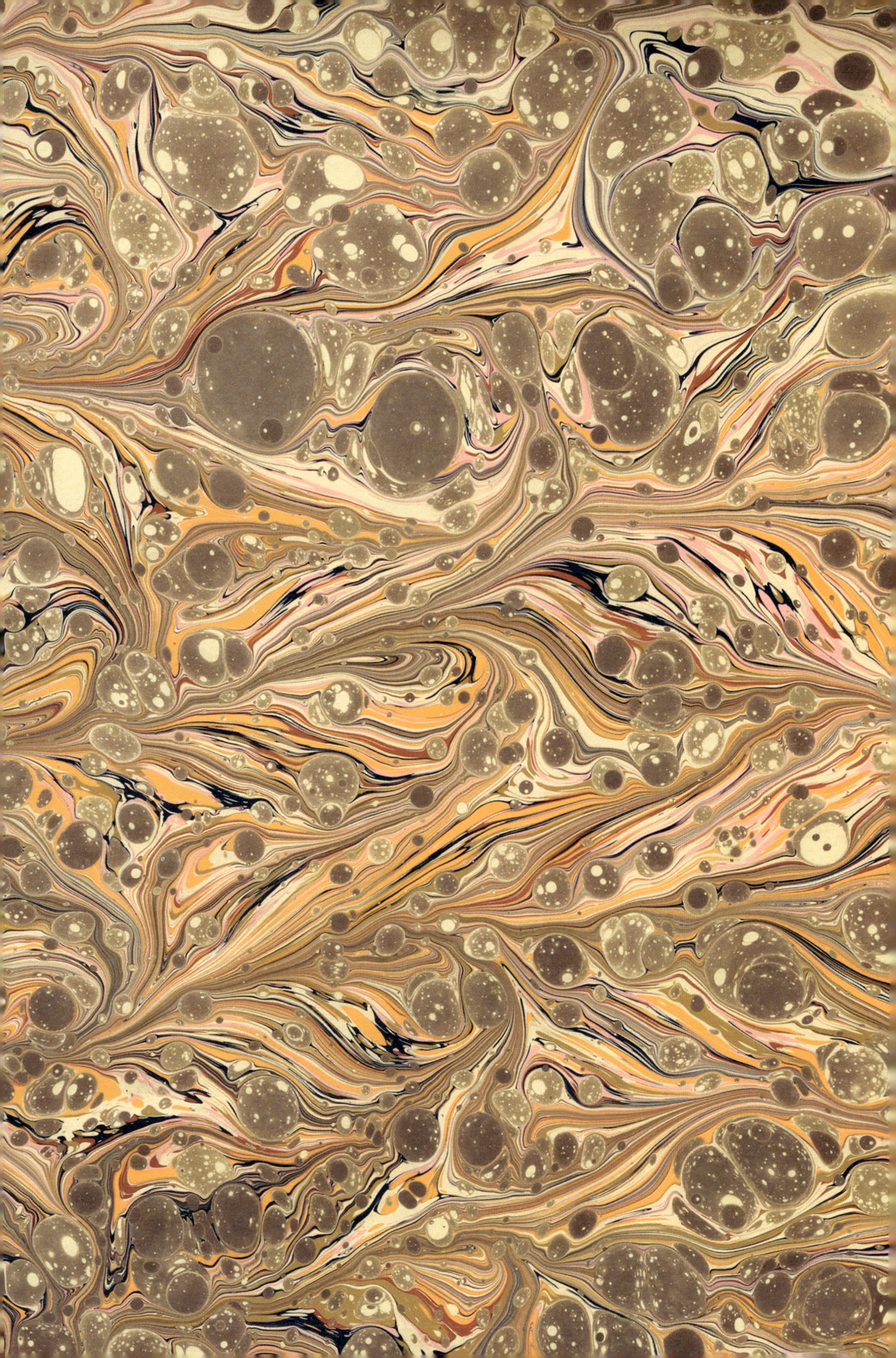

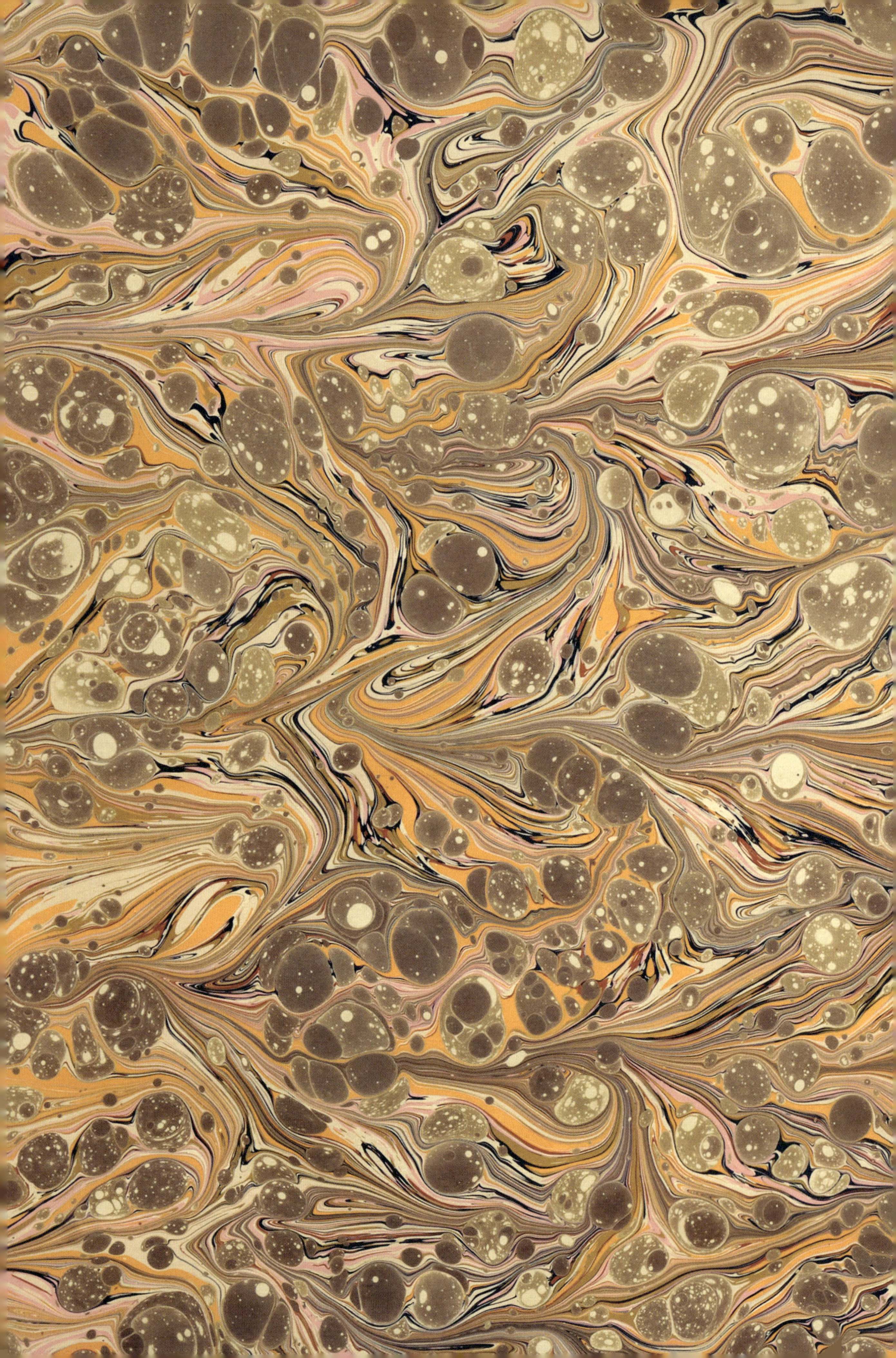